Kabbalah Demystified:

A Comprehensive Resource

Rabbi Michael Leo Samuel

ISBN

Hardcover: 978-1-967668-79-3

Paperback: 978-1-967668-78-6

Library of Congress Cataloging-in-Publication Data
Samuel, Michael Leo

1. RELIGION Mysticism /Medieval Jewish Philosophy. 3. Jewish theology

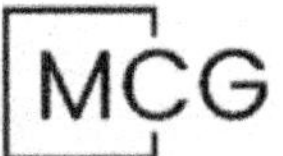

McGilligan Publishing
3707 Cypress Creek Pkwy Ste 310 #505
Houston, TX 77068
www.mcgilliganpublishing.com

Table of Contents

Kabbalah Demystified: A Comprehensive Resource

First Foreword by Rabbi Dr. Israel Drazin

Rabbi Dr. Michael Leo Samuel's book *Kabbalah Demystified: A Comprehensive Resource* is a remarkable work that I found thoroughly enjoyable and enlightening. As someone who has long admired the rationalistic philosophy of Maimonides since my youth and values rational thinking, I was pleasantly surprised by how much I appreciated Samuel's writing. His clarity, informativeness, and comprehensiveness make this book an exceptional introduction to the complex world of Kabbalah and Jewish mysticism.

Samuel's book highlights an often-overlooked fact: many contemporary Jewish thoughts, practices, and customs are deeply imbued with kabbalistic elements. For instance, the popular Shabbat hymn "*Lecha Dodi*" is commonly perceived as a celebration of Shabbat but originates from a kabbalistic perspective, reflecting the idea of God comprising ten parts. Similarly, certain rituals and songs, like those sung when Torah scrolls are taken from the ark, draw from mystical texts like the Zohar.

Even common practices like opening the door for Elijah during Passover are rooted in mystical traditions aimed at heralding the Messiah—an aspect of what scholars term "sympathetic magic." These mystical components permeate Jewish rituals, prayer books, daily routines, and every Jewish holiday.

The book explores deep questions regarding the essence of God, the origins of creation, the presence of evil, and the objectives behind the laws of the Torah. While mysticism provides unique answers to these questions, those with a rationalist perspective, like myself, might hold differing opinions. However, the value of these mystical perspectives lies in their ability to stimulate thought and introspection. Engaging with these ideas is beneficial, regardless of whether one agrees with their conclusions. Rabbi Samuel's analogies of the *Tzimtzum* are original and among the best explanations I have ever seen in writing!

In *Kabbalah Demystified: A Comprehensive Resource*, Rabbi Michael Leo Samuel provides an educational journey into the roots and impacts of Kabbalistic traditions. He details the beginnings of Kabbalah, tracing its history back to the Second Temple period, and elucidates foundational concepts like the *Sefirot*— divine emanations that symbolize different facets of God's engagement with the world. The book aims to clarify these intricate teachings, presenting them in a way that is both comprehensive and approachable for a broader audience.

Rabbi Samuel examines influential texts like the Zohar and *Sefer Yetzirah*, shedding light on the thoughts and actions they inspired, often controversial and rejected by others. He provides insights into figures like Shabbatai Sevi and Jacob Frank, whose ideas had profound and sometimes tragic consequences for their followers. The book also offers a glimpse into the world of the Hassidim, many of whom embraced certain kabbalistic ideas while rejecting others. Overall, Rabbi Dr. Samuel's *Kabbalah Demystified: A Comprehensive Resource* opens our eyes to the intricate world of kabbalistic thought, revealing the symbolic significance of letters, numbers, and shapes in Jewish mysticism. It's a must-read for anyone looking to understand the profound impact of kabbalistic ideas on Jewish life and thought.

Rabbi Dr. Israel Drazin
Targum Onkelos on the Torah:

KABBALAH DEMYSTIFIED: A COMPREHENSIVE RESOURCE

Second Foreword
By Rabbi Dr. Bernhard Rosenberg

Rabbi Dr. Michael Leo Samuel's *Kabbalah Demystified: A Comprehensive Resource* serves as your guide into the mystical depths of Jewish tradition. This book invites you into a world where ancient wisdom unfolds, decoding the intricate teachings, rich history, and profound influence of Jewish mysticism on religious thought. Each chapter reveals hidden layers of meaning— letters as cosmic codes, teachings as pathways to divine awareness— unraveling the enigmatic symbols, sacred texts, and complex ideas at the heart of this esoteric tradition. From the mysterious *Aleph* to the boundless *Ein Sof,* the narrative illuminates a realm where the spiritual and intellectual intertwine.

Beyond the esoteric, the book engages with the philosophical currents that shape this tradition. It traces the historical evolution of mystical thought, explores its symbolic language, and examines its lasting impact on Jewish spirituality. You'll encounter debates over the Zohar's origins, the provocative ideas of Jacob Frank, and the tensions within mystical literature— each offering a window into a multifaceted legacy.

Kabbalah Demystified also bridges the ethereal and the everyday, revealing the interconnectedness of existence. It probes the psychological and sociological dimensions of Jewish mysticism, mapping the soul's journey and uncovering the sacred in ordinary life. The exploration extends to numerology and symbolism, drawing striking parallels between the numerical systems of gematria and the abstract algebra of modern mathematics— an insight suggesting a hidden order to the universe.

In its later sections, the book immerses you in the "alphabet of creation," the intricacies of the soul, and the deeper meanings of biblical terms through a mystical lens. Ancient texts like the Sefer Raziel come alive, shedding light on concepts such as creation from nothing and the process of *Tzimtzum.* The narrative also reveals connections to Western esotericism, showing how these traditions intersect, while examining their influence on cultural norms, social structures, and Jewish communities across history.

This work transcends traditional theology, weaving a mosaic of universal themes that resonate with philosophy, science, and psychology—from Jung's collective unconscious to quantum theory. It draws fascinating parallels, such as *Tzimtzum*'s echo in the Big Bang or the Tree of Life's resonance with archetypes of the psyche. The book also explores mysticism's role in shaping Jewish law, ethics, and societal paradigms, offering a panoramic view of its enduring relevance.

More than a study, *Kabbalah Demystified* is a journey— a transformative adventure into Jewish mysticism that sparks curiosity and deepens understanding. Its final chapters venture into the realms of magic, folklore, and superstition, unveiling the enigma of the Golem, decoding cryptic rites, and immersing you in a world of mystic tales. With academic rigor and accessible prose, Rabbi Samuel crafts a bridge between the ordinary and the divine, presenting this tradition as both a scholarly pursuit and a path to personal growth.

This is your invitation to a realm where science meets spirituality, where ancient insights converse with modern ideas, and where timeless questions find illumination. *Kabbalah Demystified: A Comprehensive Resource* opens a gateway to the radiant heart of Jewish mysticism. Embark on this voyage, and prepare to be enlightened.

Rabbi Dr. Bernhard Rosenberg,
Echoes of The Holocaust: Survivors: and Their Children and Grandchildren Speak Out

Chapter 1

What Is the Kabbalah?

Since the dawn of Judaism, patriarchs, prophets, and seers have embarked on profound spiritual odysseys to comprehend the true essence of God and the universe. Recognizing that this quest demanded a profound understanding of the human psyche, their mystical encounters engendered a treasure trove of Judaic mystical texts. These works, steeped in enigma, were dedicated to decoding the mystery and purpose of human existence. The term קַבָּלָה "Kabbalah[1]" signifying "received" in Hebrew, alludes to this extensive body of esoteric wisdom primarily passed down through an oral tradition, transferred from master to disciple.

Rooted in the Second Temple period, the kabbalistic tradition unfurls several fundamental concepts like the *Sefirot,* divine emanations that symbolize various facets of God's interaction with the world. These ten *Sefirot*, from *Keter* (the Crown) at the apex, representing God's incomprehensible essence, to *Malkhut* (the Kingdom) at the base, symbolizing the physical world in which we dwell, offer a richly nuanced framework to contemplate divine realities.

Throughout this book, we aim to distill these intricate and profound concepts, making them accessible to a broad readership. We strive to elucidate these foundational tenets of the Kabbalah in a manner that is both engaging and comprehensible without compromising their depth and complexity. We hope that readers, regardless of their prior exposure to Judaic mystical thought, will better understand this ancient wisdom and its timeless relevance to our contemporary lives. We seek to open doors to a realm where spiritual exploration and intellectual curiosity intertwine, inviting each reader on a personal journey of discovery and enlightenment.

A Word of Advice to the Reader

As you begin your exploration of Jewish mysticism, recognize that this journey is yours alone. You're free to shape it according to your learning style, interests, and schedule. Whether you choose to immerse yourself in every detail or chart a more selective path through the text, craft an experience that feels authentic to you. The Table of Contents acts as your compass, outlining the landscape ahead and letting you pinpoint the chapters or sections that call to you most. A focused approach can make the most of your time, ensuring you connect with the wisdom that matters to you, but don't shy away from lingering where inspiration strikes. Deep, reflective study often unlocks insights and shifts that a rushed pace might miss. Both efficiency and immersion are powerful allies on this path.

Known as "The Hidden Wisdom," this tradition offers a spiritual lens to uncover the personal, profound meanings woven into Torah and Jewish heritage. The journey unfolds within your heart and mind, making each discovery as unique as your soul. Though the changes it sparks may go unseen by others, their impact can ripple through your life in lasting ways. Everyone approaches this sacred study differently— some find comfort in a step-by-step dive, others in a curated exploration. Trust the method that resonates with you, letting intuition guide you through this inner realm.

Engaging with these teachings is a deeply personal voyage, set against the rich backdrop of Jewish tradition. It's a quest that echoes the universal search for spiritual meaning, with each moment of prayer, meditation, or reflection revealing its timeless relevance. No two experiences are alike, shaped by your own blend of background and longing.

What does this body of wisdom offer today? How do its insights speak to the modern seeker? This mystical tradition invites you into your innermost self, heightening awareness in ways that are yours alone, earning its title as "The Hidden Wisdom." It acts as a mirror, reflecting the deeper significance of Torah and Jewish practices. The transformations it inspires remain subtle, internal, and as individual as you are. More than a collection of ideas, this philosophy reframes our place in the cosmos, deepening our ties to the Divine and one another. It opens a direct line to God while enriching human connections, demanding a shift in thought and action that unveils humanity's purpose and the universe's workings. Ancient and modern mystics alike have delved into its esoteric layers— crafting commentaries, treatises, meditative practices, and symbolic readings of ritual— to forge a meaningful link to the Divine. Their work seeks to decode creation, God's nature, and our existence, aiming to transform individuals and, through them, the world.

At its core lies the Tree of Life, a divine map of spiritual realms and the pathways of sacred energy. By tracing its spheres and connections, seekers uncover the soul's journey and the universe's structure, striving for enlightenment, alignment with divine will, and balance in life. This tradition offers a system to grasp our cosmic role, illuminating the origins, purpose, and destiny of our existence. Yet this isn't just theory— it's a lived practice. Meditation, visualization, and sacred texts become tools to connect with the Divine, while ethical living and kindness channel positive energy into the world. For centuries, this wisdom has guided spiritual seekers, offering a framework to explore life's hidden dimensions and strengthen our bond with the transcendent.

What is Mysticism?

The term "mystical" derives from the Greek verb *muein* (μυεῖν), which means "to close" or "to shut," often in reference to the lips or eyes. This etymology underpins the broader concept of "mystery" (*mysterion*, μυστήριον), linked to initiation rites in ancient Greek cults (e.g., the Eleusinian Mysteries), where participants were sworn to secrecy— lips closed— and often experienced revelations beyond ordinary perception— eyes metaphorically shut to the mundane.

The mystical exploration beckons us into a realm beyond precise definition. Like trying to pin down the fleeting scent of a blooming flower or the soothing sweetness of honey with words alone, its essence slips through the cracks of language, rooted in sensory richness and intangibility. This journey thrives not in verbal confines but in the quiet expanse of personal experience and reflection.[2]

From the solitary prayers of Christian hermits to the whirling dances of Sufi dervishes, the still meditations of Buddhists, or the introspective studies of Jewish Kabbalists, this pursuit reveals a universal thread— a longing to unite with the divine that spans cultures, faiths, and borders. Yet, for all its shared aim, the path remains deeply individual, shaped by the unique contours of each seeker's soul. Though its transformations are invisible, they ripple outward subtly, like a flower's fragrance shifting a room's air or honey cleansing as it sweetens. These changes reach beyond the surface, touching the core of the seeker. But like the wind— shifting in strength and direction— their impact varies, as distinct as the lives they touch.

Rituals and doctrines, vital to religious life, often take a backseat for those drawn to this inner quest. This isn't a rejection of outward practice but a turn toward a deeper, internalized bond with the divine. A Christian mystic might still attend mass, a Sufi offer his prayers, a Buddhist sit in meditation, or a Jewish seeker pore over the study of sacred Torah texts— yet their truest fulfillment lies within.

Conveying this experience to the uninitiated is like describing a burn to someone spared by fire or a sunrise to one who's never seen dawn. Words falter; the splendor of this path eludes debate or explanation, unveiling itself only to those willing to step into its depths. The term "mysticism" is but a shadow— a marker pointing to a reality grasped solely through immersive encounters. This spiritual pursuit calls us to a wisdom beyond mere thought, into a space where the soul's quiet voice resonates. It's a transformative dialogue, at once profoundly personal and universally alive, echoing in the heart's unspoken tongue.

Bound by Chains— The Ineffable Experience

In the vibrant literature of Sufi lore, a haunting tale unveils humanity's yearning for the unseen and the elusive dance of profound insight. Long ago, in a realm cloaked in enigma, a towering wall shimmered with an aura of the unknown. Whispered legends told of climbers who scaled its heights, gazed beyond, and— transformed by what they beheld— leapt into the abyss, never to return. Their vanishings hinted at a revelation so potent it severed ties to the familiar, a glimpse of the infinite's edge.

This mystery ignited the villagers' curiosity, a fire stoked by the urge to pierce its veil. They hatched a plan: tether the next seeker with chains, hauling them back to unveil the secret. A brave soul, aflame with truth's hunger, ascended, ropes binding him to the crowd below. At the summit, his face softened into a serene smile— radiance born of an encounter beyond words. Yet, when dragged down, the chains had claimed more than his freedom: his once-fluid voice fell silent. Mute, he stood— a vessel of wisdom locked within, his eyes alight with what his tongue could no longer sing.

This parable mirrors our restless quest to touch the divine, yet cling to safety's shore. The chains embody the fetters of habit and doubt, binding us to the known even as we reach for transcendence. It's a timeless tension: the soul's leap toward the boundless, tethered by the weight of the mundane. More deeply, it lays bare the frailty of language before the mystical. The silenced climber reflects a truth that a Jewish mystic, like the Kabbalists, knows well: the divine, veiled as the *Ein Sof*, eludes capture, its essence felt, not fenced. Silence here is no void but a sacred echo, a chorus resounding beyond speech. Like Maimonides' "Silence is praise to You" (Psalm 65:2), it whispers of intimacy with the unutterable.

This Sufi tale beckons us to our own quest. It challenges us to shed skepticism's bonds, to meet mystery with humility's open hand— not to seize, but to receive. In its quiet, we hear a call: to listen with the soul, where truths too vast for words ripple in the stillness, inviting us to join the infinite's silent song. "No thought can hold You" means God's essence is too vast for the mind to contain, like trying to hold the ocean in your hands. R. Sheneir Zalman teaches that while we can't grasp God, we can feel Him through the Torah and soul, turning mystery into a song of connection rather than a barrier.

"The Experience of the Ineffable"

The image captures figures ascending toward a luminous center, possibly representing enlightenment or a divine force. Encircled by the cosmos, it reflects the paradox of individual smallness and cosmic interconnectedness, resonating with kabbalistic themes of the infinite Divine (Ein Sof) and the soul's quest for divine unity. The central light likely symbolizes the origin of truth, pulling all into a harmonious spiritual ascent.

Embarking on the Interior Journey

At its heart, the mystical journey beckons seekers into a boundless inner realm, soaring past the frail boundaries of sect and creed. True mystics glimpse a golden thread of unity weaving through every such pilgrimage— a timeless pulse unshaken by the fleeting shadows of the outer world. Their encounters, whether with the soul's silent depths or faint whispers from beyond, transcend mere fancy; they are living truths, etched into the fabric of their being, as real as the breath that stirs their lips.

Yet we must sift the genuine from the fleeting. Many don the mystic's mantle, their words shimmering with promise, but lacking the weight of authentic revelation. True seekers bear a mark of unwavering resolve— a relentless fire driving them toward self-discovery and the unseen divine. This path is no idle drift; it demands a heart flung wide; a mind unshackled, eager to plumb mysteries veiled from the senses. Casual explorers falter, their steps shallow, while the steadfast press on, undeterred by the abyss of the unknown.

To walk this way is to bare our soul— to embrace the uncharted, casting off the husks of preconception, letting the invisible lead. Doubt rises like a storm, clouding faith, testing the spirit's mettle. Yet for the mystic, doubt is a fleeting mist, a forge that tempers trust in the hidden. This journey marries intellect to intuition— a delicate dance where neither arid reason nor blind leaps suffice. Scholarship alone cannot pierce these depths; it must entwine with the spirit's quiet knowing. In this harmony, truths unfurl— insights beyond the grasp of ordinary sight, painting existence in hues richer than the eye can hold. To embrace this balance is to unlock a pilgrimage both arduous and luminous.

Seekers differ as stars in the night sky, yet those who journey far share a sacred echo: the inner self, the beyond, shifts from distant theory to a felt pulse— a reality thrumming beneath the skin. Some stumble, snared by doubt's rigid chains, their hearts and minds calcified, growth stilled. Here, imagination emerges as a radiant ally. It kindles art, weaves tales, and lifts songs to the heavens; turned inward, it unveils a beauty eclipsing the outer world's glare. To skeptics demanding proof of the divine, the mystic offers imagination as a bridge— a spark igniting belief where logic alone dims. To shelter it is to starve the soul; to cradle it is to deepen our bond with the sacred, a tether to the infinite's quiet glow.

This path invites us not to seize but to surrender— to meet mystery with humility's open hand, to listen with the spirit where ears fall short. In silence, the mystic finds a symphony of the unutterable, a melody threading through doubt and wonder, calling us to join the divine dance beyond the veil— a journey inward that mirrors the infinite's eternal song.

Mystics often doubt the capacity of human language to accurately convey divine truths, considering it an inadequate vessel to contain God's grand mystery. Instead, they venture beyond the veil of words into a realm of silent knowledge. The divine truths, they believe, dwell not on the surface of the Scriptures but nestle deep within. They read between the lines. They believe the Scriptures communicate a transpersonal message to comprehend and apply. For mystics, they serve as a treasure map leading to hidden divine truths. As the Zohar attests:

> Rabbi Shimon explained further that there is a garment visible to everyone. When foolish people see someone in an attractive garment, they don't look beyond that. However, the true essence of the garment is the body it covers, and the essence of the body is the soul it houses. The same applies to the Torah. It has a body, which is the commandments of the Torah, referred to as "the physical manifestation of the Torah." This body is clothed in the stories of this world. The foolish only see this outer covering, the story of the Torah, and they don't understand anything more. They fail to look at what's beneath the garment.[3]

Commercialized Kabbalah: McMysticism

Jewish mysticism, particularly Kabbalah, is often misrepresented as a standalone spiritual system, detached from its Jewish roots. This distortion reduces a profound tradition to a fleeting fad, obscuring its depth. Far from an isolated philosophy, Kabbalah is woven into Jewish heritage, drawing vitality from the Hebrew Bible and centuries of mystical inquiry. Its timeless questions—about the Divine Presence (Shekhinah), human purpose, and cosmic harmony—captivate seekers, inviting exploration of the soul's divine connection. To grasp Kabbalah authentically, one must view it as a vital thread of Jewish tradition, not a collection of esoteric rituals.

Kabbalah explores the divine through the Bible's lens: Genesis unveils creation's mystery, Exodus kindles a sacred bond, Leviticus offers rituals for harmony, and Psalms echo the soul's longing. These texts shape Kabbalah's vision of a universe alive with divine purpose, a vision deepened by medieval mystics through texts like the Zohar, refined by 16th-century Safed scholars, and enriched by Hasidic teachers (Scholem, 1941). This rich evolution, as Gershom Scholem notes in *Major Trends in Jewish Mysticism*, grounds Kabbalah in rigorous inquiry and sacred practice, distinguishing it from superficial interpretations.

Yet, popular culture distorts this tradition, reducing Jewish mysticism to "pop Kabbalah" or "McMysticism"—a commercialized phenomenon promising instant enlightenment. McMysticism operates like a fast-food chain: mass-produced and profit-driven, it markets products like red string bracelets and Kabbalah water. The red string, a wool bracelet dyed red, is sold by The Kabbalah Centre as a talisman imbued with "protective energy," often tied to celebrity endorsements (Kabbalah Centre, 2007). Similarly, Kabbalah water, branded as "Giving Water," is sourced from a Smoky Mountains spring and promoted for its mineral content and high pH, with unverified claims of healing diseases (Kabbalah Centre, 2007). On January 9, 2008, Madonna reportedly told a friend she drank only this water, priced at $5 per bottle, highlighting its celebrity-driven allure. Kabbalah gurus have created a lucrative online business helping spiritual seekers wishing to solve their personal problems.

In authentic Kabbalah, water and symbols hold sacred meaning—purification through Mikveh immersion or ritual ties to devotion—but McMysticism transforms these into commercialized products. Unlike these distortions, authentic Kabbalah emphasizes scholarly study and ethical living, rooted in Jewish texts.

McMysticism's accessibility—through its simplified teachings, celebrity endorsements (such as those from figures like Madonna), and trendy merchandise—can indeed spark initial curiosity, drawing in spiritual novices who feel overwhelmed by Kabbalah's intricate doctrines and esoteric symbolism. This populist approach democratizes mysticism, making it seem approachable in a fast-paced world where ancient traditions might otherwise appear inaccessible. However, its commercial pitfalls, including pricey seminars and branded products, risk steering seekers toward superficial consumerism rather than genuine enlightenment, sidestepping the rigorous, disciplined study essential for true comprehension. Many introductory books and online resources exacerbate this issue by oversimplifying profound concepts like the Tree of Life or detaching Kabbalah from its intrinsic Jewish roots, thereby marginalizing its rich historical and cultural depth. This detachment can alienate earnest seekers yearning for substantive meaning, reducing profound mysticism to an exotic, fleeting novelty devoid of ethical grounding.

Authentic Kabbalah is like a meticulously crafted home-cooked meal, requiring patience, immersive study, and guidance from seasoned mentors steeped in Jewish scholarship. Unlike the fleeting appeal of "McMysticism"—a superficial, trend-driven spirituality—Kabbalah demands a disciplined journey rooted in divine wisdom (Chochmah), the call to heal the world (Tikkun Olam), and ethical living (Mitzvot). This "long way" unfolds through engagement with foundational texts like the Torah, Talmud, and Zohar, alongside practices such as meditation, prayer, and communal study (chevruta). While McMysticism's allure may spark initial curiosity, only committed exploration reveals Kabbalah's profound, enduring treasures.

The Long Way That Is Short

McMysticism's accessibility—its simplified teachings and celebrity endorsements—can spark curiosity, appealing to spiritual novices overwhelmed by Kabbalah's complexity. However, its commercial traps risk diverting seekers toward consumerism, bypassing the disciplined study needed for true understanding. Many introductory books exacerbate this by oversimplifying concepts or detaching Kabbalah from its Jewish context, sidelining its historical depth. This alienates seekers craving meaning, portraying mysticism as an exotic novelty. Authentic Kabbalah, like a well-prepared home-cooked meal, demands time, study, and guidance from seasoned mentors. It centers on divine wisdom, healing the world, and ethical living, offering profound understanding through Jewish texts and practices.

While McMysticism's allure may open doors, only dedicated study reveals Kabbalah's true treasure. Joining a community class, attending a synagogue lecture, or reading introductory texts like Gershom Scholem's works can guide novices to Kabbalah's roots, exploring mystical texts with mentors who prioritize authenticity over profit. In Jewish tradition, study thrives in community, making these steps practical and welcoming. By grounding exploration in Jewish heritage, seekers can unite the divine and human in harmony, transcending McMysticism's fleeting appeal.

The Long Way that is Short

This contrast between superficial shortcuts and deep, committed pursuit echoes a timeless Jewish teaching on the paradox of paths: the "long way" that proves short and the "short way" that turns long. Mastering the teachings of Kabbalah is not for the spiritually faint of heart, as it demands embracing the former over the latter's deceptive ease. The Talmud (Eruvin 53b) recounts a story about Rabbi Joshua ben Hananya, who encountered a young boy at a fork in the road while traveling to a city. When asked for directions, the boy replied: "This path is long but short, and that one is short but long."

Intrigued, Rabbi Joshua chose the "short but long" path, only to find it obstructed by gardens and fences, forcing him to turn back. The boy explained that he had warned him—it appeared short but ultimately proved long due to the delays.

This tale illustrates the paradox that the quickest path is not always the wisest—a lesson directly applicable to the pitfalls of McMysticism versus authentic Kabbalah. A "long way" that is "short" demands more initial effort and time but leads reliably to the goal, like a well-maintained road that avoids hazards. In contrast, a "short way" that is "long" tempts with efficiency but results in complications and setbacks, such as treacherous shortcuts filled with obstacles. The sages thus advocate foresight and patience over haste, a principle that extends to spiritual, ethical, and practical realms, reminding us that true mastery in Kabbalah comes through disciplined, authentic pursuit rather than commercialized shortcuts.

In Rabbi Sheneir Zalman of Liadi's foundational Chabad text, the Tanya, Chapter 26 describes spiritual growth as a "long way" that requires disciplined prayer, study, and ethical refinement. This path, though demanding, is ultimately "short" because it builds a lasting connection to the Divine. In contrast, seeking quick spiritual highs without discipline—a "short way"—leads to stagnation, proving "long" in achieving true closeness to God. Similarly, both the Tanya and the Ethics of the Fathers (Pirkei Avot) emphasize that ethical choices, such as choosing integrity over dishonest gains, represent the "long way." This approach ensures enduring success and spiritual fulfillment. However, pursuing hasty or unethical shortcuts—a "short way"—often results in loss and spiritual emptiness.

The study of Kabbalah and Jewish mysticism exemplifies this "long way." Unlike accessible Jewish texts, Kabbalah demands rigorous preparation, including mastery of Torah, Talmud, and Hebrew, as well as emotional and spiritual maturity. Its esoteric concepts, such as the *Sefirot* or the nature of the *Ein Sof,* require years of disciplined study to grasp, often under a qualified teacher. The Zohar and other mystical texts warn that superficial engagement—a "short way"—can lead to misunderstanding or spiritual harm. Yet, this demanding path is "short" in its profound rewards: deep insight into the Divine and alignment with God's will. The hard work of Kabbalah mirrors the Talmud's call for deliberate effort, yielding clarity only through persistence.

Psychologically, the allure of the "short way" stems from cognitive ease. The brain uses heuristics—mental shortcuts—to simplify decisions, favoring quick fixes that require less effort. However, as the Talmud cautions, these paths often backfire. For example, a high-interest loan may seem to resolve financial strain but can deepen debt. Cultural pressures amplify this, as modern society glorifies speed and instant solutions via technology and social media, making the "long way" feel inefficient. Spiritual growth demands avodah—hard, painstaking work to actualize our latent ability to become closer to the Divine.

The Talmud, Tanya, and Kabbalah collectively teach that shortcuts—driven by cognitive biases, stress, or cultural trends—often lead to setbacks. Embracing the "long way" through disciplined effort, whether in ethical choices, spiritual growth, or mystical study, yields lasting success. By aligning actions with long-term goals, as Rabbi Joshua and Rabbi Sheneir Zalman advocate, we navigate life's challenges with wisdom and purpose.

CHAPTER 2

ANCIENT ANTECEDENTS TO THE KABBALAH

I see, my dear Theaetetus, that Theodorus had a true insight into your nature when he said that you were a philosopher; for wonder is the feeling of a philosopher, and philosophy begins in wonder.

PLATO,
Theaetetus 155c-d

Love of learning is by nature curious, not hesitating to bend its steps in all directions, prying into everything, reluctant to leave anything that exists unexplored, whether material or immaterial. It has an extraordinary appetite for all that there is to be seen and heard, and, not content with what it finds in its own country, it is bent on seeking what is in foreign parts and separated by great distances.

PHILO of ALEXANDRIA, *Migration* 215

Footnotes to Plato

In *Process and Reality*, Alfred North Whitehead, a towering 20th-century philosopher, famously dubbed European philosophy a "series of footnotes to Plato," underscoring the Greek thinker's indelible imprint on Western thought. Jewish scholars, particularly

Kabbalists, push this further, boldly asserting that Plato— and Greek wisdom broadly— drew inspiration from Moses and the wellsprings of Jewish mysticism. Though no historical evidence supports this claim, it reflects Plato's vast influence while hinting at a subtle, unprovable bridge between cultures. His ideas ripple across metaphysics, epistemology, ethics, and political theory, fundamentally reshaping how we grapple with reality itself.

At the heart of Plato's philosophy lies the Theory of Forms, a vision of perfect, eternal ideals existing beyond our flawed, sensory world. This idealism— positing a higher reality beyond the tangible— and his pursuit of the Good reverberate through Aristotle, Neo-Platonism, and modern thought. Kabbalists discern echoes of their own tradition here, tying Plato's forms to the concept of divine emanation, even if direct lineage remains elusive. Both systems chase a hidden order beneath the visible, a shared quest that suggests a profound, if speculative, resonance.

This interplay deepens through figures like Philo of Alexandria, a first-century Jewish philosopher who wove Greek and Hebrew threads into a rich tapestry. Philo's fusion of Platonic concepts with Torah wisdom laid the groundwork for mystical traditions, including early Kabbalah. These currents feed into the "Great Chain of Being," an ancient framework envisioning existence as a ladder stretching from the Divine to the mundane. In Kabbalah, this aligns with the *Sefirot*— ten emanations channeling God's essence into creation, crafting a cosmos where every level pulses with interconnected purpose. Whitehead's nod to Plato thus opens a window onto this vibrant confluence. While kabbalistic claims of Plato borrowing from Jewish roots lack proof, their mutual hunger for transcendent truth binds these traditions. The "Great Chain" becomes a unifying thread— from Moses' revelations to Plato's ideals to Kabbalah's cosmic map— casting the universe as a living network of meaning. Far from static footnotes, these ideas spark a dynamic dialogue, illuminating existence for seekers across millennia.

Plato & The Kabbalah— An Old Legend

The notion that Plato or Pythagoras received their wisdom from the Kabbalah— a Jewish mystical tradition formalized in the medieval period— requires careful historical and philosophical scrutiny. The Kabbalah, as understood today, emerged in written form in the 12th–13th centuries with texts like the Zohar, long after Plato (c. 427–347 B.C.E.) and Pythagoras (c. 570–490 B.C.E) lived. However, some thinkers posited that these Greek philosophers accessed an earlier, esoteric Jewish wisdom, thinking that these oral traditions predated the Kabbalah's codification, or that their ideas paralleled Kabbalistic concepts due to a shared ancient source. This belief often stems from the Renaissance and later interpretations rather than direct evidence from antiquity. Below, we shall identify key philosophers and thinkers who advanced this view, their arguments, and the historical context, with citations drawn from scholarly sources where possible.

Was Plato a Disciple of Jewish Wisdom?

During the Renaissance, Christian and Jewish thinkers sought to synthesize Greek philosophy with Judeo-Christian traditions, often claiming that Plato drew from Jewish sources, including what they anachronistically labeled "Kabbalah." This echoed earlier assertions by ancient Jewish philosophers like Philo of Alexandria and Aristobulus of Paneas, who suggested Plato's teachings derived from Moses' wisdom. Philo often stressed how the famous Greek philosophers borrowed or stole their ideas from Moses. [4]

Among the early Christian thinkers, Justin Martyr and Tertullian also believed ancient philosophers like Socrates and Plato accessed Jewish wisdom through ancient biblical texts in Egypt, with a specific legend claiming Plato studied under the prophet Jeremiah. Such an interpretation is implausible, pointing out that Plato (c. 427–347 B.C.E.) lived long after Jeremiah (c. 650–570 B.C.E). Similarly, there is no evidence of the Septuagint (Greek Pentateuch translation) existing in Plato's time— it was made by order of Ptolemy Philadelphus (c. 285–246 B.C.E). Likewise, Alexandrian writers like Strabo (c. 64 B.C.E–24 C.E) offer no trace of Plato's alleged Jewish studies in Egypt. Such claims are exaggerated and unsupported.

Moshe Idel, a leading scholar of Jewish mysticism, explores how Renaissance Jewish thinkers, notably Isaac Abravanel and his father, repositioned Kabbalah above Greek philosophy by redefining its ties to Plato and Aristotle. In medieval times, they leveraged Plato's ideas— such as emanation and the soul's eternity— as a prestigious foil to the widely rejected Aristotelianism, aligning them with Kabbalistic concepts to enhance Kabbalah's appeal to philosophers. During the Italian Renaissance, as Platonism emerged as a theological force, Jewish intellectuals shifted from noting parallels to claiming Plato derived his wisdom from Mosaic revelation, rejecting the Florentine notion of separate Greek and Jewish knowledge streams. They argued that truth flowed from Moses to Plato, who grasped it imperfectly, while Aristotle further muddled it, a narrative bolstered by Aristotelianism's waning influence among Renaissance Jews compared to its medieval dominance.[5]

In *Mif'alot 'Elohim,* Abravanel credits Plato with recognizing emanation for angels and creation for the material world, viewing nonexistence as a return to eternal "Ideas," akin to Kabbalistic views, though he frames this as Neoplatonic influence. He asserts Plato learned from Jewish elders in Egypt, surpassing Aristotle, who lacked such roots. Isaac Abravanel builds on this, depicting Plato as a disciple of these "ancient fathers," with Aristotle as his lesser student, marking a decline from the pure Jewish origin. He links Pythagoras and Socrates to this tradition, suggesting their belief in soul transmigration stemmed from early prophets, unlike Aristotle's dismissal. Tracing creation from Adam through Moses, Abravanel underscores a continuous Jewish lineage, employing the Renaissance "ancient theology" concept to affirm Kabbalah's primacy over Greek thought, harmonizing yet elevating Jewish wisdom.

Furthermore, Idel contextualizes Leone Ebreo's conceptual framework in *Dialoghi d'Amore* against his father Isaac Abravanel's views, noting Leone's deeper familiarity with Neoplatonic literature in Latin translation. Leone employs the "ancient theology" theory, asserting that Plato, unlike Aristotle, aligned with Mosaic teachings due to instruction from Jewish "ancient fathers" in Egypt. He praises Plato's broader vision of divine wisdom as a secondary cause dependent on God, contrasting it with Aristotle's shallower grasp, which fused beauty and wisdom as the primal origin. Both father and son claim Plato derived his knowledge from Jewish sources, though Leone softens Aristotle's role, describing his comprehension as weaker rather than outright opposed, as Isaac does. Idel interprets this as a succession— Kabbalists taught Plato, who taught Aristotle— with a decline in understanding, suggesting the earliest Jewish wisdom surpasses both. Leone's closer affinity to these sages makes his Platonism a key to Jewish doctrine, particularly on ideas and the soul's antecedence, reinforcing Jewish thought's antiquity and superiority within Renaissance Italy's harmonizing trends.[6]

Idel's comment reflects his analysis of the evolving perception of Kabbalah in Renaissance Italy, using Johannes Reuchlin's work as a key example. He points out that Reuchlin, a prominent Christian Kabbalist and humanist (1455–1522), dedicated his intellectual project to Pope Leo X, aiming to recover what he believed was Pythagoras's lost philosophy through the lens of Kabbalah. Idel sees this as a significant indicator of a broader transformation in how Jewish Kabbalah was understood and valued. Initially, in the 13th century, Kabbalah arrived in Italy as a relatively obscure set of texts studied by a small circle of Jewish scholars, imported from regions like Spain or Provence, where it had begun to flourish with works like the Zohar.

By Reuchlin's time in the late 15th and early 16th centuries, it had morphed into something far more expansive in the Christian imagination— an esoteric tradition blending philosophy and magic, and one that was thought to encode Christian truths beneath its Jewish surface. Reuchlin's effort to link Pythagorean ideas (e.g., numerology, cosmic harmony) with Kabbalah exemplifies this shift, as he viewed Kabbalah not just as a Jewish mystical system but as a universal wisdom capable of illuminating ancient Greek thought and supporting Christian theology. For Idel, this dedication to the Pope highlights Kabbalah's elevated status: from a marginal Jewish import to a prestigious, multifaceted lore embraced by Christian intellectuals, signaling its integration into the Renaissance project of synthesizing classical, Jewish, and Christian knowledge. This reflects a broader trend Idel often explores— Kabbalah's dynamic adaptation and reinterpretation beyond its original Jewish context.

Giovanni Pico della Mirandola (1463–1494), a central figure in Renaissance humanism, explicitly connected Plato to Kabbalistic wisdom in his 900 Theses (1486) and Oration on the Dignity of Man. Pico argued that Plato's philosophy, alongside Pythagorean numerology, shared a common origin with the Kabbalah, rooted in a *prisca theologia* (ancient theology) revealed to Moses. He wrote, "The Kabbalah confirms the true doctrines of Plato," suggesting that Plato accessed this wisdom indirectly through Pythagoras or Egyptian intermediaries influenced by Jewish exiles. Pico's teacher, Alemanno, likely shaped this view, reinforcing the idea of a Jewish-Greek transmission.

Pico's contemporary, Marsilio Ficino (1433–1499), head of the Florentine Academy, also linked Plato to Jewish mysticism. As the first to translate Plato's complete works into Latin, Ficino saw Neoplatonism, derived from Plato, as compatible with Kabbalistic emanation theories. While he didn't explicitly claim Plato studied Kabbalah, he suggested Pythagoras and Plato tapped into a universal wisdom preserved in Jewish tradition, citing their shared emphasis on numbers and the soul's divine nature. These assertions reflect a syncretic effort to unify Christian, Jewish, and Greek thought rather than historical fact.[7]

Postscript: Plato & the Kabbalah

One might argue that many of the early medieval Judaic thinkers were indirectly complimenting Plato by claiming he derived his wisdom from Jewish sources, effectively "making him one of their own." This phenomenon reflects a mix of admiration, cultural pride, and strategic apologetics, common among Jewish intellectuals across different eras.

Plato's philosophy— his emphasis on transcendent Forms, the soul's immortality, and a structured cosmos— resonated deeply with Jewish mystical and philosophical traditions. Thinkers like Philo of Alexandria (c. 20 B.C.E.–50 C.E.) saw parallels between Plato's Logos and Jewish concepts of divine wisdom, while Renaissance figures like Isaac Abravanel and Leone Ebreo admired his metaphysical depth. By linking Plato to Moses or Jewish prophets, they implicitly praised his insights as profound enough to align with sacred revelation, elevating him to a near-prophetic status within their framework.

Claiming Plato as a disciple of Jewish figures like Jeremiah (as in Abravanel's narrative) or "ancient fathers" (per Leone Ebreo) served to "Judaize" him, folding his brilliance into the Jewish intellectual lineage. This wasn't just about asserting primacy; it was a backhanded compliment— acknowledging Plato's genius by suggesting it stemmed from the ultimate source of truth, Mosaic wisdom. It's akin to saying, "Your ideas are so great, they must have come from us," honoring Plato while reinforcing Jewish tradition's antiquity and superiority.

In Hava Tirosh-Rothschild's *Between Worlds: The Life and Thought of Rabbi David ben Judah Messer Leon,* she highlights R. David ben Messer Leon, a 15th–16th century Italian Jewish scholar, who reconciled Plato's philosophy with Kabbalah by asserting that Plato was a disciple of the prophet Jeremiah in Egypt.[8] This "historical" claim, probably inspired by figures like Isaac Abravanel, lacks a factual basis but served strategic ends during the Renaissance when Platonism surged in popularity. It justified Jewish interest in Platonic ideas by tracing them to a Jewish origin, implying no conflict with Jewish identity and encouraging their study. Additionally, by portraying Platonism as derived from Jewish wisdom, R. David shaped a Jewish *prisca theologica*— the Renaissance notion of an ancient, universal theology— rooting both Platonism and Hermeticism in Moses' divine revelation. This positioned Judaism as the fountainhead of these traditions, merging Renaissance syncretism with Jewish pride. His approach cleverly blended apologetics and cultural assertion, making Platonism a legitimate pursuit within Jewish thought.

This move also had a defensive edge. In Hellenistic times (e.g., Aristobulus), medieval debates (e.g., Maimonides' era), and the

Renaissance, Jews faced cultural competition with Greek thought. By co-opting Plato, thinkers neutralized a rival tradition, turning a potential threat into a derivative of their own heritage. This flattered Plato's stature— his ideas were worth claiming, while safeguarding Jewish identity against external influence.

Striking Parallels: Plato's Cave and Kabbalistic Ascent

R. Leon de Modena (1571–1648), a brilliant Italian Jewish thinker, dismantles the Kabbalists' claim that Plato and Aristotle drew their wisdom from Jewish prophets like Jeremiah and Simeon the Just, dismissing it as absurd and arguing instead that Kabbalah absorbed Greek philosophical influences post-Maimonides, evident in the late emergence of the Zohar. His rationalist skepticism recasts Kabbalah as a historical synthesis rather than an ancient revelation, upending its mystique as a derivative tradition.

Yet, despite de Modena's insistence on this chronological reversal, the conceptual affinities between Greek thought and Kabbalah persist as a point of intrigue, inviting exploration beyond his critique. Consider the striking parallels between Plato's "Allegory of the Cave" in *The Republic* (Book 7: 515–517) and Kabbalistic notions of ascent, where both depict a transformative journey from illusion to a higher truth, revealing an unexpected resonance that transcends questions of origin. In Plato's tale, prisoners chained in a cave perceive only shadows on a wall, mistaking them for reality; one escapes, emerging into blinding sunlight to behold the true world— a metaphor for awakening to a higher truth. Kabbalah, as articulated in the Zohar (e.g., Zohar 1:83b), mirrors this: the physical realm is a faint reflection, a shadow cast by the infinite *Ein Sof* through the *Sefirot*.

For the Kabbalists, everyday existence lacks full substance, emanating from the *Ein Sof* and structured by the *Sefirot*'s divine light. Like Plato's freed prisoner, dazzled yet transformed by sunlight, the mystic ascends in stages: the lower *sefirot* (e.g., *Malchut*) offers shadowy glimpses, akin to the cave's illusions; deeper insight through *Yesod* and *Tiferet* reveals reflections, then direct forms; and the higher *Sefirot*, like *Binah* and *Hokhmah*, shine as "moon and stars," edging toward God's essence. The ultimate goal—Plato's sun or the unreachable *Ein Sof*— blazes as full illumination, a truth too vast for mortal grasp, yet the core of all being. Both visions insist surface reality cloaks deeper depths, with the cave's liberation paralleling the Kabbalistic climb from illusion to divine unity, each step unveiling the cosmos' veiled order. Plato's dualistic universe, with its higher realm of immutable Forms led by the Form of the Good and a lower realm of imperfect copies, fits well with this structured ascent, echoing the "Great Chain of Being" reflected in Kabbalah's cosmic hierarchy. Zade

Where Kabbalah and Plato Differed . . .

Despite their similarities, the mystical tradition within Judaism diverges from Platonic philosophy in several key areas:

NATURE OF THE PHYSICAL WORLD:

❑ **Plato's** philosophy often portrays the physical world as an imperfect and transient shadow of the ideal, unchanging realm of forms. This perspective leads to a certain devaluation of the material world, favoring the spiritual or intellectual realm.

❑ **Kabbalah,** conversely, sees the physical world as an essential part of the divine plan. While acknowledging the higher spiritual realms, Jewish mystical thought emphasizes that the material world is imbued with divine sparks and is the arena for spiritual growth and fulfillment of divine commandments (*mitzvot*). The physical is not merely a shadow but a vital component of the divine structure.

PURPOSE AND GOAL OF HUMAN LIFE:

❑ **Plato:** The divine, epitomized by the Form of the Good, emerges as an abstract, impersonal pinnacle— a supreme principle rather than a deity with agency or

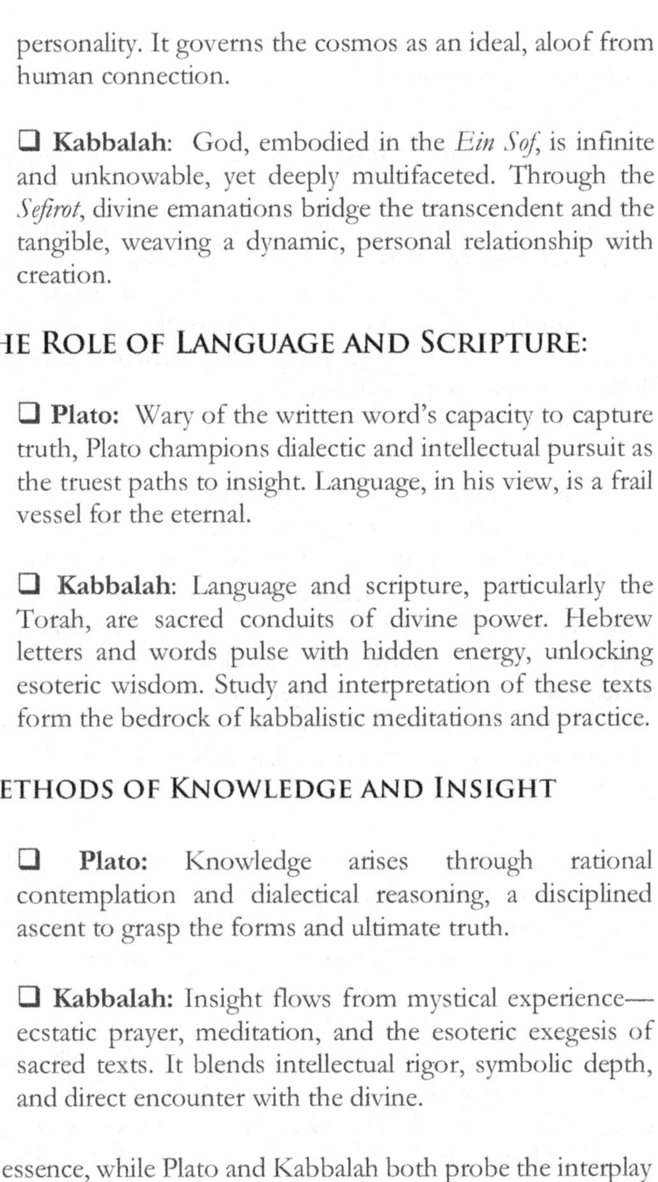

personality. It governs the cosmos as an ideal, aloof from human connection.

❑ **Kabbalah**: God, embodied in the *Ein Sof*, is infinite and unknowable, yet deeply multifaceted. Through the *Sefirot*, divine emanations bridge the transcendent and the tangible, weaving a dynamic, personal relationship with creation.

THE ROLE OF LANGUAGE AND SCRIPTURE:

❑ **Plato:** Wary of the written word's capacity to capture truth, Plato champions dialectic and intellectual pursuit as the truest paths to insight. Language, in his view, is a frail vessel for the eternal.

❑ **Kabbalah**: Language and scripture, particularly the Torah, are sacred conduits of divine power. Hebrew letters and words pulse with hidden energy, unlocking esoteric wisdom. Study and interpretation of these texts form the bedrock of kabbalistic meditations and practice.

METHODS OF KNOWLEDGE AND INSIGHT

❑ **Plato:** Knowledge arises through rational contemplation and dialectical reasoning, a disciplined ascent to grasp the forms and ultimate truth.

❑ **Kabbalah:** Insight flows from mystical experience—ecstatic prayer, meditation, and the esoteric exegesis of sacred texts. It blends intellectual rigor, symbolic depth, and direct encounter with the divine.

In essence, while Plato and Kabbalah both probe the interplay of physical and spiritual realms, their paths diverge sharply. Platonic thought privileges the abstract and rational, distilling a cosmos of impersonal ideals. Kabbalah, by contrast, offers a holistic vision: a personal, dynamic divinity infuses the material world, sanctified through practice, ethics, and the transformative power of the word. These differences illuminate their distinct approaches to the eternal.

Philo's Possible Indirect Influence on the Kabbalah

Philo of Alexandria emerges as a pivotal figure in Jewish intellectual history, deftly weaving Greek philosophy— Platonic and Neo-Platonic strands— into the fabric of Jewish theology. This first-century thinker forged a synthesis that reverberates in the mystical currents presaging Kabbalah, offering a historical lens through which to trace the roots of its esoteric exegesis and relentless pursuit of hidden truths.

Philo's signature lies in his allegorical approach to the Hebrew Scriptures, a method that resonates with Judaic esoteric practice. He peered beyond the literal, viewing texts like Genesis as reservoirs of profound meaning— a stance mirrored by mystics who plumb sacred writings for divine secrets. His concept of the Logos, a divine intermediary bridging God and creation, anticipates the *Sefirot*— Kabbalah's ten emanations that channel the infinite *Ein Sof* into the tangible world. For Philo, the Logos imposes order on reality; for the kabbalists, the *Sefirot* orchestrate the flow of divine light, harmonizing the celestial and terrestrial.

While scholars debate Philo's direct influence on Kabbalah,[9] Moshe Idel's scholarship underscores his enduring mark. Idel points to the cherubim in Jewish symbolism, interpreting them as embodiments of masculine and feminine divine traits— a duality echoed in early mystical texts.[10] Citing Edwin Goodenough and the *Midrash Tadshe*, Idel links the cherubim to the divine names Tetragrammaton (mercy) and *Elohim* (judgment), illuminating a cornerstone of early Judaic mystical thought: God's attributes converge within a unified essence. This idea finds richer expression in the 12th-century sage R. Abraham ben David of Posquières (Ravaad). His *du-partzufin* framework— "two faces"—casts divine qualities like mercy and justice as intertwined partners, not rivals, envisioning a dynamic divine order where opposites cohere. Ravaad's paradigm elevates creation as a balanced dance of binary forces, deepening Kabbalah's cosmic vision.[11]

Philo's legacy thus planted the seeds that would later flourish in Kabbalah. His Logos foreshadows the *Sefirot's* mediating role, while his allegories pave the way for mystical interpretation. Idel's analysis of the *cherubim*, paired with Ravaad's insights, traces an evolution: from Philo's interplay of divine attributes—Goodness and Sovereignty in *On the Special Laws* (210–211)—to Kabbalah's intricate exegesis of a cosmos suffused with Divine Presence. Unlike the restrained allegories of medieval Jewish rationalists, Philo's symbolic readings invite direct engagement with the divine, blending contemporary philosophy with Jewish theology.

As a conduit between traditions, Philo illuminates the historical and spiritual contours of Jewish mysticism. His work not only frames the complex interpretive landscape of Kabbalah but also underscores its enduring quest: to unveil the divine shimmering through scripture, symbol, and the infinite beyond. In this light, Philo stands as a vital link, deepening our grasp of Judaism's mystical dimensions and its dialogue with the broader intellectual world.

Philo of Alexandria

Plotinus's Influence on Jewish Mysticism

Plotinus (204–270 C.E.) expanded Plato's metaphysics into a mystical, structured system. While Plato envisioned a realm of ideal Forms crowned by the Form of the Good, Plotinus introduced "the One" as the transcendent source of all existence, emanating into the "Nous" (Intellect), which contains the Platonic Forms, and the "Soul," linking the spiritual and material realms. Unlike Plato's focus on intellectual comprehension, Plotinus emphasized a mystical ascent toward union with the One. This Neoplatonic framework— centered on emanation and the soul's return to the divine— extended Plato's ideas and laid a foundation that influenced kabbalistic thought, evident in shared concepts like a singular divine source, emanation, and spiritual ascent.

Plotinus's philosophy and Kabbalah exhibit deep connections rooted in Neoplatonism's impact on Jewish mysticism. Both posit a singular, infinite origin— the One in Neoplatonism, *Ein Sof* in Kabbalah—as the foundation of reality. Emanation is central to each: Plotinus describes the One unfolding into the Intellect and Soul, forming a hierarchical cosmos. At the same time, Kabbalah depicts the Divine emanating through the *Sefirot* to connect the infinite with the finite. This shared model portrays a universe interwoven with spiritual and material dimensions, stemming from one source. Similarly, both traditions prioritize mystical ascent— Plotinus's soul seeking one's reunion with the One parallels the Kabbalist's pursuit of unity with the Divine— reflecting a universal human longing for closeness to the ultimate Being.

The integration of Neoplatonic ideas into Jewish thought likely arose from cross-cultural exchanges among early Christian, Islamic, and Jewish scholars engaging with Greek philosophy. These interactions shaped Kabbalah's metaphysical framework, particularly its views on the universe and the divine. Yet, despite their parallels, Plotinus's Neoplatonism and Kabbalah emerged in distinct contexts: the former as a philosophical system in the Greco-Roman world, the latter as a mystical tradition within Judaism.

CHAPTER 3

THE JEWISH GNOSTIC EXPERIENCE

הַנִּסְתָּרֹת לַיהוָה אֱלֹהֵינוּ וְהַנִּגְלֹת לָנוּ וּלְבָנֵינוּ עַד־עוֹלָם לַעֲשׂוֹת אֶת־כָּל־
דִּבְרֵי הַתּוֹרָה הַזֹּאת

The secret things belong to the Lord our God, but the revealed things belong to us and to our children forever, to observe all the words of this Torah.

Deut. 29:29

גְנוֹסְטִיצִיזְם יְהוּדִי

JEWISH GNOSTICISM

A Brief Overview

A brief introduction to *Gnosticism* is indeed helpful before delving into Jewish Gnosticism. Gnosticism is a broad and complex religious and philosophical movement that provides essential context for understanding its various offshoots, including Jewish Gnosticism. By outlining Gnosticism's core concepts—such as the pursuit of gnosis (spiritual knowledge), its dualistic worldview, and its historical emergence—you establish a foundation that clarifies how Jewish Gnosticism adapts and diverges from this wider tradition. Without this background, the specific influences and characteristics of Jewish Gnosticism might feel disconnected or unclear.

Gnosticism is a diverse religious and philosophical movement that centers on *gnosis*—spiritual knowledge—believed to free the soul from the confines of the material world. It emerged around the fall of the Jerusalem Temple in 70 CE, partly as a response to Jewish apocalyptic disappointments and early Christian messianic failures, fostering a turn toward inner spiritual insight.[12] As Hans Jonas notes in *The Gnostic Religion*, Gnosticism is highly syncretic, weaving together influences from pre-Christian Iranian dualism and Greek mystery religions, such as the Eleusinian and Dionysian cults, which emphasized secret rites, initiation, and knowledge of the divine cosmos.[13]

The 1945 discovery of the *Nag Hammadi* library in Egypt—a collection of Coptic Gnostic texts—illuminated this syncretism, revealing how Gnosticism blended Christian, Jewish, Neoplatonic, and mystery religion elements.[14] At its core, Gnosticism posits a stark dualism: the spiritual realm is divine and good, while the material world is flawed or evil, estranging humanity from its true source. Gnostics sought to awaken the "divine spark" within, transcending material existence through esoteric knowledge. Though the world was seen as fundamentally good, historical evil corrupted it, making this spiritual quest urgent.

Within this broader Gnostic framework, Jewish Gnosticism emerged as a unique strand, blending these esoteric traditions with Jewish theology and mystical interpretations of texts like Genesis and Ezekiel. Gnostic Judaism intricately weaves aspects of divine speculation, deeply immersed in the profound and mysterious complexities encompassing the universe's nature and divinity. As a mystic voyage seeking communion with the spiritual and material realms, it prized firsthand exploration of cosmic origins through the mystical practices of meditation, rituals, and asceticism. Initially shrouded in secrecy, these teachings would eventually come to light, subtly echoing the tenets of the Kabbalah and magic, all aimed at unraveling the mysteries of existence and God.

At its core, this tradition revolves around two central ideas drawn from the biblical books of Genesis and Ezekiel. *Ma'aseh Bereshit,* or "the Work of Creation," explores the mystical interpretation of the creation narrative in Genesis, seeking to understand how the world came into being through esoteric readings that go beyond the literal story. *Ma'aseh Merkavah*, known as "the Work of the Divine Chariot," focuses on Ezekiel's vision of God's throne-chariot (Ezekiel 1:4-28), interpreted as a pathway to divine understanding. It involves contemplating the heavens and the Divine Presence, aiming to achieve a direct encounter with God. These teachings were considered so sacred and powerful that they were originally kept secret, shared only with a select few deemed capable of grasping their depth.

These mystical ideas likely emerged around the second century B.C.E., influenced by Babylonian and Syrian religious thought. This timeline positions Jewish Gnosticism as older than similar Christian and Judeo-Christian gnostic traditions, though its precise connections to them remain a matter of scholarly debate. Initially shrouded in secrecy, its teachings began to surface more openly over time, much like the spread of magical practices. These fragmented glimpses of this mystical tradition, preserved in early Jewish literature, betray the age-old prohibition against openly discoursing on gnosis. However, by the third to fifth centuries C.E., traces of gnostic ideas appeared in the Talmud—Judaism's central text of law and theology—likely added by later scholars who saw value in these mystical pursuits.

In its developed form during the second century C.E., Jewish Gnosticism emphasized three main elements: philosophical speculation about the divine, mystical rituals, and ascetic practices like fasting or self-denial. However, its approach to rituals set it apart from Christian Gnosticism. While Christian Gnosticism often relied heavily on rituals to access mystical knowledge, treating them as essential gateways to the divine, Jewish Gnosticism placed greater focus on philosophy and asceticism. This difference likely stemmed from Judaism's existing framework of religious laws and liturgy, which fulfilled many spiritual needs and reduced the reliance on additional mystical rituals. This blending of gnosis (mystical knowledge), theology, and occasional magical elements makes Jewish Gnosticism challenging to study directly, with much of our understanding derived from indirect sources, such as later rabbinical writings.

One of the most famous illustrations of the dangers of these mystical pursuits is found in the Talmud (BT Hagigah 14b). It recounts the story of four sages—Ben Azzai, Ben Zoma, Elisha ben Abuyah, and Rabbi Akiba—who entered PaRDeS, a term meaning "paradise" but symbolizing a profound mystical experience. Before their journey, Rabbi Akiba warned them to avoid deception, citing a verse about speaking truthfully before God. Their fates were starkly different: Ben Azzai died, Ben Zoma lost his sanity, Elisha ben Abuyah abandoned his faith, and only Rabbi Akiba emerged unscathed.[15] This parable underscores the risks of mystical exploration, suggesting that only a disciplined few can safely navigate it. PaRDeS, also refers to four levels of scriptural interpretation, reflecting the depth of esoteric knowledge: *Peshat* (literal), *Remez* (allegorical), *Derash* (homiletical), and *Sod* (mystical).

Centuries later, the Kabbalah developed concepts like the *Sefirot*, a system of ten divine attributes through which God interacts with the world, and emphasized the soul's ascent to higher spiritual realms, echoing the gnostic focus on bridging the physical and divine. The contemporary scholar Moshe Idel explicitly linked the PaRDeS story to Kabbalah, arguing that Rabbi Akiba's survival reflects Kabbalah's cautious approach to those pursuing a mystical ascent. In this view, preparation and discipline are critical to avoid the fates of the other sages. This connection highlights how Kabbalah evolved from earlier gnostic ideas, refining them into a structured system while retaining their elitist and esoteric nature.

In the end, Gnostic Judaism created an ancient mystical tradition that seeks to understand the divine through meditation, rituals, and self-discipline. Rooted in interpretations of Genesis and Ezekiel, it explores the creation of the world and visions of God's presence. Though initially secretive, its influence persisted, shaping later Jewish thought, including Kabbalah. The PaRDeS story serves as a timeless warning: the pursuit of esoteric knowledge is profound but perilous, reserved for those with the wisdom and resilience to endure its challenges.[16] [See the entry regarding Moshe Idel's View of Gershom Scholem's Views regarding Gnosticism.]

Mysticism May Not Be for Everybody

The story of the four sages entering PaRDeS serves as a powerful allegory supporting rabbinical caution regarding the study of Jewish mystical thought. It highlights the risks of prematurely delving into profound divine mysteries and underscores the need for personal readiness, maturity, and a strong foundation in exoteric religious study before embarking on such a spiritual journey. The tale of the four who entered PaRDeS—Rabbis Ben Azzai, Ben Zoma, Elisha ben Abuyah, and Akiba—and their distinct outcomes illustrate this wisdom. Three of the sages exemplify the dangers of engaging with mystical realities without adequate preparation, while one demonstrates the rewards of proper grounding.

Ben Azzai's death symbolizes the peril of being overwhelmed by the divine experience, unable to reconcile it with earthly existence. Ben Zoma's descent into madness reflects the psychological hazards of encountering profound spiritual truths without sufficient mental or spiritual resilience. Elisha ben Abuyah, who "peered and cut the plants," represents the risk of misinterpreting divine insights, leading to a break with traditional beliefs. A key figure in early Jewish gnostic thought, Elisha interpreted the recording angel Metatron—seated at the base of God's throne in *Hekhalot* literature—as evidence of Metatron's divine status (*Two Powers,* Segal, 10). This heresy illustrates how mystical experiences, if misunderstood, can disconnect one from established religious truths. In contrast, Rabbi Akiba, who entered and emerged safely, embodies the ideal practitioner of early mystical practice. His success suggests he possessed the spiritual maturity, intellectual foundation, and emotional balance required, reinforcing the need for wisdom often gained through life experience before exploring such depths.

While the PaRDeS allegory cautions against unprepared mystical pursuits, similar themes resonate in other Jewish mystical and magical traditions, many of which reflect traces of earlier gnostic concepts. Emerging during the late antique and medieval periods, texts like the *Hekhalot* and *Merkavah* literature blend Jewish theology with *Hellenistic* and other mystical influences. These works explore profound questions—the nature of divinity, the origin of evil, and the soul's ascent—through vivid accounts of heavenly journeys and celestial encounters. The relationship between Jewish Gnosticism, mysticism, and magic is intricate and fluid, with boundaries that often overlap. Jewish mystical midrashim borrowed from gnostic systems while assimilating elements from diverse traditions, evolving into a unique syncretic form.

Ultimately, Jewish Gnosticism emerges as an enigmatic tradition within Judaism, shaped by philosophical and mystical currents from beyond its borders. Though its full scope remains elusive, fragments of gnostic thought appear in early Jewish literature, and later traditions like Kabbalah and magical texts echo these ideas. For instance, the *Hekhalot* texts, with their depictions of heavenly ascents, reflect not only Jewish concerns but also *Hellenistic* influences, highlighting the interplay of mystical systems. Studying Jewish Gnosticism demands careful analysis of varied sources and an appreciation for its syncretic complexity. The tale of the four sages reminds us that while the pursuit of divine knowledge can enlighten, it requires preparation and respect for human limits—a lesson woven throughout Jewish mystical history.

The Interpretative World of PaRDeS

Once again, let us revisit what Rabbi Shimon said:

> Woe to the person who says the Torah presents mere stories and *ordinary words*! … Ah, but *all the words of Torah are sublime words,* sublime secrets! This story of the Torah is the garment of the Torah. Whosoever thinks that the garment is the real Torah and not something else—may

> his spirit deflate! He will have no portion in the world that is coming.... Fools of the world look only at the [garment] the story of Torah and nothing more. They do not look at what is under the garment.... As wine must sit in a jar, so too, Torah must sit in this garment. *So, look only at what is under the garment!* (Emphasis added.)[17]

PaRDeS is a beautiful Hebrew acronym, blossoming into *peshat* (literal or contextual meaning), *remez* (hinted meaning), *derash* (interpreted meaning), and *sod* (hidden meaning). Each signifies unique comprehension horizons, offering a varied perspective of the divine wisdom embedded within the Torah. A concept rooted in the medieval period, the term *PaRDeS* encapsulates the essence of these four layers, transforming the practice of interpretation into an expedition traversing through panoramas of comprehension.

Our exploration commences with the *Peshat*, the firm earth beneath us, the literal interpretation visible to the unassisted eye. It forms the foundation, the historical backdrop of the text, our launching pad into deeper spheres of meaning. With meticulous examination, we strive to unveil and distill the subtle implications concealed within the straightforward words of the Torah and decipher its Hebraic nuances and wisdom. *Remez's* second horizon manifests itself as a mere insinuation, a transient allusion on the brink of comprehension. Through this semi-transparent curtain, we perceive the text in a refreshed light, spotting glimpses of profound truths tucked just below the surface.

Next, we embark upon the domain of *Derash*, the interpreted meaning. The horizon broadens, beckoning us to interrogate, challenge, and wrestle with the text. This audacious endeavor unearths potential interpretations within the ambit of tradition and scholarship. *Derash* personifies a search for authenticity, proffering philosophical, theological, and moralistic insights invoked only when *Peshat* fails to untangle textual complexities. The final horizon, *Sod*, is the mystifying realm of the concealed. Swathed in divine mystique, it lures us beyond the text's immediate context, spurring us to discern the unspoken, divine secrets that only unwind to the contemplative mind. Here, personal experiences and spiritual leanings illuminate the text uniquely intimately, revealing mystical subtleties and grand themes of cosmic significance.

פַּרְדֵּס

PARDES – THE ORCHARD OF INTERPRETATION

Hebrew	Letter	Meaning
פְּשָׁט	פ (p)	*P'shat* - Simple, literal
רֶמֶז	ר (r)	*Remez* - Hint, Suggestion
דְּרָשׁ	ד (d)	*D'rash* - Insight
סוֹד	ס (s)	*Sod* - Mystery

In this complex dance of interpretation, the ancient text and the contemporary reader swirl in unison, amalgamating the objective with the subjective. These "two horizons," combining the past with the present, collide and blend, enabling us to encounter the text anew, revealing its multi-layered meanings within the sacred precincts of PaRDeS. Within this dynamic interaction, the symphony of interpretation achieves its climax, resonating within the reader's heart and mind.[18]

CHAPTER 4

KABBALAH'S SEEKERS OF UNITY

I have been a seeker and I still am, but I stopped asking the books and the stars. I started listening to the teaching of my Soul.
Enlightenment of soul, whatever it may see.
By quibbles of school logic cannot silenced be.

—RUMI, *Collected Poetic Works*

Piercing the Veil of Existence

Jewish mysticism, rooted in the Hebrew verb "to receive," unveils the hidden layers of existence, forging a deeper bond with the divine. Far from rigid doctrine, Kabbalah is a living tradition of secret wisdom passed through generations, illuminating the cosmos and the soul. Its rise owes much to bold mystics united by a vision of repairing a fractured world. This chapter, "Kabbalah's Seekers of Unity," traces its journey from a counterpoint to cold logic to a vibrant force that still draws seekers today. Through pivotal voices, it reveals how Jewish mysticism bridges the human and divine, the earthly and cosmic, guiding the self to its truest essence.

The story begins in the medieval Jewish world, where Maimonides' rationalism held sway. Blending faith with Aristotelian logic, he made reason the key to understanding God and scripture. Yet for some, this clarity fell short—they yearned for a soul-stirring encounter with the divine. Kabbalah emerged to answer that call, wielding symbols, paradoxes, and lived experience to uncover hidden currents beneath Jewish law and logic, rekindling tradition rather than rejecting it. Early Kabbalah took shape through cryptic texts and enigmatic figures. *Sefer HaBahir*, an early masterpiece, cast God as ten *sefirot*—divine emanations forming a cosmic map and a ladder for the soul. Around the same time, Isaac the Blind, the "father of Kabbalah" from Provence, envisioned the universe as an interplay of divine energies, laying the groundwork for what followed.

In the 13th century, Ramban (Nachmanides) wove mysticism into Jewish tradition. He saw creation *ex nihilo* as a purposeful divine act linking God to the cosmos, and transformed rituals like levirate marriage into mystical keys for redemption. His PaRDeS method—unveiling scripture's literal, allegorical, homiletical, and mystical layers—showed every word as a path to divine unity, embedding Kabbalah in Jewish life.

While Ramban grounded mysticism in tradition, Abraham Abulafia took a radical turn. This 13th-century Spanish mystic used the Hebrew alphabet and God's names as meditative tools to unlock prophetic visions and unite the soul with the divine intellect. His unconventional approach stirred debate but inspired Joseph Gikatilla, his student, to map the *sefirot* to God's names and attributes, turning Kabbalah into a dynamic path to transcendence. In late 13th-century Spain, Moshe de Leon—likely the Zohar's author—wove earlier threads into a vivid mosaic. The Zohar portrayed the divine as a fractured unity yearning for repair through human action, introducing *tikkun* (mending the world) as a clarion call that spread Kabbalah's influence. Later, in the 16th century, Eliyahu de Vidas grounded these cosmic ideals in daily ethics, showing how the quest for unity spanned the vast and the intimate.

Kabbalah expanded greatly with R. Isaac Luria (1534–1572), the "Healer of the Cosmos," in Safed. His cosmic drama—*tzimtzum* (God's contraction), *shevirat ha-kelim* (shattered vessels), and *tikkun olam* (world repair)—cast humanity as partners in redeeming divine sparks. Preserved by Hayyim Vital in Etz Hayyim, Luria's vision fused mysticism with purpose, urging souls to lift the world through *mitzvot*. Yet the pursuit of unity faced perils. The 17th-century Sabbatean heresy, ignited by Shabbatai Tzvi's messianic claims, began with promise but collapsed when he converted to Islam, leaving a cautionary tale of unchecked zeal. Still, Kabbalah's drive to find wholeness amid brokenness endured.

In 17th–18th-century Italy, R. Yosef Ergas defended Kabbalah's depth, while R. Moshe Hayyim Luzzatto integrated it with his thoughts about Mussar in *Mesillat Yesharim*, overcoming accusations of Sabbateanism to offer a disciplined ascent. Across Europe, R. Shneur Zalman of Liadi infused Luria's ideas into Chabad, Hayyim Volozhin weighed their risks, and Nachman of Breslov turned mysticism into art—his *Likutei Moharan* and Kafka-esque tales summoning the inner tzaddik. The Kotzker Rebbe's piercing aphorisms cut to the core.

In the 20th century, R. Abraham Isaac Kook reimagined mysticism for a modern age. His essay "Souls in Chaos" embraced evolution and atheism as steps toward truth, blending old and new in a vision of unity: "the fresh turns true, in hallowed hue." This chapter invites you into their world—from Ramban's study to Luzzatto's trials, Nachman's tales to Kook's bold embrace of now. Each seeker chased a wholeness beyond division. Kabbalah, through them, is no mere relic—it's a call to see light in shadow, oneness in multiplicity, and the divine within. Step in, and trace their paths to the infinite.

Kabbalah as a Reaction to Maimonidean Philosophy

Rav Nachman of Breslov observed, "Where philosophy ends, Kabbalah's wisdom begins." Philosophy explores life's mysteries through reason and observation, but it often falters when faced with metaphysical realities beyond its reach. Kabbalah steps boldly forward, embracing the divine and the unknown, transcending rational limits to offer a pathway into the mysteries of God and the cosmos.

Through its rich symbolism, Kabbalah constructs a comprehensive metaphysical framework—divine emanations (*sefirot*), the Tree of Life, and the interplay of light and vessels. It probes the connections between the divine and the mundane, the spiritual and the physical, the microcosm and the macrocosm, yielding profound insights into the essence of God, humanity, and the universe. Beyond theory, Kabbalah invites personal mystical experience and introspection, fostering direct encounters with the divine through contemplative practice. It is a wisdom both conceptualized and deeply felt.

Not all Jewish thinkers embraced this mystical turn. Figures like Saadia Gaon, Moses Maimonides, and Gersonides championed a rational, Aristotelian approach to Judaism, prioritizing logic over mystery. Yet this intellectualism left some unsatisfied, stirring a longing for a more spiritual, experiential faith. By the 12th century, this discontent fueled a shift, as Jewish mysticism gained traction—not just among solitary seekers, but within broader communities. Many, including influential leaders, began to view the prevailing rationalism as overly detached from the soul's needs.

Kabbalists met this yearning, emphasizing mysticism over intellectualism in stark contrast to Maimonidean philosophy. What began as a niche pursuit evolved into a vibrant spiritual movement. To align their teachings with Jewish tradition and ease skepticism from Talmudists and philosophers, Kabbalists claimed their wisdom was not new but a revival of an ancient tradition rooted at Mount Sinai. They argued that alongside the written Torah, Moses received a hidden teaching—unrecorded and subtle—passed down through the ages. This esoteric wisdom, they asserted, pierced the surface of existence, revealing the divine nature, the secrets of creation, and the universe's sacred blueprint.

The Early Kabbalah

Kabbalah, as recognized in modern scholarship, began to crystallize in the 12th and 13th centuries, emerging prominently in the regions of Provence (southern France) and Spain. During this transformative period, these Judaic mystical teachings coalesced into a substantial body of literature, distinct from—and at times diverging from—the legalistic and narrative traditions of the Talmud. Written often in a distinctive, esoteric Aramaic, these works primarily took the form of Torah commentaries, infusing scripture with mystical depth. At the heart of this evolving tradition stands the *Zohar*, a sacred text that surfaced suddenly in the late 13th century, likely through the efforts of Moshe de Leon in Spain. Its enigmatic prose and profound insights swiftly established it as the cornerstone of kabbalistic thought, shaping the tradition for centuries to come.

Kabbalists devoted themselves to probing the mysteries of the divine and the intricate bond between God and humanity. A central pillar of their inquiry was the concept of the *Sefirot*, a framework heavily influenced by Neoplatonic philosophy. The *Sefirot*—ten divine emanations—map the process by which God's infinite essence, termed *Ein Sof* (the Endless One), manifests within the finite, material world. Far from abstract theology, this system provides a dynamic lens for understanding the divine structure: a cascade of energies bridging the transcendent and the tangible. Each *Sefirah* represents a facet of God's nature, interacting within a cosmic hierarchy that mirrors the interplay between the spiritual and physical realms. This intricate model offered Kabbalists a sophisticated vocabulary to explore the universe's creation, sustenance, and ultimate purpose.

Throughout this book, we will embark on a detailed exploration of the *Sefirot*, unpacking their individual roles and collective significance within Judaic mystical thought. We begin with their foundational definitions—clarifying terms like *Keter* (Crown), *Chesed* (Loving-Kindness), and *Malkhut* (Kingdom)—before delving into their deeper meanings, symbolic resonances, and philosophical implications. Each *Sefirah* will be examined as a unique expression of the divine, revealing how attributes like wisdom, justice, or beauty interplay to form a cohesive whole.

We will trace their dynamic relationships, such as the balance between *Gevurah* (Severity) and *Chesed*, and their broader role in shaping Kabbalah's vision of existence. By illuminating their attributes and functions, this journey aims to provide a comprehensive understanding of this cornerstone of Jewish mysticism, enriching the reader's grasp of its profound theological and metaphysical framework.

Sefer HaBahir

The *Sefer HaBahir* or "Book of Brightness" stands as a cornerstone in the history of kabbalistic literature, marking a transformative period in Jewish mysticism. Its earliest mention can be traced back to 1174 in Provence, France, though it is often attributed to the 1st-century sage R. Nehunya ben HaKanah, a contemporary of R. Yochanan ben Zakai. The text was instrumental in shifting the focus of Jewish mystical tradition from the *Merkavah* and *Hekhalot* literature, which concentrated on heavenly ascents and angelology, to a more philosophically rich and symbolic kabbalistic framework. A groundbreaking aspect of the *Sefer HaBahir* was its introduction of the *Sefirot* concept—ten divine emanations or attributes through which God interacts with the universe. This idea of the *Sefirot*, later integral to Jewish mystical thought, provided a spiritual structure linking the divine, the cosmos, the utterances of creation in Genesis, and the Ten Commandments. This connection between cosmology, ethics, and the Torah's language significantly developed Jewish thought.

The *Bahir* also stands out for its use of symbolic language and imagery, particularly the metaphor of light, drawing on Platonic and Gnostic influences to describe divine emanation. It introduced groundbreaking concepts like the divine's male and female aspects, represented by the "*Ein Sof*" (Infinite) and "*Shekhinah*" in kabbalistic cosmology. The text is notable for its method of biblical interpretation, treating Torah verses as esoteric descriptions of divine realms and the soul's journey. This approach greatly influenced esoteric interpretations of the Torah and Jewish ritual, infusing them with deeper mystical meanings.

The *Sefer HaBahir* bridges Jewish mystical tradition, linking older forms of mysticism, like *Hekhalot* and *Merkavah* mysticism associated with Ezekiel's chariot vision, with the emergent kabbalistic thought. By aligning with ancient esoteric traditions, the *Bahir* sought to establish its authority and antiquity, reinterpreting older traditions within its new framework. Furthermore, the text's composition reflects its nature as a compilation, possibly with multiple authors or compilers. Its diverse literary forms, including dialogues, parables, and homilies, are characteristic of early Judaic mystical literature, where new ideas were often woven into older narratives and ascribed to revered ancient authorities.

Isaac the Blind

In the annals of Jewish mysticism, Rabbi Isaac ben Abraham of Posquières, informally referred to as "Isaac the Blind" (סגיא נהור), holds a significant position. He thrived during France's 12th and 13th centuries, marking an epoch in kabbalistic thought. Though not the inventor, Isaac's transformative effect on the Geonim's mystical traditions shaped Kabbalah as we know it today.

Renowned Kabbalist and biblical commentator R. Baḥya ben Asher, along with scholars Joseph Gikatilla and Shem-Tob ibn Gaon, revered Isaac as the "Father of the Kabbalah". To them, he received an esoteric wisdom lineage that stretched back to the revelation at Mount Sinai. Isaac's mastery lay in his systematic articulation of this wisdom. His disciples, notably Azriel Ben Menahem of Gerona, disseminated his teachings, thus promoting the resonance of the kabbalistic tradition.

- ❑ R. Isaac's profound contributions included the identification of the ten *Sefirot* or divine emanations and the unprecedented introduction of metempsychosis, the transmigration of souls.

- ❑ In his teachings, the doctrine of Sefirot held primacy. It describes the ten divine emanations through which *Ein Sof* (the Infinite) unveils Himself, forming a pillar of esoterical thought.

This doctrine offered the kabbalists a metaphysical blueprint to comprehend and relate to the divine.

- Furthermore, Isaac innovated the doctrine of *gilgul,* the reincarnation or transmigration of souls. This new layer about the soul's nature was a novelty in Jewish mystical thought then. Isaac's spiritual acumen, manifesting as an ability to ascertain a soul's age, heightened his mystique and elevated his stature in Jewish mysticism.

"Isaac the Blind" as imagined.

Isaac's blindness invites curiosity. Did it precede his birth, or was it an affliction of his later life? Despite this, his blindness did not curtail his intellectual pursuits. Rather, it augmented his spiritual insight, gaining him veneration in Jewish mystical history. In the 12th and 13th centuries, blindness was not an obstacle to intellectual accomplishments. The oral tradition valued in these societies allowed scholars like Isaac to dictate their insights to scribes, and the enhanced memory often found in such cultures likely facilitated their learning process.[19] It is plausible that Isaac's "blindness" was metaphorical, denoting his indifference to the physical world and his profound engagement with the metaphysical. Regardless of his physical condition, Isaac's influence on Kabbalah and Jewish thought was momentous.

It showcased his ability to transcend physical limitations in pursuit of scholarly endeavors. It's intriguing that Isaac, reportedly born blind, expressed vibrant color imagery in his mystic expressions. According to Jewish mystical tradition, Isaac could perceive every person's soul, nature, and history. His life and legend spawned a lineage of charismatic Jewish leaders, enhanced by the Kabbalah, who impacted Jewish spiritual life. His teachings propelled a new mystical circle in Gerona, near Barcelona, anchoring the Kabbalah's centrality in Jewish spirituality and metaphysics during the Middle Ages.

Ramban

Rabbi Moshe ben Nahman, commonly known as Nachmanides or the Ramban, is one of the most influential figures in Jewish history. He is renowned for his contributions as a Talmudic scholar, philosopher, physician, and kabbalist. His approach to Jewish mystical tradition was profoundly significant and uniquely distinguished his scholarship. Born in 1194 in Gerona, Spain, Nachmanides was steeped in a rich cultural and intellectual milieu that combined Jewish law, philosophy, and Kabbalah. He was first exposed to its esoteric teachings during the late twelfth and early thirteenth centuries, a period marked by the proliferation of early mystical texts such as *Sefer Yetzirah* (Book of Creation) and Sefer *HaBahir* ("Book of Brightness"). However, it was not merely his exposure to these texts that forged his connection with Kabbalah but his distinct method of interpretation and synthesis.

Ramban frequently includes mystical interpretations through the use of על דרך האמת *(derekh ha'emet)* based on ideas gleaned from the Kabbalah.[20] This concept stands in contrast to the more familiar exegetical term and contextual meaning known as *peshat*, contrasting with the more straightforward על דרך הפשט (*derekh ha-peshat*).[21] Such mystical insights require a background in fundamental mystical concepts to be fully understood, as Ramban indicates.[22] He is often lauded for integrating *Halakhic* (Jewish legal) discussions with esoteric kabbalistic ideas. This integrative approach became his signature style and later influenced Judaic spiritual and *Halakhic* literature. His seminal work, a commentary on the Torah, clearly demonstrates this method. Ramban elucidates some of the most complex Jewish mystical concepts within this commentary, embedding them within the broader Halakhic and *aggadic* (narrative) contexts.

A. Ramban's View of Creatio Ex Nihilo

For instance, in his commentary on the opening verses of Genesis, Ramban grapples with the cosmogonic problem of creation *ex nihilo* (creation from nothing), a topic of contention between Jewish, Christian, and Islamic philosophers of his time. His interpretation subtly marries the philosophical, the mystical, and the literal. He posits that the primordial substance described in Genesis was, in fact, the raw material for creation and served as the mystical substratum from which the physical world emerged. This concept is deeply kabbalistic, rooted in the notion of *'Ein Sof'* (the infinite), the primal source of all creation in the world of Kabbalah.

B. Ramban's View of the Levirate Marriage

Levirate marriage, known in Hebrew as *yibbum*, is a biblical mandate (Deut. 25:5–10) stipulating that if a man dies childless, his brother must marry the widow. This law aims to secure the widow's welfare and preserve the deceased's name within Israel. Ramban approached Jewish law—including *yibbum*—through a distinctive blend of Talmudic exegesis, philosophical reasoning, and esoteric insight, enriching traditional interpretations with mystical depth.

In his Torah commentary, Ramban views *yibbum* as more than a social or familial duty. Beyond supporting the widow or perpetuating a lineage, he imbues it with profound spiritual significance rooted in Kabbalah. He posits that when the surviving brother performs *yibbum*, the soul of the deceased reincarnates into the child born of this union. This idea hinges on the doctrine of *gilgul hanefesh* (reincarnation), which holds that souls may return to the physical world to complete unfinished spiritual tasks, rectify past failings, or fulfill a divine purpose curtailed by premature death.

For Ramban, *yibbum* thus transcends its legal framework, becoming a sacred act of cosmic restoration. The child conceived carries forward the deceased brother's soul, offering it a renewed opportunity to achieve its intended destiny. This perspective transforms levirate marriage into a bridge between the earthly and the divine, intertwining human relationships with the soul's eternal journey. It exemplifies Ramban's hallmark approach—melding Jewish law with mysticism to reveal the hidden spiritual currents beneath the Torah's commandments.[23]

C. Ramban's View of the PaRDeS

Ramban (Nachmanides) passionately embraced the concept of *Sod* (secret), the pinnacle of the four-tiered Pardes system of biblical interpretation—Peshat (literal), *Remez* (allegorical), *Derash* (homiletical), and *Sod* (mystical). He held that every verse of the Torah concealed profound, hidden meanings accessible through a kabbalistic lens. For Ramban, scripture was not merely a legal or historical document but a mosaic of divine mysteries, revealing the spiritual underpinnings of existence. This approach sharply distinguished him from rationalist thinkers like Maimonides, who prioritized philosophical clarity, often grounded in Aristotelian logic, over mystical exploration. Where Maimonides sought to reconcile faith with reason, Ramban leaned into the esoteric, viewing the Torah as a gateway to the divine unseen.

Yet Ramban's commitment to Kabbalah was not without nuance. Despite his deep mystical bent, he remained discerning, cautioning against the pitfalls of superficial or reckless engagement with this emerging esoteric tradition. He recognized that its complexity and allure could lead to misinterpretation or misuse, potentially distorting Jewish theology or practice. His warnings reflect a balanced stance: a champion of mysticism who valued its depth but insisted on rigorous analysis, and he grounded study to safeguard its integrity.

"Ramban" as imagined.

Ramban's influence extended far beyond his writings and personal convictions. As a towering figure in 13th-century Catalonia's Jewish community, he cultivated an environment ripe for kabbalistic inquiry. His hometown of Gerona emerged as a vibrant hub of esoteric Jewish learning, drawing scholars and mystics eager to explore the Torah's hidden dimensions. This flourishing was no accident—Ramban's leadership, intellectual stature, and teachings nurtured a generation of kabbalists, cementing Gerona's status as a key center of mystical thought alongside Provence and Castile. His Torah commentaries, infused with mystical insights, became foundational texts, bridging traditional exegesis with the burgeoning mystical tradition.

Nachmanides' contribution to Jewish mysticism is monumental. By legitimizing and refining esoteric interpretation within the framework of Jewish law and scholarship, he not only enriched the spiritual landscape of his time but also left an enduring legacy. His synthesis of Talmudic mastery, philosophical acumen, and mystical vision positioned him as a pivotal figure, shaping Kabbalah's trajectory and ensuring its integration into the broader mosaic of Jewish thought.

A Brief Biological Sketch of R. Abraham Abulafia

R. Abraham ben Samuel Abulafia (1240–1291), born in Saragossa, Spain, stands as a transformative figure in mystical thought. His spiritual odyssey began at 18, following his father's death, propelling him on a restless quest for enlightenment. He journeyed first to Israel, seeking the mythical Sambatyon River and the Ten Lost Tribes, but conflict in Acre forced him onward to Europe. After marrying in Greece, he settled in Italy, where he plunged into its esoteric study under the tutelage of prominent scholars. Among them was Hillel ben Samuel of Verona (1223–1295), a staunch defender of Maimonidean philosophy, whose influence likely shaped Abulafia's early engagement with rationalist and mystical ideas.

In 13th-century Barcelona, Abulafia fully embraced Kabbalah, convinced it unlocked prophetic insight. This conviction ignited a mystical movement, driven by his voluminous writings. Key works include *Get ha-Shemot* (Book of Names), a mystical reimagining of Maimonides' *Guide for the Perplexed*—hinting at hidden mystical depths in the rationalist's work—and *Sifrei Nevu'ah* (*Books of Prophecy*), composed under a pseudonym derived from numerical patterns in his name (gematria). His radical approach, blending linguistic mysticism with meditative techniques, stirred both inspiration and turmoil. In 1280, some disciples, swayed by teachings that echoed Christian motifs, converted to Christianity, underscoring the confusion his ideas could provoke.[24] Undeterred, Abulafia that same year audaciously attempted to convert Pope Nicholas III in Rome to his visionary ideals—an act that led to brief imprisonment. Released, he settled in Sicily, where he penned *Or HaSechel* (*Light of the Intellect*) and *Otzar Eden Ganuz* (*Treasure of*

Hidden Eden), fusing meditations on the Tetragrammaton (God's four-letter name) with introspective autobiography.

Abulafia's ambitions grew bolder still. By 1284, he claimed the mantle of Messiah, predicting the Messianic era's onset in 1290. These declarations sparked a fierce backlash, most notably from R. Solomon ben Aderet, a leading rabbinical scholar who excommunicated him for heresy; he might have also held him spiritually responsible for the apostasy of several of his students. Yet opposition could not silence Abulafia. His innovative mysticism—centered on the Hebrew alphabet, divine names, and personal transcendence—left an indelible, if controversial, legacy in Kabbalistic thought, inspiring later figures like Joseph Gikatilla while challenging the boundaries of Jewish orthodoxy.

Heinrich Graetz's View of Abulafia and His Movement

Heinrich Graetz, a prominent 19th-century Jewish historian, viewed the Kabbalah, particularly through the lens of Abraham Abulafia's life and influence, as a complex and often problematic phenomenon within Jewish mysticism. According to Graetz, Abulafia, a self-proclaimed Messiah and prophet, developed a "prophetic Kabbala" rooted in strict moral behavior, asceticism, and obscure mystical revelations. His charismatic personality and bold claims attracted followers in Sicily, where he sought to prepare a return to the Holy Land. However, his ideas faced skepticism and opposition, notably from Solomon ben Aderet, a respected rabbi who denounced Abulafia as illiterate and dangerous, prompting Abulafia to respond with a vitriolic defense that alienated many.

Graetz portrays Abulafia's Kabbalah as eccentric and delusional, noting his eventual exile to the tiny island of Comino after persecution in Sicily around 1288. There, Abulafia continued producing mystical writings—over twenty-two prophetic works—despite their origins in what Graetz calls a "diseased brain." His bitterness toward Jews who rejected his teachings, contrasted with his claim that Christians were more receptive, underscored his growing isolation. Graetz sees Abulafia's influence as contagious, sparking similar messianic fervor in Spain through figures like the prophets of Ayllon and Avila, who also claimed divine inspiration but ultimately led followers to disappointment and confusion, such as the mysterious appearance of crosses on their garments in 1295.

Graetz extends his critique to Abulafia's disciples, like Joseph Gikatilla, whose mystical works echoed his master's eccentricities, and to Moses de Leon, whom Graetz considers the most impactful yet deceptive Kabbalist. De Leon's creation of the Zohar gave the movement lasting prominence, though Graetz questions whether his motives were selfish or pious, ultimately deeming him a skilled but insincere impostor. In Graetz's view, the Kabbalah under Abulafia and his successors represented a mix of sincere delusion and manipulative fraud, producing both fascination and harmful consequences within Jewish communities, ultimately reflecting a "diseased state" of religious thought.[25]

Abulafia's Contribution to Kabbalah

Abraham Abulafia (1240–1291) stands as one of the most innovative and singular voices in the Kabbalistic tradition. Born in Saragossa, Spain, he crafted a bold and unconventional approach to Jewish mysticism, distinguishing himself from his peers. At the core of his contribution lies *Tziruf* (צֵרוּף), or "Permutation of Letters," a groundbreaking meditative technique inspired by the seminal Kabbalistic text *Sefer Yetzirah* (Book of Creation). Abulafia viewed each Hebrew letter as a distinct channel to divine energies, reimagining the alphabet as a vibrant lattice of spiritual potency.

This method signaled a profound shift in Jewish mysticism, pivoting from the cosmological focus of texts like the *Zohar*—with its *Sefirot*—to an intensely personal, experiential practice. Abulafia intertwined systematic letter permutations with the intentional formation of sacred words, peeling back hidden layers of meaning within scripture. Far from abstract wordplay, these practices fused with meditative techniques: rapid recitation of letter sequences, rhythmic chanting of divine names, controlled breathing, and precise bodily postures. This fusion transformed linguistic manipulation into a powerful conduit for divine connection, aiming to spark prophetic visions and ecstatic union with God. For

Abulafia, engaging the Hebrew language was a sacred alchemy, a bridge linking the practitioner's soul to the infinite.

Since visionary experience lay at the heart of his mystical journey, Abulafia extolled the vivid visualization of divine names, especially the Tetragrammaton (YHWH), as a direct route to divine communion. To induce this elevated state, he advocated rigorous ascetic disciplines—prolonged sleep deprivation, fasting, ceaseless letter recitation, and distinctive breathing patterns—crafted to shatter ordinary awareness and foster a mind ripe for prophetic insight. His approach married physicality and spirituality, turning the body and breath into instruments for transcending the mundane and accessing the divine intellect, a notion he borrowed from Maimonides' philosophy but infused with ecstatic zeal.

Abulafia's inquiry reached deeper still, probing the spiritual essence of the Hebrew alphabet. Through Kabbalistic tools like *gematria* (numerical word analysis), *notarikon* (acronyms), and *temurah* (letter substitution), he traced connections between words and divine names. He also pioneered "jumping" (*dilug*), a fluid process of associative leaps within defined limits, urging practitioners to break from linear thinking and expand their consciousness toward profound spiritual truths. To Abulafia, Hebrew was not merely a language but a mystical code—a *mosaic* of divine wisdom—whose decipherment could lift the soul to higher planes of awareness.

Yet, for all his ingenuity, Abulafia wrestled with a moral quandary over sharing his teachings. His prolific corpus—twenty-six books, a number mirroring the *gematria* of YHWH (10+5+6+5 = 26)—remained largely private during his lifetime, honoring the Kabbalistic custom of restricting esoteric knowledge to a select few. This tension between revelation and restraint shaped his legacy, as he weighed the impulse to illuminate against the risk of misinterpretation by the unprepared. His caution was not unfounded; his radical ideas drew scrutiny, culminating in his excommunication by Rabbi Solomon ben Aderet. Still, his influence rippled outward, leaving a lasting imprint on Jewish mysticism. In 16th-century Safed, luminaries like Moses Cordovero and Isaac Luria engaged with his concepts indirectly, weaving his ecstatic Kabbalah into broader traditions and spotlighting personal redemption over cosmic frameworks.

Abulafia's manuscripts, mostly unpublished until the late 20th century, preserve a treasure trove of mystical thought, enduring despite his polarizing reputation. His final chapter, spent in obscurity on the remote island of Comino near Malta, remains cloaked in enigma—a fitting close to a life defined by relentless spiritual questing. Through his fusion of rational philosophy and ecstatic practice, Abulafia redefined Kabbalah as a pathway to inner transformation and divine encounter, cementing his place as a visionary whose legacy transcends the controversies that shadowed him.

R. *Moshe De Leon*

Rabbi Moshe de Leon (c. 1240–1305) occupies a central role in the Kabbalistic tradition, renowned as the presumed architect of the Zohar, the cornerstone of Jewish mysticism. His life unfolded during Spain's Golden Age of Jewish culture, a vibrant era of intellectual and spiritual flourishing in the Iberian Peninsula. De Leon's profound erudition in Kabbalistic thought, coupled with his remarkable ability to unravel complex mystical concepts, elevated him as a luminary among his 13th-century peers in Castile.

De Leon's scholarly journey began with a deep engagement in religious studies and philosophy, notably captivated by Maimonides' *Guide for the Perplexed.* This rationalist foundation initially shaped his thinking, but his path soon veered toward Jewish mysticism, drawn by the esoteric currents swirling among Castilian Kabbalists. Immersed in their circles, he found a kindred spirit in their teachings, igniting a passion that fueled his prolific output. His early works, often termed the "Mystical *Midrash*," laid the groundwork for what would become the Zohar. Written in a blend of Aramaic and Hebrew, frequently under pseudonyms, these texts tackled ethics, the soul's eschatology, and the hidden meanings of scripture—offering a mystical counterweight to the era's dominant rationalism.

The Zohar, which de Leon attributed to the second-century sage Rabbi Shimon bar Yochai to imbue it with ancient authority, is widely regarded by modern scholars as his creation, possibly with input from contemporaries like Todros Abulafia or other Castilian mystics. This expansive mystical commentary reimagines Torah interpretation, probing the nature of God, creation, and reality through a Kabbalistic lens. At its heart lies the Sefirot—ten divine emanations mapping the flow of God's infinite essence (*Ein Sof*) into the finite world. Far from abstract theology, the Zohar weaves a mosaic of divine wisdom, blending narrative, allegory, and metaphysical insight to illuminate the interplay between the spiritual and material realms.

Beyond the Zohar, de Leon's literary legacy includes significant works like *Shekel ha-Kodesh* (The Holy Shekel), *Ha-Nefesh ha-Hakhamah* (The Wise Soul), and *Sefer ha-Rimmon* (Book of the Pomegranate). Each delves into distinct facets of Kabbalistic philosophy—metaphysics, the reasons behind commandments (*ta'amei ha-mitzvot*), and the soul's journey after death—enriching the tradition with depth and variety. In 1305, shortly before his death, de Leon invited the mystic Isaac of Acre to examine what he claimed was the original Zohar manuscript at his home in Ávila. Yet, his passing in Valladolid that same year left the manuscript's existence in doubt; his widow later denied its presence, fueling speculation about its origins. Despite this ambiguity, the symbiotic relationship between de Leon's broader writings and the Zohar is unmistakable, with his works serving as both a prelude and a companion to its mystical vision.

Moshe de Leon's death in 1305 marked the end of his earthly life, but his influence reverberated through the centuries. The Zohar, alongside his other writings, forms a bedrock of Kabbalistic literature, shaping its study and practice into the modern era. His ability to synthesize mystical intuition with intellectual rigor bridged the esoteric and the exoteric, offering a framework that continues to guide Jewish mystical thought. His legacy endures as a testament to the transformative power of Kabbalah, cementing his place as one of its most consequential figures.

Abulafia's Student: R. Joseph ben Abraham Gikatilla

R. Joseph ben Abraham Gikatilla was born in 1248 in Medinaceli, Old Castile. Studying under the esteemed Kabbalist Abraham Abulafia, Gikatilla's exceptional knowledge and aptitude in Jewish mystical thought led to widespread belief in his capability to perform miracles, earning him the title "*Joseph Ba'al ha-Nissim*," or the "Master of Miracles."

Gikatilla devoted his life to exploring mystical combinations and transpositions of letters and numbers, a passion he shared with his mentor, Abulafia. Despite his deep investment in mysticism, he respected philosophy and strived to harmonize it with the Kabbalah, asserting that the latter formed the basis for the former. Gikatilla's works embody an evolving progression of philosophical insight transformed into mysticism, demonstrating an extensive understanding of secular sciences and familiarity with the eminent works of Ibn Gabirol, Ibn Ezra, and Maimonides, among others. He passed away in Peñafiel sometime after 1305. Variations of his name, including "Gribzul," "Karnitol," and "Necatil," have been recorded in different manuscripts, all believed to be alterations of "Gikatilla."

Commencing his literary career at twenty-six, Gikatilla authored a considerable body of work. His first significant contribution was "*Ginnat Egoz*," a Kabbalistic treatise divided into three parts. It delved into the various names of God, the letters of the alphabet, and vowels from religious, philosophical, physical, and mystical perspectives. However, Gikatilla faced criticism from Isaac ben Samuel of Acre for his liberal use of the Holy Name in his work.

Later, Gikatilla's focus shifted to mysticism, an influence evident in his attempts to harmonize philosophy with the Kabbalah. This resulted in significant literary contributions like *Ginnat e'goz* (*Nut Orchard*), wherein he interpreted the nut as a symbol of mysticism. He also used *Ginnat* to represent the initial letters of three names for esoteric interpretation methods. His writings heavily influenced his contemporary Moses de León, the probable author of the critical Jewish mystical work, the Zohar.

Subsequently, the Zohar reciprocally influenced Gikatilla, as evidenced by his next significant work, *Sha'are' Orah* (*Gates of Light*), a treatise on Kabbalist symbolism.

Standard *Sefirot* commentaries, rooted in theosophical Kabbalah, begin with *Keter* or *Ein Sof* and descend through the *Sefirot* (*Hokhma, Binah*, etc.) to *Malkhut,* reflecting creation's unfolding. This descending path emphasizes divine powers and their role in the world's structure, often aiming to understand or influence them. Gikatilla, however, starts lower—implicitly with *Malkhut*—and moves upward to *Keter,* framing the *Sefirot* as stages in the mystic's return to the divine source. His focus on divine names as central symbols, rather than just powers, further distinguishes his approach, blending intellectual analysis with mystical intent.[26]

In his *Sha'arei Orah* ("Gates of Light"), Gikatilla presents the Sefirot—ten divine emanations—as a structured system, typically arranged in three triads (*Keter-Hokhma-Binah, Chesed-Gevurah-Tiferet, Netzach-Hod-Yesod*) plus a distinct Malkhut or Shekhina, symbolizing divine immanence. Often depicted in three horizontal lines (left, right, center) rather than a descending sequence, the top triad features *Hokhma* (Wisdom, right), linked to biblical wisdom traditions, and Binah (Understanding, left), balanced or crowned by *Keter* (Crown, center), associated with divine will or nothingness. This circular system ties *Keter* to *Malkhut* (Kingship), reflecting unity between the highest and lowest. Philosophically, *Keter* may align with *Ein Sof* (the Infinite), prompting *Da'at* (Knowledge, with intuitive undertones) as an alternative tenth *Sefirah.* Gikatilla's framework blends mysticism, Neoplatonic ideas, and Jewish symbolism, mapping the divine-human connection in a dynamic, accessible way.[27]

Gikatilla's *Sha'are Orah* ("Gates of Light") is considered a monumental work in Jewish mystical thought, where he provides an extensive analysis of the divine names within the context of the ten sephiroth, or the ten divine emanations. Each chapter is devoted to one *Sefirah*, providing a comprehensive guide for understanding the divine attributes and manifestations according to Kabbalistic philosophy. Gikatilla's works played a substantial role in popularizing and expanding Jewish mystical thought during the medieval period, and they continue to be studied for their philosophical and mystical insights.

Judah Abarbanel: Mystic's Echoes in a Philosopher's Voice

Judah Abarbanel (1465-1521), known to the world as Leone Ebreo, stands as a bridge between worlds—Jewish and Christian, medieval and Renaissance, rational and mystical. Born in Lisbon to the illustrious Abarbanel family, he was the son of Isaac Abarbanel, a towering figure in Jewish scholarship whose biblical commentaries and theological writings often engaged with Kabbalistic ideas. Judah's life was marked by upheaval: the expulsion of Jews from Spain in 1492 forced him into exile, first to Naples, then across Italy, where he penned his philosophical masterpiece, *Dialoghi d'amore.* This work, a series of dialogues on the nature of love, blends Neoplatonism with Jewish tradition, raising the question: how deeply did Kabbalah, the esoteric heartbeat of Jewish mysticism, shape his thought? To explore this, we must consider his heritage, his intellectual context, and the text itself, tracing the threads of mystery that weave through his legacy.

Judah's father, Isaac Abarbanel (1437–1508), provides the first lens. A statesman, financier, and scholar, Isaac was steeped in Jewish learning, including Kabbalah, which had flourished in Spain during the 13th and 14th centuries with texts like the Zohar. Isaac's commentaries on the Torah, such as his work on Deuteronomy, occasionally reflect Kabbalistic concepts, like the *Sefirot* (divine emanations) or the interplay of divine unity and multiplicity. He was not a full-fledged Kabbalist like Moses de León or Isaac Luria, but he respected the tradition, integrating its insights into his exegesis while prioritizing rational analysis. Growing up in this household, Judah would have been exposed to Kabbalah as part of a broader Jewish intellectual tapestry. His education likely included the Torah, Talmud, and philosophical works alongside mystical texts, a blend mirrored in the Renaissance humanism he later encountered in Italy. This familial grounding suggests Kabbalah was a familiar melody in Judah's life, even if he didn't sing it as his primary tune.

The *Dialoghi d'amore*, written in Italian and published posthumously in 1535, offers the clearest window into Judah's relationship with Kabbalah.[28] Structured as a conversation between Philo (lover) and Sophia (wisdom), the text explores love as a cosmic force binding the universe, from the divine to the human, the intellectual to the physical. This framework owes much to Neoplatonism, a philosophy popularized by figures like Marsilio Ficino and Pico della Mirandola, whom Judah likely encountered in Italy's humanist circles. Neoplatonism posits a hierarchy of existence emanating from the One, a concept strikingly parallel to Kabbalah's *Ein Sof* (the Infinite) and its Sefirot. In the *Dialoghi*, Judah describes love as originating in God, descending through celestial intelligences, and animating the material world—a flow reminiscent of Kabbalistic emanation. For instance, he writes of God as the "first cause" whose beauty and goodness permeate creation, a notion that echoes the Zohar's depiction of divine light cascading through the Sefirot to sustain reality.

Yet, Judah's treatment of these ideas diverges from traditional Kabbalah in tone and method. Where Kabbalists like Isaac Luria delve into intricate metaphysical systems—*tzimtzum* (divine contraction), the breaking of vessels, and the repair of the world—Judah remains philosophical, not esoteric. He doesn't cite the Zohar or employ Kabbalistic terminology explicitly; instead, he universalizes the concept of divine unity and love, making it accessible to a Renaissance audience of Jews and Christians alike. This suggests a selective engagement: he draws on Kabbalah's mystical sensibility—its vision of an interconnected cosmos infused with Divine Presence—but reframes it in a rational, Neoplatonic idiom. His father's influence likely shaped this approach; Isaac, too, balanced mysticism with reason, using Kabbalah to enrich exegesis without surrendering to its speculative depths. Judah, then, inherits a Kabbalistic awareness but adapts it to a broader philosophical stage.

The Renaissance context amplifies this dynamic. In Italy, Judah lived amid a cultural ferment where Jewish mysticism met Christian and pagan thought. Pico della Mirandola, a contemporary admirer of Kabbalah, argued that it proved the divinity of Christ, blending it with Neoplatonism and Hermeticism. While there's no direct evidence Judah met Pico, their shared milieu—Naples, Venice, and humanist salons—implies he was aware of such syntheses. The *Dialoghi* reflects this cross-pollination: its emphasis on love as a unifying force mirrors Kabbalah's focus on divine harmony, yet its style aligns with the humanist quest for universal truths. Some scholars, like Moshe Idel, suggest Judah's work contains "Kabbalistic echoes," such as the idea of the soul's ascent to God through love, akin to the Kabbalistic goal of *devekut* (clinging to the divine). Others, like Gershom Scholem, see him as more Neoplatonist than Kabbalist, noting the absence of specific mystical practices or texts.

Judah's personal trials, exile, and the forced baptism of his son by Portuguese authorities may also have informed his relationship with Kabbalah. The *Dialoghi* often explores love as a redemptive force, a theme resonant with Kabbalah's *tikkun* (repair of the world). After losing his child to Christian coercion, Judah's focus on cosmic harmony could reflect a yearning to mend a fractured existence, a subtle nod to Kabbalistic restoration. Yet, he never frames this in explicitly Jewish terms; his exile pushed him toward a universal language, perhaps distancing him from the particularism of Kabbalistic tradition. His son's fate, a wound he carried through Italy, might have made the esoteric less urgent than a philosophy that could speak across divides.

So, what was Judah Abarbanel's relationship with Kabbalah? It was neither that of a devoted *mekubbal* (traditional Kabbalist) nor a complete outsider. He stood at a crossroads, absorbing Kabbalah's mystical resonance through his father's teachings and the Jewish heritage of Spain, then refracting it through the prism of Renaissance humanism. The *Dialoghi d'amore* hums with Kabbalistic undertones—divine unity, emanation, the soul's journey—but these are harmonized with Neoplatonic chords, not played in the distinct key of the Zohar or *Sefer Yetzirah*. Unlike his father, who engaged Kabbalah within a Jewish framework, Judah's exile and intellectual encounters led him to a broader stage, where mysticism became a universal song rather than a secret doctrine. His work invites us to hear the echoes of Kabbalah, not as a system he mastered, but as a melody that enriched his vision of love's eternal dance.

Judah's story offers a bridge: he shows how mystical ideas can ripple beyond their origins, touching even those who don't wear the Kabbalist's mantle. His relationship with Kabbalah was one of influence, not immersion—a dialogue, not a doctrine—reminding us that mystery, like love, flows through many channels, harmonizing the human and the divine in unexpected ways.

R. Moshe Cordevero

Rabbi Moses Cordovero (1522–1570), known as the Ramak, was a pivotal Kabbalist in *Safed*, a 16th-century center of Jewish mysticism. Born likely of Spanish descent, he studied Jewish law under Rabbi Joseph Caro (1488–1575), author of the *Shulchan Aruch*, who lauded his legal insight in a responsum (*She'eloth Uteshubhoth, 'Abhkath Rokhel*, No. 91), citing Proverbs 23:15. From age twenty, his mystical training came from his brother-in-law Solomon Alkabetz (d. c. 1580), composer of the Sabbath hymn *Lekha Dodi*, a ritual born in *Safed's* ascetic circle who welcomed the Sabbath in white. Together, they practiced *gerushin*—pilgrimages to ancient Kabbalists' graves—documented in Cordovero's *Sefer Gerushin*, seeking inspiration from sacred proximity.

Cordovero led *Safed's* Kabbalah school before Isaac Luria (1534–1572), his student who later surpassed him with new interpretations, yet still honored him as "master." His key works, *Pardes Rimonim* and *Tomer Devorah*, shaped Jewish mysticism. *Pardes Rimonim* systematically organizes Kabbalistic concepts like the *Sefirot*, while *Tomer Devorah* offers an accessible, poetic guide to ethical living, urging emulation of divine attributes (*middot*)—compassion, patience, love—for *Tikkun Olam* (world repair). His *Safed* brotherhood embraced strict piety, banning profane thoughts, speaking only Hebrew, and mourning the Temple nightly, as reflected in moral precepts he drafted (noted by Solomon Schechter).

Tomer Devorah focuses on imitating the divine attributes, or *middot,* described in Judaic esoteric thought, providing practical advice on cultivating traits like compassion, patience, and love. This work is notable for its poetic language and deep insights into the nature of God and humanity, offering a unique blend of spiritual and ethical guidance. It suggests that by emulating these divine qualities, individuals can contribute to *Tikkun Olam*, the repair of the world, thus emphasizing a spiritually grounded social responsibility.[29]

"Rabbi Moshe Cordevero" as imagined.

The concept of imitating God, central to Rabbinic ethics, finds roots in biblical verses like Leviticus 19:2 ("Be holy, for I am holy") and Deuteronomy 11:22 ("walk in His ways"). Rabbinic texts, such as the Sifre interpret this as emulating God's attributes—mercifulness and compassion—while Hama b. Hanina (3rd century) expands it to practical acts like clothing the naked or visiting the sick, citing Genesis 3:21 and 18:1 (Sotah 14a). Abba Saul (2nd century) reads Exodus 15:2 as "be like Him," and Maimonides[30] explains divine epithets (e.g., "merciful") as models for human behavior, not literal qualities of God. For Rabbis, unsystematic in philosophy, God's Torah command suffices without deeper inquiry into why or how.

Kabbalah, however, reframes this doctrine through the Ten *Sefirot*, divine emanations revealing God's qualities—mercy, power, beauty—within the "Supernal Man," after whose image humans are made (Genesis 1:27). Unlike Maimonides' symbolic view, where anthropomorphisms reflect God's acts, not His essence (Guide I.54), Kabbalists distinguish *Ein Sof* (the unknowable Infinite) from the revealed God of scripture. The *Sefirot* bridge this gap, channeling the Infinite into creation, blending Neoplatonic and Gnostic influences (*Mishnat Ha-Zohar*, pp. 101–102). By embodying mercy and compassion, humans activate these qualities in the upper worlds, reinforcing divine unity, likened to water taking a bottle's color without changing, against dualistic missteps.

Philosophers like Maimonides see God as an unchanging First Cause, beyond human traits, making biblical descriptions symbolic aids for understanding His acts, not His nature. Kabbalists, preserving Jewish monotheism, assert that imitating *Sefirot's* revealed attributes aligns human action with cosmic purpose, distinct from the Rabbis' practical focus or philosophy's abstraction.

Initially, Cordovero's teachings became the dominant strain of Kabbalah in *Safed*, but after he died in 1570, his direct student, Rabbi Isaac Luria (also known as the Ari or Arizal), proposed new interpretations in Jewish esoterism that came to be more widely accepted. Nonetheless, Cordovero remains a significant and highly respected figure in Jewish mystical history. His works continue to be studied, and his systematic approach influenced the understanding of Judaic mystical thought.

Cordovero's mystical insights exerted an influence on Christian Kabbalists, like Johannes Reuchlin and Pico della Mirandola, who had already begun integrating Jewish mysticism into Christian thought by the Renaissance, focusing on divine attributes and human-divine connection—themes central to *Tomer Devorah*. Cordovero's emphasis on compassion and cosmic harmony likely indirectly influenced later Christian mystics, such as Jakob Böhme, whose works echo Lurianic notions of divine retraction and restoration, though no explicit citation exists.[31]

His disciples, including Elijah de Vidas (*Reshith Hokhmah*) and Samuel Gallico (*Asis Rimmonim*), carried his legacy, as did Menahem Azariah da Fano in Italy, who valued his manuscripts. Cordovero's influence reached Christian Kabbalists like Reuchlin and Pico della Mirandola, and possibly Jakob Böhme, echoing themes of divine harmony, though his God-in-all concept diverged from Spinoza's pantheism. Legends of his sanctity—reincarnation as Eliezer, a pillar of fire at his death (seen by Luria)—enhanced his fame. Prolific with around thirty works, including the vast *Or Yakar*, praised by Abraham Azulai as divinely inspired, Cordovero remains a towering figure in post-Zoharic Kabbalah.

R. *Eliyahu de Vidas*

Rabbi Eliyahu de Vidas (1518–1587), a prominent 16th-century Kabbalist from Safed, left an indelible mark on Jewish mysticism and ethics through his masterpiece *Reishit Hokmah* ("The Beginning of Wisdom"). A disciple of Rabbi Moses Cordovero, de Vidas flourished in Safed's vibrant mystical community, blending scholarly depth with practical spirituality. *Reishit Hokmah* explores kabbalistic theology, focusing on divine attributes—such as mercy and kindness—and their reflection on human conduct.

De Vidas links ethical behavior to the cosmic battle between good and evil, arguing that personal actions shape the spiritual realm. He urges readers to emulate God's qualities, aligning this practice with *tikkun olam* (world repair), as a means to spiritual enlightenment. Drawing from sources like the Zohar and weaving in vivid tales of repentance, the work bridges complex mysticism with everyday ethics, making it both a scholarly treasure and a guide for lived faith. De Vidas' writings radiate deep spirituality and a commitment to ethical living, rooted in spiritual principles. His accessible yet profound teachings on moral growth and divine connection resonate beyond *Safed*, enduring in Jewish study and practice worldwide. *Reishit Hokmah* remains a testament to his legacy, uniting mystical insight with actionable wisdom for generations.

Healer of the Cosmos: Isaac Luria

Rabbi Isaac Luria (1534–1572), widely known as "*Ari Ashkenazi*," emerged as a towering figure in Jewish mysticism from 16th-century *Safed*. Born in Jerusalem to an Ashkenazi father from the prominent Luria family and a Sephardic mother of the Frances lineage, Luria's diverse heritage foreshadowed his far-reaching influence. After his father's early death, his mother relocated them to Egypt, where Luria's intellectual journey began. Under the guidance of renowned *Halakhic* scholars R. David ibn Abi Zimra (1479–1573) and R. Bezalel Ashkenazi (1520–1592), he excelled in legal studies, co-authoring works with Ashkenazi. Yet, in Egypt, Luria turned to mysticism, retreating to an island in the Nile near Cairo. There, he immersed himself in the Zohar and the writings of R. Moses Cordovero, laying the groundwork for his revolutionary mystical vision.

In 1569, Luria settled in *Safed*, a hub of Judaic mystical thought, joining Cordovero's circle. After Cordovero died in 1570, he gathered disciples, teaching a bold cosmology that reframed creation as a drama of divine withdrawal and restoration. Central to Lurianic Kabbalah is the *tzimtzum*—God's contraction of the infinite *Ein Sof* to create space for existence. This "empty space" received a ray of divine light, forming the *Sefirot* within Adam Kadmon ("Primordial Man," see the entry or glossary). Yet, the vessels holding this light shattered (*shevirat ha-kelim*), scattering holy sparks amid broken shards. Humanity's role, Luria taught, is *tikkun olam*—cosmic repair—lifting these sparks through ethical deeds and *mitzvot* to mend the fractured cosmos. His meditations on divine names and *Sefirot* unification aimed to connect souls with the righteous and unravel creation's mysteries.

Luria's eloquence and reverence for Jewish law infused his teachings with moral urgency, addressing crises like the Spanish Expulsion (1492). Though he wrote little himself, disciples like R. Hayyim Vital preserved his ideas in works such as *Etz Hayyim*, ensuring their spread. His vision of exile, rupture, and renewal captivated Jewish communities, offering hope amid persecution. From *Safed*, Lurianic Kabbalah reached Turkey, Italy, Holland, Germany, and Eastern Europe, notably Poland, shaping Jewish spirituality. Lawrence Fine notes that Luria's mysticism rekindled purpose in a hostile world (Physician of the Soul, 2003, p. 12). Today, the Ari remains a cornerstone of Kabbalistic thought, his concepts—*tzimtzum, shevirah, and tikkun*—integral to its legacy.

One of the central themes of Lurianic kabbalistic is the concept and metaphor of the "*Tzimzum*," the process of divine contraction, or withdrawal. According to Luria, the *En Sof,* or God, had to withdraw to allow space for creation since divine light pervaded all, leaving no room for creation to occur. This idea reframes the act of creation as a paradoxically negative one, demanding divine withdrawal. After this withdrawal, a line of light flowed from God into the "empty space," adopting the form of *Sefirot* in the shape of *Adam Kadmon.*

"Rabbi Isaac Luria" as imagined.

Luria's concept of divine contraction, the shattering of vessels, the dispersion of sparks, and cosmic repair have since become integral components of subsequent Judaic mystical thought. Although Luria's direct literary contribution was limited, his disciples collected and wrote down his teachings, ensuring his continued influence within the Kabbalah tradition. Even today,

Isaac Luria remains an emblematic figure in the history of Jewish mysticism.

This process resulted in the creation of vessels, eternal structures that gave specific characteristics to each emanation. However, these vessels were insufficiently robust to contain such pure light, and they shattered. This breaking caused an upheaval in the nascent emanations, dividing the "empty space" into two parts. The upper realm held the escaped pure divine light, while the broken vessels, with clinging sparks, constituted the first part. Luria perceived humanity as the battleground for good and evil, central to the necessary *tikkun*, or cosmic repair, following the cataclysmic shattering of the vessels. Observance of God's commandments was seen as a form of repair; ethical deeds could redeem the fallen divine sparks. Thus, each prayer and moral action, according to Luria, carried a spark. Jewish adherence to religious and ethical law would redeem these sparks and elevate them.

In his important study on Isaac Luria, the scholar Lawrence Fine observed that Luria's mystical visions breathed new life into the Jewish people's spirit, casting a beacon of hope and instilling a renewed sense of purpose amidst a world hostile to their faith. The echoes of Luria's teachings resonated far and wide, journeying first to the sun-bathed lands of Turkey and the Near East, then making their way to the bustling hearts of Italy, Holland, and Germany, and eventually seeping into the rich cultural soil of Poland and Eastern Europe.

How did his students regard him? Samson Bacchi says we have important corroborating testimony in language strikingly similar to Hayyim Vital. In one of several letters that he sent from *Safed* in the early 1580s, Bacchi wrote as follows about Luria:

> He used to understand the language of trees, the sounds of birds and animals, and the rushing of water. And when he would gaze upon an individual's shadow [*be-tselha-'adam*)], that is the external aura that is outside the person's body, he could recognize the good inclination and the evil inclination that constantly accompany an individual. And he used to discern all the transgressions that that individual had committed, and he would

> tell him what he had done even in the most concealed places [*be-hadrei hadarim*]. He could also recognize in detail the transmigration of souls of every individual. And by his great holiness, he would converse with the holy souls in this land. In this way, the concealed mysteries and secrets of Kabbalah, as well as other wondrous things, were revealed to him.[32]

R. Isaac Luria's Greatest Student: R. Hayyim Vital

In 1570, Hayyim Vital (1543–1620), a young scholar, joined the circle of Rabbi Isaac Luria, the "Ari," in *Safed*, a thriving kabbalistic center. Lawrence Fine notes that Vital saw himself as Luria's foremost disciple, listing himself first among peers.[33] Joseph ibn Tabul, a key figure possibly second only to Vital, was relegated to the list's end, suggesting rivalry. Vital also named ten others—Moses Alsheikh, Moses Najara, Isaac Orcha, Solomon Saban, Mordechai Gallico, Jacob Masud, Joseph Altun, Moses Mintz, Moses Yonah, and Abraham Gukil—forming a second tier. Their bond solidified after Luria's 1570 arrival from Egypt, though Vital dated it later, around February 1571. Following Luria's death in 1572, Vital emerged as his chief interpreter, preserving and expanding his master's teachings.

Lawrence Fine recounts:

> Vital regarded himself as the leading disciple and thus placed himself at the head of the list. Joseph ibn Tabul, who was actually an exceedingly important disciple, perhaps second only to Vital in influence, is placed at the end of the list. Undoubtedly, Vital regarded ibn Tabul as a rival and thus sought to relegate him to a relatively insignificant place in the hierarchy of disciples. In the second grouping, Vital includes the following ten names: Moses Alsheikh, Moses Najara, Isaac Orcha, Solomon Saban (or Avsaban), Mordechai Gallico, Jacob Masud, Joseph Altun, Moses Mintz, Moses Yonah, and Abraham Gukil.[34]

Vital's journey took him from Safed to Egypt in 1577, then back to Ottoman Syria, settling briefly in *Ein Zeitim* near *Safed* before moving to Jerusalem. By the 1590s, he led Damascus's Sicilian Jewish community, where he wrote his first independent work—an esoteric treatise on clouds, planets, the Seven Heavens, and their metals. Ordained by R. Moshe Alshich in Jerusalem (1590), Vital faced a year-long illness, during which he authored *Shaar HaGilgulim (Gate of Reincarnations*), later part of *Shemonah She'arim* (*Eight Gates*). While bedridden, his brother Moshe was bribed with 500 gold coins by disciple R. Yehoshua ben Nun to share Vital's manuscripts. Yehoshua hired 100 scribes, copying over 600 pages in three days. Though Vital disavowed these copies, they circulated as Luria's teachings, forming *Shemonah She'arim* and, later, the structured *Etz Hayyim* ("Tree of Life"), asserting Kabbalah's role in hastening the Messiah.

Vital revered Luria as his ultimate teacher, though he also honored R. Moses Cordovero, claiming visions of him in dreams. Convinced Luria relocated from Egypt to *Safed* solely to mentor him, Vital believed he alone could fully interpret the Ari's teachings. When Luria died in 1572, Vital took up this mantle, collecting notes from fellow disciples, whom he deemed less capable, while asserting his exclusive insight into Luria's mystical system.

Vital's life was marked by restless movement and prolific output. After Luria's death, he traveled to Jerusalem, then briefly to Egypt in 1577, before returning to Ottoman Syria, settling in *Ein Zeitim* near Safed. By 1594, he established himself in Damascus as a leader of the Sicilian Jewish community, delivering nightly lectures on Kabbalah until failing eyesight in 1604 preceded his death in 1620 at 77. Ordained by Alshich in 1590, Vital faced criticism from figures like Menahem Lonzano (*Imrei Emet*), yet his influence grew. In 1587, a severe illness left him bedridden; during this time, his brother Moshe accepted 500 gold coins from disciple R. Yehoshua ben Nun to share Vital's manuscripts. Yehoshua hired 100 scribes, who copied over 600 pages in three days. Vital disavowed these copies, but they circulated widely via Palestine to Europe as *Etz Hayyim* ("Tree of Life"), shaping Western Lurianic Kabbalah—distinct from *Safed's* tradition.

Lawrence Fine highlights Vital's two-decade effort to transcribe Luria's teachings across *Safed*, Damascus, and Jerusalem, culminating in *Shemonah She'arim* (Eight Gates) (*Physician of the Soul, 2003,* p. 159). This work—encompassing Luria's writings, oral lessons, and other disciples' accounts—spans foundational concepts to advanced doctrines like reincarnation (*Shaar HaGilgulim*). Revered by Sephardi Kabbalists, Etz Hayyim reflects Vital's deep engagement with Jewish esotericism, cementing his enduring legacy despite contested dissemination.

Rabbi Hayyim Vital's mystical interests, as reflected in the *Eight Gates* of his work, cover a broad and profound spectrum of Lurianic study and practice. These gates demonstrate his deep engagement with the esoteric dimensions of Judaism, ranging from foundational concepts to advanced doctrines:

❑ *Sha'ar ha-Hakdamot* (*The Gate of Introductions*) reveals his dedication to laying a solid groundwork for understanding the intricate principles of Kabbalah, aligning with his foundational text, *Etz Hayyim.*

❑ *Sha'ar Mamarei RaShB"I* (*The Gate of RaShBI's Teachings*) indicates his study and interpretation of the Zohar, and suggests his engagement with the deeper secrets and commentaries of this text.

❑ *Sha'ar Mamarei R' Ari'zal* (*The Gate of Talmudic Sages' Teachings*) likely contains his expositions on the teachings of the *Ari'zal*, Rabbi Isaac Luria, one of the most influential Kabbalists, and would reflect his interest in the evolution of kabbalistic thought post-Zohar.

❑ *Sha'ar ha-Pesukim (The Gate of Bible Verses*) showcases his interest in the mystical interpretations of scriptural verses, an essential aspect of esoteric study that seeks to uncover the hidden dimensions of the divine wisdom in the Torah.

❑ *Sha'ar ha-Mitzvot* (*The Gate of Commandments)* points to his focus on the esoteric aspects of the mitzvot (commandments), exploring how each commandment relates to the divine structure and spiritual rectification.

❑ *Sha'ar ha-Kavvanot* (*The Gate of Meditations*) emphasizes the practical applications of Kabbalah in daily Jewish practice, particularly in prayer, where specific meditative intentions (*kavvanot*) are directed toward mystical union and divine worship.

- *Sha'ar Ruach ha-Kodesh* (*The Gate of the Holy Spirit*) suggests his explorations into the prophetic and revelatory aspects of mysticism, including the attainment of higher states of consciousness, as well as practical Lurianic applications such as healing and understanding the divine flow through physical creation.

- *Sha'ar ha-Gilgulim* (*The Gate of Reincarnations*) reflects his profound interest in the soul's journey through multiple lifetimes, a central doctrine in Lurianic Kabbalah, which involves understanding the soul's correction and elevation through successive existences. These gates collectively affirm Rabbi Hayyim Vital's commitment to exploring the full breadth of Lurianic wisdom, from theoretical doctrines and scriptural exegesis to practical mysticism and spiritual transformation.

After Vital's demise, his son Shmuel, born in 1598 and residing until around 1677, undertook the task of restructuring his father's seminal work, Etz Hayyim. Shmuel's revision gave birth to the compendium titled *Shemonah She'arim*, or the "Eight Gates." He dissolved the initial gate, categorizing Luria's writings into the rest of the sections. Similarly, he assimilated the teachings gathered from other students, previously appended to various gates by his father, into the extant sections based on their themes. However, in this endeavor, Shmuel eliminated any references that could be traced back to the source, be it Ari, his father Hayyim Vital, or any other Lurianic disciples. Consequently, in his quest for organization and clarity, the chronology and origins of the teachings inadvertently lacked an organized structure.

Despite the trials and tribulations, Vital's dedication to preserving the teachings of his master remained unwavering. His works reflect not only the wisdom of the "Ari" but also the intellectual and spiritual interests of the *Safed* group. These works delve into a range of subjects that continue to captivate us today, including dreams and their interpretations, meditation and its spiritual implications, altered states of consciousness, and parapsychology. Through Vital's writings, we get a glimpse into the provocative strands of mystical thought and exploration that characterized this group's spiritual journey. Hayyim Vital's life and works continue to inspire and guide those who seek to understand the mysteries of Kabbalah. His journey, marked by dedication, rivalry, and resilience, serves as a testament to his unwavering commitment to preserving the teachings of his master, Isaac Luria. His legacy lives on in his writings, which continue to be studied and revered by scholars and seekers of wisdom alike.

A Brief Word About the Sabbatean Heresy

To fully appreciate the significance of Jewish mysticism from the 18th century onward, it is essential to consider the profound influence of Shabbatai Sevi, the most renowned false messiah of modern Jewish history. Shabbatai Sevi's story is not just one of individual charisma but a movement that gripped the imagination and faith of an entire generation of Jews across the world. His rise and fall left a deep imprint on Jewish thought, paving the way for subsequent spiritual movements and shaping the course of Jewish history in complex and enduring ways.

The impact of Shabbatai Sevi's messianic claims cannot be overstated. He brought hope to Jewish communities during a time of immense suffering and upheaval, only for those hopes to be dashed when his claims unraveled. This phenomenon created a vacuum that later Jewish mystics and movements sought to fill, often in reaction to the disillusionment his failure caused. While his story is intricate and multifaceted, we will attempt to summarize its key elements and significance in a concise yet meaningful exploration.

Shabbateanism, the largest and most significant messianic movement in Jewish history after the destruction of the Temple and the Bar Kokhba Revolt, gained widespread appeal due to two key factors. Firstly, it tapped into the enduring Jewish longing for political and spiritual redemption, deeply rooted in Jewish religious tradition and thought. Secondly, specific conditions in 1665, marked by political and social challenges in the Jewish Diaspora, fueled the momentum of this movement. At its core, the Shabbatean movement was profoundly religious, arising from a transformation in Judaism's religious landscape centered in *Safed* during the 16th century. The rise of Lurianic Kabbalah integrated striking concepts with messianic ideas. This fusion of "messianism in mysticism" introduced a new tension element into traditional mystical practices, which were more contemplative.

Lurianic Kabbalah emphasized a connection between religious observance, prayer, and the messianic message, focusing on the Jewish people's role in restoring the universe to harmony. It believed the final redemption would be achieved through a series of activities. While political liberation was seen symbolically, there was no conflict between the messianic idea's national and political content and its new spiritual and mystical aspects.

The popularity of Lurianic Kabbalah, in the 1630s-40s, fueled messianic fervor and became integrated with the Shabbatean movement's ideology. Its widespread appeal across various Diaspora centers can be attributed to the intense promotion of Lurianic ideas, creating a climate conducive to the release of messianic energies, even in places where Jews faced less oppression. These locations became hubs of Shabbatean activities. Sevi's charisma and strategic replacement of religious leadership with his appointees amplified his influence. Mystical happenings further propelled his reputation, such as the alleged sighting of a Hebrew-unscripted ship manned by Hebrew-speaking sailors. This period of uncertainty and upheaval for European Jewry, exacerbated by devastating pogroms, made the promise of a savior, a Messiah, an appealing prospect.

With the help of a talented publicist named Nathan of Gaza, this young, self-appointed prophet exhibited remarkable skills that would have made the apostle Paul blush in comparison. Nathan circulated letters throughout the Jewish diaspora and managed a group of missionaries. As a result, within a year, Sabbatia Sevi's assertion of being the Messiah had gained widespread acceptance, fulfilling his initial intentions. Speculation surrounding the advent of the Messiah spread like wildfire across the civilized world. Jewish communities in Greece, Italy, Syria, Egypt, and Turkey began to liquidate their properties in anticipation of migrating to the Holy Land.

His charismatic personality inevitably caught the Ottoman authorities' attention, leading to his incarceration in 1666 in Gallipoli. Offered the choice between death and Islam, Shabbatai Sevi chose conversion, jolting his followers. Despite his apostasy, he continued clandestine Jewish practices, retained a fraction of followers, and inspired the Donmeh sect's formation. Despite its dramatic denouement, his movement catalyzed a significant shift within the Jewish communities and, even in controversy, persists as an influential epoch in Jewish history.

What was Shabbatai Sevi's rationale for his seeming apostasy to Islam?

As we previously discussed, the notion of "liberating the sparks" from the Lurianic Kabbalah offers a valuable lens through which we can discern the motivations underpinning this seemingly paradoxical behavior. This mystical concept posits that fragments of divine essence are interspersed throughout the physical world, embedded within the material forms we encounter in our daily existence. According to this metaphysical framework, a cardinal spiritual duty incumbent upon Jews is to extricate these divine shards, facilitating their assembly and ultimate reunion with the holistic divine entity.

Shabbatai Sevi's apostasy, within this spiritual context, can be perceived not as a renunciation of his faith but rather as a calculated transition into Islam. He intended to liberate the divine sparks clandestinely embedded within this distinct religious tradition, a step toward their spiritual redemption. His acolytes in Salonika, profoundly influenced by his spiritual voyage, construed his conversion not as a departure but as a divine mandate. Consequently, they felt duty-bound to emulate his religious transition. This act of assuming a new religious identity was perceived to facilitate a more comprehensive emancipation of the divine essence, thereby aligning their lives more closely with the mission of spiritual liberation prescribed by the Lurianic Kabbalah.

Rabbi Isaiah Horowitz (c. 1565–March 24, 1630), known as the *Shelah HaKadosh* (the Holy Shelah), became revered because his popular magnum opus Shenei Luchot HaBrit ("Two Tablets of the Covenant") was a pivotal figure in synthesizing *Ashkenazic* rabbinic scholarship with the numinous traditions of *Safed.* Born in Prague, educated in Poland under luminaries like Meir of Lublin and Solomon Leibush, and later serving as a rabbi across Europe before settling in Jerusalem in 1621, Horowitz's life culminated in a deep engagement with the mystical teachings of Isaac Luria, Moses Cordovero, and Joseph Karo.

His writings, particularly *Shenei Luchot HaBrit* and *Sha'ar HaShamayim,* reflect a profound commitment to integrating Kabbalah into rabbinic literature, making esoteric wisdom accessible while grounding it in halakhic and ethical frameworks. Below is an exploration of his core teachings as they pertain to Kabbalah and rabbinical literature, emphasizing his theological innovations and their lasting impact.

Horowitz's approach to Kabbalah was shaped by the Lurianic revolution, which he encountered fully upon arriving in the Holy Land. Unlike some predecessors who guarded its secrets, Horowitz believed in their public dissemination, driven by a messianic urgency. In *Shenei Luchot HaBrit,* he argues that revealing Kabbalah's mysteries hastens redemption, a stance reflecting his view of history as nearing its eschatological climax. He writes that the "time has come" to share these teachings, not just with an elite, but with the broader Jewish community, to elevate collective spiritual consciousness. This democratization of mysticism distinguishes him from earlier Kabbalists like Cordovero, whose *Pardes Rimmonim*, who systematized Kabbalah for scholars, and aligns him with Luria's emphasis on practical application through *mitzvot.*

R. *Isaiah ben Avraham HaLevi Horowitz*

A. Mitzvot as Cosmic Repair (Tikkun)

A cornerstone of Horowitz's teachings is the Lurianic notion of *Tikkun*—cosmic restoration—achieved through mitzvot. He views commandments not merely as legal obligations but as mechanisms to mend the fractured vessels of creation, a process Luria described as rectifying the *Shevirat HaKelim* (Breaking of the Vessels). In *Shenei Luchot HaBrit,* Horowitz explains that each *mitzvah* elevates a spark of holiness trapped in the material world, contributing to the Shechinah's reunification with God. This practical mysticism transforms daily observance into a sacred act, a theme he illustrates with examples like the meticulous laws of *tzitzit* and *tefillin*, which he details under "*BT tractate Ḥullin*." Here, he blends *halakhic* precision with mystical intent, arguing that their physical forms symbolize the *Sefirot* and channel divine energy.

Horowitz's rejection of excessive *pilpul* (casuistic debate akin to sophistry) in favor of straightforward Torah study further ties his Kabbalah to rabbinic literature. He critiques the overcomplication of Talmudic analysis, advocating a return to the text's plain meaning enriched by mystical insight. This approach, rooted in his father's *Emeq Berakhah*, which he annotated with esoteric glosses in 1590, bridges the rationalism of Moses Isserles with the mysticism of *Safed*, creating a holistic Torah study that serves both intellectual and spiritual ends.

B. Prayer as Mystical Praxis

In *Sha'ar HaShamayim*, Horowitz elevates prayer to a spiritual discipline, infusing traditional liturgy with esoteric significance. He interprets the morning prayer (*Shacharit*) as an appeal to divine mercy, *linked* to the growing light symbolizing *Chesed* (the outflow of divine kindness), and the afternoon prayer (Mincha) as an invocation of *Din* (the withholding of divine compassion), tied to declining light. Drawing on Luria's emphasis on *kavannah* (intent), he assigns each prayer a role in unifying the *Sefirot*, particularly through the Shema's declaration of divine unity (Deut. 6:4). In a rare departure from his reluctance to commit Lurianic secrets to writing, he praises Luria as the "divine kabbalist" whose teachings on the *Shema* reveal an "inner dimension" too profound for the masses, yet vital for the adept. This selective disclosure reflects his nuanced stance: while advocating broader access to the Kabbalah, he reserves its deepest layers for those spiritually prepared. Horowitz's prayer commentary also integrates rabbinic *aggadic* homilies with mysticism. He cites Talmudic legends—like David's death—to reinforce ritual stringency, yet interprets them through a hidden lens, finding symbolic resonance with the *Sefirot*. His ethical teachings, such as advising advocates to trust in God over earthly power, further weave Kabbalah into practical rabbinic guidance, emphasizing humility and divine dependence.

C. Influence of Safed's Triumvirate

Horowitz's reverence for Safed's kabbalistic triumvirate—Luria, Cordovero, and Karo—shapes his synthesis of mysticism and rabbinic tradition. In a letter from Jerusalem, he describes them as "supernal great ones" visited by angels and prophets, their graves forming a sacred triangular arrangement he kissed in devotion. While his writings lean heavily on Cordovero's systematic framework, his encounter with Lurianic manuscripts, such as *Etz Chayyim* via Samuel Vital in Damascus, marks a shift toward Luria's dynamic cosmology. He marvels at Luria's ability to illuminate "the secrets of the Lord" (Psalm 25:14), particularly in prayer and mitzvot, yet maintains Cordovero's influence in his structured exposition. Karo's *Maggid Mesharim*,[35] with its mystical revelations, also informs *Shenei Luchot HaBrit*, where Horowitz excerpts Karo's dialogues with the *Shechinah* to underscore prayer's transformative power. This synthesis is evident in his treatment of the Ten Sefirot, which he finds mystically encoded in the human body (e.g., the fingers' bones) and rabbinic law. Unlike Cordovero's theoretical focus or Luria's esoteric depth, Horowitz grounds these concepts in accessible practice, aligning them with Talmudic narratives and halakhic rulings to create a unified religious system.

D. Legacy in Rabbinic and Mystical Traditions

Horowitz's works, especially *Shenei Luchot HaBrit*, rejected Talmudic obscurantism and focused on ethical mysticism, as seen in teachings like sanctifying the mundane through Torah, resonated with the Baal Shem Tov's later ideals. The *Tefillat HaShelah*, a prayer for children's righteousness, exemplifies his pastoral application of Kabbalah, blending parental concern with mystical intent, and remains a staple in Jewish liturgy.

In rabbinic literature, Horowitz's integration of Kabbalah with halakha challenged the dominance of pure legalism, offering a model where law and spirit coexist. His strict adherence to ritual, tempered by exalted ethical insights, reflects a belief in Torah as both divine command and cosmic blueprint. Horowitz's core teachings fuse Kabbalah's esoteric depths with rabbinic literature's practical breadth. Through *Tikkun*, prayer, and Torah study, he sought to sanctify the world, viewing exile's trials as reflections of the *Shechinah's* plight. His legacy endures in Jewish spirituality, where his writings continue to inspire a holistic approach to faith, law, and mysticism.

Kabbalah in 17-18th Century Italy

A. R. Yosef Ergas

Rabbi Yosef Ergas (1685–1730), a prominent Jewish philosopher and Kabbalist from Italy, made significant strides in

Jewish thought during the early 18th century. After his birth in Rome, he eventually moved to Livorno, a center for Jewish learning. His most notable work, *Shomer Emunim* ("Guardian of the Faith"), was published posthumously in 1736 and stands out for blending philosophical insights with Lurianic mysticism. The work's systematic clarity has rendered the Arizal's concepts more accessible, earning it widespread acclaim and study in yeshivot, and cementing its place as a key text in Jewish mysticism.

Shomer Emunim is renowned as an excellent introduction to Jewish mysticism. In it, Ergas robustly argues for Kabbalah's authenticity within the rabbinical tradition, using the narrative of the four rabbis entering the *Pardes* as a foundational text. He also addresses how the Sabbatean movement misinterpreted various elements of Lurianic Kabbalah. The work gained wide acceptance across diverse Jewish communities, transcending various religious ideologies, and continues to be a vital resource in understanding the depth and nuance of Jewish mystical thought.

Shomer Emunim is structured into two parts. The first part offers a philosophical exploration of faith and the human intellect's limitations in comprehending the divine. Ergas emphasizes the importance of using rational thought to acknowledge God's existence and unity as a precursor to deeper mystical studies. The second part examines the intricate aspects of Jewish esoteric thought, particularly the *Sefirot*, the ten divine emanations in kabbalistic theology. He discusses the complex relationship between *Sefirot* like *Chesed* ("Divine love") and *Gevurah* ("Divine judgment"), illustrating their interplay in maintaining cosmic balance.

Rabbi Ergas dedicated himself to studying rabbinical and Judaic mystical texts throughout his life. His deep understanding and creative interpretation of esoteric principles, combined with his logical and accessible writing style, have significantly impacted the development and broader comprehension of Jewish mysticism. The author also provides deep insights into Luria's concept of "*Tzimtzum*," the Kabbalistic concept of God's self-contraction to allow for the existence of a universe separate from divine reality. He grapples with this profound paradox of God's omnipresence and simultaneous absence, shedding light on the intricate dynamics between the Creator and the created universe. Overall, the examples within Ergas' "*Shomer Emunim*" demonstrate his keen ability to make complex esoteric concepts of Jewish mysticism accessible and understandable, using clear and logical argumentation. His work remains a central text for students of Jewish mysticism to this day.

"R. Yosef Ergas" as imagined

B. R. Moshe Hayyim Luzzato

Rabbi Moshe Hayyim Luzzatto, widely known by his acronym "*Ramchal*," stands out as one of the most intriguing Italian Kabbalists of the 18th century. Born in Padua in 1707, Luzzatto demonstrated exceptional intellectual abilities from a young age, earning him a reputation as a prodigy in a vibrant Jewish community. As he matured, his scholarly prowess became universally recognized, encompassing a remarkable range of disciplines: Bible studies, Midrash, Talmud, Halakhah, and proficiency in Western languages. His mastery of Talmudic and classical Judaic mystical literature was particularly extraordinary, especially considering he achieved this expertise in his youth. Beyond religious studies, there is evidence suggesting that Luzzatto may have pursued secular knowledge, possibly including medicine at the prestigious University of Padua, reflecting the era's growing interest in bridging faith and science.

Luzzatto's upbringing in Padua, a hub of intellectual and cultural activity, provided fertile ground for his development. From his early years, he immersed himself in Jewish texts, quickly surpassing his peers in understanding the intricacies of the Talmud and the esoteric depths of Kabbalah. His linguistic skills extended to Western languages such as Italian and possibly Latin, which were essential for engaging with the broader academic world of his time. If he indeed studied medicine at the University of Padua—an institution renowned for its contributions to science—this would underscore his versatility and his alignment with the Enlightenment ideal of synthesizing diverse fields of knowledge.

One of the most distinctive aspects of Luzzatto's career was his formation of a study circle composed of medical scholars dedicated to exploring Kabbalah. This group, led by the youthful and clean-shaven Luzzatto, embodied a striking fusion of mysticism and rational inquiry. In the early 18th century, during the Enlightenment, such intersections were not unheard of, as thinkers across Europe sought to reconcile spiritual beliefs with empirical investigation. Luzzatto's leadership of this circle highlights his innovative approach, drawing devout Italian students into a dual exploration of the scientific and the mystical. This endeavor likely contributed to his reputation as a forward-thinking scholar, though it also set the stage for the controversies that would later define his life.

Luzzatto's unconventional methods and bold claims soon drew scrutiny. A minor but telling critique, preserved in an account from the Lubavitcher yeshiva, pointed to his decision to forgo a beard—a choice that, while symbolic, hinted at his broader departure from traditional norms.[36] However, the real storm of controversy arose from his mystical assertions. Luzzatto claimed to receive revelations from a *maggid*, a spiritual guide or an angelic mentor, and declared his intention to create a "new Zohar," positioning his writings as a modern successor to the foundational text of Kabbalah. These assertions alarmed religious authorities, who viewed his visions and teachings as potential threats to established doctrine.

The backlash was severe. Accused of heresy by some, Luzzatto faced persecution from prominent rabbis, which forced him to leave Italy in 1735. He eventually settled in Amsterdam, where he found a more tolerant environment to continue his work. Despite the opposition, his literary output during this period was profound, including masterpieces like *Mesillat Yesharim*, a seminal work on Jewish ethics, and *Derech Hashem*, a systematic treatise on Jewish theology. These texts, blending mystical insight with practical guidance, reveal the depth of his thought and the breadth of his influence.

Rabbi Moshe Hayyim Luzzatto's life was marked by brilliance and controversy, yet his contributions to Jewish thought remain enduring. His works, particularly *Mesillat Yesharim*, continue to be studied widely in yeshivas and religious circles, serving as cornerstones of the Mussar movement, which emphasizes ethical self-improvement. His ability to weave complex Lurianic concepts into accessible frameworks has secured his place as a pivotal figure in Jewish mysticism. Though his career was shadowed by disputes over his visions, his writings, and even his appearance, Luzzatto's legacy transcends these conflicts, offering a rich synthesis of spirituality, intellect, and ethics that resonates to this day.

A. An Anti-Sabbatean Storm Brews

A disciple of Rabbi Moses Chaim Luzzatto (*Ramchal*)—perhaps Jekutiel, though history cloaks his name and ties to Vilna in shadow—stood awestruck by his master's mystic fire and intellectual blaze. With fervor, he penned a vivid chronicle of

Ramchal's kabbalistic feats and teachings, destined for Rabbi Mordechai Jaffe in Vienna. Yet fate twisted the thread: the letter veered into the grasp of Rabbi Moses Hagiz of Altona-Hamburg, a fierce hunter of Sabbatean heresy. This misstep ignited a storm, thrusting *Ramchal's* circle into a crucible of suspicion and debate.

Rabbi Moshe Hayyim Luzzatto

In 1730, Hagiz dispatched the pupil's words to Venice's rabbis, a torch to dry tinder, urging a probe into *Ramchal's* messianic glint. The era pulsed with dread—Shabbatai Sevi's 17th-century shadow loomed large. Sevi, self-proclaimed Messiah, had electrified Jewish hopes in 1665, only to shatter them with his 1666 conversion to Islam under Ottoman duress. His fall birthed a fractured legacy: some followers faded, others burrowed underground, nursing secret faith in his return. By the early 18th century, any whiff of *messianic* zeal in Jewish mysticism sparked alarm, a specter of Sabbatean revival haunting rabbinic councils. *Ramchal's* plunge into Kabbalah—his visions of *Sefirot* and redemption's dawn—stirred this fear, even if his path diverged from Sevi's. To Hagiz, the pupil's glowing account was a flare in the dark.

The spark flared wider with Rabbi Raphael Yisrael Kimhi, *Ramchal's* defender, who testified before Venice's rabbinate. "No formal Sabbatean charge stands," Kimhi swore, yet his words betrayed whispers already afoot. Scholar Isaiah Tishby later confirmed it: Venetian rabbis eyed *Ramchal's* circle with unease, sensing echoes of forbidden fervor. Hagiz fanned the flames, accusing *Ramchal* of winking at Sevi's apostasy—a damning claim, given Sevi's infamy as Judaism's false dawn.

Enter Rabbi Jacob Emden, a polemicist with a blade-sharp pen, slashing at Sabbatean roots. Emden pounced, arguing Ramchal's critique of Sevi lacked teeth—too soft for a heretic's stain. He spun a bolder thread: perhaps Ramchal cast Sevi as Messiah ben Joseph, the warrior precursor, while crowning himself Messiah ben David, the final redeemer. Emden seized on *Ramchal's* use of *tsedek* (justice)—a Sabbatean codeword, he claimed—tying it to the Davidic messiah. Evidence was thin, a lattice of guesswork, but Emden's voice thundered, swelling the controversy's roar.

Ramchal stood firm, his quill a shield. His *Kin'at Hashem Tseva'ot* ("The Zeal of the Lord of Hosts") blazed against Sabbateanism and Christianity alike, a clarion call rooted in Torah's bedrock. His Mesillat Yesharim wove ethics with mystic ascent, with no hint of Sevi's taint. Yet the Italian rabbinate, rattled by his mystical depths—Zohar's secrets spilling from his pen—saw smoke where he swore no fire burned. They tightened the vise: cease teaching Kabbalah, surrender your manuscripts. Rabbi Isaiah Bassan, *Ramchal's* mentor and shield, bore the bitter task—delivering those sacred pages to Hagiz, who torched them, ash rising as a grim seal on *Ramchal's* stifled voice.

This clash wasn't a mere squabble but a tremor in Kabbalah's soul. *Ramchal's* dance with messianic hope—Sefirot as rungs to *Ein Sof*—clashed with a world scarred by Sevi's fall. His pupil's letter, a spark of awe, lit a firestorm, revealing the razor's edge where mystic vision meets rabbinic dread.

D. How Did Luzzatto Differ from Shabbtai Sevi?

My research owes much to Batya Gallant's insightful article, "The Alleged Sabbateanism of Rabbi Moshe Hayyim Luzzatto," published in Tradition. Gallant draws heavily on Meir Benayahu's *Kitvei ha-Kabbala shel Ramchal*,[37] a comprehensive collection of Rabbi Moshe Hayyim Luzzatto's (*Ramchal*) kabbalistic writings. In an analysis likely titled "The Messianic Descent into the Realm of Evil" (possibly mistranslated as "into Evil"), Benayahu carefully distinguishes Luzzatto's theology from Sabbatean ideology, dismantling Isaiah Tishby's claim that Luzzatto's framework was inherently Sabbatean. This debate illuminates Luzzatto's unique contribution to 18th-century Jewish mysticism, rooted in his life in Italy and Amsterdam amid post-Sabbatean tensions.

The Sabbatean movement, ignited by Shabbatai Sevi in the 17th century, shook Jewish communities with its radical theology. Sevi's 1666 conversion to Islam was cast by followers, notably Nathan of Gaza, as a messianic plunge into the *kelippah*—the realm of evil—to redeem divine sparks (*nitzotzot*) trapped there. This doctrine framed apostasy as a redemptive necessity, sparking fervor and division. Luzzatto, however, offered a starkly different vision. He acknowledged the messiah's descent into the *kelippah* as a theological necessity but redefined it as a spiritual, not physical, act. Within his system, the messiah confronts evil metaphysically, purifying sparks without transgression or moral stain. Unlike Sabbateans, who linked Sevi's historical apostasy to prophecy, Luzzatto maintained the messiah's soul remains pure, needing no *tikkun* (rectification), and explicitly rejected Sevi's conversion as messianically irrelevant.

Tishby, a leading scholar of Jewish mysticism, argued that Luzzatto's ideas strayed from Isaac Luria's foundational Kabbalah, pointing to Nathan of Gaza's influence. Luzzatto admitted familiarity with Nathan's writings, selectively integrating valid mystical concepts while disavowing Sabbatean heresy. Gallant and Benayahu highlight this transparency, countering Tishby by framing Luzzatto's theology as a critical synthesis, not a derivative. His portrayal of the Messiah, son of Joseph—a figure of struggle and preliminary redemption—echoes Sevi's adversity motif but remains abstract, focused on the spiritual liberation of sparks, not historical upheaval. Gallant and Benayahu affirm Luzzatto's originality, distancing his work from Sabbateanism's tumult. His spiritualized redemption, emphasizing ethical purity and metaphysical depth, enriches Kabbalah, offering a resilient response to a fractured era.

B. *Embattling Sabbatean Accusations—Past & Present*

The concept of *averah lishmah* (עֲבֵירָה לִשְׁמָה), meaning "a sin committed for a holy purpose," represents a strikingly radical innovation introduced by the Sabbatean movement in the 17th century. Sabbateans employed this theological principle to justify the controversial actions of their leader, Shabbatai Sevi, particularly his conversion to Islam in 1666, which they interpreted as a necessary descent into the realm of evil (*kelippah*) to redeem divine sparks. In his treatise *Kin'at Hashem Tseva'ot*, Rabbi Moshe Hayyim Luzzatto (commonly known as *Ramchal*) directly confronts this notion, firmly asserting that a transgression can never be classified as a *mitzvah* (a pious religious act). Nevertheless, *Ramchal* concedes that under exceptional circumstances, a sin committed with pure and virtuous intent might contribute to significant *tikkun* (spiritual rectification).

Ramchal illustrates this nuanced position with the biblical example of Yael, who seduced and killed the Canaanite general Sisera to protect the Israelite people (Judges 4–5). He categorizes her actions as a *hora'at sha'ah* (הוֹרָאַת שָׁעָה), a temporary ruling sanctioned by divine will for a specific esoteric purpose. *Ramchal* stresses, however, that such measures are not generalizable; they apply only to unique situations and cannot be replicated once those extraordinary conditions no longer exist. Moreover, he insists that only individuals possessing exceptional scholarship and piety—masters of both *Halakhah* (Jewish law) and spiritual insight—can legitimately discern when a *hora'at sha'ah* is warranted. This qualification underscores *Ramchal's* intent to limit the application of such exceptions and safeguard against misuse.

Tishby finds *Ramchal's* treatment of *averah lishmah* intriguing, especially given that it appears in *Kin'at Hashem Tseva'ot,* a work explicitly aimed at refuting Sabbatean ideology. He further observes that *Ramchal's* framework surprisingly aligns with conventional Jewish thought, despite its anti-Sabbatean context. He draws a parallel between *Ramchal's* concept of *hora'at sha'ah* and its use by Nathan of Gaza, a key Sabbatean thinker, who invoked it to rationalize Shabbatai Sevi's transgressions as part of a redemptive mission. Tishby argues that the boundary between a divinely sanctioned temporary act (*hora'at sha'ah*) and the Sabbatean doctrine of redemption through sin is blurry and not as robust as *Ramchal* suggests. He labels *Ramchal's* reliance on this distinction a "weak reed" in his polemic against Sabbatean heresy, contending that it fails to decisively dismantle their theological claims.

Tishby further critiques *Ramchal's* position that *tikkun* may occasionally require violating the law, warning that this idea risks a dangerous inversion of traditional Jewish values. He posits that such a stance could undermine the moral and legal foundations of Judaism if not tightly constrained. While *Ramchal* imposes strict conditions on these "holy sins"—requiring precision, virtuous intent, and temporality—Tishby deems these safeguards inadequate to address the inherent perils of legitimizing transgressions, particularly in light of the Sabbatean precedent.

Meir Benayahu sharply rebuts Tishby's interpretation, defending *Ramchal's* integrity and orthodoxy. He points to *Ramchal's* unequivocal denunciation of Sabbatean antinomianism in *Kin'at Hashem Tseva'ot,* where *Ramchal* writes:

> "Know and understand that the entire edifice which was fabricated by those transgressors (the Sabbateans) is false and in vain… they violate the entire Law… turning words of a living God into wormwood and gall."

Benayahu acknowledges that Ramchal may have initially entertained the possibility that Shabbatai Sevi could have been a potential messianic figure. However, he argues that Ramchal ultimately rejected this view, concluding that Sevi's Halakhic violations and subsequent conversion disqualified him from any redemptive role. Benayahu emphatically asserts that Ramchal neither regarded the converted Sevi as the messiah nor subscribed to core Sabbatean tenets, such as *averah lishmah* or the messiah's descent into evil. While Ramchal did not deny being influenced by certain peripheral ideas linked to Sabbatean theology, Benayahu maintains that this does not implicate him as a Sabbatean.

Benayahu expresses outrage at Tishby's critique, accusing him of besmirching Ramchal's reputation more severely than even Ramchal's contemporary adversaries did. He portrays Tishby as an unrelenting prosecutor who twists Ramchal's scholarly merits into liabilities to prop up a shaky intellectual argument. In a pointed rebuke, Benayahu suggests that Tishby's accusations might reflect Tishby's own scholarly failings. He charges Tishby with engaging in intellectual contortions—fabricating connections, glossing over contradictions, and constructing an elaborate but fragile thesis that risks collapsing under scrutiny, exposing his theories as illusory.

Ramchal's *Kin'at Hashem Tseva'ot was* composed amid intense controversy, as he faced accusations of Sabbatean sympathies from the Venetian rabbinate in the early 18th century. These charges, rooted in suspicion of his kabbalistic writings and associations, were eventually resolved in his favor. However, the academic dispute between scholars like Tishby and Benayahu has kept the question of Ramchal's relationship to Sabbatean thought alive. Tishby's critique highlights potential ambiguities in Ramchal's theology, while Benayahu's defense underscores his orthodoxy and contributions to Jewish thought, such as his ethical masterpiece *Mesillat Yesharim*. This ongoing scholarly contention reflects the broader complexity of interpreting Ramchal's legacy within the turbulent landscape of post-Sabbatean Jewish intellectual history.

C. Graetz's Critical View of Luzzatto

Heinrich Graetz's portrayal of Moshe Hayyim Luzzatto (1707–1747) in his *History of the Jews* intertwines admiration for his literary brilliance with sharp censure of his mystical turn. Born to affluent Paduan parents, Luzzatto's elite education in Hebrew and Latin fueled his poetic gifts—Latin lending elegance, Hebrew a sublime depth. Graetz casts him as a prodigy, his "delicately-strung soul" resonating like an Aeolian harp. Early works, such as a drama on Samson at seventeen and 150 hymns by twenty, showcase Hebrew's vitality, unmarred by the era's excesses. His second play, *The High Tower*, though immature and Italian-influenced, foreshadows greatness. Graetz marvels at Luzzatto's revitalization of Hebrew, likening him to Jehuda Halevi but enriched with Italian musicality, a potential renewer of Jewish poetry.

This promise sours in 1727 when Luzzatto embraces Kabbalah. Enthralled by the Zohar's style, which he mimics with uncanny precision, he deems his creativity divine—a delusion Graetz blames on his teacher Isaiah Bassan's "mystical poison" and the Kabbalah-drenched ghetto milieu. Immersed in Lurianic texts, Luzzatto crafts a *Zohar Tinyana* and envisions himself as a Messianic figure, a shift Graetz mourns as a squandering of genius. He attributes this to a desperate, esoteric bid to rationalize Judaism's woes, forsaking reason for "cobwebs of the mind." Luzzatto's revelations ignite a following—Venetian Kabbalists and the reckless Yekutiel of Wilna—whose zeal provokes rabbinic alarm. Excommunicated in 1730 by figures like Moses Chages, he vows to abandon Kabbalah but relapses amid personal crises, facing renewed persecution. By 1734, the Venetian rabbinate, stung by his critique of Leon Modena and rumors of sorcery, burns his works and exiles him. Graetz notes the irony: tolerance in prosperity, condemnation in ruin.

In Amsterdam, supported by the Portuguese Jewish community, Luzzatto polishes lenses and crafts *Glory to the Virtuous* (1743)—a mature, flawless drama reflecting life's lessons, though tinged with mystical echoes. Drawn to Palestine in 1744, he succumbs to plague in 1747 and is buried in Tiberias, his legacy tainted as followers revive his kabbalistic fervor in Italy and Poland. Graetz frames this as a cautionary tale: a brilliant mind, influential to poets like David Franco Mendes, ensnared by Kabbalah's irrational allure, reflecting broader Jewish intellectual tensions.

In essence, Graetz exalts Luzzatto's poetic mastery while decrying his mystical descent as a tragic fall from reason, his Messianic claims, and Zohar imitation as mere "chimeras" born of a Kabbalah-obsessed age. *Glory to the Virtuous* offers partial redemption, yet his life remains a testament to mysticism's corrosive pull, aligning with Graetz's disdain for its sway over Jewish thought.[38]

D. *Modern Scholars' Critique of Graetz's View of Luzzatto*

Isaiah Tishby, a leading scholar of Jewish mysticism, critiques Graetz's portrayal as overly reductive, arguing it misrepresents Luzzatto's kabbalistic depth. In *The Wisdom of the Zohar* (1989), Tishby asserts that Graetz's "rationalist prejudice" blinds him to Luzzatto's theological sophistication (Vol. 1, 35). Far from a mere imitator, Luzzatto developed an original mystical system, blending Lurianic Kabbalah with ethical teachings, as seen in works like *Mesillat Yesharim.* Tishby notes that Graetz's dismissal of Luzzatto's *Zohar Tinyana* as "meaningless" overlooks its role in advancing Judaic mystical thought, which influenced later *Hasidic* movements. Graetz's focus on Luzzatto's Messianic claims as delusional ignores their cultural context—18th-century Jewish hope for redemption amid persecution—casting him as a fanatic rather than a visionary responding to his time.

Jonathan Garb, in *A History of Kabbalah: From the Early Modern Period to the Present Day*), further criticizes Graetz for projecting his anti-mystical agenda onto Luzzatto's biography (p. 45). Garb argues that Graetz's narrative—Luzzatto's talent ruined by Kabbalah—serves his historiographical goal of championing rational Judaism against mysticism's "excrescences."[39] By emphasizing Luzzatto's excommunication and the Venetian rabbinate's reaction, Graetz amplifies a moral tale over historical nuance. Garb highlights Luzzatto's Amsterdam period, where he produced *Glory to the Virtuous* alongside Kabbalistic works, as evidence of sustained productivity, contradicting Graetz's view of a life derailed. Garb suggests Graetz's reliance on rabbinic critics like Moses Chages biases his account, sidelining Luzzatto's supporters who saw his mysticism as legitimate.

Why does Graetz err?

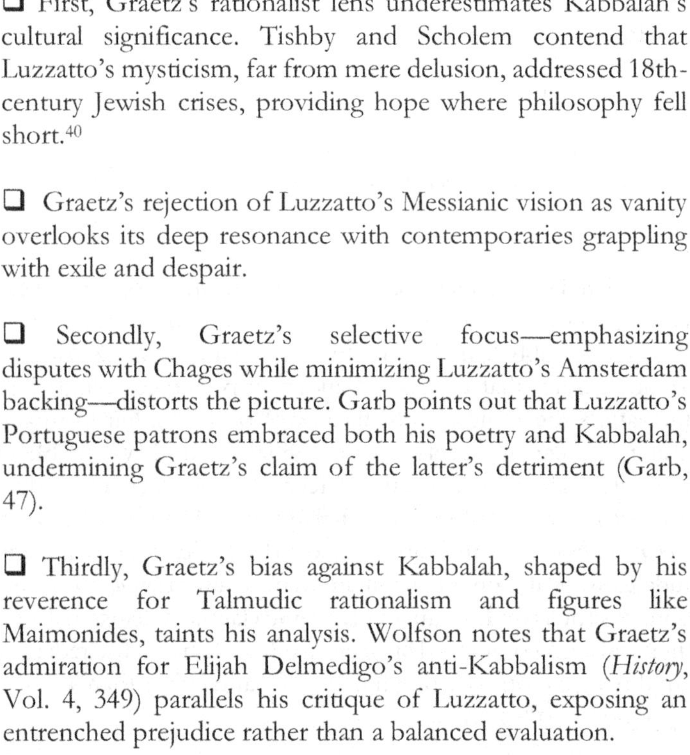

❑ First, Graetz's rationalist lens underestimates Kabbalah's cultural significance. Tishby and Scholem contend that Luzzatto's mysticism, far from mere delusion, addressed 18th-century Jewish crises, providing hope where philosophy fell short.[40]

❑ Graetz's rejection of Luzzatto's Messianic vision as vanity overlooks its deep resonance with contemporaries grappling with exile and despair.

❑ Secondly, Graetz's selective focus—emphasizing disputes with Chages while minimizing Luzzatto's Amsterdam backing—distorts the picture. Garb points out that Luzzatto's Portuguese patrons embraced both his poetry and Kabbalah, undermining Graetz's claim of the latter's detriment (Garb, 47).

❑ Thirdly, Graetz's bias against Kabbalah, shaped by his reverence for Talmudic rationalism and figures like Maimonides, taints his analysis. Wolfson notes that Graetz's admiration for Elijah Delmedigo's anti-Kabbalism (*History*, Vol. 4, 349) parallels his critique of Luzzatto, exposing an entrenched prejudice rather than a balanced evaluation.

Moreover, Graetz misreads Luzzatto's intent. Scholem argues that Luzzatto's *Zohar Tinyana* and Messianic claims aimed to renew Jewish spirituality, not deceive, building on Lurianic ideas with originality. Graetz's charge of "self-deception" overlooks Luzzatto's ethical focus, evident in *Mesillat Yesharim*, which integrates Kabbalah with practical piety—a synthesis Graetz ignores. Finally, his historical context limits him. Writing in the 19th century, Graetz seeks to align Judaism with modernity, viewing Kabbalah as a regressive force. Such an anachronism distorts Luzzatto's 18th-century reality, where mysticism was a vibrant intellectual current, not a relic.

In conclusion, critics see Graetz's judgment of Luzzatto as flawed by his anti-Kabbalistic bias, selective historiography, and failure to appreciate mysticism's legitimacy. Far from a fallen genius, Luzzatto emerges in modern scholarship as a creative synthesizer whose Kabbalah enriched Jewish thought, a legacy Graetz's rationalist lens could not fully grasp.

G. Postscript: Luzzatto Vindicated at Last

Amsterdam proved to be a fertile period for Ramchal. His most well-known works, *Mesillat Yesharim, Derech HaShem, and Da'at Tevunot*, were all composed during his decade-long residence in the city. And like Spinoza, he took up the humble trades of diamond cutting and lens grinding. Following his exile in Amsterdam, Ramchal relocated to Israel. Tragically, his stay was cut short as a plague claimed the lives of his entire family within three years. He died at the tender age of 40, and his remains lie in Tiberias, adjacent to the tomb of Rabbi Akiba.

The persecution of Ramchal reflects the broader tensions within 18th-century Jewish communities, still reeling from the fallout of the Sabbatean movement. Even though Ramchal's teachings were grounded in normative Kabbalistic traditions and he actively distanced himself from Sabbatean ideology, his focus on mystical and messianic themes made him a target in a climate of heightened vigilance. The controversy eventually forced Ramchal to leave Italy. He relocated to Amsterdam, a more tolerant environment, where he continued his scholarly and spiritual pursuits. Later, he settled in the Land of Israel, in Acre, where he composed some of his most enduring works before his untimely death in 1747 at the age of 39. Ramchal's ordeal underscores the challenges faced by Jewish mystics in the post-Sabbatean era, where innovation in Kabbalah was often met with suspicion. His legacy, however, endures through his prolific writings, such as *Mesillat Yesharim* ("The Path of the Just"), which remain foundational texts in Jewish thought.

Rabbi Yaakov Emden, initially a critic, suggested heresy in Luzzatto's teachings, stating, "It is quite evident that there was significant heresy *(minut)* at Luzzatto's doctrine's core, taking malignant roots in this world." However, after Rabbi Moshe Chaim Luzzatto's death, Rabbi Emden regretted his former stance against Ramchal and conceded that he merited significant recognition for his insightful writings. He admitted that he considered Ramchal so holy that those who persecuted him did so with genuine intentions to eliminate the destructive influence of the Shabbatai Sevi heresy. In 1743, he left Europe for Tiberias, Israel.

Renowned rabbi and prominent kabbalist, Rabbi Eliyahu of Vilna, also known as the Vilna Gaon (1720–1797), held high regard for Luzzatto's compositions. He is often celebrated as the most authoritative Torah scholar of the modern era. Upon engaging with "*Mesillat Yesharim*," he reputedly proclaimed that, if Luzzatto were still among the living, he would have journeyed from Vilna to sit at Luzzatto's feet for learning. Further testament to his admiration, he remarked that the initial ten chapters of the work were so meticulously crafted that they did not contain a single superfluous word."

His successor was Rabbi Dov Baer of Mezritch, known as the *Maggid.* A learner once asked why the Ramchal had passed away so young. He replied that the generation of those days had not been worthy to receive his teachings.

In Rabbi Michal Gavin's witty *Kotzk Blog,* he cited the observation of David Sclar, who wrote about Luzzatto:

> The printer of an 1834 edition of *Mesillat Yešarim* informed readers that Luzzatto had received revelations from the prophet Elijah. Luzzatto, the printer continued, had also been the next link in the kabbalistic chain of redeemers, a successor to Isaac Luria. Although early-eighteenth-century rabbis had regarded these statements, which Luzzatto himself had made, as cause to silence Luzzatto, nineteenth-century rabbinic authorities apparently accepted their validity as they came into greater contact with Luzzatto's writings.[41]

Despite facing opposition from traditional rabbinical circles, Ramchal surprisingly gained recognition among secular leaders of the *Haskalah*. Moses Mendelssohn, a prominent figure of the Enlightenment, acknowledged Ramchal's intellectual prowess in a letter to Johann Gottfried Herder in 1781. Mendelssohn lamented the unjust treatment Ramchal suffered due to the jealousy of certain rabbis, which ultimately led to his early demise. He also mentioned Ramchal's composition of the new edition of the Psalms, highlighting the diversity of his talents and contributions. This adulation from Enlightenment leaders signified a unique respect for Ramchal, often attributed to his profound knowledge and command of the Hebrew language. He was lauded as the "father of Modern Hebrew," illustrating the esteem he held within these circles and his significant contributions to the Hebrew literary tradition.

Ramchal's life was a fascinating mosaic of deep religious scholarship, mystical exploration, controversy, and tragedy. His monumental impact on the field of Jewish mysticism and his enduring influence in the evolution of the Modern Hebrew language underscore his critical role in Jewish intellectual history. Despite his hardships and the bitter controversy surrounding his teachings, Ramchal's remarkable contributions and enduring legacy have transcended these historical confines to leave an indelible mark on the texture of Jewish thought and culture.

H. Luzzatto's Integration of Kabbalah & Mussar in Spiritual Growth

In the opening passages of *Mesillat Yesharim,* Rabbi Moshe Hayyim Luzzatto (Ramchal) lays the foundation for a profound integration of Kabbalistic spirituality and the ethical discipline of Mussar. Far from a mere preface, his introduction serves as a manifesto that articulates the essence of his spiritual philosophy. Luzzatto writes:

> I have written this work not to teach you anything new but to remind you of truths you already know—truths so clear and self-evident that you likely hold no doubts about them. Yet it is precisely because these truths are so well-known that they are also so easily forgotten. My goal is not to present fresh ideas or revelations but to help you recall what you may have allowed to

slip from your awareness. The value of this work does not come from a single reading, where you might feel there is little here that you did not already know. Instead, its benefit lies in regular review and persistent study, reminding you of those essential truths and duties that are so easily overlooked and helping you take them to heart in a way that transforms your daily life.

The purpose of *Mesillat Yesharim*, therefore, is not to introduce novel concepts but to reawaken awareness of these fundamental principles. He stresses that the work's true value emerges not from a single reading, where one might feel little has been added to prior knowledge, but through consistent review and dedicated study, which anchor these truths in the mind and transform them into lived practice.

Luzzatto defines the ultimate purpose of human existence as achieving closeness to God and experiencing the joy of His Presence. This perspective resonates deeply with Kabbalistic teachings, which view creation as a vehicle for souls to draw near to the Divine. He asserts that this joy represents the fullest realization of life, attainable completely only in the World to Come, while this world functions as the preparatory arena. Human actions, then, are pivotal—they align individuals with Divine will, contribute to the rectification of the world, and pave the way for spiritual perfection. Drawing on the Talmudic framework of Rabbi Pinchas ben Yair, Luzzatto outlines a structured path to holiness, beginning with Torah study and progressing through stages such as vigilance, diligence, and purity, ultimately culminating in saintliness, humility, and intimacy with God. This systematic approach underscores his conviction that spiritual growth requires intentionality and discipline.

Luzzatto offers a measured critique of scholars and thinkers who excel in intellectual domains—philosophy, astronomy, and even Torah study—yet often fail to prioritize the practical cultivation of virtues like fear of God, love of God, and Divine service. He attributes this neglect to a flawed assumption: that these spiritual principles are too elementary to merit serious attention. As a result, true saintliness remains misunderstood, both by the intellectual elite, who may dismiss it as simplistic, and by those of humbler minds, who may confuse it with outward displays of piety. For Luzzatto, however, true saintliness is neither about extreme asceticism—such as prolonged fasting or physical mortification—nor about unreflective zeal. Rather, it entails the rational, deliberate pursuit of moral and spiritual perfection, achieved through the consistent refinement of one's character and actions.

Acknowledging the challenges posed by worldly distractions and human frailty, Luzzatto emphasizes the necessity of practical tools to cultivate virtues such as love and fear of God, purity of heart, and the correction of personal flaws. These qualities, he insists, do not emerge spontaneously; they demand active effort and persistent reflection. Without such focus, even those who recognize their importance may let them fade amid life's demands. By internalizing these principles through study and practice, individuals not only foster their own growth but also inspire and uplift their communities, contributing to a collective spiritual elevation.

Luzzatto redefines wisdom, distancing it from abstract intellectualism or theoretical speculation. True wisdom, he argues, lies in a profound commitment to Divine service, rooted in the fear of God—an idea he supports with biblical and rabbinic sources, such as the statement in Job that "the fear of God, that is wisdom" (Job 28:28). He critiques the tendency to favor philosophical inquiry over the practical work of character refinement, urging readers to dedicate time to this essential study as a priority rather than a secondary pursuit.

At its core, *Mesillat Yesharim* masterfully weaves together the mystical aspirations of Kabbalah and the ethical pragmatism of Mussar. Luzzatto transforms esoteric spiritual ideals into an accessible framework, achievable through rational, disciplined effort. His work bridges the gap between the lofty and the everyday, providing a clear roadmap for spiritual perfection that is grounded in ethical conduct, mindfulness, and a deepening connection to God. By following this path, individuals can elevate simple, often overlooked truths into a transformative way of life, fulfilling the ultimate purpose of existence and participating in the broader rectification of the world.

Kabbalah in 18th-19 Century Eastern Europe Baal Shem Tov. R. Yisrael ben Eliezer

In the rugged landscape of 18th-century Eastern Europe, where Jewish communities reeled from pogroms, economic despair, and the disillusionment of Shabbetai Tzvi's failed messianism, a humble mystic emerged to ignite a spiritual revolution: Rabbi Israel ben Eliezer, known as the *Baal Shem Tov*, or "Master of the Good Name." (a.k.a. "Besht") Born around 1698 in Okopy, a speck of a village in modern-day Ukraine, his early years blur into myth—orphaned as a child, nurtured by communal kindness, and drawn to the wilds where he reportedly meditated among nature's whispers.

By the 1730s, he settled in Medzhybizh, Podolia, revealing himself as a healer and mystic whose reputation for wielding divine names in miracles earned him the title "*Baal Shem*." Yet the Besht's enduring mark isn't in these tales of wonder but in founding *Hasidism*, a movement that swapped the dry rigor of Talmudic debate for a vibrant, heartfelt connection to God, revitalizing a Judaism weighed down by formality and despair.

Unlike Maimonides or other giants of Jewish thought, the Besht left no systematic writings; his teachings flowed orally, captured after his death in 1760 by disciples like Rabbi Jacob Joseph of Polonnoye and Rabbi Dov Ber, the Maggid of Mezritch. Texts such as *Tzava'at Harivash* ("The Testament of the Baal Shem Tov") and *Keter Shem Tov* ("Crown of the Good Name") preserve his wisdom, a patchwork of sayings and parables that pulse with immediacy (Jacobs, *Hasidic Prayer,* 1972, p. 23)

. At the heart of his philosophy lies a radical vision of divine immanence: God isn't confined to the heavens or the synagogue's ark but permeates every corner of existence—every rustling leaf, every flicker of candlelight, every human sigh. He often cited Isaiah 6:3, "The whole earth is full of His glory," not as abstract theology but as a daily truth to live and breathe (*Tzava'at Harivash*, Section

8). This wasn't mere sentiment; it drew from Kabbalah's deep well, particularly Isaac Luria's concept of divine sparks (*nitzotzot*) scattered across creation, though the Besht reshaped this into a call for joy rather than solemn repair.

Devekut According to the Baal Shem Tov

Central to his teachings is *devekut,* a state of cleaving to God with unrelenting devotion. For the Besht, prayer wasn't a rote recitation but a ladder to the divine, climbed through fervor and focus. "When you pray," he taught, "let your heart be ablaze, and let no stray thought interrupt your bond with the Creator" (*Keter Shem Tov*, Part 1, Section 45). This wasn't reserved for scholars hunched over Talmudic tomes; the Besht flung open the gates of spirituality to the unlearned-the woodcutter, the tailor, the shepherd—insisting that sincerity trumps erudition. Where the elite *Mitnagdim*, his rationalist foes, prized intellectual mastery of Torah, he saw holiness in a farmer's heartfelt song or a widow's tearful plea. This democratization of faith, rooted in the belief that every soul houses a divine spark,
shook the Jewish establishment, earning him both disciples and detractors.

The Besht's embrace of joy as a spiritual path set him apart further. "Serve God with happiness," he urged, echoing Psalms 100:2, for melancholy dims the soul's light (*Tzava'at Harivash,* Section 43b). He saw sadness as a barrier to *devekut,* a trick of the *yetzer hara* (evil inclination) to sever one's connection to the divine. Stories abound of him dancing with villagers or lifting their spirits with tales—like the one where he turned a tavern brawl into a prayer circle by humming a *niggun* (wordless melody) until fists unclenched and voices joined in. This wasn't escapism; it reflected his conviction that joy unearths the hidden sparks Luria described, elevating the mundane to the sacred. A broom sweeping a floor, a cup raised in cheer—these, too, were acts of *tikkun* (repair), mending the world one gleeful moment at a time.

Baal Shem Tov's Practical Approach to the Kabbalah

His approach to Kabbalah was practical, not esoteric. While steeped in Lurianic ideas—*tzimtzum* (divine contraction), the *Sefirot,* and the breaking of the vessels—the Besht sidestepped complex meditations favored by earlier mystics like Abraham Abulafia. Instead, he taught that God's Presence flows through the Sefirot into everyday life, accessible via simple acts. "The world is a mirror of the divine attributes," he said, linking *Chesed* (kindness) to a generous hand, *Tiferet* (beauty) to a balanced heart (*Keter Shem Tov,* Part 2, Section 19). This grounded mysticism resonated with the masses, who found in Hasidism a Judaism they could touch and feel, not just study. Yet he didn't discard Torah learning; he reframed it as a means to *devekut*, urging scholars to infuse their logic with soul rather than let it dry into pedantry.

The Besht's emphasis on the *tzaddik* (righteous leader) as a spiritual conduit also defined his legacy. He saw the *tzaddik* as a bridge between heaven and earth, channeling divine blessings to the community. "The *tzaddik* is the foundation (*Yesod*) of the world," he declared, echoing Proverbs 10:25 in a Kabbalistic key (*Tzava'at Harivash,* Section 63). Unlike the aloof rabbis of his day, his *tzaddikim*—later formalized in Hasidic dynasties—were shepherds of souls, healing with stories, prayers, and personal counsel. Critics like the Vilna Gaon decried this as cultish, fearing it elevated men over Torah (Etkes, *The Gaon of Vilna,* 2002, p. 87), but for the Besht, it was practical theology: if God dwells in all, why not in a holy guide who lifts the fallen?

His life, ending in 1760, was modest—teaching, healing, wandering—but his death birthed a movement that swept Eastern Europe. Disciples like the Maggid of Mezritch systematized his ideas, spreading *Hasidism's* warmth to Poland, Galicia, and beyond. The Besht's parables, like the one of a man lost in a forest finding God in a bird's song, became *Hasidic* gospel, urging followers to seek the divine in the ordinary. His teachings on intention (*kavanah*) transformed rituals—eating, dancing, even sleep—into sacred acts when done with God in mind.[42] This pantheistic streak, tempered by Jewish monotheism, insists the material isn't separate from the spiritual; it's a vessel for it.

Historically, the Besht answered a crisis. Post-Shabbetai Tzvi, Jews craved hope; post-pogroms, they needed joy. Hasidism met those needs, though it clashed with Mitnagdic rationalism, sparking bans and debates. Yet its staying power—seen today in Chabad, Breslov, and other branches—proves its appeal. The Besht's genius lay in simplicity: God is near, joy is holy, every soul matters. "A person must see himself as nothing before God, yet everything as His creation," he taught (*Tzava'at Harivash*, Section 34), balancing humility with purpose. His miracles—real or embellished—pale beside this message, which turned a downtrodden people into dancers in the divine embrace.

The Baal Shem Tov's teachings endure because they humanize the mystical. Where Kabbalah once soared in abstract heights, he brought it to the *shtetl*, the marketplace, the heart. His legacy isn't in books but in lives—generations chanting niggunim, praying with fire, finding God in a child's laugh or a friend's embrace. As he reportedly said, "The greatest Torah is to love your fellow as yourself, for in this all commandments are fulfilled" (*Keter Shem Tov*, Part 2, Section 88). In a world of rules, he offered a relationship; in a time of gloom, he lit a spark. That spark still burns, a testament to a man who saw the divine not just above, but within us all.

Parallels Between Baal Shem Tov and Jesus of Nazareth

Across centuries, the Baal Shem Tov, a mystic of 18th-century Eastern Europe, and Jesus of Nazareth, a 1st-century Judean preacher in the Synoptic Gospels (Matthew, Mark, Luke), rise as beacons of renewal amid rigid traditions. From *shtetls* to Galilee, their unwritten teachings—captured by disciples—defied the powerful, weaving wonder and love into *Hasidism* and early Christianity, a shared fire echoing a hunger for the Divine. Their voices stirred the humble, wielded miracles, and faced scorn, striking a timeless chord that invites us to explore their parallel paths and distinct flames. Stripping away the Gospel of John's divine veneer, the Synoptic Gospels (Matthew, Mark, and Luke) reveal Jesus as a teacher, healer, and provocateur, a portrait that resonates with the Besht's mystic fervor and communal zeal.

A. SPIRITUAL RENEWAL THROUGH THE COMMON FOLK: Both the Baal Shem Tov and Jesus rekindled faith by embracing the marginalized. The Besht, in 18th-century Eastern Europe, sidestepped rabbinic elitism, teaching peasants and sinners that joy and prayer touch the divine—e.g., sanctifying a shepherd's whistle (*Shivchei HaBesht*). Jesus, in 1st-century Judea, reached fishermen, tax collectors, and outcasts (Matthew 4:18–22, Luke 5:27–32), his parables like the Good Samaritan (Luke 10:25–37) opening holiness to all. Each shifted the sacred to the humble.

R. Israel ben Eliezer "Baal Shem Tov (a.k.a. "Besht")

B. INNER FAITH OVER RITUAL: Both prized devotion over formalism. The Besht's *devekut* (cleaving to God) exalted love and intention (*kavanah*) above *rote mitzvot*: "Serve God with all your heart" and Jesus echoed this thought by citing Deuteronomy 6:5—"Love the Lord your God with all your heart" (Matthew 22:37)—and decrying empty piety (Matthew 23:27–28). Faith was a living bond, not a ledger.

C. MIRACULOUS PERSONA AND HEALING: Miracles defined their legacies. The Besht, a *tzaddik,* healed through prayer, curing a woman with dance (Shivchei HaBesht), and banished demons, channeling divine power. Jesus restored sight (John 9:1–7) and cast out spirits (Mark 5:1–13), his acts heralding God's kingdom. Both wielded wonders to awaken faith.

D. NO WRITTEN LEGACY: Neither left writings, relying on disciples. The Besht's teachings live in oral tales, recorded by followers like Rabbi Nathan Sternhartz (*Keter Shem Tov*). Jesus' words, unwritten in life, emerged in the Gospels (e.g., Mark, c. 70 CE). This oral thread fueled *Hasidism* and Christianity.

E. MESSIANIC ECHOES AND MUTUAL ELEVATION: Both inspired transformative ideals with messianic hues. The Ebionites urged disciples to be "Christlike to each other" (John 13:34–35: "Love one another as I have loved you"), each a messiah for their world. The Besht taught every Jew holds a "spark of the Messiah" (Shivchei HaBesht), the tzaddik lifting others—a collective ascent to holiness.

F. CASTIGATION BY THE STATUS QUO: Each faced rebuke from entrenched powers. The Besht riled the *Mitnagdim*, who saw his ecstatic worship as heresy; the Vilna Gaon's 1772 ban branded *Hasidim* threats (*Iggeret HaGra*). Jesus clashed with Pharisees and Sadducees, his Sabbath healings (Mark 3:1–6) and claims sparking blasphemy charges (John 10:33). Both defied norms, castigated for their boldness.

G. TRANSFORMATIVE LEADERSHIP: Their charisma birthed enduring movements. The Besht's *Hasidism*, spread by disciples like the Maggid, infused Judaism with mysticism. Jesus' Gospel, carried by apostles, launched Christianity. Each reshaped their faith's soul.

Rabbi Dov Baer of Mezritch

In the shadowed aftermath of the Baal Shem Tov's death in 1760, as *Hasidism* teetered on the edge of fading into memory, a frail yet luminous figure stepped forward to carry its torch: Rabbi Dov Ber of Mezritch, known simply as the Maggid. Born around 1704 in Lukatch, a modest town in what is now Ukraine, his early life unfolded in obscurity—likely a Talmudic scholar and teacher, plagued by ill health, perhaps lameness, that confined him to a quiet existence. Around 1750, drawn by tales of the Besht's miracles, he journeyed to Medzhybizh seeking healing, only to find something greater: a spiritual awakening that bound him to the Besht as disciple and, eventually, successor. By 1761, settled in Mezritch, Poland, the Maggid transformed a fledgling movement into a robust theological force, earning his title—Maggid, or preacher—for his electrifying discourses that melded Kabbalistic depth with Hasidic fervor, cementing *Hasidism's* place in Jewish history.

Unlike the Besht, whose teachings danced through oral parables and joyous outbursts, the Maggid was a systematizer, a mystic-philosopher whose frail body belied a towering intellect. His words, preserved by students like Rabbi Shneur Zalman of Liadi in *Maggid Devarav LeYaakov* (*The Maggid's Words to Jacob*) and *Likkutei Amarim* (*Collected Sayings*), reveal a mind steeped in Lurianic Kabbalah, sharpened by rigorous thought. Where the Besht saw God in every blade of grass, the Maggid peered deeper, into the void before creation, teaching that all existence emerges from *ayin*—nothingness—a divine nullity that paradoxically births everything. "Before the world was created, there was only God, and God was *ayin*," he said, framing reality as a contraction of divine infinity into finite form.[43] This wasn't abstract navel-gazing; it was a call to perceive the world as a thin veil over the infinite, a lens he inherited from the Besht but polished into a metaphysical cornerstone.

The Maggid's doctrine of *bittul*—self-nullification—flows from this. To cleave to God (*devekut*), one must shed the ego, dissolving the "I" into the divine *ayin*. "Man must become as nothing before the Creator," he taught, "for only in nothingness does he find the All."[44] Unlike the Besht's buoyant devekut, fueled by song and dance, the Maggid's path was introspective, demanding meditation and inner silence. He urged his followers to strip away distractions—worldly pride, stray thoughts—until their souls mirrored the primal void, uniting with God's essence. This wasn't ascetic gloom; it was liberation, a return to the source where human and divine merge. Stories tell of him sitting motionless, eyes closed, lost in contemplation, his voice later erupting in sermons that left listeners weeping or trembling.[45] His *bittul* elevated *Hasidism* from a folk revival to a mystical discipline, bridging the Besht's warmth with a rigorous spiritual framework.

Prayer, for the Maggid, was the crucible of this union. He saw it as a cosmic act, not a rote plea. "When you pray, lift your words beyond the world, to the place where all is one," he instructed.[46] Each syllable, infused with *kavanah* (intention), could pierce the *Sefirot*, channeling divine light downward—a theurgic echo of Luria's *tikkun*. Where the Besht turned prayer into a heartfelt shout, the Maggid made it a disciplined ascent, urging focus on the letters of God's names (like YHWH) to awaken the soul's higher tiers—*neshamah, chayah, yechidah*. This wasn't for the elite alone; though cerebral, he retained the Besht's populism, teaching that even the unlearned could reach God through pure intent. "A simple man's prayer with a broken heart is greater than a scholar's without soul," he affirmed, ensuring *Hasidism's* broad embrace.[47]

The Maggid's vision of the *tzaddik* evolved the Besht's model into a linchpin of *Hasidic* life. He cast the *tzaddik* as a "conduit" (*tzinnor*), channeling divine bounty to the community, a role rooted in *Yesod,* the *Sefirah* of connection. "The *tzaddik* descends to lift the fallen, binding their souls to the Infinite," he taught.[48] Unlike the Besht's folksy *tzaddik*, a healer among the people, the Maggid's was a mystical intermediary, a figure of awe whose meditations repaired cosmic fractures. This shift birthed the *Hasidic* court—disciples flocking to Mezritch, seeking his blessings or a glimpse of his trance-like *devekut.* Critics, like the Mitnagdim, saw this as idolatry, but for the Maggid, it was symbiosis: the tzaddik needed the people as much as they needed him, a mutual elevation (Scholem, 1941, p. 352).

His leadership wasn't just spiritual; it was organizational genius. From Mezritch, he dispatched emissaries—Rabbi Menachem Mendel of Vitebsk to Israel, Rabbi Shneur Zalman to Lithuania—spreading Hasidism across Eastern Europe.[49] His home became a hub, drawing hundreds to hear his Shabbat discourses, where he wove Kabbalistic threads into practical wisdom. "The world is a garment hiding God; peel it back with faith," he'd say, urging followers to see divinity in the mundane.[50] Though physically weak—often bedridden, dictating from a cot—he radiated authority, his voice soft yet piercing, his presence magnetic. By his death in 1772, *Hasidism* wasn't a flicker but a flame, poised to ignite dynasties like Chabad and Breslov.

The Maggid's teachings deepened the Besht's legacy with intellectual heft. Where the Besht reveled in joy, the Maggid plumbed silence; where the Besht embraced the material, the Maggid sought its dissolution. Yet both shared a core: God's nearness. "Every thought is a spark; direct it to Him, and it blazes," he taught, echoing the Besht's spark-lifting but framing it in meditative terms.[51] His Kabbalah wasn't Luria's dense cosmology but a lived encounter—ayin as both origin and goal, the Sefirot as pathways to unity. This balance of mysticism and accessibility made his *Hasidism* enduring, appealing to scholars and simpletons alike.

Historically, the Maggid bridged a gap. The Besht sparked *Hasidism* amid crisis—post-Shabbetai despair, pre-industrial upheaval—but the Maggid gave it structure, fending off Mitnagdic bans with a theology too potent to dismiss His disciples fanned out, adapting his ideas—Shneur Zalman's rationalism, Levi Yitzchak of Berditchev's love—ensuring *Hasidism's* survival. His parables, like one of a prince lost in illusion returning to his father through silence,[52] distilled his message: strip away the self, find God within.

Rabbi Dov Ber died on December 19, 1772, leaving no books but a movement. His frail frame belied his titan's soul, turning Mezritch into Hasidism's beating heart. His teachings—*bittul, devekut*, the *tzaddik*'s role—wove the Besht's joy with Kabbalistic rigor, offering a path where silence speaks and nothingness shines. "The world is but a shadow; step into the light," he urged, a call that echoes in *Hasidic* courts today. In his hands, *Hasidism* grew from a spark to a fire, illuminating a Judaism where God isn't sought but found—everywhere, always.[53]

R. *Shneur Zalman of Liadi*

Rabbi Shneur Zalman of Liadi (1745–1812) (a.k.a. RSZ) stands as a towering figure in Jewish history, leaving an indelible mark on spirituality, philosophy, psychology, ethics, and law. Initially wary of Rabbi Dov Baer of Mezritch, the leading Hassidic master, Zalman's skepticism dissolved upon meeting him, drawing him into Dov Baer's inner circle. His formative years in Mezritch deepened his grasp of *Hassidic* mysticism and *Halachah*, forging a seamless fusion of spiritual fervor and intellectual rigor that would define his legacy.

Renowned for his scholarly brilliance, RSZ, was entrusted with revising the *Shulchan Aruch*, the *Code of Jewish Law*. Integrating two centuries of commentary, this monumental work cemented his reputation as a preeminent legal authority. As the founder of Chabad-Lubavitch, he confronted fierce opposition to Chassidism in Lithuania, wielding his vast Talmudic erudition to overcome resistance. Beyond the spiritual, RSZ's leadership embraced the practical, promoting agricultural initiatives and sustaining Hassidic settlements in Israel. His Chabad philosophy, rooted in intellectual engagement with faith, carved a unique path within Chassidism, balancing mind and soul.

At the heart of his teachings lies the *Tanya*, a cornerstone of Chabad thought that weaves intellect, emotion, and action into a transformative vision. This seminal work probes mystical theology and the psychology of religious life, exploring the tension between the animal soul, driven by instinct, and the divine soul, yearning for transcendence. Unlike abstract metaphysics, the *Tanya* grounds itself in the soul's practical dynamics, offering a roadmap for ethical conduct and spiritual ascent. RSZ introduces the *Benoni*, an intermediary state of heightened awareness attainable by all, emphasizing universal potential for growth.

A. RSZ and Spinoza: A Dance of Intellect and Soul

Rabbi Shneur Zalman of Liadi (1745–1812), the founder of Chabad-Lubavitch sect, and Baruch Spinoza (1632–1677), the

Dutch philosopher excommunicated from his Jewish community, share a striking intellectual kinship—yet their visions of God, the human soul, and spiritual life diverge profoundly. Both thinkers elevate reason as a pathway to the Divine, but where Spinoza's *amor dei intellectualis* (intellectual love of God) unfolds as a speculative ideal within a pantheistic framework, RSZ's teachings, crystallized in the *Tanya* and in his other esoteric writings, ground rationality in a dynamic, practical mysticism aimed at transforming human conduct and ushering in Divine Presence.

B. Shared Rationalist Threads

Spinoza's philosophy, articulated in his *Ethics*, casts God as an impersonal, infinite substance—identical with nature (*Deus sive Natura*)—knowable through reason alone.[54] The noted Spinoza scholar Steven Nadler interprets Spinoza's *Ethics* as a radical redefinition of God and Nature as one indivisible substance (*Deus sive Natura*). Spinoza argues that Nature is infinite, uncaused, and the only true whole, with nothing existing outside it.[55] All things arise within it through deterministic necessity.[56] God, as this unique, active, and infinitely powerful substance, is Nature itself—not a separate creator.

Nadler emphasizes that this identity strips away traditional religious roles. Unlike the Judeo-Christian God, Spinoza's God/Nature has no purposes or will.[57] The universe's order follows from God's attributes (thought and extension) with strict necessity, not design.[58] Talk of divine intentions is, Spinoza insists, a human fiction, leaving purposes only to human endeavors. Nadler thus sees Spinoza's system as a rationalist challenge to theism—profoundly unified, yet impersonal and devoid of teleology.[59]

His *amor dei intellectualis* emerges as a serene, intellectual apprehension of this unity, free from emotional turbulence or personal attachment. RSZ, too, prizes the intellect, rooting his Chabad ideology in the triad of *Hokhmah* (wisdom), *Binah* (reason), and *Da'at* (knowledge)—the "*ChaBaD*" of his movement's name. In the *Tanya*, he frames the divine soul's mastery over the animal soul as a rational endeavor, guided by contemplation of God's grandeur rather than fleeting emotion. Both thinkers, then, see the mind as a bridge to the eternal, echoing King Solomon's ascent through wisdom (Proverbs 3:13–18) rather than blind fervor. Yet this shared thread unravels in application.

Spinoza's God is static and abstract—an unfeeling totality encompassing all existence, leaving little room for personal connection or ethical action beyond detached understanding. RSZ, by contrast, imbues reason with fervor, insisting that intellectual insight ignite a passionate yearning for divine unity. His oft-quoted plea, "I desire You alone, to be absorbed in Your Holy Being," reveals a soul ablaze, not merely a mind at rest. Where Spinoza speculates on the nature of being, RSZ applies intellect to the soul's ascent, crafting a living guide for his Hasidim.

Rabbi Shneur Zalman of Liadi

Divergent Visions of God

Spinoza's pantheism dissolves the boundary between God and the world, rendering the divine immanent yet impersonal—a cosmic order without agency or intimacy. Zalman's theology, steeped in Kabbalistic tradition, presents the *Ein Sof* (the Infinite) as utterly transcendent, beyond human grasp, yet dynamically accessible through the *Sefirot*—emanations that bridge the infinite and the finite. In the *Tanya*, he likens comprehending the *Ein Sof* to the gap between thought and matter: just as matter cannot seize a thought, humans cannot fathom divine wisdom's essence. This analogy underscores a paradox—God's transcendence coexists with immanence, a personal Divine Presence woven into creation.

Unlike Spinoza's deterministic universe, where human freedom bends to necessity, RSZ's God invites interaction. Prayer, a cornerstone of Hassidic life, becomes a conduit for divine influence, potentially hastening the Messiah, elevated by RSZ into a structured, disciplined act. He refined his community's worship to avoid excesses critiqued by opponents, blending ecstasy with order, a far cry from Spinoza's rejection of ritual as superfluous to rational insight.

Awe Over Fear

Both thinkers critique fear-based devotion, but their alternatives diverge. Spinoza dismisses fear of God as irrational, favoring a calm acceptance of divine necessity. RSZ, too, rejects fear tied to self-interest—serving God for reward or escape from punishment—yet champions an awe born of contemplating creation's marvels. In the *Tanya*, he frames this awe (*yirah*) as a visceral response to God's infinite artistry, fueling a love (*ahavah*) that propels the soul upward. Spinoza's love is cerebral; RSZ's is both cerebral and fervent, a synthesis of mind and heart. RSZ's teachings bridge ancient Kabbalistic wisdom with a modern sensibility, offering a framework that endures in Chabad's global reach.

The *Tanya*'s focus on the soul's psychology and ethical orientation—elevating humanity through disciplined understanding and passionate devotion—stands in stark relief to Spinoza's speculative solitude. While Spinoza's God is an idea to be grasped, RSZ's is a presence to be sought, a relationship nurtured through prayer, study, and acts of kindness. His contributions reshape Jewish spirituality, blending the intellectual rigor of a philosopher with the soulful depth of a mystic.

Enduring Resonance

RSZ's approach echoes yet diverges from philosophers like Spinoza, whose *amor dei intellectualis* (intellectual love of God) shares a rationalist thread. Where Spinoza speculates, RSZ applies—prioritizing the soul's mastery through wisdom (*Hokhma*), reason (*Binah*), and knowledge (*Da'at*) over mere emotion, though his faith burns with passion. He invokes King Solomon's ascent through wisdom and critiques fear of God rooted in self-interest, advocating instead an awe inspired by creation's grandeur. This yearning shines in his words: "I desire You alone, to be absorbed in Your Holy Being," a plea for unity with the divine.

Bridging ancient wisdom and modern sensibility, RSZ's teachings endure. Tanya's focus on the human mind and its ethical orientation offers not just a mystical framework but a living guide, elevating the soul to a higher plane through disciplined understanding and fervent devotion. Prayer, a cornerstone for Hasidim, is elevated by RSZ as the essence of Torah and a conduit for divine influence, potentially heralding the Messiah. He refined its practice with structured liturgy, ensuring his followers' devotion avoided the excesses criticized in *Hasidic* worship. His ethics, rooted in tolerance—learned from personal persecution—stress accepting diverse minds as we do bodies, a principle he lived through patience and forgiveness. His doctrine of *Tzedakah* (acts of benevolence), though less emphasized by other Kabbalists fixated on the soul's eternity, completes his practical idealism, urging care for the body alongside the spirit, diverging from their ascetic neglect.

While sharing Spinoza's intellectual bent, RSZ's God transcends emotion and nature, accessible through reason yet immanent, contrasting Spinoza's impersonal pantheism. His moralism, not metaphysics, seeks a way of life, blending ecstatic prayer with actionable ethics for his *Hasidim*. In terms of his metaphysical views, Shneur RSZ asserted that the *Ein Sof*, the infinite aspect of the Divine, posits that comprehending *Ein Sof* is akin to the relationship between thought and matter; just as matter cannot grasp a thought, humans cannot fathom *Ein Sof*'s wisdom. This analogy underscores the transcendental nature of divine wisdom and the limitations of human comprehension. RSZ's contributions have significantly shaped Jewish spiritual and philosophical landscapes, offering deep insights into the nature of the divine and the human pursuit of spiritual understanding.

Kabbalists like Moses Cordovero, Isaac Luria, and Shneur RSZ of Liadi wrestled with how a spiritual God *(Ein Sof)* could create a material world without losing immateriality. Cordovero and Luria proposed *Tzimtzum* (see the entry on this theme), suggesting God contracted His infinite light to make space for creation, a view Dob Baer accepted. Shneur RSZ, wary of implied duality, refined this: creation didn't emerge directly from God but from a radiated spiritual force, preserving divine perfection while distancing God from the material world's origin. Creation derived not from God's essence, but from his ethereal light.[60]

Rabbi Dov Ber of Lubavitch

In the wake of *Chabad Hasidism's* founding by Rabbi Shneur Zalman of Liadi, the Alter Rebbe, a new luminary emerged to steer its course: Rabbi Dov Ber of Lubavitch, known as the *Mitteler Rebbe*, or "Middle Rebbe," for his pivotal place between his father's establishment and his nephew's expansion. Born on November 24, 1773, in Liozna, Belarus, Dov Ber was the eldest son of the Alter Rebbe, groomed from youth in the nascent Chabad philosophy—a fusion of Kabbalistic mysticism and rational inquiry. By 1812, following his father's death during Napoleon's retreat, he assumed leadership at age 39, moving the movement's center to Lubavitch, a small Russian town that would become synonymous with Chabad. A frail man plagued by health issues—often bedridden, his voice a whisper—he nonetheless radiated intellectual fire, authoring voluminous works that deepened Chabad's theological framework and cemented its identity as a "mindful" *Hasidism*, distinct from the emotive fervor of other sects.

Unlike the Besht's oral exuberance or the Maggid of Mezritch's meditative silences, the *Mitteler Rebbe* was a prolific writer, leaving a legacy of texts that marry mystical insight with systematic analysis. His major works—*Derech Chaim* (*The Way of Life*), Shaarei Teshuva (*Gates of Repentance*), and *Imrei Binah* (Words of Understanding)—pulse with Chabad's hallmark: *Hokmah, Binah, and Daat* (wisdom, understanding, knowledge), the intellectual triad he inherited from his father and refined.

Where the *Alter Rebbe's Tanya* laid Chabad's foundation, Dov Ber's writings expanded it into a sprawling edifice, dissecting the soul's journey and God's unity with a precision that rivals medieval philosophers. He taught that God's essence, the *Atzmut,* transcends even *Ein Sof*, the infinite light of Kabbalah, permeating creation not as a distant force but as its very reality. "All is God, and God is all," he wrote, echoing Lurianic monism but grounding it in rational terms.

This vision fueled his core teaching: contemplative prayer as a path to divine union. For the *Mitteler Rebbe*, prayer wasn't a quick recitation but a marathon of *hitbonenut*—introspection—where one meditates on God's greatness until the mind grasps His omnipresence. "Begin with *Hokmah*, the spark of awe, expand it through Binah's analysis, and root it in Daat's connection," he instructed (*Imrei Binah*, Introduction), guiding followers to dwell on concepts like *tzimtzum* (divine contraction) or the Sefirot's interplay until their souls ignited with *devekut* (cleaving to God). His own prayers, disciples recalled, could last hours—eyes shut, body swaying, voice murmuring as he plumbed cosmic depths. This wasn't the Besht's joyous shout or the Maggid's silent ascent; it was a cerebral pilgrimage, demanding focus and stamina, yet open to all who'd undertake the mental trek.

A. Dov Baer's Stoic Approach to Worship

Louis Jacobs, a prominent Jewish scholar, provides a detailed depiction of Dov Baer of Lubavitch, the second leader of the Habad (Chabad) Hasidic movement, in his writings. Dov Baer, who succeeded his father Shneur Zalman of Liadi (the founder of Habad), is portrayed as a figure of rigorous intellectualism and discipline, particularly in his approach to divine worship. Jacobs contrasts Dov Baer's strict, contemplative style with that of Rabbi Aaron of Starosselje, a contemporary and rival within the Habad movement, highlighting their differing interpretations of Shneur Zalman's teachings.

Dov Baer is characterized as having an uncompromising stance against what he saw as "*sham* emotion" in religious practice. He rejected superficial or exaggerated displays of feeling during worship, viewing them as inauthentic and contrary to the deeper spiritual goals of Habad *Hasidism*. His father, Shneur Zalman, had emphasized the primacy of the contemplative life—intellectual reflection on divine concepts such as God's unity and uniqueness—as the path to genuine spiritual elevation. Dov Baer took this teaching to an extreme, interpreting it in a "severely intellectual fashion." For him, true religious experience arose from profound mental engagement rather than emotional indulgence.

While Dov Baer did not outright dismiss religious emotion or mystical ecstasy, he was deeply critical of what he considered "spurious emotions"—feelings that were artificially provoked or self-centered rather than arising naturally from contemplation of the divine. He believed that wallowing in such emotional religiosity undermined the core Habad principle of overcoming the self (ego) in worship. Jacobs notes that Dov Baer's own prayer practice reflected this philosophy: he is said to have recited his prayers in "complete stillness and immobility," embodying a disciplined, inward-focused devotion.

B. Rabbi Aaron of Starosselje vs. R. Dov Baer on Prayer

Rabbi Aaron of Starosselje, a disciple of Shneur Zalman and a contemporary of Dov Baer, shared some of Dov Baer's views but diverged significantly in emphasis and temperament. Aaron did not reject Dov Baer's critique of inauthentic ecstasy, but he adopted a more tolerant attitude toward it. Where Dov Baer prioritized intellectual rigor and restraint, Aaron's approach to worship was marked by intense emotional expression. Jacobs describes Aaron's prayers as having a "frightening intensity," an "outpouring of religious fervor and enthusiasm" that manifested physically in a "mighty roar." This starkly contrasted with Dov Baer's stillness, reflecting their differing interpretations of how to achieve unity with the Divine. These differences were not merely personal but philosophical, rooted in their respective understandings of Habad teachings. The divergence was significant enough that, after Shneur Zalman's death in 1812 and Dov Baer's succession as leader in Lubavitch, Aaron established a rival Hasidic "court" in Starosselje in 1813. This split gave rise to two factions: the Lubavitcher *Hasidim*, loyal to Dov Baer, and the Starosseljer Hasidim, who followed Aaron. Both groups claimed to be the true heirs of Shneur Zalman's Habad legacy, though their practices and emphases diverged.

Jacobs underscores that Dov Baer's intellectual rigor and rejection of emotional excess became more emblematic of the mainstream Habad tradition, particularly as it evolved under Menahem Mendel and later leaders. Aaron, despite his prominence and contributions, such as his discourses compiled in Avodath Ha-Levi, remained a secondary figure in the movement's later history. His writings, while respected, did not achieve the same authoritative status as those of Dov Baer, Menahem Mendel, or other key Habad exponents like R. Yitzhak Isaac Ha-Levi Epstein of Homel and R. Hillel ben Meir Ha-Levi of *Parits.*

In Louis Jacobs' depiction, Dov Baer of Lubavitch emerges as a stern, intellectually driven leader who prioritized contemplation over emotion, seeking to purge divine worship of any hint of falsity or self-indulgence. His approach, rooted in his father's teachings, stood in contrast to Rabbi Aaron's more emotionally expressive and tolerant style. This tension not only shaped their personal practices—stillness versus fervor—but also led to a schism within Habad *Hasidism*, with lasting implications for its development. Dov Baer's legacy aligned more closely with the movement's enduring identity, while Aaron's influence, though significant, waned over time.

The Mitteler Rebbe's anthropology of the soul was built on Chabad's five-tiered model—*nefesh, ruach, neshamah, chayah, yechidah*—but he emphasized their interplay with the intellect. "The soul's light shines through the mind," he taught, seeing *Daat* as the bridge linking divine essence (*yechidah*) to human action (*nefesh*) (*Shaarei Teshuva*, Part 2, Chapter 12). Unlike the Maggid's *bittul* (self-nullification), which dissolved the ego into *ayin* (nothingness), Dov Ber's approach retained the self as a vessel, refining it through understanding. He introduced the *beinoni*—the "intermediate man" from *Tanya*—as a universal ideal: not a saint free of struggle, but one who masters his animal soul (*nefesh habehamit*) through reason, never sinning despite temptation. This practical spirituality spoke to the everyman, offering a roadmap to holiness without requiring mystic trances or saintly perfection.

His leadership style reflected this balance of depth and accessibility. In Lubavitch, he established a thriving court—hundreds of followers crowding his home for Shabbat, their questions met with marathon discourses that could stretch past midnight. He formalized Chabad's farbrengen, a communal gathering where teachings flowed alongside schnapps, fostering unity and introspection. Yet his tenure wasn't without strife: in 1826, Russian authorities arrested him on trumped-up charges of sedition—likely stoked by Mitnagdic rivals—only releasing him after 52 days, an ordeal he endured with calm resolve. This victory, celebrated as *Yud Kislev*, bolstered Chabad's resilience, proving its ideas could withstand external storms.

The Mitteler Rebbe's Kabbalah leaned heavily on Luria—*tzimtzum, Sefirot, tikkun*—but he reframed it through Chabad's lens of comprehension. "The *Sefirot* are not just divine attributes but windows to grasp God's unity," he wrote, urging study of their dynamics (e.g., Chesed's overflow, Gevurah's restraint) to mirror them in the soul. Where the Besht saw sparks in a broom's sweep, Dov Ber saw them in a mind's clarity—lifting them through disciplined thought rather than ecstatic leaps. His *tzaddik* wasn't the Maggid's cosmic conduit but a teacher, guiding followers to self-reliance via intellect. "The *tzaddik* lights the path, but you must walk it," he said (Shaarei Teshuva, Part 1, Chapter 19), a shift that empowered Chabad's laity.

His life, cut short on November 16, 1827, at 53, left a towering legacy. Buried in Niezhin after falling ill en route to a health spa, he passed leadership to his son-in-law, Rabbi Menachem Mendel, the Tzemach Tzedek, who built on his work. Dov Ber authored over 30 works, many unpublished in his lifetime, their breadth daunting even to scholars, some discourses spanning hundreds of pages, dissecting a single verse (Mindel, 1982, p. 112). His emphasis on *hitbonenut* birthed Chabad's meditative tradition, still alive in yeshivas today, where students pore over his texts to ignite their souls.

Historically, the Mitteler Rebbe bridged Chabad's infancy and maturity. Facing Mitnagdic bans and Tsarist suspicion, he fortified Hasidism with a philosophy too lucid to dismiss. His move to Lubavitch—a backwater turned spiritual capital—symbolized Chabad's rootedness, while his arrest and release galvanized its identity. His teachings, dense yet practical, shaped successors like the *Rebbe Rashab* and the Seventh Rebbe, embedding Chabad's "thinker" ethos. "God is found in the mind that seeks Him," he wrote, a credo that turned mysticism into a science of the soul.[61]

Rabbi Dov Ber's frail body masked a titan's spirit. His writings—marathons of insight—demand effort, yet reward with clarity: the infinite is knowable, the soul trainable, holiness attainable. For him, every thought can be a prayer, every deed a spark, echoing the Besht's immanence but through a rational lens. He died young, but his Chabad endures—synagogues chanting his *niggunim*, students wrestling his ideas, a movement thriving on his call to think deeply and live fully. In Lubavitch's quiet streets, his voice still whispers: God is near, if only we ponder Him.

Zalman's theory casts God as the immanent "Inner Cause," sustaining all existence like a flame within a candle. The cosmos—thought, action, good, evil—radiates from and returns to this unity, dependent on God's constant presence, unlike a potter's independent vessel. Though suggesting pantheism, Zalman diverges from Spinoza's *deus sive natura*: his God transcends nature, wields purpose (*takhlith*), and enables miracles, rejecting Spinoza's eternal matter, determinism, and impersonal laws. For Zalman, virtue follows Torah and Jewish tradition, not nature's fixed order, and immortality is vivid, not vague. Spinoza's dispassionate philosophy contrasts with Zalman's ecstatic mysticism, rooted in a living God revered by his Hasidic followers.

R. Hayyim Volozhin: Differing Views Concerning Kabbalah

Rabbi Hayyim Volozhin stands as a monumental figure in Jewish intellectual history, celebrated for founding the Volozhin Yeshiva in 1802 and reshaping Jewish education. A devoted disciple of the Vilna Gaon, Rabbi Hayyim embraced an approach rooted in intellectual discipline and a structured commitment to Torah study, reflecting his mentor's emphasis on rigorous scholarship over mystical fervor.

The Vilna Gaon, Rabbi Hayyim's revered teacher, was a vocal critic of the burgeoning *Hasidic* movement. His disapproval stemmed from several grievances: the Hasidim's altered prayer practices, their alleged disparagement of Torah scholars, and their unconventional interpretations of the Zohar, a foundational Kabbalistic text. Historical accounts, such as those from Immanuel Etkes, highlight a pivotal moment in 1772 when the Gaon refused to meet with prominent *Hasidic* leaders Rabbi Menahem Mendel of Vitebsk and Rabbi Shneur Zalman of Liadi. This decision followed reports of Hasidic innovations, which the Gaon interpreted as disrespectful to traditional scholarship and informed by a supposed divine revelation from Elijah. Viewing the Hasidim as heretics, the Vilna Gaon's stance galvanized opposition within the Vilna community, ensuring the controversy persisted throughout his lifetime.[62] This resistance was not unique to him; other traditionalist groups, as noted by Gershon Scholem, shared similar concerns about *Hasidism's* divergence from established norms.

While Rabbi Hayyim Volozhin aligned intellectually with the Mitnagdim—the opponents of Hasidism led by the Vilna Gaon—his approach was markedly more tolerant. Unlike his mentor's blanket rejection, Rabbi Hayyim distinguished between Hasidic ideology, which he critiqued, and individual *Hasidim*, whom he welcomed with greater openness. This pragmatism manifested in his *yeshiva*, where he permitted certain Hasidic customs, reflecting a willingness to engage with diverse perspectives within a controlled framework. His seminal work, *Nefesh Ha-Hayyim*, articulates this stance, championing rigorous Talmudic study as the cornerstone of spiritual growth—a direct counterpoint to the Hasidic emphasis on emotional and mystical experiences.

Rabbi Hayyim's teachings diverged significantly from those of Rabbi Shneur Zalman of Liadi, the founder of Chabad Hasidism and one of the *Hasidic* leaders rebuffed by the Vilna Gaon. While Rabbi Shneur Zalman infused the Kabbalah intricately into his philosophy, Rabbi Hayyim valued Kabbalah but subordinated it to the study of Torah and *Halakha.* He cautioned against allowing mystical pursuits to overshadow foundational Jewish learning, advocating instead for analytical scholarship and rational engagement with sacred texts. This conviction led him to exclude Kabbalah from the Volozhin Yeshiva's curriculum, ensuring students mastered traditional texts before, if ever, exploring mystical dimensions—a strategic choice amid the theological debates of his era.

Despite his criticisms of Hasidic ideology, Rabbi Hayyim cultivated an inclusive environment at Volozhin, welcoming students from varied backgrounds, including *Hasidim.* This openness underscored his belief in the synergy of intellectual and moral development. He insisted that Torah study be paired with ethical growth, fostering a holistic approach to Jewish practice. In *Nefesh Ha-Hayyim,* he reinterpreted Kabbalistic concepts to support a devotional life grounded in disciplined study and everyday actions, challenging the *Hasidic* prioritization of ecstatic spirituality.

Rabbi Hayyim's theology grapples with a profound paradox: God's omnipresence contrasted with His elusiveness to human perception. He posited that God permeates all creation, yet our finite understanding struggles to apprehend His direct presence. Through *Nefesh Ha-Hayyim,* he proposed that intellectual pursuit and Torah study bridge this gap, transforming mundane acts into expressions of devotion. His concept of Torah *lishmah*—studying Torah for its own sake—encapsulates this vision, presenting scholarly rigor as a form of worship that nurtures a deep connection with the Divine.

Rabbi Hayyim Volozhin's legacy endures as a synthesis of rationalism and spirituality, offering a disciplined yet devotional path within Judaism. His emphasis on critical analysis and structured learning resonated with the Mitnagdim, providing a robust counterpoint to Hasidic mysticism. His teachings continue to inspire scholars and practitioners, illuminating a way to encounter the Divine that harmonizes the mind and the heart. Through the Volozhin Yeshiva and *Nefesh Ha-Hayyim*, Rabbi Hayyim crafted an enduring model of Jewish life—one that values intellectual depth, ethical integrity, and a thoughtful approach to the sacred.

Vilna Gaon

The Vilna Gaon: A Nietzschean Analysis

In *The Birth of Tragedy* (1872), Friedrich Nietzsche framed the Apollonian and Dionysian as opposing forces fueling human culture and creativity. The Apollonian, linked to Apollo, the Greek god of the sun, represents order, reason, and individual clarity. The Dionysian, tied to Dionysus, god of wine and revelry, channels chaos, emotion, and collective passion. For Nietzsche, the interplay of these poles drives artistic and cultural vigor. This lens illuminates a pivotal 19th-century Jewish intellectual rift: the Vilna Gaon and his disciple Rabbi Hayyim Volozhin's resistance to the Hasidic movement—a clash of disciplined tradition against ecstatic spirituality.

The Vilna Gaon (Elijah ben Solomon Zalman, 1720–1797) and Rabbi Hayyim Volozhin (1749–1821) embody Nietzsche's Apollonian ideal. The Gaon, a prodigious scholar, mastered Jewish texts with razor-sharp precision, from halachic rulings to meticulous Talmudic corrections. His approach—rooted in rational analysis and strict adherence to tradition—prized intellectual rigor over emotional excess. Rabbi Volozhin extended this legacy. In 1802, he founded the Volozhin Yeshiva, a hub of Talmudic study that drew students across Europe with its focus on textual depth and logical debate. His book *Nefesh Ha-Hayyim* casts disciplined scholarship as a sacred act, reinforcing an Apollonian ethos of structure, reason, and individual achievement.

Contrast this with the *Hasidic* movement, ignited in the 18th century by the *Baal Shem Tov. Hasidism* pulsed with Dionysian energy—ecstatic prayers, fervent dances, and soulful *niggunim* (wordless melodies) filled *shtiebels* across Eastern Europe. It favored emotional connection to the divine, communal ritual, and spiritual spontaneity over rigid intellect. Followers sought transcendence through joy and shared fervor, dissolving individual boundaries in a tide of collective passion. To the Gaon and Volozhin, this exuberance bordered on chaos, even subversion.

The movement, shaped by the Maggid of Mezritch (Dov Ber, d. 1772), often balanced reason and emotion, tempering excessive mysticism. Yet Rabbi Abraham of Kalisk (1741–1810), a fiery disciple, leaned hard into the Dionysian. Embracing the Maggid's teachings on *bittul* (self-nullification) and *devekut* (cleaving to God), he led a group of young men in the early 1770s through a radical regimen of austerity, self-mortification, and ecstatic worship. Their wild prayers—marked by dancing, gestures, and occasional frenzy—clashed with Hasidism's typical restraint.[63] Rumors of such behavior, including headstands and mockery of Torah scholars, fueled the Vilna Gaon's suspicions. Trusting credible informants, he saw Hasidism as a threat to Jewish law's intellectual core.[64]

Rabbi Abraham's circle provoked the Mitnagdic critics—sober Talmudists whose scholarly gravity they deemed smug apathy. Through ridicule, they aimed to shake these opponents awake, amplifying Hasidism's emotional pulse into a defiant stance. After the Maggid's death, Rabbi Abraham joined Rabbi Menachem Mendel of Vitebsk in 1777 to settle in Tiberias, becoming a linchpin in Hasidism's spread to the Holy Land. There, his ecstatic style clashed with emerging rationalist branches like Chabad, led by R. Shneur Zalman, who favored structured contemplation. Rabbi Abraham's letters from Tiberias defended his emotive path, exposing a rift within Hasidism's evolution. His brief but intense Kalisk experiment highlights the movement's early diversity and adaptability, blending passion with the Maggid's vision.

The Vilna Gaon's wariness peaked in 1772 when he refused to meet *Hasidic* emissaries, fearing their mystical fervor undermined tradition's rational bedrock, as historian Immanuel Etkes observes. Rabbi Volozhin doubled down, positioning his yeshiva as a counterweight to *Hasidism's* spread, emphasizing analytical study amid rising enthusiasm. Their Apollonian stance—order over ecstasy, reason over passion—stood in sharp contrast to *Hasidism's* Dionysian swell.

Yet this tension wasn't mere opposition; it enriched Jewish life, echoing Nietzsche's vision. The Gaon's critiques clarified tradition's boundaries, while Volozhin's *yeshiva*, though a Mitnagdic stronghold, drew Hasidic students, sparking unintended dialogue. *Hasidism*, far from anti-intellectual, wove Torah study into its mystical fabric—think Rabbi Nachman of Breslov's blend of scholarship and storytelling. Even *Nefesh Ha-Hayyim* subtly bridges the divide, reworking Kabbalistic ideas—like the soul's cosmic role—into a rational framework, hinting at a synthesis of Apollonian and Dionysian impulses.

Through Nietzsche's lens, the Vilna Gaon and Rabbi Volozhin's resistance to *Hasidism* reveals a creative clash that deepened Jewish thought. Their Apollonian commitment to reason met the Dionysian surge of *Hasidic* passion, igniting a dynamic interplay. Far from breaking Judaism, this tension fortified it, forging a tradition where disciplined inquiry and fervent emotion could coexist. In 19th-century Jewish history, as in Nietzsche's philosophy, it's the dance between order and chaos that sustains enduring vitality.

Rav Nachman of Breslov

Rabbi Nachman of Breslov (1772–1810), a great-grandson of the *Baal Shem Tov*, stands as a transformative figure in Jewish spirituality, whose teachings on joy, faith, and personal connection with God continue to resonate today. Born into the fiery legacy of *Hasidism*—a movement sparked by his great-grandfather in 18th-century Ukraine—Nachman sought to renew its mystical traditions, making them accessible to all. His life, a mosaic of spiritual triumphs and profound tragedies, shaped a philosophy that blended mystical depth with practical wisdom, leaving an indelible mark on Jewish thought.

From childhood, Nachman displayed an extraordinary spiritual intensity, immersing himself in prayer, fasting, and meditation. Unlike many peers who prized scholarly debate, he chased direct encounters with the divine, wandering Ukrainian towns to share his vision. At 26, he undertook a daring pilgrimage to the Land of Israel in 1798, a journey he described as a spiritual ascent. This experience deepened his teachings, but it also drew skepticism from established *Hasidic* leaders. They bristled at his rejection of dynastic succession—a cornerstone of *Hasidic* tradition—and his emphasis on personal spirituality over communal norms. Undeterred, Nachman returned with a sharpened resolve, cementing his role as a bold innovator.

Nachman placed *simchah* (joy) at the heart of his philosophy, declaring, "It is a great *mitzvah* to be happy always."[65] For him, joy was a sacred act of faith, a bulwark against despair, which he saw as a barrier to God. His teachings sprang from personal experience, as he wrestled with despair yet urged followers to transform darkness into light. Scholar Arthur Green, in Tormented Master, suggests these struggles might reflect manic-depressive tendencies—a modern interpretation not shared by Nachman's contemporaries, who viewed his intensity as spiritual fervor.

Equally radical was *hitbodedut*, or secluded personal prayer. In an age dominated by synagogue worship, structured and communal, Nachman urged followers to speak to God in their own words, saying, "The main thing is speech with God."[66] Practiced alone, often in nature, *hitbodedut* offered an intimate, unscripted dialogue with the divine, starkly contrasting the formal prayers of the time. This empowered individuals to forge a direct relationship with God, a hallmark of his revolutionary approach.

Nachman's storytelling further enriched his legacy. In *Sippurei Ma'asiyot*, tales like "The Seven Beggars"—where each beggar at a wedding offers a unique blessing—unfold as allegories of the soul's journey, making profound truths vivid and relatable. His life was shadowed by hardship. He lost his first wife, Sashia, to illness and mourned several children's deaths, including two who died young. These losses, alongside his own battles with despair, shaped his teachings on resilience. Rather than hide his struggles, he shared them, showing that faith and joy could redeem suffering—a message that struck a chord with his followers.

Nachman died of tuberculosis in 1810 at 38, but his vision endured thanks to Reb Nathan of Breslov). Reb Noson compiled Nachman's works—like *Likutey Moharan* and *Sichot HaRan*—and wrote his own, such as *Likutey Halakhot*, expanding on his master's ideas. He organized the Breslov community without a living rebbe, as Nachman wished, creating a unique, decentralized movement sustained by teachings alone. Today, thousands flock to Nachman's grave in Uman, Ukraine, for Rosh Hashanah, drawn by his promise of renewal. Breslov Hasidism thrives as a testament to his timeless call for personal empowerment and spiritual authenticity.

A. Nachman's Approach to Contemplative Prayer

Rabbi Nachman of Breslov viewed הִתְבּוֹדְדוּת (*hitbodedut*), or personal seclusion in prayer, as a profound spiritual practice that allowed a worshiper to tune into the divine harmony underlying all creation. He believed that the world is imbued with God's presence and that every part of creation sings a unique song to its Creator. This concept reflects mystical teachings that portray all beings as contributors to a cosmic symphony of praise to God.

Through *hitbodedut*, individuals remove themselves from the distractions of daily life, enabling the mind and heart to quiet down. In this state of solitude, they can begin to perceive the spiritual essence of the world. Nachman emphasized that only by stepping away from external noise could one hear the "silent song" of creation. He encouraged practicing *hitbodedut* outdoors, in natural settings like fields or forests, where the rhythms of nature reflect divine harmony. With its sights and sounds, the natural world serves as a medium through which worshipers can connect to the Creator's will and hear the hidden song emanating from all elements of creation.

This practice is deeply tied to listening to one's inner voice and the voice of creation itself. Nachman described a mystical process where *hitbodedut* elevates spiritual awareness, enabling the worshiper to realize that every component of the universe participates in praising God. This idea resonates with Psalms 19:2, which states, "The heavens declare the glory of God, and the sky above proclaims His handiwork." Through *hitbodedut*, the mundane is transformed into the sacred as individuals recognize the divine essence within every grass, stone, and star blade. Nachman taught that even a blade of grass has an angel encouraging it to grow, symbolizing that all parts of creation contribute to the universal symphony of divine service.

The practice also fosters a sense of unity and healing. By hearing the song of creation, individuals experience a profound connection with the world and God, bringing inner joy, peace, and an awareness of their place within the divine order. Nachman emphasized that each person has a unique melody or spiritual note that contributes to the grand harmony of creation. Through *hitbodedut*, worshipers refine their personal song and learn to harmonize it with the greater cosmic symphony.[67] For Rabbi Nachman, *hitbodedut* was not just a tool for introspection but a gateway to experiencing the sacred song of existence. Through solitude and heartfelt dialogue with God, individuals transcend the material world and align themselves with the divine music permeating all creation, finding meaning and purpose in its rhythm.

B. Rabbi Nachman's Lekutei Maharan

Rabbi Nachman of Breslov's interpretation of the Shulchan Aruch uniquely combines *halachic* observance with spiritual and mystical depth, distinguishing it from Rabbi Yosef Karo's codified legalism and Rabbi Joseph B. Soloveitchik's intellectual rigor. While Nachman upholds the *Shulchan Aruch* as the foundation of Jewish law, he reimagines it as a means to achieve divine connection, joy, and spiritual transformation.

Rabbi Yosef Karo's *Shulchan Aruch* codifies Jewish law for universal application, emphasizing clarity and practicality. Nachman, however, views this legal structure as an opportunity for aligning one's soul with God. While Karo seeks uniformity, Nachman highlights personal engagement with the *mitzvot*, encouraging individuals to experience them as transformative acts. Nachman's approach differs considerably from Rabbi J.B. Soloveitchik's analytical approach explores the philosophical and covenantal dimensions of *halacha*, but Nachman shifts the focus toward emotional authenticity, emphasizing the heartfelt experience of mitzvot over intellectual analysis.

Nachman's teachings frame the *Shulchan Aruch* as a mystical bridge between the physical and spiritual realms. Each *mitzvah* holds cosmic significance, serving as a channel for *tikkun olam* (repairing the world) and drawing divine light into creation. In *Likutei Moharan*, Nachman underscores the deeper spiritual meaning embedded in even the smallest laws, urging practitioners to see their observance as a pathway to divine will. Central to Nachman's approach is the joy and simplicity of fulfilling *mitzvot*. He warns against viewing halacha as a burden, emphasizing the vitality of performing commandments with enthusiasm and gratitude. His teachings on joy—epitomized in his famous statement, "It is a great *mitzvah* to be happy always"—reframe *halachic* practice as a celebration of connection with God, making it accessible to all, regardless of intellectual ability.

While Karo's *Shulchan Aruch* provides a universal framework, Nachman stresses personalization. He complements formal *halachic* observance with practices like *hitbodedut*, encouraging individuals to build a direct and unique relationship with God. Nachman imbues *halacha* with mystical significance, teaching that each *mitzvah* corresponds to divine truths and cosmic realities. In his view, observing *halacha* becomes an act of participation in the divine order, enabling spiritual growth and alignment with God's will. This mystical interpretation inspires practitioners to find sacred meaning in even the most mundane laws.

Nachman teaches that the laws of the *Shulchan Aruch* correspond to divine truths. Observing these laws is a way of participating in the divine order and fostering spiritual growth. This perspective imbues *halachic* practice with a sense of sacred mystery, encouraging practitioners to see beyond the surface and engage with the divine energy present in each commandment. Nachman addresses religious observance's emotional and psychological challenges, such as feelings of inadequacy or despair. In *Likutei Moharan*, he reassures followers that even imperfect observance has immense value, advocating persistence and reliance on God's mercy. This compassionate approach contrasts with the more rigid interpretations of halacha that might discourage those who struggle with its demands. Rabbi Nachman's integration of halachic observance with joy, mysticism, and personal spirituality redefines the *Shulchan Aruch* as more than a legal code—it becomes a transformative journey toward divine connection. His teachings emphasize that halacha is about fulfilling obligations and discovering a dynamic, living relationship with God. This approach inspires those seeking a rigorous and uplifting path, making halacha a source of spiritual vitality and connection.

C. Getting in Touch with One's Inner Tzaddik

Nachman also stressed the infinite potential of every individual. He taught that each person has a unique role to play in the world and that even the smallest *mitzvah* (good deed) can have cosmic significance. He encouraged people never to give up on themselves, regardless of their past mistakes or spiritual failings. His concept of "never despairing" (אֵין שׁוּם יֵאוּשׁ בָּעוֹלָם כְּלָל = *ein shum ye'ush ba'olam klal*) is a cornerstone of Breslov philosophy, offering a message of hope and resilience that continues to resonate with people today.

The concept of the צַדִּיק (*tzaddik* =righteous person) also plays a central role in Nachman's teachings. He saw the *tzaddik* as a spiritual leader, a channel for divine light, and a source of inspiration for others. While Nachman rejected the dynastic leadership model common in other *Hasidic* groups, he viewed his teachings as a legacy for his followers, guiding them on their spiritual journeys.

Nachman believed deeply in the coming of the Messiah and the world's ultimate redemption. He saw his teachings as paving the way for this messianic era. His famous statement, "My fire will burn until the coming of the Messiah," highlights his conviction that his teachings were timeless and essential for all generations. The annual pilgrimage to Nachman's grave in Uman, Ukraine, especially during *Rosh Hashanah*, is a hallmark of Breslov piety. Nachman himself emphasized the spiritual significance of visiting his gravesite, promising to intercede on behalf of those who come there to pray and recite the *Tikkun HaKlali* (Ten Psalms). This pilgrimage has become a central expression of devotion for

Breslov *Hasidim*, drawing thousands of people from around the world each year.

Nachman's influence continues to grow, particularly in modern times. His teachings resonate with individuals seeking spiritual meaning, inner peace, and resilience in a world often filled with challenges and uncertainties. Though relatively small in number compared to other Hasidic groups, Breslov *Hasidim* are known for their fervent devotion and active efforts to spread Nachman's teachings. In summary, Rabbi Nachman of Breslov's legacy extends far beyond his short life. His teachings, centered on joy, prayer, and unwavering faith, continue to inspire and uplift individuals across the spectrum of Jewish life and beyond. Whether through the practice of *hitbodedut*, his mystical tales, or his call to live with hope and resilience, Nachman offers a timeless roadmap for spiritual seekers. His message that "there is no despair in the world at all" speaks to the depths of the human condition, offering solace, connection, and a path towards a more meaningful and fulfilling life. Through his works and the dedication of his followers, Rabbi Nachman's fire indeed continues to burn brightly, illuminating the path for those seeking to deepen their relationship with God and find joy amid life's complexities.

D. Stories as a Path to the Soul

Rabbi Nachman of Breslov, a 19th-century *Hasidic* master, wove tales that fuse mysticism, allegory, and deep spiritual insight. More than mere stories, they map the soul's journey through exile, madness, and redemption. Let's explore two of his most iconic works: *The Lost Princess* and *The Turkey Prince.*

In *The Lost Princess*, A king's cherished daughter vanishes, symbolizing the soul's estrangement from its divine root. He dispatches a viceroy to retrieve her, but the quest brims with trials—dense forests, fleeting distractions, and crushing despair. The viceroy nearly succeeds but dozes off at a pivotal moment, stalling the rescue. The tale ends unresolved, dangling a haunting question: will the princess ever be found?

Three spiritual and mystical themes emerge from this story:

- **Exile and Redemption**: The princess is the divine spark within us, lost to the material world. The viceroy's mission reflects our struggle to reclaim it.
- **Perseverance**: Setbacks reveal spiritual growth as a winding path, demanding resilience amid failure.
- **Open-Ended Hope**: The ambiguity invites us to join the search, casting ourselves as seekers of wholeness.

This story stirs us to rouse from spiritual lethargy and pursue unity, however distant it feels.

In the story of the "Turkey Prince," A prince, seized by madness, insists he's a turkey. Naked, he crouches under a table, pecking at crumbs. The king's advisors—some stern, others gentle—fail to sway him. A sage arrives with an odd tactic: he strips, joins the prince beneath the table, and declares, "I'm a turkey too." The prince, startled but curious, warms to him. Gradually, the sage probes: "Can a turkey wear a shirt?" "Can a turkey sit at the table?" Each "yes" nudges the prince toward human habits, until his delusion fades completely.

Three spiritual and mystical themes emerge from this story:

- ❑ **Empathy as Healing**: The sage meets the prince in his depths, forging trust through shared vulnerability rather than force.

- ❑ **Gradual Transformation**: Recovery unfolds in patient steps, honoring the individual's pace.

- ❑ **The Tzaddik's Role**: The sage mirrors the Hasidic ideal of a guide who descends into darkness to lift others up, unshaken by the plunge.

This quirky parable doubles as a psychological masterpiece, showing how presence and understanding heal fractured identities. In *The Turkey Prince*, the sage's descent reflects Nachman's view of the *tzaddik*—a spiritual leader who enters another's struggle without losing their footing, offering a lifeline to redemption. The prince's turkey delusion captures alienation, a disconnect from self or soul, resolved through compassionate acknowledgment. This aligns with modern psychology's emphasis on trust and nonjudgmental support, a link noted by Martin Buber, who saw relational healing in the tale, and Meyer Levin, who brought its depth to Western readers.

Both stories pulse with Nachman's genius: *The Lost Princess* urges us to seek the divine amid life's tangles, while *The Turkey Prince* reveals transformation through empathy and patience. Together, they affirm his belief that the human spirit, no matter how lost or broken, can find its way back—with persistence, connection, and the right guide. These timeless lessons transcend their *Hasidic* roots, speaking to anyone navigating the chaos of existence.

E. Rav Nachman and Franz Kafka

Rabbi Nachman of Bratslav and Franz Kafka (1883-1924) share a deep resonance in their lives and literary works, revealing striking parallels despite their vastly different worlds—one rooted in *Hasidic* mysticism and the other in secular modernity. Both men were storytellers of exceptional vision, using narrative as a vehicle to grapple with profound existential questions, transcending their specific contexts to explore universal themes.

At the heart of their shared creative and spiritual endeavors is a relentless search for meaning in a world marked by absurdity and alienation. Nachman's tales often depict individuals on mysterious journeys, facing trials and searching for redemption, symbolizing the soul's yearning for closeness to the Divine amidst the concealment of God's presence. Similarly, Kafka's characters navigate surreal, often oppressive landscapes, confronting impenetrable systems of power and logic that seem designed to thwart their understanding or agency. Both writers delve into the human condition's paradoxes, probing the tension between striving for transcendence and the inescapable reality of human limitation.

Nachman and Kafka broke with traditional narrative forms, inventing new modes of storytelling that blurred the boundaries between realism and allegory, dream and reality. Nachman's tales, such as "The Lost Princess," employ mystical symbolism and layered meanings, speaking to both the spiritual seeker and the ordinary reader. Kafka's works, such as *The Trial* and *The Metamorphosis,* similarly operate on multiple levels, portraying surreal situations that resonate as allegories for modern existential and societal dilemmas. Both writers invite their audiences into interpretive engagement, leaving their works open to varied readings.

Franz Kafka (1883-1924)

On a personal level, both Nachman and Kafka were introspective, solitary figures, deeply aware of the fragility of human existence. Nachman's teachings often emphasized the importance of faith and joy in the face of despair, born from his own struggles with depression and spiritual restlessness. Kafka, haunted by self-doubt and alienation, infused his works with a sense of existential loneliness and the weight of unfulfilled aspirations. For both, their isolation became a crucible for creativity, shaping their ability to articulate the ineffable aspects of human experience.

Both men died young from tuberculosis, a shared fate that underscores their common fragility and sense of impermanence. Despite their untimely deaths, their legacies endured, largely through posthumously published works. Intriguingly, both instructed that their unpublished manuscripts be destroyed—Nachman with his final writings and Kafka with the manuscripts left in the care of his friend Max Brod. This shared ambivalence toward their creative output speaks to their humility and the personal torment they associated with their works.

While Nachman was a mystic deeply immersed in faith, and Kafka often wrestled with doubt and estrangement from organized religion, both engaged with themes of divine absence and presence. Nachman's stories frequently explore the hiddenness of God and the need for perseverance in faith, while Kafka's works reflect a modern, secular grappling with an elusive higher power or ultimate truth. In their different ways, both articulate their times' spiritual and existential crises, making their works profoundly relatable across generations.

Both Nachman and Kafka demonstrate the transformative power of imagination, using it to transcend their personal struggles and illuminate larger truths. Nachman's fantastical narratives offer spiritual guidance and a pathway to redemption, while Kafka's surreal scenarios provide insights into the absurdities of modern existence. Through their storytelling, both created spaces where readers could confront their own questions about meaning, identity, and the nature of existence.

Nachman and Kafka's continued relevance lies in their ability to speak about the universal human experience. Both tap into a deep vein of existential questioning, addressing themes of purpose, suffering, and the search for connection in ways that resonate across cultures and eras. Their works challenge readers to confront the mysteries of life with courage, creativity, and humility. Though separated by nearly a century and divergent contexts, they share a profound kinship as visionaries who grappled with the eternal questions of existence. Their legacies, rooted in their struggles and creativity, continue to inspire and provoke, offering wisdom for those navigating the complexities of life and the mysteries of the human spirit.

The Rebbe of Kotzk

Rabbi Menachem Mendel of Kotzk (1787–1859), a.k.a. *the Kotzker Rebbe,* stands as a profound and enigmatic figure in Hasidic thought, revered for his relentless pursuit of truth and authenticity. Born in Poland, he studied under leading Hasidic masters like the Seer of Lublin and Rabbi Simcha Bunim of Pshischa, inheriting a tradition emphasizing individuality and introspection. Settling in Kotzk, he gathered a devoted circle of disciples, challenging them to strip away self-deception and confront their inner lives with unflinching honesty.

Rabbi Mendel's philosophy centered on *Emet* (truth), not as an abstract ideal but as an existential imperative. He demanded a spiritual life free of pretense, warning against hollow religiosity and mechanical observance. For him, faith was a struggle requiring courage and introspection. He famously declared, "God dwells where one lets Him in," a call to confront oneself without illusions. His teachings often critiqued the superficiality of communal piety, asserting that true worship required sincerity and personal engagement.

In A *Passion for Truth*, Abraham Joshua Heschel portrays Rabbi Mendel as a prophetic figure, uncompromising in his demands for spiritual integrity. Heschel admires his rejection of mediocrity and his protest against complacency in religious life. The Kotzker's later withdrawal into seclusion, Heschel argues, was not retreat but defiance—a refusal to condone the spiritual compromises of his time.

Comparisons with Søren Kierkegaard illuminate the existential depth of Rabbi Mendel's thought. Both emphasized the importance of individual faith over institutional religion and saw religious truth as deeply personal. Kierkegaard's notion of the "leap of faith," requiring risk and confrontation with doubt, parallels Kotzker Rebbe's insistence that true belief arises from inner struggle. Both critiqued the shallowness of organized religion, advocating for a return to authentic, personal engagement with the divine. Rabbi Mendel's legacy endures in his sharp insistence on honesty and his demand for a faith rooted in self-examination. His teachings resonate with modern seekers grappling with authenticity and questions of spiritual depth. Though his uncompromising vision challenges those who approach it, his insistence on truth offers a path to a profound connection with God for those willing to embrace the struggle. The Kotzker Rebbe's life and teachings remain a timeless call to integrity and the courage to face one's own soul.

A. Heschel's Insight on the Kotzker Rebbe's Legacy

Heschel observed that the Kotzker Rebbe envisioned a spiritual revolution akin to Elijah's prophetic moment at Mount Carmel, when the people exclaimed, "The Lord, He is God!" (1 Kgs. 18:39). This vision reflects a longing for an unambiguous, pure acknowledgment of divine truth, free from pretense or idolatry. For the Kotzker, such clarity required complete honesty and self-sacrifice, rejecting all falsehood and mediocrity.[68]

The Kotzker's spiritual demands arise from his acute sensitivity to the world's cruelty and deceit. For the Kotzker Rebbe, the profound ugliness and suffering in human existence made superficial joy or complacent happiness intolerable. His worldview was a relentless confrontation with reality, driven by a prophetic zeal to cleanse the soul and the world of hypocrisy. Heschel notes that Jewish tradition similarly values a balanced approach to life. The Torah calls for a life guided by piety and ethical action within the bounds of normalcy, not a constant state of spiritual heroism. The principle of "you shall live by them" (Leviticus 18:5) underscores the importance of life and the expectation that Jews fulfill their religious obligations while embracing the world. Martyrdom, while revered in exceptional circumstances, is not the norm.

In sharp contrast, the Kotzker Rebbe's demands were unyielding. His spiritual philosophy insisted on absolute authenticity, rejecting even the smallest trace of compromise, self-seeking, or pretense. He demanded total self-sacrifice in the face of extraordinary trials and as a constant way of life. This approach was merciless to the self and others, as it required an almost superhuman commitment to honesty, integrity, and excellence. Heschel acknowledges that the Kotzker's views, though deviating from the more compassionate and balanced norms of Jewish tradition, echo the voices of the prophets. Like the prophets, the Kotzker called for a rejection of idolatry, falsehood, and complacency. However, his insistence on relentless self-sacrifice placed his teachings in tension with the divine attributes of love and compassion, which are central to the biblical God.

Heschel's analysis highlights the dual nature of the Kotzker Rebbe's teachings: on the one hand, a powerful call to spiritual authenticity and rejection of mediocrity; on the other, a departure from the biblical emphasis on joy, gratitude, and balance. The Kotzker's unrelenting demands resonate with the prophetic mission to root out falsehood. Still, they also reveal the cost of such radicalism—a vision of spirituality that, while inspiring, is difficult to reconcile with the broader tradition's more humane and accessible path. Heschel invites us to wrestle with these tensions, appreciating the Kotzker Rebbe's profound insights while recognizing the need for balance and compassion in spiritual life.

B. Memorable Wisdom Aphorisms

Rabbi Menachem Mendel of Kotzk's aphorisms urge uncomfortable and transformative self-examination. They challenge us to strip away our pretense and face the truth about our actions, motivations, and relationship with God. Kotzker Rebbe's teachings are not merely theoretical; they demand that we confront our inner selves and live authentically.

- ❑ **When we consider his statement, "If I am I because I am I, and you are you because you are you..."** -- We are reminded of how often our identities are shaped by external influences—societal expectations, comparisons, and validation from others. The Kotzker pushes us to reflect on who we are at our core, beyond our roles or the standards we measure ourselves. True identity, he teaches, is built from within, unshaken by the opinions of others.

- ❑ **Where is God? God is only where you let Him in,** challenging us to examine how much space we create for the divine in our lives. It is easy to go through the motions of religious practice without genuinely opening ourselves to God's presence. This teaching reminds us that our relationship with God is dynamic and reciprocal. We must actively invite God into our thoughts, actions, and decisions, shaping our lives around that sacred connection.

- ❑ **All that is thought should not be said, all that is said should not be written…**— is a profound lesson in the value of restraint and intentionality. In an age where words are often shared without consideration, we are reminded to weigh their impact carefully. The Kotzker Rebbe teaches us that words have power and that not every thought need expression. Wisdom lies in knowing when to speak and when to remain silent.

- ❑ **People are accustomed to looking at the heavens and wondering what happens there. It would be better if they would look within themselves to see what happens there.** — This aphorism challenges us to prioritize introspection over speculation. Instead of being preoccupied with lofty ideas or distant mysteries, we are called to turn inward and examine our character and motivations. The Kotzker reminds us that genuine spiritual growth begins with an honest appraisal of ourselves.

❑ **There is nothing so whole as a broken heart** — a paradoxical but deeply comforting teaching. It reminds us that our moments of vulnerability and brokenness are often the most transformative. When we come before God with humility and an awareness of our flaws, we open ourselves to true healing and connection. The Kotzker reframes brokenness not as a sign of failure but as an opportunity for renewal.

❑ **Do not be satisfied with the speech of your lips and the thought of your heart... Rather you must arise and do!** —The Kotzker Rebbe's emphasis on action involves a call to move beyond good intentions. While reflection and planning are important, real change comes through action. This teaching reminds us that spirituality is not merely about what we feel or think but about what we do. Transformation requires deeds, not just aspirations.

❑ **If I am I because I am I, and you are you because you are you, then I am I and you are you. But if I am I because you, are you, and you are you because I am I, then I am not I, and you are not you."** — This aphorism emphasizes the importance of self-definition and reminds us that true identity arises from within; independent of external validation or comparison. This teaching challenges us to cultivate a sense of self deeply rooted in self-awareness and internal conviction. In a world often dominated by social pressures and the need for approval, Kotzker's words call us to resist the tendency to base our self-worth on how others perceive us. Instead, we are encouraged to develop a grounded, intrinsic understanding of ourselves. His critique of this external focus invites us to engage in honest introspection, recognize the unique qualities that define us, and embrace them fully.

This brilliant teaching extends beyond the personal, urging us to build communities and relationships that value authenticity over conformity. By advocating for individuality and intrinsic self-worth, the Kotzker Rebbe offers timeless wisdom that challenges us to lead lives of purpose and inner strength, unshaken by the shifting judgments of others. His words inspire us to live with integrity, continually striving to align our actions and beliefs with the truth that lies within.

Rabbi Menachem Mendel of Kotzk's aphorisms continue to resonate because they challenge conventional thinking and demand spiritual authenticity. Each statement reflects his sharp intellect and uncompromising commitment to truth, offering relevant insights. His teachings call on us to confront our inner selves, refine our actions, and seek a spirituality rooted in honesty, humility, and transformative effort. Through his timeless words, the Kotzker Rebbe invites us to embark on a journey of self-discovery and divine connection.[69]

A 20th Century Kabbalist: Abraham Isaac Kook

Rabbi Abraham Isaac Kook, widely known as Rav Kook, emerged as a seminal figure in Jewish thought during the early 20th century. Born in 1865 in the Russian Empire and later appointed as the first Ashkenazi Chief Rabbi of British Mandatory Palestine, he is revered for his multifaceted roles as a philosopher, mystic, poet, and leader who adeptly merged traditional Jewish principles with modern thought.

Rav Kook's interpretation of Kabbalah is distinguished by its integration of spiritual insights with everyday life. He saw the world as innately sacred, identifying the divine within religious and secular spheres. In his view, modern developments were inevitable and valuable opportunities for spiritual evolution. His teachings on Jewish mysticism transcended theoretical study, offering a practical and experiential guide for a spiritually engaged life.

His insights extended beyond personal spirituality, envisioning a collective journey toward national and universal redemption, deeply influenced by Kabbalistic ideals. He perceived the Jewish return to Israel as pivotal in the world's spiritual ascent. Rav Kook's perspective on secular Zionism was revolutionary; he regarded it as a latent element in a divine schema endowed with profound spiritual importance. Thus, his teachings bridged the mystical and the mundane, underscoring humanity's role in shaping a spiritually unified world.

Rav Kook's legacy continues to inspire, connecting ancient mystical wisdom with the nuances of modern life. His unique blend of traditional and contemporary, individual and communal, spiritual and practical, has established him as a towering influence in 20th-century Jewish thought. His works remain a beacon, guiding the harmonization of Jewish life and philosophical elements.

A. Abraham Isaac Kook's Essay: "Souls in Chaos"

In his essay "Souls of Chaos," Rabbi Abraham Isaac Kook explores the interplay between two realms: the ordered world of tradition and the chaotic sphere of rebellion against established norms. Kook posits that chaos, though initially disruptive, holds the potential for profound transformation and enlightenment when guided constructively. He expresses empathy for youthful rebels drawn to ideologies like Zionism or Marxism, acknowledging the fear they provoke while advocating for their inclusion and patient engagement. Kook believes these "souls of chaos," though temporarily adrift, are vital to societal progress and can be redirected toward holiness and order.

This journey from *Olam HaTohu* (the world of chaos) to *Olam HaTikkun* (the world of repair) reflects a collective striving for unity amid diversity, order within chaos, and hope amid uncertainty. It is humanity's enduring narrative, weaving a dynamic tapestry of progress through time.

B. Rabbi Abraham Isaac Kook's Theology of Kabbalah

Here are a few key points from Rav Kook's philosophy that may shed light on his perspective:

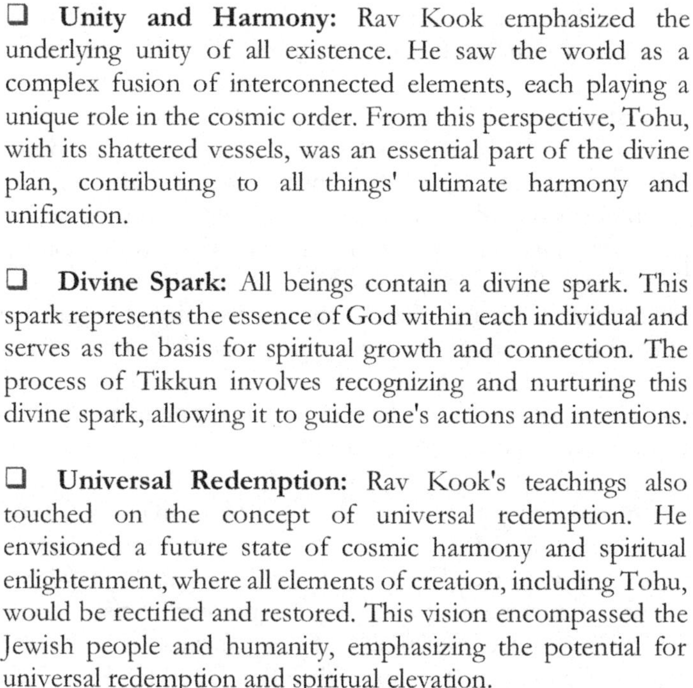

- **Unity and Harmony:** Rav Kook emphasized the underlying unity of all existence. He saw the world as a complex fusion of interconnected elements, each playing a unique role in the cosmic order. From this perspective, Tohu, with its shattered vessels, was an essential part of the divine plan, contributing to all things' ultimate harmony and unification.

- **Divine Spark:** All beings contain a divine spark. This spark represents the essence of God within each individual and serves as the basis for spiritual growth and connection. The process of Tikkun involves recognizing and nurturing this divine spark, allowing it to guide one's actions and intentions.

- **Universal Redemption:** Rav Kook's teachings also touched on the concept of universal redemption. He envisioned a future state of cosmic harmony and spiritual enlightenment, where all elements of creation, including Tohu, would be rectified and restored. This vision encompassed the Jewish people and humanity, emphasizing the potential for universal redemption and spiritual elevation.

C. Abraham Isaac Kook's View of Atheism

Rav Abraham Isaac Kook, in this text, presents a nuanced and unconventional perspective on atheism, considering it as an essential step in the progression toward a more enlightened and pure form of faith rather than viewing it as an outright rejection of God or a threat to religion. Kook sees atheism as a response to a distorted, superficial understanding of God and religious practice. When faith is practiced without genuine enlightenment and deep understanding (like following rituals without grasping their profound spiritual meaning), it leads to a detached, lower form of piety. This creates a distorted view of God that is far from reality, causing confusion, depression, and spiritual alienation. In this context, atheism arises as a corrective force. It rejects this false, distorted image of God and strips away the misconceptions that have clouded religious faith.

It purges the divine understanding of anthropomorphisms, corporeal ascriptions, and empty rituals, thereby facilitating a return to a more authentic, pure form of faith. Kook sees this "denial" of God as a transition toward a higher religious understanding. While atheism may initially appear to be a negation of God's existence, in Kook's view, it is, in fact, a profound affirmation of God's transcendence beyond human comprehension. It's a shift from perceiving God in the limited terms of human existence to recognizing God as the Source and Essence of all existence, a God Who is beyond any attribute we can ascribe. Ultimately, Kook views atheism not as an end in itself but as a transitional phase or a necessary 'cleansing process' leading toward an enlightened knowledge of God. He maintains that this process restores religious faith's respect, strength, and purity and elevates it to its true, profound state.

In this context, atheism arises as a corrective force. It rejects this false, distorted image of God and strips away the misconceptions that have clouded religious faith. It purges the divine understanding of anthropomorphisms, corporeal ascriptions, and empty rituals, thereby facilitating a return to a more authentic, pure form of faith. Kook sees this "denial" of God as a transition toward a higher religious understanding.

While atheism may initially appear to be a negation of God's existence, in Kook's view, it is, in fact, a profound affirmation of God's transcendence beyond human comprehension. It's a shift from perceiving God in the limited terms of human existence to recognizing God as the source and essence of all existence beyond any attribute we can ascribe. Ultimately, Kook views atheism as a transitional phase or a necessary 'cleansing process' leading toward an enlightened knowledge of God. He maintains that this process restores the respect, strength, and purity of religious faith and elevates it to its true, profound state.

D. Abraham Isaac Kook's View of Evolution

Rav Abraham Isaac Kook, alongside philosophers Pierre Teilhard de Chardin and Henri Bergson, each wove the concept of evolution into their philosophical frameworks, crafting distinct yet resonant visions of a dynamic, unfolding creation. For them, the universe was not a static artifact but a living tapestry, shaped by the interplay of time, spirit, and purpose. While Bergson and Teilhard infused their ideas with intellectual and spiritual vitality, Rav Kook rooted his perspective in the mystical depths of Kabbalah, seeing evolution as a sacred journey from chaos to divine harmony.

Rav Kook (1865–1935), the first Chief Rabbi of British Mandatory Palestine, viewed creation as an ongoing process, rich with spiritual meaning. Drawing from Kabbalistic thought, he interpreted the primordial state of Tohu—chaos—as a realm of raw, unformed potential, yearning for refinement through divine will. Evolution, in his eyes, was not merely biological but a cosmic ascent toward unity and holiness, with humanity, particularly the Jewish people, playing a pivotal role as co-creators in this divine drama.

Henri Bergson, the French philosopher, approached evolution as a creative unfolding, driven by an élan vital—a vital impulse that propelled life forward. For Bergson, each moment of existence was a fresh stroke on the canvas of reality, revealing the intellectual and psychological growth of humanity. His vision celebrated the novelty and unpredictability of life's progression, emphasizing the artistry inherent in its continuous blossoming.

Pierre Teilhard de Chardin, a Jesuit priest and paleontologist, saw evolution as a purposeful trajectory toward greater complexity and consciousness, culminating in the Omega Point—a state of ultimate unity he identified with "Christ consciousness." Like Rav Kook, Teilhard imbued evolution with spiritual significance, envisioning humanity as active participants in a grand, teleological narrative. While Rav Kook framed this journey within a Jewish mystical context, Teilhard's lens was distinctly Christian, yet both shared a belief in a creation infused with divine intent.

What sets Rav Kook apart is his unwavering faith in God as the foundation of existence, not a hypothesis to be proven, but an axiom that illuminates all else. He rejected the notion of a spiritually barren world as a partial sketch, missing the full brilliance of life's design (Letters I 44). In Jewish morning prayers, gratitude for God's merciful illumination of the Earth coexists with an appreciation of physics, not as a contradiction but as a complementary truth. For Rav Kook, God is the eternal artist, ceaselessly shaping creation—a conviction that welcomes scientific inquiry rather than recoiling from it. He insisted that a deeper grasp of science was not a threat but a prerequisite for a corresponding expansion of spiritual understanding.

First Chief Rabbi of British Mandatory Palestine

Rav Kook saw the rise of atheism among evolutionary thinkers not as a flaw in science but as a reflection of religious inadequacy. Darwin's theories, he argued, posed no inherent challenge to faith; rather, they exposed the limitations of a rigid or uninspired theology. His response was not to refute biology but to enrich faith through the mystical wisdom of Torah: "When an idea comes to negate some teaching in the Torah, we must not reject it, but build the edifice of the Torah above it, and thereby we ascend higher" (*Letters* I 124). For Rav Kook, the task of religious Jews was not to dismantle Darwin's work but to construct a vibrant, living faith—one that could stand alongside science as an equally compelling narrative.

While Bergson reveled in the creative spontaneity of life's impulse and Teilhard charted its march toward a transcendent endpoint, Rav Kook fused these threads into a Jewish tapestry of cosmic purpose. He saw evolution as a divine process, bridging the material and the spiritual, with humanity as both subject and artist. His philosophy radiates optimism, urging a synthesis of knowledge and faith that elevates both. In Rav Kook's world, science and spirituality are not adversaries but partners, each illuminating the other in the ongoing masterpiece of creation.

E. Old Finds New, the Fresh Turns True, in Hallowed Hue

Rav Kook's statement, הַיָּשָׁן יִתְחַדֵּשׁ וְהֶחָדָשׁ יִתְקַדֵּשׁ "The old will be made new, and the new will be made holy," provides profound insight into his unique and progressive approach to religious thought and practice. When he says, "The old will be made new," Rav Kook suggests that our traditional religious practices and concepts should not be seen as static or unchanging. Instead, they should be reexamined and revitalized to suit the changing times and circumstances. He encourages us to look at our ancient traditions with fresh eyes, seeking new interpretations and applications that resonate with our contemporary experiences and understanding. This isn't to suggest that we should discard our traditions, but rather breathe new life into them to ensure they remain relevant and meaningful.

In saying, "The new will be made holy," Rav Kook addresses the often-suspected tension between tradition and innovation. He asserts that new ideas, insights, and practices can also be sanctified and incorporated into the religious sphere. New developments in society, science, and culture need not be seen as threats to our faith. Instead, they can be harnessed and consecrated, broadening and enriching our understanding of the divine and our practice of religion. Thus, Rav Kook's statement becomes a rallying call for a dynamic and evolving approach to religious life that respects and renews the old while also welcoming and sanctifying the new. It highlights his inclusive and progressive vision, affirming the possibility of religious growth and evolution without compromising the essence of our spiritual heritage.

(1865--1935)

Martin Buber

Martin Buber (1878–1965), an Austrian-born Jewish philosopher and theologian, crafted a philosophy that reshaped how we think about human relationships and spirituality. His work, blending existentialism, Jewish mysticism, and a focus on dialogue, offers a rich framework for understanding life through connection.[70]

Buber's philosophy hinges on two fundamental ways we engage with the world: I-Thou and I-It. He lays this out vividly in *I and Thou*, where he describes the I-Thou relationship as a direct, mutual encounter. Here, you meet another person—or even a tree, an animal, or a piece of art—as a unique presence, not reducible to parts or purposes. Buber puts it this way: "When I confront a human being as my Thou… he is not a thing among things, nor does he consist of things."[71] This is about being fully present, open, and receptive, with no agenda clouding the moment. It's a two-way street—both sides engage, and something real happens between them. On the flip side, the I-It mode treats the other as an object: something to use, study, or manage. Think of checking your phone while someone's talking to you—that's I-It territory. Buber doesn't say I-It is evil; it's just practical, like when you measure a table or pay a bill. But if that's all you do, life gets shallow and disconnected. He pushes for a balance, where I-Thou moments bring depth and meaning to our existence.

This focus on relationships isn't just about personal interactions—it's about the nature of being itself. Buber drops a bold line: "In the beginning is the relation."[72] He's saying that existence starts in the "between"—that alive, electric space where two beings meet. This flips the script on Western philosophy's obsession with the lone individual, pondering life in a vacuum. For Buber, we're not isolated; we're defined by how we connect. In an I-Thou encounter, you don't come with a checklist or a script—you show up fully, and so does the other. That's transformative. He saw modern life heading the opposite way, though—people reduced to roles or numbers, like cogs in a machine. Buber calls us to resist that, to meet others as whole beings, not just their job titles or what they can do for us. This isn't just nice advice; it's an ethical stance. How we relate shapes who we become.

Then there's the spiritual layer, which ties everything together. Buber, steeped in Jewish mysticism, brings in the Eternal Thou, a concept that gives his philosophy a cosmic reach. He writes, "Every particular Thou is a glimpse through to the eternal Thou."[73] What he means is that every genuine I-Thou moment—whether with a friend, a sunset, or a quiet thought—points to something bigger: a relationship with God. But this isn't God as a distant rule-maker or a dusty theology textbook. For Buber, God is right here, in the thick of life, met through these encounters. It's not about reciting creeds; it's about experiencing a presence that runs through everything. This makes his spirituality practical and alive, open to anyone willing to show up fully to the world. It's a bridge between the everyday and the infinite, and it's why his ideas hit home even if you're not religious.

Buber's teachings speak loudly today, especially when you look at how modernity can strip away connection. He saw technology and systems—like assembly lines or endless paperwork—turning people into "its," and that's only gotten truer with screens and algorithms running our lives. His answer? Be present. See others as ends, not tools. It's a simple ethic, but it cuts through the noise of a world obsessed with efficiency and likes. He's not naive—he knows we can't live in I-Thou bliss all the time—but he insists those moments are what make life worth living.

So, where does this leave us? Buber's major teachings boil down to this: life's meaning comes from dialogue—with people, with the world, with the divine. The I-Thou and I-It distinction shows us how to relate; his relational view of existence flips the focus from "me" to "us"; and the Eternal Thou ties it all to a living spirituality. Through I and Thou, he challenges us to ditch the habit of objectifying everything and step into a life of presence, mutuality, and awe. It's a tall order, but it's also a lifeline in a fragmented age.

A. Between Martin Buber and Carl G. Jung

Martin Buber and Carl Jung, two influential thinkers of the 20th century, approached the human experience from fundamentally different perspectives, leading to significant philosophical and methodological disagreements. Buber, a Jewish existentialist philosopher, is best known for his concept of "I-Thou" relationships, which emphasize authentic, mutual encounters between individuals or between a person and the divine. Carl Jung, a Swiss psychiatrist and the founder of analytical psychology, explored the inner workings of the psyche, focusing on the unconscious, archetypes, and the process of individuation. While both sought to address profound questions about existence, their differences, particularly regarding the nature of religious experience, the role of relationships versus the individual, and the application of psychology to spirituality, created a notable rift. This essay examines these divergences over approximately two pages, drawing on their public disagreement in the 1950s and their broader intellectual frameworks.

One of the most prominent points of contention between Buber and Jung emerged in their differing interpretations of religious experience, spotlighted by their clash over Jung's 1952 book

Answer to Job. In this work, Jung analyzed the biblical story of Job psychologically, viewing God's actions as expressions of the unconscious mind and exploring the archetype of the divine within humanity. Buber fiercely criticized this approach, arguing that it reduced the divine-human relationship to a mere psychological construct. For Buber, religious experience was a direct, relational encounter with the "Eternal Thou"—a transcendent presence that could not be explained or contained by psychological analysis. He wrote in I and Thou, "The Thou, on the other hand, cannot be sought, for it meets one through grace" (emphasizing the mystery and immediacy of this connection.[74]

Jung, however, maintained that his psychological perspective did not deny the reality of religious experience but rather illuminated its inner dimensions. He argued that understanding the unconscious underpinnings of spirituality could enhance, not diminish, its significance. In *Psychology and Religion*, Jung stated, "I do not deny the validity of religious experience; I merely suggest that it is accessible to psychological understanding" (*Jung,* 1953, p. 174). For Buber, this analytical stance missed the essence of the divine encounter, reducing a sacred relationship to an object of study. Their disagreement thus hinged on whether religious experience should remain an irreducible mystery or be integrated into a psychological framework.

Another core difference lies in their emphasis on relationships versus the individual. Buber's philosophy centers on the "between"—the space where meaning arises through genuine encounters. He famously declared, "All real living is meeting" suggesting that human existence is defined by connection with others. In his view, the self is inherently relational, fully realized only in the presence of a "Thou," whether human or divine. By contrast, an "I-It" relationship, where others are treated as objects, represents a lesser mode of being.

Jung, conversely, focused on the individual's inner journey through the process of individuation—the integration of conscious and unconscious elements of the psyche to achieve self-realization. The goal of individuation is to divest the self of the false wrappings of the persona and the suggestive power of the unconscious. While

Jung recognized that relationships could influence this process, his primary concern was the internal development of the individual. Buber might have viewed this focus as potentially isolating, arguing that it prioritized selfhood over connection, whereas Jung saw it as a necessary foundation for authentic relationships. This contrast reflects their divergent priorities: Buber looked outward to the relational, while Jung delved inward to the psychological.

Buber's critique of Jung extended to a broader discomfort with psychoanalysis, which he believed risked objectifying individuals. He argued that interpreting unconscious motives, a hallmark of Jung's analytical psychology, could undermine the possibility of an "I-Thou" relationship, even in therapy. In *The Knowledge of Man,* Buber expressed concern that psychoanalysis might turn the patient into an object of investigation. He noted, "The patient cannot equally well experience the relationship from the side of the therapist or the pupil from the side of the teacher without destroying or fundamentally altering the relationship.

This does not mean that the therapist, for example, is reduced to treating his patient as an object, an *It.* The one-sided inclusion of therapy is still an I-Thou relationship founded on mutuality, trust, and partnership in a common situation, and it is only in this relation that real therapy can take place. If all real living is meeting as Buber argues in *I and Thou,* all true healing also takes place through meeting,[75] thus disrupting the mutual presence he deemed essential to human connection.

Jung, as a psychoanalyst, defended the value of exploring the unconscious, seeing it as a pathway to wholeness. He viewed the unconscious not merely as a repository of repressed material but as a source of growth and spiritual insight. For Jung, psychological analysis enriched understanding of the self and its relation to the divine, whereas Buber feared it distanced individuals from the immediacy of encounter. This disagreement underscores their differing views on psychology's role: Jung embraced it as a tool for illumination, while Buber saw it as a potential barrier to authentic experience.

These specific disputes reflect deeper philosophical divides. Buber, influenced by existentialism and Jewish *Hasidic* mysticism, emphasized the uniqueness of each encounter and resisted reducing human experience to systematic analysis. His thought celebrates presence and dialogue as pathways to meaning. Jung, while also engaging with mysticism, approached it through a psychological lens, seeking universal patterns—archetypes—that underlie human behavior across cultures. His work aims to map the psyche, offering a structured framework for understanding the self.

Their views on the Self, further illustrate this divide. For Buber, the Self emerges through relationship, transcending individuality in moments of connection. For Jung, the Self is a complex system striving for integration, achieved through the internal process of individuation. Buber's "I-Thou" invites a move beyond the ego, while Jung's individuation seeks to harmonize it—a subtle but significant distinction in their visions of human fulfillment.

Martin Buber differed from Carl Jung primarily in their approaches to religious experience, the balance between relational and individual focus, and the role of psychology in spiritual life. Buber championed the sanctity of direct encounter, wary of analytical methods that might dissect the ineffable. Jung, while respecting the mystery of existence, believed psychological insight could deepen our grasp of both self and spirit. His public disagreement over *Answer to Job* and its broader intellectual stances reveal a tension between existential presence and analytical understanding. Yet, both sought to heal the alienation of modernity—Buber through connection, Jung through self-realization. Their differences enrich the dialogue between philosophy and psychology, challenging us to reflect on whether we approach the world as a mystery to meet or a puzzle to solve.

B. The Theology of "Meetings"

Martin Buber's *Meetings: Autobiographical Fragments*[76] is not a traditional autobiography but a collection of vivid vignettes that illuminate the pivotal encounters shaping his life and philosophy.

These "meetings" are moments of genuine connection with people, nature, ideas, and the divine. They embody Buber's core belief, famously articulated in *I and Thou*, that authentic human existence emerges through "I-Thou" relationships. Unlike "I-It" interactions, where others are treated as objects for use or observation, "I-Thou" encounters involve mutual presence and dialogue, creating a shared space of meaning. Each fragment in Meetings serves as both a personal memory and a lens into Buber's broader ideas, rooted in existentialism and Jewish mysticism, about the transformative power of relating to others as full beings.

The narrative opens with Buber's early years, shadowed by a sense of disconnection. As a child, he felt like an outsider, struggling to engage with his surroundings. This shifted during a formative encounter on his grandfather's estate, where he would stroke a horse's mane and feel an inexplicable unity—a bond beyond mere affection. He describes this as his first "I-Thou" experience, noting, "What I experienced in touching the horse was the Thou."[77] Here, the animal was not an "It" but a living presence met with openness, planting the seed for Buber's lifelong exploration of relationality and the "between"—the space where meaning arises in authentic connection.

As he grew, Buber's meetings extended to human relationships that shaped his intellectual and personal growth. He recalls his grandfather, Solomon. a Jewish scholar and a university professor who introduced him to philosophy. These were not mere teachers; they engaged him in true dialogue—open, reciprocal exchanges alive with mutual presence. He writes of these interactions as vibrant and formative: "In the atmosphere of such a dialogue, I found myself changed" (Buber, 1967, p. 28). For Buber, genuine learning and living stemmed from active engagement, not passive receipt, a theme central to his philosophy that relationships thrive when we approach others with full attention.

Buber's spiritual encounters further enrich his narrative, revealing his connection to the "Eternal Thou"—his term for the divine. During World War I, amid chaos and despair, he experienced a profound sense of being addressed by God, not through words but through an overwhelming presence. He reflects, "I felt myself touched by the eternal."[78] These moments were lived realities, not abstract theology, reinforcing his belief that the divine is immanent, woven into every authentic meeting. Whether with people or nature, each "I-Thou" encounter offers a glimpse of this ultimate relationship, accessible through vulnerability and openness.[79]

Yet Buber candidly acknowledges his failures. One haunting memory involves a student who sought his guidance while he was a professor. Distracted, Buber responded half-heartedly, only to learn later that the student, in deep distress, had taken his own life. He recounts this with regret: "I was not there wholly for him."[80] This failure underscored the stakes of his philosophy: treating another as an "It" squanders the potential for transformation. Every meeting matters, demanding intention and presence to fulfill its promise.

Even in everyday moments, Buber finds significance. In Martin Buber's *Meetings,* he shares a casual but profound conversation from a journey with an observant Jew while travelling on a train. The discussion centers on a disturbing biblical story from the Book of Samuel, where God commands King Saul to annihilate the Amalekites, including their king. Saul spares the king, prompting the prophet Samuel to declare that Saul's dynasty will end and to execute the Amalekite king himself. Buber reveals his lifelong unease with this tale, stating, "I have never been able to believe that this is a message of God. I do not believe it."

The Jew, shocked, challenges Buber: "You do not believe it?" Buber stands firm, replying, "No," and explains, "I believe that Samuel has misunderstood God." After a tense pause, the man's initial anger fades, and he quietly agrees, "Well, I think so too." This exchange bridges their perspectives, showing that even a traditional believer can question scripture when it clashes with a personal sense of divine mercy.

Buber later reflects on whether his bold stance was right. He deems it suitable for the dialogue, as it sparked mutual understanding, but uses the moment to explore a larger theme: humans often misinterpret God's will, blending divine guidance with their own biases—even in sacred texts. For Buber, faith is personal, guided by conviction rather than an objective standard to distinguish divine truth from human error. This story captures his philosophy of dialogue, where honest exchange fosters shared insight, and highlights the challenge of discerning God's intent amid scripture and tradition.[81]

Through these vignettes, Buber ties his personal experiences to his philosophical framework. In *I and Thou*, he contrasts "I-Thou" relationships—marked by presence and dialogue—with "I-It" interactions, where others are reduced to utility: "All real living is meeting". While "I-It" is inevitable in practical life, overreliance fosters alienation; "I-Thou" encounters, though rare, infuse existence with meaning. Connections with nature, like a tree's vitality, or art's resonance, can be as profound as human dialogue, each a bridge to the "Eternal Thou."[82]

Buber's reflective, often poetic prose invites readers to consider their own meetings—those cherished, missed, or yet to come. In an era of distraction and isolation, *Meetings* delivers a timeless message: "Only in man, however, does this interrelatedness transform itself and issue into the reality of meeting in which the one exists over against the other as his Other, as one able in common presence at once to withstand him and confirm him. "To live is to be open to the possibility of meeting" (Buber, 1967, p. 105). His philosophy challenges us to move beyond objectification, embracing a way of being that values mutuality and reverence. These moments, however fleeting, offer a counterpoint to a disconnected world, beckoning us toward a richer, more relational existence.

C. The Way of Man

Martin Buber's *The Way of Man* is a remarkable and concise work that distills the profound wisdom of *Hasidism*, a mystical Jewish movement that emerged in Eastern Europe during the 18th and 19th centuries, into a universally accessible exploration of the human spirit. In this slim yet deeply impactful book, Buber draws upon *Hasidic* tales and teachings to guide readers on a journey of self-discovery, spiritual fulfillment, and authentic connection. Far from being a dry philosophical treatise, *The Way of Man* is alive with storytelling, weaving together simple narratives and profound insights in a way that resonates with both the heart and the mind. Its timeless message speaks to anyone seeking meaning in a world often marked by disconnection and superficiality, making it a treasure worth revisiting.

At the core of Buber's philosophy in *The Way of Man* is the "I-Thou" relationship, a concept that underscores the transformative power of genuine encounters. Buber contrasts this with the "I-It" mode of interaction, where others are treated as objects or tools rather than as beings worthy of deep connection. He argues that it is through "I-Thou" relationships—with other people and with the divine—that we truly awaken to our humanity and experience the sacred. This idea is not presented as an abstract theory but is brought to life through relatable *Hasidic* stories, each one carefully chosen to reveal layers of meaning. For example, Buber tells of a man who spends years searching for spiritual treasure only to discover it buried in his own backyard. This tale beautifully illustrates that fulfillment lies not in distant pursuits but within the depths of our own hearts and the ordinary moments of life.

In Martin Buber's story about Rabbi Shneur Zalman, the rabbi, imprisoned by the Mitnagdim in Petersburg, engages in a profound conversation with the chief of the gendarmes. While awaiting trial, the gendarme, intrigued by the rabbi's meditative demeanor, poses a question about God's inquiry to Adam, "Where art thou?" The rabbi responds by emphasizing that the Scriptures are eternal and that God calls each person throughout history to reflect on their journey and progress in life. This exchange highlights self-reflection and the spiritual significance of one's existence.

The narrative continues to illustrate a key principle in Jewish thought: the focus is not on self-salvation but on contributing to the greater purpose of creation. Buber notes that the pursuit of personal salvation can lead to self-centeredness, which Hasidism rejects. Instead, the essence of one's spiritual journey is to engage deeply with the world and work towards the Kingdom of God, promoting the well-being of creation rather than merely seeking individual fulfillment. Ultimately, the story serves as a reminder that true spiritual attainment arises from our actions for the greater good rather than a preoccupation with one's own fate.[83]

The power of *The Way of Man* lies in Buber's ability to use these stories as vessels of wisdom, making complex spiritual truths accessible and compelling. Each chapter centers on a narrative—often featuring a wise rabbi or a humble seeker—that Buber unpacks to explore themes like personal responsibility, community, and the interplay between the mundane and the sacred. In one story, a rabbi teaches that every individual has a unique path to God, tailored to their specific gifts and struggles. Yet Buber emphasizes that this personal journey is not solitary; it is woven into the broader tapestry of humanity, where every person's role contributes to the whole. This balance between individuality and interconnectedness is a recurring thread, offering a vision of spirituality that is both deeply personal and profoundly collective.

Buber also delves into the idea of "resolution," the ongoing commitment to align one's life with higher values. Through the story of a flawed man who transforms himself through sincere repentance, Buber highlights the possibility of redemption and the strength that comes from a resolute heart. This theme of inner transformation is paired with a call to self-awareness in another chapter, where a rabbi, asked why he doesn't try to change the world, responds that he is still working on himself. This teaching strikes at the heart of personal responsibility: true change begins within, and by improving ourselves, we naturally contribute to the betterment of the world. Buber's prose here is both poetic and precise, inviting readers to reflect on their own lives without preaching or prescribing.

Yet Buber is careful not to let self-focus tip into self-absorption. In a cautionary tale, he describes a man so consumed by his spiritual practices that he neglects his duties to others, illustrating the danger of becoming preoccupied with oneself. This story serves as a counterpoint, advocating for a spirituality that engages with the world rather than retreating from it. Buber suggests that authentic living requires a delicate balance: tending to our inner growth while remaining open and compassionate toward those around us. This nuanced perspective is one of the book's strengths, offering practical wisdom that feels both grounded and inspiring.

Perhaps the most poignant message of *The Way of Man* comes in its final reflection, where Buber urges readers to find the divine in the present moment. He recounts the story of Rabbi Eizik, the son of Rabbi Yekel of Cracow. who, after a long quest for enlightenment, realizes that what he sought was with him all along, "here where one stands."[84] This encapsulates the essence of Buber's teaching: the spiritual journey is not about chasing a distant ideal but about being fully present in the now, recognizing the sacred in every encounter and every breath. It's a simple yet radical idea, delivered with a quiet power that lingers long after the book is closed.

Buber's writing style enhances the impact of these teachings. His prose flows with a poetic rhythm, blending narrative, philosophy, and spiritual insight into a seamless whole. The stories are memorable not just for their lessons but for their humanity—rabbis and seekers stumble, question, and grow, mirroring our own imperfect journeys. This accessibility is part of what makes *The Way of Man* so effective; it doesn't demand prior knowledge of *Hasidism* or philosophy but meets readers where they are, inviting them into a deeper conversation about life's purpose.

What sets *The Way of Man* apart is its timeless relevance. Though rooted in a specific Jewish tradition, its themes—authentic relationships, personal growth, the search for meaning—transcend cultural and religious boundaries. In today's fast-paced, often fragmented world, Buber's emphasis on presence, connection, and inner transformation feels like a balm. His approach is refreshingly non-dogmatic; he doesn't dictate a rigid path but encourages each person to find their own way, trusting that the divine has laid out a unique journey for everyone. This inclusivity broadens the book's appeal, making it a welcoming companion for seekers of all backgrounds, whether they identify as religious or simply yearn for something more.

Ultimately, *The Way of Man* is a masterpiece of spiritual literature, compact yet overflowing with insight. It challenges readers to look beyond the surface of their lives, to question how they relate to themselves and others, and to seek the divine in the everyday. Buber's gift is his ability to take the esoteric and make it intimate, to transform ancient wisdom into a living, breathing guide for modern life. The book is not a one-time read but a resource to return to, each visit revealing new depths. For anyone longing to deepen their understanding of themselves and their place in the world, *The Way of Man* offers a path that is as profound as it is approachable, a quiet call to live more fully, more authentically, and more presently.

R. Zalman Schachter-Shalomi

My personal history with Reb Zalman Schachter-Shalomi (1924-2014) began in 1970 when I first met him in Berkeley, California. As a young Lubavitcher Hasid, I was struck by his rainbow-colored *tallit*—a vivid contrast to the traditional black and white—and wondered what had led him away from the Lubavitcher *Hasidic* movement. Over the years, we grew close, and though I no longer believe in the concept of a Rebbe, I must admit that Reb Zalman possessed an extraordinary pastoral gift, connecting deeply with people from all walks of life, including myself. Our friendship deepened throughout the rest of his life, especially after I left the Chabad movement to chart my own spiritual journey.

Reb Zalman Schachter-Shalomi, born in Poland in 1924 and later an immigrant to the United States, was ordained as a rabbi in the Lubavitcher Hasidic tradition. His early life reflected both deep ties to tradition and bold aspirations, as captured in a well-known Chabad anecdote: as a young man, he asked the Lubavitcher Rebbe if he could succeed him, only to hear the Rebbe express hope that the *Moshiach* (the Jewish Messiah) would take that role instead. This exchange highlights Reb Zalman's ambition and the traditional messianic focus he initially inhabited.

Yet, Reb Zalman's spiritual journey soon led him beyond strict orthodoxy. Seeking to revitalize Judaism for a modern audience, he drew from its mystical core—particularly Kabbalah—and founded the Jewish Renewal movement. This approach emphasized personal spiritual experience, inclusivity, and accessibility, opening Jewish mysticism to seekers of all backgrounds. Though he never became the Lubavitcher Rebbe, Reb Zalman emerged as a "*Rebbe*" in a broader sense—a spiritual guide whose teachings and pastoral care touched several generations. His transformative influence continues to shape modern Jewish spirituality.

Kabbalah delves into the nature of God, the universe, and the soul through symbolic interpretations of sacred texts, emphasizing direct, personal experiences of the divine. Reb Zalman's teachings not only reflect core Kabbalistic principles but also expand upon them, adapting ancient wisdom to contemporary spiritual needs. His approach to prayer and meditation is deeply rooted in practical Kabbalah, encouraging personal encounters with the divine. He viewed prayer as a direct connection to God and adapted Kabbalistic meditation practices to foster spiritual growth and self-awareness.

A hallmark of Reb Zalman's philosophy was his integration of other spiritual traditions. He incorporated insights from Eastern philosophies and modern thought, not as a departure from Kabbalah but as an expansion of its principles, making ancient wisdom relevant to today's seekers. This openness enriched his teachings and broadened their appeal. Central to his work was a vision for personal and communal transformation.

Reb Zalman believed Judaism should evolve to meet the needs of its practitioners, reflecting the Kabbalistic ideal of *tikkun olam*—repairing the world. He emphasized individual growth alongside collective responsibility, inspiring a dynamic, living tradition. Reb Zalman's impact on Jewish spirituality is profound. Through his innovative approaches to prayer, meditation, and the integration of diverse spiritual insights, he revitalized Judaism for a modern audience. His teachings continue to inspire seekers of all backgrounds, demonstrating the enduring relevance of Kabbalistic wisdom in fostering personal and communal renewal.

A. Schachter's Approach to Prayer and Meditation

Schachter's approach to prayer, which he termed "*davvenology*," lies at the heart of his teachings and exemplifies his deep connection to Kabbalistic mysticism. For Schachter, prayer was far more than a ritual obligation—it was a dynamic, experiential practice designed to foster a direct connection with the divine. This perspective resonates strongly with the Kabbalistic concept of *devekut*, or cleaving to God, where the practitioner seeks to transcend the mundane and unite with the Divine Presence. Traditional Kabbalah employs practices like *hitbodedut* (solitary meditation) and *kavvanah* (focused intention in prayer) to achieve this state of spiritual elevation. Schachter built upon these methods, encouraging worshippers to engage in prayer with emotional authenticity and intentionality, rather than merely reciting words by rote.

In his prayer services, Schachter urged participants to express their emotions freely—whether through tears, laughter, or quiet contemplation—emphasizing that authentic spiritual experience originates in the heart. This focus mirrors the Kabbalistic belief that the soul's yearning for God is central to religious practice. Additionally, Schachter incorporated visualization techniques into his teachings, a practice directly inspired by Kabbalistic meditation. Kabbalists have long used imagery, such as meditating on the divine name or the *sefirot* (the ten emanations of God), to deepen their divine connection. Schachter adapted these techniques for contemporary seekers, simplifying them while preserving their mystical essence. Through *davvenology*, he sought to democratize these once esoteric practices, making the transformative power of Kabbalistic prayer accessible to ordinary people, not just scholars or mystics.

This emphasis on personal experience over external performance is consistent with Kabbalah's ultimate goal: the direct apprehension of the Divine. Schachter's innovative approach thus serves as a modern bridge to Kabbalistic traditions, ensuring that their spiritual depth remains relevant in today's world. He taught that dreams, occurring when the mind is still during sleep, offer a glimpse of divine insight, a fraction of prophecy.[85] He distinguished prayer from Torah study, noting that while Torah study engages analytical thought, prayer requires dissolving the self, a challenge due to persistent thoughts and desires.

To calm the mind, he advised:

Observe thoughts briefly for a few minutes until they slow.

Focus on a holy phrase, such as "*Ribbono Shel Olam*," to align the quiet mind with holiness.

Pray gently for needs like strength or faith.

He recommended softly affirming God's oneness with words like:

"I believe with perfect faith that You, the Most High, are the only One in Existence, and all is Your effulgence."

This should be said gently, not forcefully, to avoid stirring the ego.

For correcting flaws, he suggested affirming positive traits, like zeal, instead of negating laziness. Alternatively, one could gaze at a watch to still the mind, inviting Divine Presence and deepening faith. With practice, expressions like "This is my God, and I will beautify Him" gain profound meaning.[86]

B. Integration of Other Spiritual Traditions and Modern Thought

Schachter's teachings are distinguished by their openness to wisdom from other spiritual traditions and modern scientific paradigms, a stance that both reflects and expands upon the Kabbalah's historical tendencies. While rooted in Jewish mystical texts, Kabbalah has always been somewhat syncretic, drawing from Neoplatonism, Gnosticism, and other philosophical systems to enrich its understanding of the divine. Schachter continued this tradition of synthesis, engaging with Buddhism, Sufism, and Christian mysticism, among others. He believed that different faiths could mutually enrich one another, a perspective that echoes the mystical notion of divine unity transcending cultural and religious boundaries. For example, he recognized parallels between Buddhist meditation and Jewish contemplative practices, using these insights to enhance his interpretation of Kabbalah and make it more relatable to a spiritually diverse audience.

Beyond interfaith dialogue, Schachter was keenly interested in the intersection of spirituality and modern science. He explored how emerging scientific paradigms, such as quantum mechanics, could provide new metaphors for ancient mystical concepts. The concept of non-locality in quantum physics—where particles remain interconnected across vast distances—resonates with the kabbalistic view of the unity of all creation and God's immanence in the universe. Schachter saw these parallels as opportunities to update and rearticulate Kabbalah for the modern age, ensuring its relevance in a world shaped by scientific discovery.

As he wrote in *Paradigm Shift*, "We need a God who is both the Creator of the universe and the intimate presence in our hearts," a statement that encapsulates the kabbalistic balance between God's transcendence (as *Ein Sof*, the infinite) and immanence (manifest through the *sefirot*). This integrative approach demonstrates Schachter's commitment to evolving Kabbalah beyond its traditional boundaries. By weaving together insights from other traditions and contemporary thought, he created a more inclusive and dynamic mystical framework, while staying true to its foundational principles of divine unity and spiritual exploration.

C. Vision for Personal and Communal Transformation

Schachter's vision for personal and communal transformation is where his kabbalistic roots shine most brightly, particularly in his alignment with the concept of *tikkun olam*—repairing the world. According to Judaic mystical wisdom, humans are seen as partners with God in the ongoing process of spiritual and material redemption, tasked with elevating the divine sparks scattered throughout creation. Schachter embraced this mission, advocating for social justice, environmental stewardship, and spiritual growth as interconnected aspects of *tikkun*. His concept of "spiritual eldering" exemplifies this ethos, guiding individuals through the later stages of life to rectify their souls and contribute to the world's healing—an application of spiritual ideas about the soul's journey and its role in cosmic repair.

Schachter's eco-spirituality further reflects Kabbalistic teachings, particularly the notion that God is immanent in the world. He viewed nature as a manifestation of the divine, encouraging his followers to approach the environment with reverence and responsibility. This perspective aligns with Kabbalah's depiction of creation as a reflection of the sefirot, where every element of the material world contains divine light waiting to be redeemed. Schachter's emphasis on ecological awareness thus extends the kabbalistic vision of unity between the spiritual and physical realms.

Additionally, Schachter envisioned a "New Age" Judaism that was inclusive, egalitarian, and spiritually vibrant—qualities he sought to cultivate through the Jewish Renewal movement. He was a passionate advocate for women's rights and LGBTQ inclusion, challenging the patriarchal structures of traditional Kabbalah. While this progressive stance diverges from historical practice, it can be seen as an evolution of its mystical emphasis on unity and the dissolution of barriers between the human and divine. By broadening access to spiritual practice, Schachter fulfilled his goal of democratizing Kabbalah, making its teachings available to all, regardless of gender or identity.

Schachter's transformative vision also incorporated a sense of joy and celebration, deeply rooted in *Hasidic* traditions, which drew its inspiration from Lurianic Kabbalah. He believed that spirituality should uplift and inspire, a sentiment captured in Jewish with Feeling, where he writes, "The old models of spirituality are no longer sufficient. We need to find ways to experience the divine in the here and now, in our bodies, in our relationships, in our world." This call to bring the divine into everyday life reflects Kabbalah's mission to reveal God's presence in all aspects of existence.

Zalman Schachter's teachings represent a profound and innovative engagement with Jewish mysticism, tailored to the complexities of modern life. Through his approach to prayer and meditation, he revitalized Kabbalistic practices, emphasizing personal experience and emotional authenticity. His integration of other spiritual traditions and modern science continued Kabbalah's syncretic legacy, while his vision for personal and communal transformation embodied the Kabbalistic ideal of *tikkun olam*. By addressing contemporary issues such as ecology, psychology, and inclusivity, Schachter ensured that Kabbalah remains a living tradition, capable of inspiring and transforming individuals and communities alike. His work stands as a bridge between ancient mysticism and the present day, demonstrating the enduring relevance of Kabbalistic wisdom in a rapidly changing world.

CHAPTER 5

DEBATES OVER THE HISTORICITY OF THE KABBALAH

"Nonsense is nonsense, but the history of nonsense is scholarship."

— GERSHOM SCHOLEM, *New Republic, April 1957*

"For God does not want to be believed in, to be debated and defended by us, but simply to be realized through us."

— MARTIN BUBER, *On Judaism*

Rivash's Criticism of Kabbalah

As the mystical teachings of Kabbalah started to spread, it was met with varying responses from scholars and religious leaders within the Jewish community. Maimonides had taken a dismissive approach to one of the controversial kabbalistic texts, the *Shi'ur Komeh* [see our entry]. But he was hardly alone. Rabbi Yitzchak ben Sheshet Perfet (1326–1408), also known as *Rivash*, voiced his concerns regarding the widespread study of Jewish mystical thought among the public.

In *Theology in the Responsa,* Louis Jacobs notes that the dissemination of the Kabbalah's mystical teachings evoked diverse reactions within the Jewish community. While Maimonides openly dismissed certain controversial texts like the *Shi'ur Komeh,* he was not the sole critic. Rabbi Yitzchak ben Sheshet Perfet, also known as *Rivash,* expressed reservations about popularizing Jewish mystical thought among the general public.[87]

Rivash further invoked the memory of R. Samson of Chinon, known as a leading scholar in his time, whose approach to prayer was characterized by simplicity, much like a child's. He did not incorporate complex Kabbalistic intentions, unlike those who alternated their focus between different *Sefirot* during prayers. Perfet critically examined the Kabbalistic interpretation of rabbinic teaching that suggested facing north for wealth and south for wisdom, attributing these directions to specific *Sefirot.* Such an interpretation was considered foreign and even hinted at dualism by non-Kabbalistic individuals.

He related a conversation he had with a philosopher who criticized the Kabbalists for believing in "ten," a concept they found more problematic than the Christian belief in the Trinity. Striving for understanding, Perfet sought the wisdom of Don Joseph ibn Shoshan, a respected Talmudic scholar, philosopher, Kabbalist, and saint. He asked how Kabbalists could shift their focus between *Sefirot* during prayers without committing idolatry.

Ibn Shoshan explained that the prayers were directed to the Cause of all causes, God, and not to the *Sefirot* per se. The focus on different *Sefirot* was likened to a subject appealing to a king through the appointed prince. The intent was not to pray to the *Sefirot* but to ask God to exert His divine influence through them. Despite appreciating the subtlety of this explanation, Perfet maintained his skepticism. He argued for the simplicity of praying to God directly without seemingly trying to manipulate His actions through the *Sefirot.*

As Jewish mystical literature grew and influenced Jewish thought, it traversed a landscape shaped by intellectual giants like Perfet, Rivash, and others. Their interaction with Kabbalah, whether direct or indirect, reflected the dynamic and diverse nature of Jewish religious thought. This historical journey reflects Judaism's intellectual tradition marked by constant evolution, introspection, and pursuit of understanding. Beyond philosophers, other factions within Jewish society, particularly the Talmudic scholars, resisted Kabbalistic teachings, considering them inconsistent with the conventional Jewish legal tradition, *Halakha*.

And yet, not all Jewish philosophers opposed Kabbalah; some even integrated it with their philosophical notions. Acceptance and resistance to Kabbalistic ideas varied across communities and eras, influenced by societal contexts and local religious climates. While Kabbalah faced considerable opposition from various quarters, especially Aristotelian-Maimonidean philosophers and Talmudic scholars, the response was not uniform. This diversity of reactions showcases the rich intellectual traditions within Judaism and the dynamic interplay of mysticism and rationalism within the Jewish philosophical landscape.[88]

Paradoxically, the initial wave of criticism directed at Kabbalah benefited its evolution and maturation. By challenging its teachings, these early skeptics inadvertently served the field great. They compelled Kabbalah scholars and practitioners to confront and articulate responses to various theological issues that had previously been overlooked or insufficiently addressed.

Such scrutiny led to a deeper exploration and clarification of esoteric doctrines, fostering a more robust and thoughtful development of its theological framework. As a result, the Kabbalah emerged stronger and more refined, with a clearer understanding and expression of its spiritual and philosophical underpinnings. This critical engagement thus enhanced the credibility and depth of kabbalistic thought, contributing to its enduring influence and relevance.

The Zohar: A Turning Point

Arguably, the most transformative work in Kabbalah is the *Zohar* (*Book of Splendor*), penned by the Spanish Kabbalist Moses de León in the late 13th century but attributed to the 2nd-century

Rabbi Shimon bar Yochai. The Zohar offered a detailed exploration of the *Sefirot*. It introduced many mystical concepts like the four spiritual worlds, divine feminine (*Shekhinah*), and the dynamic relationship between different aspects of divinity. The Zohar's compelling mythical narratives and allegorical exegesis greatly expanded the scope of Kabbalah, rendering it the quintessential text of Jewish mysticism. The Zohar may well have the most important new Midrashic composition of the medieval era.

Controversies Over the Publication of the Zohar

The Zohar, a fundamental text in Jewish mysticism and Kabbalah has sparked significant debate regarding its authorship. Traditionally considered a mystical commentary on the Pentateuch, Song of Songs, and the Book of Ruth, the Zohar frequently attributes its teachings to Shimon bar Yochai, a 2nd-century Tannaitic sage. In the text, he is often depicted unveiling profound mystical secrets, often through dialogues with his disciples.[89]

However, the true authorship of the Zohar remains a subject of scholarly contention. While the tradition of Shimon bar Yochai as the author is longstanding, many modern scholars, including Gershom Scholem and others, argue for a later origin. They suggest that the Zohar was actually composed by the 13th-century Spanish Kabbalist Moses de León.

This theory is supported by the text's linguistic, stylistic, and contextual analysis, which aligns more closely with 13th-century Spanish culture and religious thought than with 2nd-century Judea. The earliest manuscripts of this work date to the late 13th century, with no evidence of the text existing earlier. Additionally, references to the Zohar in other Jewish writings only appear from this period. After Moses de León's death, his wife reportedly claimed that he authored the Zohar, as noted in a letter by Isaac of Akko, a contemporary Kabbalist. [90]

The Catholic Church's Love of the Zohar

The Zohar was first promulgated in 1553 when the Catholic Church burned the Talmud. It might seem counterintuitive that the Catholic Church would support the publication of the Zohar, a core text of Jewish mysticism, especially given its history of suppressing Jewish texts like the Talmud. However, historical context can provide some insight into this seemingly contradictory stance.

The Israeli scholar Yehuda Liebes, noted that the Zohar frequently describes the Godhead as a threefold unity, a concept that aligns with traditional Judaism's tenfold structure of the Kabbalistic *sefirot.* However, Liebes, contends that Christian trinitarian doctrine may have influenced these tripartite formulations in the Zohar. He argues the Zohar's interest in three-part structures results from Christian influence.

Liebes illustrates his point with the Zohar's interpretation of the divine names in the verse "Hear O Israel, the Lord our God, the Lord is One" (Deuteronomy 6:4). The *Zohar* (II, 53b) suggests that these three names—*Adonai, Eloheinu, Adonai*—while distinct, form a single unity. This unity is likened to a voice, which, though one, consists of three elements: fire, air, and water. These elements merge into one in the voice's mystery, just as the three Divine manifestations merge into a single unity. This concept is central to the daily act of unification in Jewish prayer, where the intention is to unify all, from the Infinite (*Ein-Sof*) to the end of creation, a secret revealed through the holy spirit.[91]

Some Christian scholars, such as Guillaume Postel in the 16th century, believed that Kabbalah, the Jewish mystical tradition in which the Zohar plays a central role, held universal truths and could be used to demonstrate the truth of Christian doctrine, especially because of its fondness for the number three. For example, regarding the passage, "Hear, O Israel, *Adonai Eloheinu, Adonai* is one" (Deut. 6:2). These three are one. How can the three Names be one? Only through the perception of faith: in the vision of the Holy Spirit, in the beholding of the hidden eye alone."[92] It is hardly any wonder why the Church believed that this Zoharic passage would lead Jewish believers to accept the Trinitarian theology of Christianity!

Other scholars felt that if the Zohar were widely disseminated, books would fall into the hands of Christian scholars, who would use them to persuade Jews to give up their Judaic faith. The general view held that mystical literature, in general, should remain secretive since its content is beyond most people's capacity to understand.

Joseph Dan, another leading scholar of Jewish mysticism, identifies what he considers the earliest evidence of kabbalistic exegetical methods contributing to their conversion to Christianity, found in the work of Abraham Abulafia (b. 1240). Abulafia, a 13th-century Spanish kabbalist known for his ecstatic Kabbalah, refers to a group of students he taught in Capua, Italy, who later converted to Christianity. Dan notes that these students likely employed Abulafia's technique of letter rearrangement (*tzeruf*) to reinterpret Song of Songs 2:3, where "in his shadow" (*b'tzilo*, בצלו) appears. They reshaped *b'tzilo* into *b'tzaluv* (בצלוב), meaning "in the shadow of the crucified," thus transforming the phrase into a Christian reading such as "I live happily in the shadow of the crucified" or "I love the crucified." This shift turned a Jewish poetic image into a reference to Jesus' crucifixion.

Dan clarifies that this conversion arose from Abulafia's interpretive approach—manipulating Hebrew letters for mystical insight—not his theological framework, which remained Jewish and focused on prophetic ecstasy. The students' apostasy likely reflects the Christian milieu of medieval Italy, where such a reinterpretation could align with prevailing beliefs, rather than any Christian intent in Abulafia's teachings. This case marks a rare, early instance of kabbalistic tools inadvertently facilitating a religious crossover.[93]

The Lion Who Roared

Leon Modena (1571–1648), a multifaceted Italian rabbi, philosopher, and critic from Venice, stands out for his incisive critique of Jewish mysticism, particularly the Zohar and Kabbalah, articulated in his 1639 work *Ari Nohem* ("The Roaring Lion"). Living in a vibrant intellectual milieu, Modena challenged the revered status of these mystical texts and their philosophical system, arguing they diverged from authentic Jewish tradition. Far from ancient revelation, he posited that Kabbalah, as embodied in the Zohar, was a medieval construct, shaped by later mystics rather than rooted in the teachings of the Tannaitic era (1st–2nd centuries C.E). Through *Ari Nohem*, Modena not only questioned their origins but also critiqued their pervasive influence on Jewish thought and ritual, offering a rational lens that contrasts sharply with Kabbalah's esoteric appeal.

Modena's central argument rests on meticulous historical and textual analysis. He highlights anachronisms in the Zohar, traditionally attributed to Rabbi Simeon bar Yochai in the 2nd century C.E.[94] For instance, he points to references to post-Talmudic events, such as the Spanish Expulsion of 1492, which suggest a composition date no earlier than the 13th century—likely in Spain under Moses de León, a figure often credited with its authorship.[95]. Modena further scrutinizes the Zohar's language, noting its Aramaic is laced with medieval Spanish and Portuguese terms, unlike the purer dialect of earlier works like the Talmud *or Sefer Yetzirah.* This linguistic hybridity, he argues, betrays a later origin, aligning with a Iberian medieval context rather than a 2nd-century Palestinian one, a conclusion that dismantles claims of its antiquity.[96]

Equally compelling is Modena's skepticism toward the Zohar's origin story: bar Yochai's 13-year cave exile with his son, where he purportedly penned the *Secrets of the Torah.* Modena finds this tale implausible, emphasizing the absence of writing materials—paper, ink, or tools—in such a setting. Surviving on carob and spring water, buried in sand up to their necks, they faced conditions prioritizing bare existence over scholarly output. He questions how, under such duress, bar Yochai could have produced a complex mystical text, suggesting the narrative's logistical flaws undermine its credibility. By stripping away this miraculous veneer, Modena champions a practical, evidence-based approach, exposing Kabbalah's foundations as human rather than divine.

Modena's critique reflects his broader intellectual courage, a trait that resonates with modern readers. His work not only challenged the mystics of his day but also enriched Jewish discourse, balancing tradition with critical inquiry in a time of flux. [97]

The Zohar as Pseudepigraphal Literature

R. Leon Modena and Gershom Scholem highlight the Zohar as a key example of pseudepigraphal literature, a genre that thrived during the Second Temple period and the early Christian era. The term "pseudepigrapha," from the Greek *pseudēs* ("false") and *epigraphē* ("inscription"), describes texts falsely attributed to notable historical or legendary figures. This practice, widespread in Jewish and Christian traditions, often involved ascribing works to revered figures—such as biblical patriarchs, prophets, or apostles—to enhance their authority and authenticity. In religious contexts, where a text's perceived origins shaped its influence, this attribution was particularly impactful.[98]

Pseudepigrapha served various purposes. Authors might adopt pseudonyms to shield themselves from controversy or persecution while sharing their ideas. Additionally, this approach allowed them to present new theological perspectives or narratives through the voice of a respected figure, blending innovation with tradition. By aligning their work with established authority, they ensured greater acceptance among their audiences.

The Zohar, traditionally linked to the 2nd-century sage Rabbi Shimon bar Yochai, exemplifies this strategy. Attributing the text to such a venerated figure boosted its credibility and appeal, especially in communities that prized the wisdom of ancient sages. Moses de León, widely regarded as the likely author, probably used this tactic to counter skepticism about the Zohar's mystical content. By framing it as Rabbi Shimon bar Yochai's work, de León facilitated its dissemination and acceptance, embedding innovative mystical ideas within the framework of traditional Jewish teachings. Thus, the Zohar's pseudepigraphal nature reflects a deliberate effort to secure its influence and transmission.

Did Abraham write the Sefer Yetzirah?!

Leone Modena applied a similarly skeptical approach to *Sefer Yetzirah*, an early Jewish mystical text traditionally attributed to Abraham. Modena questioned this claim, arguing that it was unlikely for Abraham—a nomadic figure who traveled from the Negev to Beth El—to have written such a work. He doubted Abraham would have recorded instructions on parchment, skin, or bark, given his circumstances. Furthermore, Modena pointed out that Abraham's contemporaries were not suitable recipients of such esoteric teachings, making a written text unnecessary. If intended for his son Isaac, verbal transmission would have sufficed for such profound secrets of prophecy and divinity.

Modena further refuted the likelihood that Rabbi Akiba, a second-century Tanna, wrote *Sefer Yetzirah.* He dismissed the slightly more refined claims that Rabbi Akiba taught *Sefer Yetzirah* based on traditions passed down from Abraham. He questioned the assertion that at a time when the Oral Torah wasn't committed to writing, the deepest secrets would be inscribed in a book, accessible to all, both young and old, near and far. This wide dissemination of esoteric secrets would contradict Rabbi Akiba's likely intentions.

Theological Questions on the Kabbalah

Modena also takes issue with the philosophical and theological content of the Zohar and Kabbalah. He accuses Kabbalistic thought of introducing a form of polytheism into Judaism by suggesting that there are ten divine *sefirot* or emanations rather than a single unified God. Modena sees this as a dangerous deviation from monotheism, undermining the core tenets of Judaism. Historically, apologists for the Kabbalah also dispute Modena's claim that the concept of the "*sefirot*" contradicts monotheism. They argue that the *sefirot* are not separate deities but rather aspects or manifestations of the one God. As such, they believe Kabbalah offers a sophisticated and nuanced understanding of divine unity, rather than undermining it.

Modena, with a keen intent, sought to persuade the Jews of Venice to retreat from their increasing affinity for an emergent form of Jewish polytheism, deemed irrational in his eyes. He aimed to rekindle their commitment to the traditional Judaism espoused by Maimonides. Modena's invocation of reason, embodied by Maimonides' *Guide,* was not just a rhetorical device; it held a deep spiritual significance for him. It symbolized an intrinsic element of Jewish tradition that he esteemed and served as a formidable instrument to refute the parallel authenticity claimed by proponents of Kabbalah.

Yaakov Dweck's biography, *The Scandal of Kabbalah: Leon Modena, Jewish Mysticism, Early Modern Venice,* examines Leon Modena's sharp critique of Kabbalah in the context of seventeenth-century Venice. Modena challenged the authenticity of Kabbalah by rejecting a story claiming that Maimonides, a revered Jewish philosopher, retracted his earlier writings after discovering Kabbalah late in life. Modena argued that this tale was a fabrication by kabbalists, asserting that if Kabbalah were a genuine tradition from the prophets, like the Oral Torah, Maimonides would have been taught it from his youth by his teachers. He viewed the story as an attempt by kabbalists to claim Maimonides' authority while ignoring his *Guide of the Perplexed*, which condemned practices central to Kabbalah, such as letter combinations, numerology, and theurgic invocations of God's names. For Modena, this "kabbalization" of Maimonides was a greater offense than Kabbalah itself, revealing his deep frustration with what he saw as baseless inventions.

Modena's critique drew strength from his collaborative study of Maimonides' *Guide of the Perplexed* with his student Joseph Hamiz, a partnership that deepened his engagement with key theological questions. Through this lens, he tackled issues like prayer's purpose, heresy's boundaries, Abraham's significance, the rationale for commandments, and the Oral Torah's transmission—all areas where he found Kabbalah lacking. In *Ari Nohem*, particularly chapter 27, Modena cites the *Guide (*Part 3:51), invoking Maimonides' parable of the palace: those seeking divine wisdom without proper grounding—like kabbalists with their unmoored mysticism—wander further from truth, deluded into thinking they approach it. He criticized Kabbalistic practices such as letter combinations, numerology (*gematria*), and theurgic invocations of God's names, which the *Guide* condemns as irrational deviations (e.g., 2:37). For Modena, Maimonides' methodical approach to metaphysics—rooted in reason and tradition—stood as the gold standard, starkly opposing Kabbalah's speculative leaps.

"R. Leon Modena as imagined.

Dweck situates Modena's arguments within Venice's cultural ferment, where Renaissance humanism and Jewish scholarship intersected. His reliance on the *Guide* not only fortified his intellectual stance but also reflected his broader mission: to safeguard Jewish thought from what he saw as a mystical drift eroding its foundations. By rejecting the Maimonides myth and Kabbalah's claims, Modena championed a rationalist legacy, leaving an indelible mark on early modern Jewish critique.[99]

Modena's Thoughts on Kabbalistic Prayer

> Indeed, I heard, but I did not understand, the sin someone commits when he directs his prayer to God without [directing his thought] to the sefirot, for because of His absolute unity, He

cannot change His will. But even the least of the preachers can solve this [quandary] to understand the ignoramus, [using] a simple parable. This [problem] is similar to the [situation of] someone on a ship in a river who throws a cable on a pillar or a tree on the shore and strongly draws the ship and so brings it near to the shore. But whoever sees this may say that he draws the banks of the river to the ship, and so he comes near to the shore. But the matter is not so, since the ship comes near to the shore by drawing, whereas the shore stands forever. So is the prayer [like] a cable which is seized above on His will, which does not change itself, but the one praying who was at first remote comes near to his prayer to his God.

Let us then elevate our very selves by our prayers to the higher ascent of the divine and good rays as if a luminous chain being suspended from the celestial heights and reaching down hither, we, by ever clutching this upwards first with one hand and then with the other, seem indeed to draw it, but in reality, we do not draw it down, it being both above and below, but ourselves are carried upwards to the higher splendors of the luminous rays. Or, as if, after we have embarked on a ship, and are holding on to cables, reaching from some rock, such as are given out, as it were, for us to seize, we do not draw the rock to us but ourselves in fact and the ship to the rock.[100]

Kabbalists often thought that when one prays without considering the *Sefirot,* they are committing a mistake, because they are ignoring the fact that God, in His absolute unity, cannot change His will. The text then presents a parable to elucidate this idea: the act of praying is compared to a person on a ship, throwing a cable onto the shore to draw the ship closer. However, it might seem to an observer as if the person is pulling the shore toward the ship. In reality, the shore is constant and unchanging—similar to God's will—while it is the ship, or the person praying, that moves and comes closer to the shore or God. This illustrates that prayer does not change God or His will but instead brings the one who prays closer to God.

Modena stressed that prayer is likened to a luminous chain extending from earth to heaven. When we pray, we may seem to be pulling the chain—or Divine Presence—down to us, but in reality, we are pulling ourselves upward toward divine illumination. This metaphor underscores the transformative power of prayer in elevating our spiritual state and bringing us closer to the divine realm, rather than compelling God to descend to our level.

The last metaphor returns to the ship imagery but with a slight variation. Here, we are aboard a ship, holding onto cables attached to a rock. We don't pull the rock toward us, but rather, we pull ourselves and the ship toward the rock. This metaphor reiterates that in prayer, we are not pulling God toward us but rather drawing ourselves closer to God. These metaphors emphasize that the purpose and power of prayer lie not in changing God or His will but in transforming ourselves and drawing us closer to the Divine Presence.

Modena Urges a Return to Maimonidean Faith

Underscoring the historical paradox engendered by the widespread embrace of esotericism, Modena issued an unambiguous appeal for a return to the bedrock principles of Maimonidean rationalism. To bolster his argument, he diligently assembled an array of medieval sources, thereby introducing a tradition of anti-kabbalism into premodern Judaism. In this regard, *Ari Nohem* can be viewed as an extraordinarily ambitious work, constituting a robust challenge to the ascendant cultural influence of Kabbalah. Modena's criticism of Kabbalah was not merely a casual dismissal; he meticulously crafted an argument against a trend he perceived as contrary to the fundamental tenets of Judaism. This underscores the depth of his commitment to a rationalist interpretation of Jewish tradition and his resolute stance against what he perceived as an irrational departure from it.

Modena's Prescient Warning About the Kabbalah

Leon Modena's critique of Kabbalistic studies, particularly his examination of the Zohar in *Ari Nohem*, stemmed from deep concerns about the impact of these mystical teachings on traditional Jewish scholarship. He observed a shift in focus within Jewish intellectual circles from the rigorous analysis and debate of Talmudic studies to the esoteric and mystical elements of

Kabbalah. Modena viewed this shift as a significant departure from the established norms of Jewish learning and intellectual tradition.

Modena's worries centered around the drift from logical reasoning and critical thinking toward mystical interpretations in Kabbalistic studies. He feared that this trend could lead to an increase in superstitious beliefs and practices, potentially undermining the longstanding intellectual foundations of Jewish scholarship. This concern was not just theoretical; the rise of Shabbatai Sevi, a self-proclaimed Messiah whose appearance coincided with Modena's death, resulted in widespread messianic fervor and societal disruption. This event illustrated the risks that Modena had cautioned against, where unbridled mystical speculation, unchecked by rational analysis, could lead to significant upheavals within the Jewish community.

Despite these criticisms, Modena held a nuanced view of the Zohar. He acknowledged its literary and interpretive strengths, praising its midrashic composition and the depth it brought to scriptural interpretation. Modena admired the Zohar for its refined style, orderly structure, and the way it interwove stories and teachings, considering it unparalleled in its ability to inspire devout religious observance. However, he was cautious about accepting its allegorical and mystical narratives without critical analysis and contextual understanding. He advocated for a balanced approach to studying the Zohar and Kabbalah, integrating them with traditional Jewish learning and rational thought.

Modena Praises the Zohar as Inspiring Judaic Literature

Despite whatever reservations Modena had about the Kabbalah's historicity, he nevertheless extended praise and glory to the Zohar, lauding it as a work that excelled in exposition and surpassed all other compositions in his esteem. Through these affirmations, Modena revealed an ambivalent attitude toward the Zohar, expressing both admiration for its literary merits and reservations about its philosophical implications.

He acknowledges that they contain valuable ethical and spiritual teachings. Still, he insists that these should be approached critically and grounded in a firm understanding of traditional Jewish texts and rational thought. In this sense, Modena's critique can be seen as part of a broader project of integrating and reconciling different strands of Jewish thought. This project continues to be a vital part of Jewish intellectual life today. Modena advocated integrating secular knowledge with religious study, and his critique of the Zohar and Kabbalah should be seen in this light. His objections to the Zohar's authenticity and the Kabbalah's divergence from monotheism can be seen as a broader critique of what he saw as a trend toward irrationalism and superstition in Jewish thought.

Leon of Modena's critique of the Zohar and Kabbalah in his *Ari Nohem* provides a provocative and influential perspective on these texts and their role in Jewish life and thought. Modena challenges both the authenticity of the Zohar and the philosophical and social implications of Kabbalistic thought. While not all scholars or practitioners of Judaism agree with Modena's views, his critiques continue to inspire debate and reflection on the nature and place of mysticism in Judaism.

Age Limits on the Study of Kabbalah

Although the term "Kabbalah" did not appear in literature before the 11th century, and given the pseudonymous nature of the Zohar and most Kabbalistic writings, many medieval and modern scholars treated Kabbalah with skepticism and from a rationalistic standpoint. An animus against esoterism has long been evident since Late Antiquity, such as Ben Sira's saying:

פְּלָאוֹת מִמְּךָ אַל תִּדְרוֹשׁ, וּמְכֻסֶּה מִמְּךָ אַל תַּחְקוֹר
בַּמֶּה שֶׁהוּרְשֵׁיתָ הִתְבּוֹנֵן, וְאֵין לְךָ עֵסֶק בְּנִסְתָּרוֹת.
בְּיוֹתֵר מִמְּךָ אַל תַּמֵּר, כִּי רַב מִמְּךָ הָרְאֵיתָ.

Do not pursue what’s too hard for your might,
Nor delve into mysteries hidden from sight.
Focus instead on the tasks you’ve been given,
For what’s concealed isn’t yours to be driven.

Steer clear of matters that lie far away,
For there's much beyond what you grasp today.
Reflect on the wisdom that's been shared with you,
And let go of thoughts that you cannot construe.

Ben Sira 3:19-23

The Book of Ben Sira (also known as Ecclesiasticus) offers profound wisdom on the importance of focusing on what is within one's grasp or understanding and not meddling in matters that surpass human comprehension. This sage counsel finds resonances in Jewish traditions, particularly concerning the study of Jewish esoteric mysticism.

Jewish mystical tradition is replete with complex and profound spiritual and metaphysical concepts that explore the nature of God, the universe, and the soul. Due to the intricacies and profound nature of Kabbalah, traditionally, it has been suggested that it should not be studied until a person reaches forty.[101] The rationale behind this norm is multilayered. Firstly, age forty is considered a milestone in the maturity of an individual in Jewish tradition, not only physically but also emotionally, intellectually, and spiritually. By this age, an individual is expected to have garnered enough life experience, wisdom, and a robust foundation in Jewish law and philosophy to handle the profound and complex teachings of Jewish mystical tradition.

Let us repeat Ben Sira's words: "What is too sublime for you, don't search into things beyond your strength." (Ben Sira 3:21). These words mirror this sentiment, implying that one should not delve into knowledge or wisdom that might be too overwhelming or challenging to understand. This also reflects the danger of misinterpretation or misunderstanding, a risk inherent in exploring profound mystical concepts.

In the verse "Where the pupil of the eye is missing, there can be no light; and where there is no knowledge, there can be no wisdom," Ben Sira seems to propose that without an essential understanding (the "pupil of the eye"), there can be no true enlightenment ("light"). This parallels the perspective that, without a solid grounding in Jewish law and philosophy, there can be no proper understanding of the wisdom Kabbalah offers. Thus, the prohibition against studying Kabbalah before age 40 is designed to safeguard individuals from potentially misguided interpretations and ensure that those who engage with its teachings have the necessary foundation and maturity. This prohibition resonates with Ben Sira's wisdom, underscoring the importance of patience, maturity, and understanding in the pursuit of wisdom, particularly in matters of spirituality and mysticism.

The idea that Kabbalah should not be studied until age 40 is traditionally attributed to latter rabbinic authorities, though no single individual is definitively credited with establishing this rule. It emerges from a broader Jewish scholarly caution about engaging with esoteric mysticism without sufficient maturity and grounding in foundational texts like the Torah and Talmud. The earliest explicit mention of an age restriction tied to mystical study appears in the Talmud (BT Hagigah 11b), where R. Yohanan warns against expounding the *Ma'aseh Merkavah* (Ezekiel's chariot vision, a precursor to Kabbalistic thought) to an individual unless he is wise and discerning. Later, medieval Kabbalists formalized this caution, linking it to age 40—a milestone symbolizing wisdom and life experience, as Moses began his prophetic mission at 40 (Exod. 7:7).

The specific 40-year threshold is most prominently cited in the writings of R. Shabbatai ben Avraham HaKohen (a.k.a. the Shach, 1621–1662), a 17th-century Talmudist and jurist. In his commentary on the *Shulchan Aruch* (*Yoreh De'ah* 246:6), he states that Kabbalah study should be reserved for those over 40 who have mastered Talmud and Halakha, reflecting a consensus among earlier authorities like the Ari (Isaac Luria), who restricted esoteric teachings to mature scholars. This restriction aimed to ensure intellectual and spiritual readiness, preventing misinterpretation or misuse of Kabbalah's profound concepts. While not universally enforced—exceptions like Luria himself, who began younger, exist—it became a widely accepted norm in traditional Jewish circles, balancing reverence for mysticism with disciplined preparation.

19th Century Critics of the Kabbalah
Leopold Zunz

Leopold Zunz, a foundational figure in the 19th-century *Wissenschaft des Judentums* ("Science of Judaism") movement, offered a nuanced and critical perspective on the Kabbalah that significantly influenced scholarly views throughout the century. In 1818, at the age of twenty-four, Zunz articulated a key distinction in an essay published in Jedidjah. He separated the early Kabbalah, exemplified by the Zohar, which he saw as having some original theological value for Judaism, from the later Lurianic Kabbalah, which he dismissed as descending into "obscure superstition." He described the Zohar as the "first and most brilliant representative" of Kabbalah, a synthesis of neo-Platonic ideas and oriental magic rooted in Palestinian origins, drawing both Talmudic and gentile philosophy into its "magical circle." However, he criticized its inability to address textual (Masoretic) questions, arguing it "worshipped the letter more than the word," reflecting a superficial reverence for form over meaning.

Zunz traced the origins of Jewish mysticism to a blend of ancient Jewish and Alexandrian thought, which evolved into a cosmogonic and theosophical system. He argued that Kabbalah imposed mystical interpretations—either traditional or invented—onto biblical and Talmudic teachings, expanding into diverse philosophical systems. He emphasized the individuality of these systems, noting that nearly every Kabbalistic author created a unique framework, often using pseudo-epigraphy (attributing works to ancient figures like biblical personalities or angels) to gain authority or avoid scrutiny. This practice, he suggested, undermined the label "Kabbalah" (meaning "tradition"), as the ideas were often new and personal rather than truly traditional.

Historically, Zunz placed the emergence of Kabbalah in 12th-century Italy and southern France, asserting that the Zohar itself was a late compilation, partly from writings around 1300, rather than an ancient text. He highlighted medieval critiques of Kabbalah, which accused it of idolatry and inauthenticity, reinforcing his view of its questionable legitimacy. His primary scholarly contribution lay in his meticulous philological approach, particularly his focus on pseudo-epigraphy. Zunz's analysis avoided deep theological engagement, focusing instead on historical and textual critique. He left the doctrinal debates to others, such as Graetz, who viewed Kabbalah more harshly as a product of delusion or deceit, and Abraham Geiger, while passing the philological baton to Moritz Steinschneider. Zunz's work thus framed Kabbalah as a relatively modern phenomenon with roots in ancient thought but marred by later excesses, shaping the Wissenschaft scholars' skeptical yet systematic approach to Jewish mysticism.

Abraham Geiger

In 1840, Abraham Geiger, a young German Jewish scholar of the "Science of Judaism" movement, explored Kabbalah's historical and theological dimensions through a biography of Joseph Solomon Delmedigo, a 17th-century critic of Kabbalah who rejected the Zohar's attribution to Rabbi Shimon bar Yochai. Geiger used a letter from Delmedigo to argue his deep opposition to mysticism, prefacing the biography with an analysis of Jewish mysticism's origins. He saw Kabbalah emerging from a clash between Talmudic tradition and philosophical reason, an irreconcilable conflict that Maimonides' harmonizing efforts couldn't resolve. Mysticism, Geiger argued, borrowed metaphysical exegesis from philosophy but rejected its rational God-concept, instead starting "from above" with divine intuition, using philosophical terms loosely and ascribing natural effects to divine emanations rather than causal chains. This approach viewed the Torah's laws as tools for holiness, not just knowledge, contrasting with both Talmudic legalism and philosophy's intellectualism.

Geiger contrasted philosophy's dissection of nature with mysticism's holistic view, where all merges into the infinite "*Ein-Sof*," unlike philosophy's reification of concepts into entities. Mysticism oscillated between pantheism, emanation, and theism, seeking spiritual ascent. It warped Scripture, akin to the Talmud and philosophy, yet transformed words into spiritual powers, harmonizing with the authority of tradition. By the 13th century, as philosophy stagnated, mysticism gained ground, claiming its ideas as ancient "Kabbalah" (tradition). Geiger credited Moses de Leon with crafting the Zohar around this time, and he rejected the claim that it was authored by Shimon bar Yochai. He admired its literary flair but called it a "deception," a view later echoed by Graetz and contested by Scholem. Geiger observed that the Zohar's success was remarkable, rapidly spreading a subjective and degraded form of mysticism disguised as holy tradition.

Kabbalah's Lack of Originality and Intellectual Weakness

Geiger argued plainly that Kabbalah lacked originality, claiming it "never produced anything new" but instead relied on existing ideas, which it twisted and distorted. He viewed it as a parasitic system that drew heavily from earlier Jewish philosophers like Maimonides, Judah Halevi, and Solomon Ibn Gabriol, only to warp their concepts with what he termed "fantasies" or Hirngespinste. Far from being true successors to these thinkers, Geiger insisted that kabbalists did not build on their work in any meaningful or progressive way. He rejected the notion that Kabbalah was a legitimate heir to the rational, systematic thought of these figures, portraying kabbalists instead as shallow imitators who borrowed elements from these philosophical giants without grasping or preserving their depth and rigor.

Geiger saw Kabbalah as a product of intellectual decay, thriving in times when education and cultivation—Bildung—were weak, rather than as a valid alternative to rationalism. He rejected the romantic idea that it was a soulful rebellion against sterile logic, arguing instead that both shallow rationalism and mysticism stemmed from the same lack of intellectual vigor. For him, Kabbalah and its popularity reflected a broader decline, not a noble resistance.

A central pillar of Geiger's critique was Kabbalah's lack of a coherent system. He contrasted it sharply with philosophy, which he categorized into two disciplined streams: the empirical-synthetic approach of Aristotle and the idealistic-analytic method of Plato. Kabbalah, he argued, had no such structure—no deductive reasoning or organized framework. While he acknowledged that early mystical works like *Sefer Yetzirah* blended elements of both philosophical traditions, he believed that by the Middle Ages, Kabbalah had deteriorated into a chaotic, sensual jumble, heavy on imagination but light on analytical depth. This absence of rigor made it, in his eyes, intellectually untrustworthy and incapable of advancing true understanding.

Geiger also charted what he saw as Kabbalah's historical decline. He tied its rise in the late 13th century to the fading of original Jewish philosophy, a time when thinkers like Maimonides were no longer setting the pace. Kabbalah, he claimed, took scraps of philosophical thought and mixed them with wild, fantastical speculation—elaborate cosmologies, angelic hierarchies, and esoteric twists on scripture. Here, "fantastic" doesn't mean impressive; it means unreal, conjuring images of a disordered stew of ideas with no unifying logic.

Far from being successors to Jewish philosophers, kabbalists were, in Geiger's view, mere imitators, cobbling together a "fantastic ragout" of absurdity that lacked the clarity or substance of their predecessors. For Geiger, Kabbalah's greatest failing was not just its intellectual messiness but its ethical emptiness. Instead of fostering moral growth, it either disconnected people from practical life or puffed up an elitist few with arrogance. In his judgment, it offered no real contribution to human progress—only a retreat into confusion and self-importance.[102]

Nachman Krochmal's Positive View of the Kabbalah

Nachman Krochmal (1785-1845), a 19th-century Jewish philosopher and historian from Galicia, viewed Kabbalah as an integral and valuable part of Jewish tradition, approaching it through a rational and historical lens rather than the purely mystical perspective of traditional kabbalists. Unlike his German Wissenschaft contemporaries, Krochmal, an orthodox Jew writing in Hebrew, was shaped by Eastern European Jewish enlightenment and German idealism, drawing on thinkers like Hegel and Kant in his seminal work, *Moreh Nevukhe ha-Zeman* ("Guide for the Perplexed of the Time") to reconcile Jewish thought with modern philosophy.[103] He aimed to defend Judaism against secular critique by reinterpreting its traditions historically, seeing Judaism as subject to universal cycles—rise, maturity, decline—yet enduring through its connection to the "Absolute Spirit," a divine essence permeating Jewish history and religion.

Krochmal argued that each era of Jewish history had its own "mode of investigation" to adapt external ideas and reinterpret revelation, positioning Kabbalah as a sophisticated tradition that, when critically understood, preserved esoteric wisdom and enriched faith through a conceptual grasp of the divine. He treated Kabbalah as a legitimate "science of the faith" (חָכְמוֹת הָאֱמוּנָה = *hokhmot ha-emunah*), akin to Maimonidean philosophy or Neoplatonism, linking its "secret of unity and faith" (סוֹד הַיִּחוּד וְהָאֱמוּנָה = *sod ha-yihud v'ha-emunah*) to speculative traditions and even Gnosticism, anticipating Gershom Scholem's theory. He valued its reflection of profound spiritual truths, such as divine self-confinement—God creating the world out of Himself—theologically matching his own ideas about the infinite-to-finite transition, which distinguished him from rationalist critics like Heinrich Graetz.

Krochmal emphasized avoiding extremes in Torah interpretation—overly literal or excessively mystical—through a balanced, historical-philosophical understanding of this "science of faith." He drew on a rabbinic metaphor: "This Torah is like two paths: one of fire, the other of ice and snow. If a man goes in one direction, he will die in the fire; in the other direction, death from freezing awaits him. What then should he do? Go in the middle" [Guide, p. 10]. In his creative exegesis, he suggested the rabbis foresaw interpretative extremism and advocated a moderate path integrating reason and faith, reflecting his historicist approach where Kabbalah is a legitimate speculative tradition when approached critically rather than as literal mysticism.

His engagement with Kabbalah deepened with Lurianic doctrines like the *tzimtsum* (divine contraction) and *tikkun* (cosmic restoration), which resonated with his "Absolute Spirit" concept [Luria, as cited in Scholem]. However, he critiqued Lurianic Kabbalah's mythological imagery—vivid depictions of divine withdrawal and repair—as too sensual and unrefined, lacking the rational abstraction he deemed essential, a stance rooted in Kantian terms. This mirrored his rejection of Hasidism and early Jewish Gnosticism, which he believed degenerated into excesses, undermining authentic religious thought in his era.

Krochmal's preference for reason over mythical thinking, reflects a 19th-century tension between inclusivity and rationalism. He saw Kabbalah as a bridge between faith and reason, beginning with reason but degenerating into excess, yet still contributing to Judaism's spiritual vitality and adaptability when critically engaged. His nuanced stance influenced Scholem, who built on his historicism while embracing Kabbalah's irrational vitality, reframing the *Wissenschaft des Judentums*' groundwork into a "counter-history" of Jewish mysticism. Thus, Krochmal's philosophy balances speculative depth with critical reason, offering a distinctive perspective that neither fully endorses mysticism nor dismisses it, underscoring Kabbalah's role in Judaism's enduring strength.

Heinrich Graetz's View of the Kabbalah

Heinrich Graetz, the preeminent Jewish historian of the 19th century, approached Kabbalah with a blend of scholarly fascination and sharp critique, significantly advancing its study despite his critical view of its role in Jewish history. In his monumental *History of the Jews*, particularly Volume 7 (1863), he labeled Kabbalah—alongside phenomena like the Essenes and *Heichalot* literature—as "mysticism" (Kohler 2018, 107–130). Yet, he rarely leaned on this term as his primary lens, preferring "secret doctrine" (*Geheimlehre*) to capture its esoteric nature (Graetz 1863, vol. 7, 73), a phrase already used to describe Kabbalah's hidden teachings. Graetz envisioned Judaism's essence as a "*kernel*"—a transcendent, extra-mundane God, distinct from pagan immanence—evolving progressively toward the rational scholarship of the Wissenschaft des Judentums, which he championed. Kabbalah, with its mystical and often anthropomorphic divine depictions, clashed with this rationalist trajectory, leading him to dismiss it as a deviation, an irrational reaction to the philosophies of Maimonides or Saadia Gaon, and a "shell upon a shell" lacking organic ties to Judaism's true core.

Graetz's critique sharpens in his analysis of the Zohar, Kabbalah's foundational text, which he dissects in *History of the Jews* (Volume 7, pp. 73–77). He argues that it's not an ancient revelation from Shimon bar Yochai, the 2nd-century sage traditionally credited as its author, but a medieval forgery by Moses de Leon, a

13th-century Spanish Jew. He notes that the Zohar's use of Aramaic ("*Chaldee*") instead of Hebrew was a deliberate choice—its obscure, otherworldly tone suited a text claiming secret wisdom, masking its contemporary origins from Kabbalists who might recognize a Hebrew echo of their own era. Graetz portrays de Leon as a cunning manipulator, staging Shimon bar Yochai in splendor—halo and all—teaching a select circle of disciples amid celestial fanfare, with Elijah, angels, and the *Sefirot* unveiling Messianic secrets. These theatrical flourishes, he suggests, were designed to dazzle credulous readers and cement the Zohar's mystique as a "notorious forgery" that deceived Jews for centuries and even gained traction among some Christians.

The Zohar's extravagant praise of Shimon bar Yochai is, for Graetz, a glaring sign of its inauthenticity. Dubbed the "holy light" and elevated above Moses, Shimon boasts of surpassing the prophet, seeing beyond Sinai and knowing his face shines. The text ties divine favor to his presence, lamenting the woe of any generation without him, and his disciples hint at his divinity, fulfilling a call to "appear before the lord." Graetz finds this self-deification absurd and strategic: it preempts skepticism about why such wisdom, long hidden by cautious Kabbalists, surfaced suddenly. The Zohar claims Shimon's era was uniquely blessed, nearing the Messianic age, justifying the unveiling of its secrets—a clever but flimsy excuse, in Graetz's view, to dodge historical scrutiny.

Despite its flaws, Graetz marvels at the Zohar's enduring influence. He describes it as a sprawling, formless "*farrago*"—lacking a clear beginning or end, with uncertain divisions between its three main parts, appendices, and later additions. Its wild, sonorous style defies categorization as a Pentateuch commentary, theosophic manual, or sermon collection, inviting imitations that spawned "counter-forgeries." Yet, few works have shaped Jewish thought so profoundly, a testament to its remarkable, if chaotic, impact. Graetz sees this lack of structure as a weakness, reflecting Kabbalah's broader failure to align with Judaism's rational essence, which he ties to ethical reason and a transcendent God.

Graetz's engagement with Kabbalah built on earlier Orthodox scholarship, like Jacob Emden's proto-modern Zohar critique in the 18th century, and 19th-century traditionalists such as M. H. Landauer, D. H. Joel, and Eljakim Milzahagi. Adolf Jellinek's Bet ha-Midrash, with its meticulous, unbiased studies of the Zohar's authorship, particularly influenced Graetz and later Gershom Scholem, bridging traditional and modern approaches. While accepting Jellinek's findings, Graetz's historicist lens—stripping myth to reveal truth—casts Kabbalah as a secondary, disruptive force, not a legitimate strand of Jewish tradition. Unlike Abraham Geiger, who saw mysticism as pure degeneration, Graetz treats it as a flawed but significant artifact, worthy of study yet not reverence, balancing his rationalist ideals with a grudging nod to its cultural weight.

Elijah Benamozegh vs. Samuel David Luzzatto Debate

The intellectual confrontation between Samuel David Luzzatto (1800–1865), known as Shadal, and Elijah Benamozegh (1823–1900), two towering Italian Jewish scholars of the 19th century, stands as a defining moment in the modern Jewish struggle to reconcile rationalism with mysticism. Centered on the Zohar—the foundational text of Kabbalah—their debate unfolded through a rich exchange of correspondence and published works from the late 1850s to early 1860s, revealing not only personal convictions but also the broader stakes for Jewish identity amid the Enlightenment and secularization. Marked by mutual respect yet unyielding disagreement, their clash derailed a planned collaboration by the end of 1859, sparking a broader "storm" that illuminated enduring fault lines in Jewish thought.

Shadal, a biblical exegete and a unique voice within the *Haskalah* (Jewish Enlightenment), blended a conservative rabbinic outlook with rigorous historical criticism. Unlike mainstream *Haskalah* figures like Heinrich Graetz, who broadly rejected mysticism, Shadal's opposition to the Zohar stemmed from a deep commitment to the Torah's literal meaning and a reverence for simple, unadorned faith. In his seminal 1852 work, *Vikuach al Chokhmat ha-Kabbalah* ("Dialogue on the Wisdom of Kabbalah"), originally drafted in 1827, he dismantled the traditional claim that the Zohar was authored by the 2nd-century sage Shimon bar Yochai.

Instead, he pinpointed its origins to 13th-century Spain, likely under Moses de León, marshaling a formidable array of evidence: linguistic anachronisms in its Aramaic, late Hebrew grammatical forms, and references to post-Talmudic innovations like Hebrew vowel-points and accents, which the Zohar imbued with mystical significance. He drew striking parallels to Dante's *Divine Comedy*, composed around the same period, noting shared motifs of cosmic journeys and divine hierarchies as further proof of its medieval context.

For Shadal, the Zohar's historical inauthenticity was only part of the problem. He saw Kabbalah as a corrosive force that undermined Judaism's ethical and communal essence—simple monotheism and moral compassion. He argued that its esoteric doctrines, with their focus on numerology (*gematriot*), acronyms (*rashei tevot*), and the cosmic ramifications of *mitzvot* (commandments), distracted scholars from the Torah's practical legal and spiritual depth, where every word and letter carried tangible weight. In his view, Kabbalah fostered superstition, intellectual decline, and an elitist arrogance, as mystics speculated boldly about God's essence, creation, and governance—topics he deemed disrespectful and baseless.

Similar to Graetz, Shadal traced its rise to a backlash against medieval rationalist philosophy, particularly Maimonides, whom he daringly criticized despite the Haskalah's veneration of him. Yet he reserved his sharpest rebuke for kabbalists, writing in Vikuach that they "did more evil than the philosophers" by perverting true faith. In a November 3, 1859 letter to Benamozegh, he quipped, "To believe that the Zohar predates Dante is to willfully close one's eyes," a pointed jab at mystical naivety delivered with a mix of affection and exasperation.

The genesis of *Vikuach* added a personal layer to Shadal's critique. Written as a fictional dialogue between himself and a Polish scholar who dismantles the Zohar's claims, the work initially saw Shadal defending the text before conceding defeat—a rhetorical device showcasing his intellectual honesty. In an addendum, he revealed that its 1852 publication, 25 years after its drafting, was spurred by a real encounter with a Polish student. This student, alarmed by Hasidism's growing influence in Eastern

Europe—where the Zohar fueled what Shadal saw as misguided piety—urged him to share the critique, believing it could restore Torah-centric faith among "tens of thousands of pseudo-pietists." This context underscored Shadal's mission: not to dismantle tradition wholesale, but to safeguard Judaism's core from mystical excess.

Elijah Benamozegh, a kabbalist and polymath, mounted a spirited counteroffensive in *Sefer Ta'am Leshad* (1863), also crafted as a dialogue to mirror Shadal's style. He rejected the notion that the Zohar's late appearance—traditionally dated to its 13th-century publication—negated its antiquity, arguing it distilled ancient oral and written traditions passed down through generations. He pointed to traces of these ideas in pre-Zoharic literature, such as the Talmud and midrash, and suggested its delayed emergence reflected the Jewish people's historical prioritization of national identity over mystical speculation. For Benamozegh, Kabbalah was no aberration but a vital complement to Jewish thought, weaving diverse influences—biblical, rabbinic, and even philosophical—into a cohesive theology. He envisioned Jews as a "priestly people" with a universal ethical mission, a role enriched by Kabbalah's cosmic perspective on mitzvot. Dismissing Shadal's rationalism as a reductive echo of Moses Mendelssohn, he warned that stripping Judaism of its mystical depth risked flattening its spiritual richness.

Their disagreement crystallized around three pivotal issues: historicity, intellectual coherence, and ethical impact. On historicity, Shadal demanded concrete, empirical evidence for the Zohar's antiquity, dismissing unwritten tradition as unreliable, while Benamozegh embraced esoteric continuity as a hallmark of Jewish resilience. On coherence, Shadal, aligned with Graetz's view of Kabbalah as a disjointed "mishmash," decried its lack of logical rigor; Benamozegh celebrated its synthetic brilliance, arguing it harmonized Judaism's multifaceted heritage. Ethically, Shadal feared Kabbalah bred superstition and an aloof elitism, disconnecting *mitzvot* from their communal purpose; Benamozegh countered that it elevated Jewish practice into a universal moral framework, countering rationalism's cold utilitarianism. Shadal likened Benamozegh's stance to "blind faith," while Benamozegh saw Shadal's approach as a sterile overcorrection that threatened tradition's vitality.

Their exchange, documented in part by *Hakirah* (2022), never bridged this chasm. Shadal's critique, rooted in linguistic precision and historical analysis, marked an early triumph for Wissenschaft des Judentums, the scientific study of Judaism, influencing skeptics like Graetz and later scholars who confirmed the Zohar's medieval origins. Benamozegh's defense, though unable to overturn this consensus, offered a nuanced apologia that prefigured 20th-century mystics like Rav Abraham Isaac Kook, who similarly sought to fuse tradition with modernity. His reflections on the Zohar's late circulation—tied to the Jewish focus on nationhood rather than sectarian theology—remain a compelling, if speculative, contribution to kabbalistic scholarship.

The Benamozegh-Luzzatto debate left no definitive victor but etched a lasting divide in Jewish thought. Today, their arguments reverberate in tensions between Orthodoxy's mystical currents and rationalist strains, as well as in questions about whether *mitzvot* serve cosmic mysteries or earthly communities. Shadal's vision of a Torah-grounded faith, untainted by speculation, contrasts sharply with Benamozegh's embrace of Kabbalah as Judaism's spiritual heartbeat. As Daniel Klein aptly notes, their "sparks flew" not merely over the Zohar, but over the soul of Judaism in a world tilting toward reason and away from wonder.[104] Their stormy yet respectful dialogue—preserved in letters, books, and the echoes of their ideas—remains a testament to the complexity of Jewish intellectual life, a clash worthy of study for its depth, passion, and enduring relevance.

20th Century Scholarship & Beyond

A. Gershom Scholem

Among modern 20th-century scholars, Gershom Scholem both builds on and departs from Graetz. Like Graetz, Scholem embraces a historicist definition of Judaism as the sum of its historical manifestations, not a fixed theological construct. Where Graetz saw mysticism as a dangerous byproduct of philosophical progress, Scholem sees it as a vital, autonomous strand of Jewish history. Graetz's rationalism blinded him to the Kabbalah's significance, forcing him to denigrate it as un-Jewish or marginal, whereas Scholem argues that these "irrational" elements—often flirting with myth, pantheism, or polytheism—coexisted with and enriched the monotheistic tradition Graetz prized.

Scholem positions himself as fulfilling Graetz's unfinished project. Graetz's historicism faltered under the pressures of his era, where rationalism and the need to defend Judaism against assimilationist or Christian critiques compelled him to sideline mysticism. Scholem, working in the context of a Jewish national homeland, claims he can complete this program by giving equal weight to the irrational currents that Graetz suppressed. While Graetz saw Jewish history as a linear progression toward rational reflection, Scholem views it as a dynamic interplay of contradictory forces—rational and mystical, transcendent and immanent. For instance, Graetz dated the Zohar late and dismissed its value due to its pseudepigraphic nature, interpreting it as a sign of mystical regression. Scholem, while accepting a similar dating, revalues pseudepigraphy as a creative religious act, not a flaw, and elevates the Kabbalah as a legitimate expression of Jewish vitality.

In essence, Scholem is both indebted to and critical of Graetz. He adopts Graetz's historicist foundation but rejects his rationalist lens, arguing that a true history of Judaism must embrace its full spectrum, including the mystical traditions Graetz scorned. Where Graetz's framework was constrained by a transcendent God guiding history toward reason, Scholem's immanent historiography allows for a richer, more conflicted narrative—one that Graetz, despite his ambitions, couldn't achieve within the intellectual confines of 19th-century Europe. The perception that Gershom Scholem single-handedly invented the field of Kabbalistic scholarship often stems from the starkly negative stance that many prominent 19th-century scholars of the *Wissenschaft des Judentums* ("Science of Judaism") took toward irrational elements in Jewish history, such as mysticism. This group, dedicated to the scientific study of Judaism, tended to favor rationalism and often dismissed or marginalized the Kabbalah as an aberration.

However, while Scholem's contributions were groundbreaking, he didn't start from nothing. He leaned heavily on the work of predecessors who, despite their biases, laid the critical groundwork, supplying historical and philological tools and even engaging directly with Kabbalistic texts. Figures like Moritz Steinschneider, who cataloged countless Kabbalistic manuscripts in European libraries, provided the bibliographical foundation that Scholem later built upon. Even Heinrich Graetz, known for his harsh critiques of mysticism, displayed a deep familiarity with mystical sources, a knowledge that Scholem drew from despite his sharp disagreements with Graetz's conclusions.

B. Scholem as an "Accountant" of Jewish Mysticism

In his widely popular book, *Nine and a Half Mystics: The Kabbala Today,* Herman Weiner's reflection on the Jerusalem rabbi's remark about scholars of Jewish mysticism, particularly in the context of Gershom Scholem and the Kabbala, points to a distinction between intellectual knowledge and experiential or spiritual ownership. The rabbi's metaphor of scholars as "accountants" suggests that these academics, like Scholem, possess a deep understanding of the Kabbala's teachings, historical significance, and philosophical richness—they know "where the wealth is, its location and value." However, the rabbi implies that this knowledge remains theoretical and detached. The "wealth" of the Kabbala, its spiritual and transformative power, cannot be fully accessed or "used" by scholars who approach it solely as an object of study rather than as a lived, mystical practice.[105]

In Scholem's case, Weiner is exploring how this tension might have shaped his personal life and thought. Scholem, a preeminent scholar of Jewish mysticism, meticulously studied the Kabbala's texts and historical development, but the rabbi's remark raises the question of whether Scholem engaged with it as a spiritual path or remained an "accountant," cataloging its profundity without claiming its spiritual benefits. The comment underscores a broader critique of academic approaches to sacred traditions, suggesting that intellectual mastery does not equate to the personal, transformative engagement that true practitioners experience.

Scholem's *Major Trends in Jewish Mysticism* exemplifies this "accountant" role. His meticulous scholarship—reconstructing manuscripts, unmasking pseudoauthors, uncovering heresies, and linking the Kabbala to phenomena like the French Revolution and early Reform Judaism—demonstrates unparalleled mastery. He emphasizes that mysticism is tied to specific religious systems, describing how mystics reshape canonical texts through a "fiery stream of mystical consciousness," often approaching heresy by engaging with suppressed spiritual cravings. The Kabbala, Scholem notes, reintroduced pagan superstitions, theurgic rites, and gnostic heresies, serving as a vehicle for these impulses.

Historical examples, from the Essenes' covenant communities to the Talmudic Descenders of the Chariot's visions of divine hierarchies, illustrate the Kabbala's experiential nature. Medieval Hasidim combined fiery imagery with God's immanence, believing in the semimagical power of prayer, while Abraham Abulafia's meditative system used Hebrew letters to achieve dvekut (intimate clinging to God). The Zohar's esoteric teachings further reflect this lived tradition. Scholem's scholarship illuminates these practices but, as the rabbi's metaphor implies, focuses on cataloging rather than participating in their spiritual depth.

To Weiner's credit, his exploration into the mind of Gershom Scholem (and similar academicians) underscores a broader critique: academic mastery of sacred traditions, while profound, differs from the transformative engagement of practitioners. The Kabbala's diverse, practice-driven nature demands personal commitment, suggesting that scholars, despite knowing the "wealth," may not "use" its spiritual power.

C. The History of Nonsense is Scholarship

Saul Lieberman once introduced Gershom Scholem at a famous lecture in the 1940s at the Jewish Theological Seminary with the quip, "Nonsense is nonsense,[106] but the history of nonsense is scholarship."[107] This remark, made during a notable lecture, reflects Lieberman's nuanced take on esoteric traditions like Kabbalah, dismissing their content as irrational yet affirming their historical study as legitimate. For Scholem, the pioneering historian of Jewish mysticism, this encapsulates both a critique and an endorsement of his life's work. Scholem transformed Kabbalah from a fringe subject into a respected academic field by treating its "nonsense"—fantastical claims like the Zohar's celestial visions—as a rich historical tapestry, not a theological truth to defend.

Lieberman's first clause, "Nonsense is nonsense," highlights his skepticism. Rooted in the precise, text-critical world of Talmudic study, he viewed Kabbalah's speculative leaps—its divine emanations and Messianic promises—as lacking the rational grounding of halakhic reasoning. To him, these were intellectual fluff, a sentiment echoing traditionalist doubts about mysticism's worth. But the second clause, "the history of nonsense is scholarship," shifts the perspective, recognizing that even if Kabbalah's doctrines are dubious, their evolution and impact warrant serious inquiry. This aligns directly with Scholem's mission in works like *Major Trends in Jewish Mysticism* (1941), where he traced Kabbalah's development—from medieval Spain to Sabbateanism—not to validate its miracles but to reveal Judaism's dynamic undercurrents as a scholarly pursuit.

Scholem's approach embodies this duality. Rebelling against his assimilated Berlin upbringing, he immersed himself in Jewish texts, focusing on Kabbalah despite its dismissal by figures like Heinrich Graetz as a medieval aberration. Where Graetz saw forgery, Scholem saw creativity, analyzing the Zohar's 13th-century origins under Moses de Leon as a response to historical crises like the 1492 Spanish expulsion. He explored its "nonsense"—*Sefirot* and Messianic visions—as human artifacts with symbolic weight, making them historically meaningful. Lieberman's quip mirrors this: Scholem didn't need to believe in Kabbalah to find its history valuable.

Their dynamic adds depth to the statement. Colleagues in Jerusalem after Scholem joined the Hebrew University in 1925, Lieberman and Scholem represented contrasting temperaments—traditional philology versus secular mysticism. The remark may have been a gentle jab at Scholem's focus on what Lieberman deemed marginal, yet it concedes his success in proving Kabbalah's historical study rigorous. Scholem, in *From Berlin to Jerusalem* (1977), recalls defending mysticism against superstition charges, a stance Lieberman's words unwittingly bolster: he turned "nonsense" into a cornerstone of Jewish scholarship. This reflects a broader 20th-century tension in Jewish studies. The *Wissenschaft des Judentums*, which Scholem critiqued, favored rationalism, sidelining Kabbalah as Graetz had. Scholem reclaimed it, bridging "nonsense" and "scholarship," a legacy later expanded by Moshe Idel beyond historicism. Lieberman's quip, both critique and validation, captures the skepticism Scholem faced and his triumph in elevating Kabbalah's history to academic prominence, cementing its intellectual weight.

The statement also hints at a subtle tension between Scholem and Lieberman, who were contemporaries and colleagues in Jerusalem after Scholem joined the Hebrew University in 1925. Lieberman, a traditionalist rooted in Talmudic philology, and Scholem, a secular Zionist fascinated by mysticism, represented contrasting scholarly temperaments. Anecdotes suggest Lieberman respected Scholem's erudition but remained skeptical of Kabbalah's worth. The quip, often cited in Scholem's work, may have been a playful jab at Scholem's obsession with what Lieberman saw as marginal or dubious. Yet it also concedes Scholem's point: the history of such "nonsense" could indeed be a field of rigorous inquiry, as Scholem proved through decades of meticulous research.

D. Moshe Idel's Post-Scholem View of Kabbalah

Moshe Idel, a leading Kabbalah scholar, offers a groundbreaking perspective in Kabbalah: New Perspectives (1988), critiquing earlier historians like Heinrich Graetz and Gershom Scholem while reframing Kabbalah's emergence in 12th–13th century Provence and northern Spain. His work engages a central question: Why did Kabbalah arise amid the Maimonidean controversy, a debate sparked by Maimonides' rationalist reinterpretation of Jewish tradition in works like The Guide for the Perplexed? Idel's nuanced synthesis positions Kabbalah as a creative response to Maimonides' Aristotelian philosophy, bridging rationalism and mysticism through continuity with earlier Jewish esoteric traditions.

Heinrich Graetz, in his History of the Jews (1863), viewed Kabbalah as a defensive reaction to Maimonides' rationalism, which threatened traditional Jewish spirituality. Influenced by the Wissenschaft des Judentums movement's rationalist bias, Graetz dismissed Kabbalah as a superstitious setback, famously branding the Zohar a "book of lies" forged by Moses de Leon. Despite this, his expansive surveys of kabbalistic literature were pioneering, outstripping contemporaries. Yet his perspective, echoed by 17th-century critic Leone da Modena, framed Kabbalah as a deliberate counterweight to philosophy, born of necessity rather than organic growth.

Gershom Scholem, in *Major Trends in Jewish Mysticism* (1941), rejected Graetz's reactive model, arguing Kabbalah emerged from a fusion of ancient Gnostic and Neoplatonic traditions with Jewish mysticism. He emphasized its internal evolution, downplaying external triggers like Maimonides' influence and presenting Kabbalah as a natural outgrowth of Jewish mystical currents. While Scholem's work elevated Kabbalah's academic legitimacy, his historicist lens—tying its development to crises like the 1492 Spanish expulsion—overemphasized foreign influences and dramatic ruptures, such as Lurianic innovations and Sabbatian messianism.

E. Idel's Synthesis: A Silent Controversy

Idel stakes a middle ground, arguing Kabbalah was neither a reactive invention (Graetz) nor a spontaneous mystical flowering (Scholem), but a structured response to Maimonides' rationalism. Maimonides sought to reinterpret Jewish esotericism through an Aristotelian lens, sidelining mystical traditions like theurgy (ritual acts to influence divine realms) and myth. Idel posits that Kabbalah reclaimed and systematized these displaced elements into a coherent alternative, drawing on pre-existing Jewish practices, such as those in Heikhalot literature (early mystical texts on heavenly ascents). This "silent controversy" unfolded not through direct polemics—early kabbalists rarely attacked Maimonides—but through a mystical counter-narrative. Later kabbalists, like R. Shem Tov ibn Shem Tov and R. Hayyim Vital, explicitly critiqued Maimonides' philosophical dominance, while anti-kabbalists like R. Elijah del Medigo championed his rationalism, highlighting this tension. For Idel, Kabbalah emerges as a creative synthesis, bridging rational and mystical facets of Judaism.

F. Idel's Critique of Historicist Kabbalah

Moshe Idel refines and challenges Gershom Scholem's historicist approach to Kabbalah, which overemphasizes external influences and historical ruptures. Scholem portrays Kabbalah as a Gnostified Judaism, shaped by discontinuous historical events, overlooking its organic continuity within Jewish tradition. Idel counters that core practices like devekut (mystical union) and motifs like the merkabah chariot, prominent in *Heikhalot* texts and later echoed in the Zohar, are inherently Jewish. These elements not only predate but likely influenced Gnosticism, persisting through undocumented yet enduring channels. Idel argues that figures like Nahmanides, deeply rooted in Jewish tradition, would not have embraced foreign doctrines, bolstering kabbalists' claims of an ancient esoteric lineage. Through meticulous textual analysis of Midrash, Talmud, and later works, Idel traces a coherent evolution, spotlighting figures like Abraham Abulafia, whose ecstatic Kabbalah enriches the dominant theosophical tradition. Contra Heinrich Graetz's view of Kabbalah as a medieval aberration, Idel reclaims its vitality as an integral, dynamic thread of Jewish spirituality.

Idel also reassesses 19th-century Jewish scholarship, noting that Graetz's rationalist bias obscured Kabbalah's vitality, yet his surveys laid the groundwork for future study. Scholars like Nachman Krochmal, who explored mystical dimensions of Jewish history, and Adolphe Franck, who produced early translations of kabbalistic texts, showed greater sympathy for Kabbalah than Scholem acknowledged. Their contributions, alongside Moritz Steinschneider's detailed studies of figures like Abulafia, provided a foundation for modern research, though often overshadowed by Scholem's influence.

Overall, Idel's third hypothesis reframes Kabbalah as a vital response to Maimonides' rationalist challenge, rooted in Jewish continuity and enriched by dialogue between tradition and innovation. By critiquing Graetz's reductive rationalism and Scholem's historicist speculations, Idel offers an evidence-based, phenomenological understanding of Kabbalah's origins, cementing its place as a dynamic force in Jewish intellectual history.

CHAPTER 6

BEHIND THE VEIL OF TZIMTZUM

Know that before the Source of Emanation emitted its emanations which are now emanated, created, and made, the Infinite filled this whole place in which the four worlds, atzilut, beriah, yetzirah, 'assiah, stand, and there was nothing outside of Him. And behold, since everything was filled with that light which is called the Infinite, then there was no empty place; the Infinite was forced to contract Its presence and to withdraw Its light and leave an empty space to emanate the worlds within it. Indeed, that contraction was not in one of His sides, but only at a central point within it. And it contracted itself to the sides equally on all sides, and a free space remained in the center.

—Rabbi Hayim Vital, Mavo She' a rim, Chapter 1, fol. la)

When it occurred to His simple will to create the worlds and to emanate the emanations and to actualize the completeness of His actions and His names and appellations, for this was the reason for the creation of the worlds .... Then the Infinite contracted Itself in a central point which is truly in the center of the light, and that light was contracted and withdrew to the sides around the central point. Then an empty place remained with air and empty space.

—Etz Hayim, Heykhal I, p. 22

The light of the blessed Infinite One is endless, without limit or measure. It fills everything, and in contrast to it, no existence other than it can exist - "nothing but Him". At the beginning of the creation of the world, the Infinite One contracted a part of His light for us, and set a limit and measure for it, in order to give the possibility of existence to creation and creatures, and so that we, the limited beings, could comprehend something from His illumination. Contraction is a term of covering, as in the language of our sages: "And she contracted her face" (Bereishit Rabbah end of chapter 45), meaning—the Infinite One covers Himself from us, and reveals to us only limited revelations, but He Himself—no contraction or limit has been imposed on Him. The measure and limit of the contraction... [the text cuts off here].

—*Sha'are Ramchal s.v. Tzimtzum*

צִמְצוּם

TZIMZUM

Antecedents to Luria's Tzimtzum

The Kabbalistic concept of *tzimtzum*, central to Lurianic Kabbalah, delves into the intricate process of divine contraction and creation. At its core, *tzimtzum* is more than a simple withdrawal of God's light to create a vacated space for the universe; it represents a profound theological and spiritual principle, encapsulating the paradox of an infinite God making room for a finite world.

This notion of *tzimtzum*—divine contraction to enable creation—gains its fullest expression in Lurianic Kabbalah, yet it wasn't Luria's invention. As Moshe Idel has demonstrated, earlier kabbalists employed this idea in diverse forms, suggesting it evolved across Jewish mystical thought long before Luria (16th century, Safed) elevated it to prominence.

❑ Nahmanides (13th century): In his Commentary on *Sefer Yetzirah*, Nahmanides, a towering medieval Jewish thinker, describes the *kavod* ("divine glory") between the cherubim as contracting. This usage aligns with Luria's later idea of

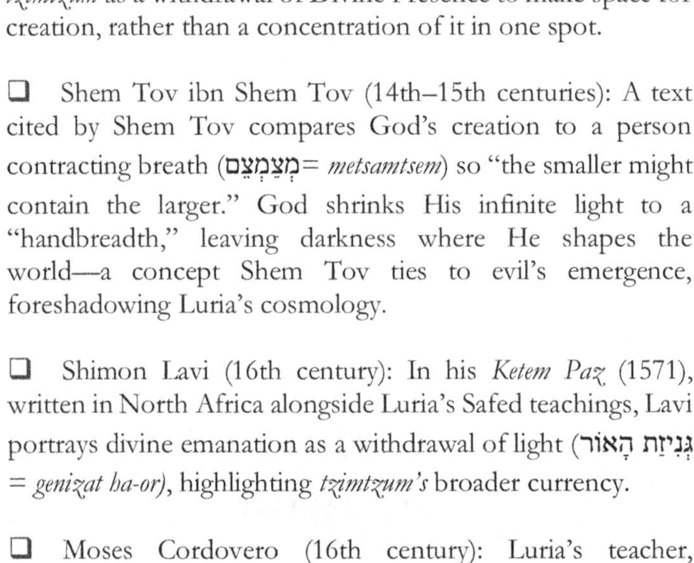

tzimtzum as a withdrawal of Divine Presence to make space for creation, rather than a concentration of it in one spot.

- Shem Tov ibn Shem Tov (14th–15th centuries): A text cited by Shem Tov compares God's creation to a person contracting breath (מְצַמְצֵם= *metsamtsem*) so "the smaller might contain the larger." God shrinks His infinite light to a "handbreadth," leaving darkness where He shapes the world—a concept Shem Tov ties to evil's emergence, foreshadowing Luria's cosmology.

- Shimon Lavi (16th century): In his *Ketem Paz* (1571), written in North Africa alongside Luria's Safed teachings, Lavi portrays divine emanation as a withdrawal of light (גְּנִיזַת הָאוֹר = *genizat ha-or)*, highlighting *tzimtzum's* broader currency.

- Moses Cordovero (16th century): Luria's teacher, Cordovero, also taught *tzimtzum* as divine retraction, though it played a less central role than in Luria's system.[108]

The Kabbalistic concept of *tzimtzum*, central to Lurianic Kabbalah, delves into the intricate process of divine contraction and creation. At its core, the *tzimtzum* is more than a simple withdrawal of God's light to create a vacated space for the universe; it represents a profound theological and spiritual principle.

Kabbalists caution against a purely literal interpretation of *tzimtzum*, suggesting instead a conceptual approach. In this view, t*zimtzum* is not about God creating physical space but rather about a metaphysical process. It involves God's self-imposed limitation, allowing for the existence of 'lack' or 'darkness' within the otherwise omnipresent divine light. This conceptual 'space' facilitates human free will and achievement, providing a stage for the dynamic interaction between the divine and the created.

Central to this discussion is the concept of *Or Ein Sof*, "the light of Ein Sof." *Ein Sof*, or "The Limitless One," symbolizes the ultimate unity of the Divine, transcending human understanding. *Or Ein Sof*, the emanation from this infinite source, is the aspect of the Divine we can perceive. It is a uniform, simple light, the initial creative force of the universe, and serves as the highest divine manifestation within our conceptual grasp.

In essence, *Or Ein Sof* is a crucial intermediary in the Kabbalistic understanding of the creation process. It is through this 'light' that the Divine expresses itself in a form that allows for the existence of a diverse and multifaceted universe, while still remaining rooted in the unity of *Ein Sof.* This concept underscores the deep interconnectedness between the Creator and creation, with *Or Ein Sof* acting as the medium through which the divine essence is both concealed and revealed in the world. However, the *Or Ein Sof* inherits the infinite nature of *Ein Sof.* As such, while it filled all existence, it left no room for anything else. Although it had the energy potential to birth an infinite number of universes, the totality of *Or Ein Sof,* like mathematical infinity, could neither be added to nor subtracted from. Consequently, the existence of anything independent was impossible within *Or Ein Sof.*

The subsequent step in creation, therefore, was the fabrication of a concept of 'lack' or a 'negative light' that would serve as a barrier against God's own light. This created the חָלָל הַפָּנוּי the "Vacated Space" or *Chalal HaPanui.* The Zohar refers to this concept as בּוֹצִינָה דֶּה קַרְדְנוּתָה (*botsinah deh qardenuthah*) the "Lamp of Darkness." This divine contraction within *Or Ein Sof* creates something akin to a negative energy field. It's a 'lamp' that radiates 'darkness,' blocking out everything that could potentially exist but doesn't. In essence, *Or Ein Sof* symbolizes the omnipresent divine light before creation, a state of existence where nothing else can coexist. Through *tzimtzum,* God creates a metaphysical space for creation and free will, setting the stage for the dynamic interplay between the divine and the created.

This concept of the *tzimtzum* goes beyond the creation of the physical universe. It offers a profound pathway for understanding our spiritual journey. The process of *tzimtzum* mirrors the human quest for spiritual growth: just as God concealed part of His essence to allow creation to emerge, we, too, must navigate through layers of concealment and limitation to uncover the divine spark within us. This journey is not linear but cyclical, echoing the rhythmic contractions and expansions of the universe itself. In practical terms, the *tzimtzum* challenges us to find a balance between the recognition of God's overwhelming omnipresence and the acknowledgment of our agency. It invites us to engage in spiritual practices that deepen our awareness of the Divine, while also cultivating our unique path and purpose within creation. This dynamic tension between the divine and the human, the infinite and the finite, is at the heart of the Kabbalistic path, encouraging a continual process of self-discovery and divine communion.

In essence, the concept of *tzimtzum* in Kabbalah is not just a theological or cosmological doctrine; it is a living, breathing spiritual paradigm. It urges us to explore the depths of our being, to embrace the mysteries of the Divine, and to actively participate in the ongoing act of creation. *Tzimtzum,* thus, becomes a metaphor for our spiritual evolution, reminding us that within the "empty space" of our perceived limitations lies the potential for profound growth and divine revelation."

In Kabbalistic teachings, especially as articulated by Rabbi Moshe Chaim Luzzatto, the process of God's creation and governance of the world is portrayed not as a display of unfettered omnipotence, but rather as a gradual and deliberate unfolding, similar to the way humans act. This concept is central to understanding the *tzimtzum*, where the Infinite (*Ein Sof*) intentionally contracts His light. This contraction represents a choice by the Divine to create in a measured, step-by-step manner, rather than through the overwhelming force of His unlimited power. This methodical approach is crucial for making the process of creation comprehensible to human minds.

This act established two paths of divine action: the path of omnipotence and the path of graduality. Before creation, only the former existed, but intending to create the world, God initiated the latter. The concept of *Ein Sof* pertains to God's supreme, perfect will, while the *Sefirot,* which emerged through this process, represents gradations of divine influence. The Emanator, or first existence, limited His all-powerful will to facilitate a gradual process of creation, leading to the revelation of the *Sefirot* and their diverse aspects.

In essence, the Lurianic doctrine of *tzimtzum* presents a profound and dynamic framework for understanding the creation process and the nature of the Divine. It highlights the balance between God's omnipresence and the independence of creation, setting the stage for the interplay between the divine and the mundane. The idea of *tzimtzum* has significantly impacted Jewish mysticism, profoundly shaping perceptions of the universe and humanity's role within it. It illuminates the complex interplay between the Infinite and the finite, offering deep insights into the nature of creation and existence. In the following subsections, we will delve into the intricate details of the *Tzimtzum* process, exploring its nuances and implications.

Semantical Views Regarding the Tzimzum

As previously noted, the concept of *tzimtzum*, or Divine contraction, has generated considerable controversy. Kabbalists have long wondered whether this concept is predicated upon an actual contraction and withdrawal of the Divine, which gave rise to the phenomenal universe, or whether the *Tzimtsum* is merely a metaphor that describes in spatial terms that people can analogically understand.

Let us consider the divergent interpretations of the Lurianic concept of *Tzimtzum*. Post-Lurianic Kabbalists such as R. Yosef Ergas, R. Immanuel Hai Ricchi, the Vilna Gaon (R. Elijah ben Solomon Zalman), R. Shneur Zalman of Liadi, and R. Hayyim Volozhin debated the extent to which this concept should be interpreted literally. Their differing views highlight the essential role of metaphor in interpreting and understanding mystical ideas within Jewish thought, especially in Kabbalah. These discussions reflect the ongoing challenge of deciphering esoteric teachings and the role of metaphor in bridging the gap between the mystical and the comprehensible.

- R. I. RICCHI AND THE LITERAL INTERPRETATION OF TZIMTZUM: Ricchi, in "*Yosher Leivav*,"[109] views *Tzimtzum* as a physical contraction of the Divine Light, creating space for the universe. He felt, wrote that logic dictated that it is disgraceful for the Divine to be found in a dirty place. This interpretation hints that God exists within spatial confines; a notion some deem heretical.[110]

❑ R. YOSEF ERGAS AND THE FIGURATIVE INTERPRETATION: Contrasting Ricchi, Ergas argues in his *Shomer Emunim* against a literal *Tzimtzum,* seeing it as metaphorical. He suggests a withdrawal of God's full manifestation, where the Divine Light is present but concealed within creation, like a dimmed light.

❑ R. SHNEUR ZALMAN OF LIADI also favors a non-literal interpretation, seeing *Tzimtzum* as a dynamic process of divine revelation and concealment. In one letter, he wrote regarding the Vilna Gaon's strident position that the notion "'He fills all worlds' and 'there is no place devoid of Him' literally, and in his eyes, this is complete heresy, to say that He, blessed be He, is literally found in lowly and inferior things, and for this reason . . ." And for this reason, he had the Tanya burnt.[111]

❑ RABBI ELIJAH BEN SOLOMON ZALMAN, THE VILNA GAON, conversely asserts that the *Tzimtzum* signifies God's partial withdrawal but maintains the integrity of His infinite essence. This view emphasizes divine transcendence, suggesting an active divine involvement in creation through hidden channels. He thus leans toward a literal interpretation but with nuances, viewing *Tzimtzum* as a metaphorical withdrawal rather than a physical event.[112] See the entry on HaMakom for more details of his position.

R. HAYYIM VOLOZHIN (the foremost student of the Vilna Gaon) interprets the Kabbalistic concept of *Tzimtzum* (contraction), originating from the teachings of the ARI, uniquely. Instead of viewing *Tzimtzum* as the withdrawal of the divine essence to make space for creation, he sees it as the divine essence donning material "garments." These garments mask the Divine Presence of human perception, leading people to view the universe as a complex system of diverse and seemingly contradictory elements. This perception underlies the need and potential for *Halakhah*, as it sets the boundaries between the sacred and the profane in a world perceived to be filled with contrasting elements.

The image shows a simple, abstract representation of the Tzimtzum, depicting what appears to be a central space or void, with layers of contraction around it. This could be interpreted as the divine essence or the initial spark of creation that remains after God's self-contraction. The surrounding squares may represent the successive stages or veils of concealment that God enacted during the Tzimtzum, creating a structured, finite reality from His infinite essence. The progressive, squared spiral moving inward toward the Aleph suggests a journey back to unity with the divine, reflecting the mystical path of return in Kabbalistic thought.

Later, Kabbalists urged against interpreting *Tzimtzum* in a purely literal sense. They remind us that applying spatial concepts to God is fundamentally flawed. Instead, they suggest understanding *Tzimtzum* on a conceptual level. God's omnipresent light signifies every conceivable notion of perfection, unified in His pure, unadulterated essence. *Tzimtzum,* in this context, represents God's self-imposed limitation of His infinite perfection. This contraction allows for the introduction of "lack" or "darkness," creating a metaphysical "space" for human free will and achievement.

Ricoeur's Lamp in the Tzimtzum Labyrinth

The Lurianic concept of *Tzimtzum*, or Divine contraction, has haunted the halls of Kabbalah for centuries. Is it a literal withdrawal, carving space for the universe? Or a metaphorical dance, veiling and revealing the infinite in the finite? Paul Ricoeur's illuminating ideas on metaphor offer a lamp in this labyrinth, allowing us to navigate the complexities of *Tzimtzüm* with fresh eyes.

Ricoeur saw metaphors as more than rhetorical flourishes. They are cognitive bridges, connecting the abstract to the concrete, the ineffable to the imaginable. *Tzimtzum*, a concept grappling with the very act of creation, demands such bridges. Is it not, to borrow Ricoeur's words, a "cunning distortion," defying literal translation yet pulsating with meaning?Through this lens, we see the richness of diverse interpretations. Ricchi's literal *Tzimtzum*, a physical shrinking of the Divine Light, sparks discomfort. Does it imply spatial limitations to God? Ricoeur offers a different picture, suggesting a self-limitation of God's infinite perfection, not a physical retreat. This "lack" or "darkness" then becomes the canvas for creation, the space for human agency to flourish.

Ergas' metaphorical *Tzimtzum*, a dimming of the divine light within creation, resonates with this dynamic play of presence and absence. It evokes the mystical experience, where God is felt not as an external object, but as an inner spark, veiled yet vibrant. Similarly, Volozhin's "garments" metaphor paints a picture of the divine cloaked in the material world, its essence hidden within the intricate mosaic of existence. This veiling, Ricoeur reminds us, does not diminish the divine; it invites exploration, a mystical quest to peel back the layers and glimpse the infinite within the finite.

The Vilna Gaon's nuanced stance, a partial withdrawal that preserves God's infinite essence, further underscores the value of metaphor. Literal interpretations, Ricoeur warns, can lead to theological pitfalls. Instead, the metaphor allows for ambiguity, paradox, and ongoing contemplation. *Tzimtzum*, in this light, becomes an invitation to wrestle with the unanswerable, to grapple with the enigmatic relationship between the divine and the cosmos.

Ultimately, Ricoeur's contribution is not to settle the *Tzimtzum* debate but to enrich it. His metaphorical lens reminds us that Kabbalah is not a dry doctrinal manual, but a poetic mosaic woven with paradox and mystery. It invites us to engage with *Tzimtzum* not as a fixed answer, but as a living question, an evolving narrative that speaks to the human yearning for connection with the ineffable.

This approach, as Ricoeur suggests, fosters not only intellectual rigor but also imaginative flexibility. It allows us to embrace the multiple shades of meaning within *Tzimtzum,* the dance of concealment and revelation, the interplay of infinite and finite that lies at the heart of divine-human connection. With Ricoeur's lamp in hand, we can move beyond literal pitfalls and enter the labyrinth of *Tzimtzum*, not as tourists seeking answers, but as seekers embracing the mystery.

Paul Ricoeur's insights on metaphor enrich this discussion, suggesting that metaphors are cognitive tools bridging the abstract with the concrete. *Tzimtzum*, thus, can be seen as a "cunning distortion" that defies literal interpretation, inviting deeper contemplation of the divine and the universe. Ricoeur's perspective allows for a richer understanding of *Tzimtzum*, advocating for metaphorical interpretations that avoid theological pitfalls and open up new avenues for spiritual exploration.

Although Ricoeur's approach does not resolve the *Tzimtzum* debate, but adds depth to it. His metaphorical lens shows that Kabbalah is not just a set of doctrines but a poetic exploration of divine mysteries. *Tzimtzum* becomes a living question, encouraging intellectual rigor and imaginative exploration of the divine-human connection. With this understanding, we can approach the *tzimtzum* not merely for answers but as a part of a journey into the heart of mystical thought.

Tzimtzum as a Feminine Process

The Kabbalistic doctrine of *Tzimtzum,* traditionally conceptualized as a masculine act of divine self-withdrawal, has long captivated and challenged theological and philosophical minds. However, a fresh and inclusive interpretation rooted in feminist thought offers a compelling reimagining of this concept. This perspective compares the *Tzimtzum* to the contractions experienced by a woman during labor. Such an analogy significantly broadens our comprehension of *tzimtzum*, depicting it as a cosmic birthing process, intricately tied to the feminine qualities of the Divine.

This metaphorical approach positions *Tzimtzum* as not just a contraction or concealment of the Divine but as an essential and rhythmic process akin to the natural cycles of childbirth. In this process, akin to a mother's labor pains facilitating the emergence of new life, the *Tzimtzum* becomes a dynamic, life-giving act. It transforms the understanding of creation from being a mere act of making space into a nurturing and generative process, where the feminine aspects of divinity are vital and central. It's crucial to note that when we speak of the Divine in terms of "feminine" or "masculine," we tread in the realm of metaphor. These terms are not meant to anthropomorphize God or ascribe literal gender, but rather to express the diverse attributes and energies inherent in the Divine nature. In Kabbalistic thought, the balance and interplay of masculine and feminine qualities are essential to understanding the complex nature of the Divine and the universe.

In this feminist reading, the concepts of Malchut and Shekhinah in Jewish mystical thought, traditionally associated with the feminine Divine, gain deeper significance. *Malchut,* representing the manifestation of the Divine in the physical world, mirrors the role of the womb during childbirth — a receptive and nurturing space where life is formed and realized. *Shekhinah*, often seen as the indwelling Presence of God, parallels the active nurturing force in the birthing process, embodying the care and connection essential to bringing forth new existence.

This reinterpretation of *Tzimtzum* challenges and enriches traditional perspectives, highlighting the importance of the feminine in the creative divine act. It suggests that creation is not merely a top-down, paternal process but a deeply maternal one, involving nurture, care, and connection. The metaphor of childbirth in *Tzimtzum* brings to light the profound interconnectedness and reciprocity between the Creator and creation, akin to the bond shared between a mother and her child.

Religious imagery is tailored to the imaginative faculties of the human mind and soul. This black and white image symbolically captures the essence of the Shekhinah, a concept in Jewish mysticism representing the Divine Presence. The ethereal, almost intangible form at the center exudes a radiant glow, suggesting a divine and transcendent nature. The figure is enveloped by gentle, flowing shapes that evoke a sense of spiritual connection and unity with the cosmos. The soft, indistinct features of the figure transcend specific human form, embodying a universal spiritual essence. This is accentuated by the minimalist background, using light and shadow to create an atmosphere of peace, grace, and spiritual profundity. The overall composition of the image invites a contemplation of the Divine, reflecting the Shekhinah's role as a bridge between the earthly and the heavenly.

In conclusion, the metaphor of childbirth in the context of *Tzimtzum* offers a powerful, feminist lens through which we can explore and appreciate the diversity and complexity of the Divine. This approach not only adds depth and nuance to our understanding of Kabbalistic concepts but also invites us to embrace a more holistic view of the Divine, recognizing and celebrating the harmonious coexistence of both masculine and feminine aspects within the realm of the sacred... SEE THE ENTRY ON THE *SHEKHINAH.*

חָלָל

THE CHALAL: THE DIVINE EMPTINESS

The concept of "*Chalal*" (חלל), often translated as "empty space" or "vacuum," is central to the Kabbalistic doctrine of *Tzimtzum*, introduced by the 16th-century mystic Rabbi Isaac Luria, also known as the Ari. In Lurianic Kabbalah, *Tzimtzum* describes a process where God, *Ein Sof* (the Infinite), voluntarily contracted Himself to create a conceptual space for the universe to exist.

The *Chalal* represents this metaphorical space that emerged as a result of God's self-contraction. It is not "empty" in the usual sense, as it does not imply the absence of God. Rather, it is a state where God's presence is hidden or diminished to allow for the existence of a finite, diverse world that is not overwhelmed by divine omnipresence. This concealment is necessary for creation to maintain its distinct existence and for free will to operate.

In this mystical framework, the creation of the *Chalal* is seen as a necessary precondition for the subsequent stages of creation. After the *Tzimtzum* and the formation of the *Chalal*, divine light was reintroduced into this space in a controlled and limited manner through the Sefirot, the ten attributes or emanations of God in *Kabbalah*. These Sefirot structure the flow of divine energy into the *Chalal*, giving rise to all of creation.

The concept of *Chalal* is deeply philosophical and symbolic. It deals with paradoxes such as how the finite can emerge from the Infinite, and how God's omnipresence can coexist with a world that appears to be separate from its Creator. This concept underscores the Kabbalistic view of the dynamic interplay between divine transcendence and immanence, and the ongoing relationship between the Creator and creation.

Analogies to Understand the "Chalal"

The concept of the "empty *Chalal*" in Kabbalistic thought can be challenging to comprehend, as it deals with abstract ideas of Divine Presence and absence. To better understand this concept, here are three analogies:

- ❑ THE CANVAS AND THE ARTIST: Imagine an artist with a blank canvas. The canvas represents the "empty space," and the artist symbolizes the Divine. Initially, the canvas is empty, void of any images or colors, just as the *Chalal* is void of any finite forms or manifestations. The artist's decision to leave a part of the canvas blank allows for the creation of a distinct image. Similarly, in *Tzimtzum*, God contracts to leave a "space" where creation can unfold, distinct from His overwhelming presence.

- ❑ THE SILENCE IN MUSIC: Consider a piece of music where the power of the composition is not just in the notes played, but also in the pauses or silences between them. These moments of silence can be likened to the *Chalal* – a necessary absence that allows the notes (the creation) to be appreciated and understood in their distinct form. The silence doesn't mean the absence of the music; rather, it is an integral part of the musical expression, just as the "empty" space in *Tzimtzum* is an essential aspect of God's creative process.

- ❑ A PARENT AND A CHILD'S GROWTH: Think of a parent teaching a child to ride a bike. Initially, the parent holds the bike, guiding and supporting the child. However, there comes a moment when the parent must let go, creating a space for the child to ride independently. This action is similar to the *Chalal*; God "contracts" His presence, creating a space where creation can exist and function independently, allowing for free will and individual growth within the divine plan. These analogies are meant to provide a metaphorical understanding of the complex Kabbalistic concept of the *Chalal* and are not to be taken as literal explanations. They illustrate the idea of creating a necessary space or absence for the manifestation and appreciation of distinct, independent entities or experiences.

- A TEACHER AND STUDENT RELATIONSHIP: The analogy of a teacher creating space to introduce a sophisticated idea to a student can indeed be likened to the Kabbalistic concept of *Chalal* within the doctrine of *Tzimtzum*. This comparison provides a relatable and concrete way to understand a deeply abstract and mystical concept. In the context of education, when a teacher introduces a complex or advanced idea to students, they often have to first create a conceptual space in the students' minds. This involves clearing away or setting aside pre-existing notions or simpler concepts to make room for new, more sophisticated ideas. The teacher might do this by simplifying or holding back certain elements of the full concept initially, allowing the students to grasp the foundational aspects before delving into more complex details. This process mirrors the *Tzimtzum*, where God's contraction is seen as a necessary precondition for creation and comprehension within a finite realm.

Further Thoughts on the Teacher-Student Analogy

Let us expand on the last illustration. Just as God contracted His infinite light to create a space where the finite universe could exist, a teacher must create an intellectual environment conducive to learning new concepts. This might involve simplifying explanations, using metaphors, or connecting new ideas to familiar ones, thereby making the learning process more accessible and less overwhelming.

In Lurianic Kabbalah, after the initial *Tzimtzum* and formation of the *Chalal,* the divine light is reintroduced in a controlled and measured way through the *Sefirot.* Similarly, a teacher introduces complex ideas gradually, building upon what students already know and can comprehend. This step-by-step approach allows students to absorb and integrate new knowledge without being overwhelmed, much like the controlled reintroduction of divine light.

The creation of the *Chalal* in Kabbalah is not merely about the absence of the divine, but about enabling the existence of a realm where free will and independent exploration are possible. In a classroom setting, once the initial groundwork is laid, students are encouraged to explore, question, and engage with the new concepts on their own. This independent exploration is crucial for deeper understanding and personal growth. Just as the *Chalal* represents a state of hidden or diminished Divine Presence, a teacher guides students through the known (familiar concepts) and the unknown (new, complex ideas). This journey helps students understand and appreciate the depth and breadth of the subject matter.

Ultimately, the analogy of a teacher creating space for a sophisticated idea is a potent way to grasp the essence of *Tzimtzum* and *Chalal.* It underscores the necessity of creating a receptive space for growth and understanding, whether in the cosmic sense of creation or a student's intellectual development. This comparison demystifies the Kabbalistic concept and highlights the dynamic interplay between teaching and learning, revelation and concealment, and the expansion of knowledge within a structured environment.

רֵשִׁימוֹ

THE RESHIMU: THE "DIVINE TRACE"

In Kabbalistic thought, the concept of *Reshimu*, which roughly translates as "imprint" or "trace," is often compared to notation in a book. This metaphorical comparison illustrates the subtle yet significant role of *Reshimu* in the process of creation as described in the Lurianic Kabbalah.

- Just as notations in a book serve as a foundational guide for the development of ideas, *reshimu* represents the foundational divine imprint left after the *Tzimtzum* (the 'contraction' of the divine light). It provides a template or a basic outline for the subsequent process of creation.

❑ In addition, notations in a book are usually brief, subtle hints or marks, yet they hold the potential for more complex development. Similarly, the *reshimu,* being the faint residual presence of the Divine Light, is subtle but contains the potential for the entire structure of creation to unfold.

❑ Notations in a book imply something beyond themselves; they point to a larger body of knowledge or content that is not immediately present. In a similar sense, the *reshimu* is the remaining trace of the withdrawn divine light, signifying the presence within absence— the hidden presence of the Divine in the post-*Tzimtzum* void.

❑ Furthermore, just as notations can act as a blueprint for further writing, the *reshimu* acts as a divine blueprint for the unfolding cosmos. It's the initial, abstract template from which the detailed and varied forms of the universe eventually emerge.

In essence, this comparison to notations in a book helps to convey the idea that *reshimu*, while a mere "trace," plays a crucial role in the Kabbalistic understanding of creation. It is the initial, subtle hint of the Divine Presence that lays the groundwork for the complex and diverse manifestations of the material and spiritual universe.

הַמָּקוֹם -- HaMakom

God as the Omnipresent One

Since the time of biblical writers, Judaic thought and Jewish thinkers such as Philo have long contemplated the theme of God's Presence and absence in the world. In Jewish mysticism, the term הַמָּקוֹם "the *Makom*," translated as "Omnipresent One," posits the Divine as the fundamental existential space in which the universe is situated. This profound conception, while it underscores God's omnipresence, also skirts the edge of pantheistic interpretations, potentially obfuscating the essential distinctions between the sacred and the secular and between good and evil.

As we noted earlier, R. Shneur Zalman of Liadi, Hasidic Judaism, articulated the notion of divine immanence with potent vigor. Reflecting the ideas of the Baal Shem Tov and his teacher, R. Dov Baer of Mezritch, RSZ's teachings conveyed the monistic idea that God's Presence suffuses all creation, implying that every element of the material world, no matter how mundane or lowly, is a manifestation of the Divine. This perspective intimates that there exists no true reality apart from God and, by extension, suggests that even entities traditionally viewed as "evil" are infused with a divine essence, albeit in a concealed or diminished form.

The Mitnagdim view the *Tzimtzum* as God's deliberate self-limitation, carving a metaphysical void where the universe could stand apart. This doctrine draws a sharp line: the infinite Creator retracts His essence, birthing a finite realm that, to us, feels separate—a chasm preserving divine transcendence. The Hasidim, by contrast, see *Tzimtzum* as no literal retreat but a veil, a dimming of *Ein Sof's* boundless light. For them, God doesn't withdraw—He hides, His Presence pulsing through every layer of existence, a radiant thread weaving the infinite into the finite. Where Mitnagdim guard the divide, Hasidim blur it, whispering of divinity's nearness in all things.

Kabbalistic Disputes Regarding Divine Immanence

R. Elijah ben Solomon Zalman (a.k.a. the Vilna Gaon [GRA]), an 18th-century rabbinical authority, voiced significant concerns regarding the Hasidic interpretation of divine immanence. He perceived a looming danger in the Hasidic portrayal of God as pervading all aspects of creation, including the most profane. The GRA feared that such a view could lead to a dilution of the distinction between holiness and impurity, potentially resulting in theological confusion and ethical ambiguity, as seen repeatedly during the apostasy of Shabbatai Sevi and Jacob Frank, who believed in a concept Gershom Scholem described as "redemption through sin."[113] Indeed, many of the early Hasidim often disregarded normative Jewish law regarding prayer and other ritual observances. The GRA's critique of Hasidism centered on their view of divine immanence as potentially heretical and behaviorally dangerous, fearing it could lead to a loss of value discrimination.

Furthermore, the GRA challenged the Hasidic understanding of the biblical verse, בָּרוּךְ כְּבוֹד־יְהוָה מִמְּקוֹמוֹ "Blessed be the glory of the Lord from His place" (Ezek. 3:12). He argued that this verse does not speak of God's immanence, or His Presence within all things, but rather it highlights God's transcendence and His providential care over creation. The GRA posited that the essence of God cannot be contained within the physical realm, and the verse should be understood as praising God's overarching authority and Presence throughout the universe.

The Hasidic belief that God can be served through every facet of life, transforming even the most mundane elements into sacred opportunities, was groundbreaking. Rooted in the conviction of God's omnipresence, Hasidism taught that the physical world could be a conduit for spiritual growth. The Baal Shem Tov (BESHT), the founder of Hasidic Judaism, emphasized that during moments of spiritual focus, such as prayer or Torah study, even fleeting or distracting thoughts could become pathways to divine connection

Yet, this monistic view of an all-pervading divinity posed significant philosophical challenges. The Vilna Gaon countered that normative Judaism traditionally emphasizes the importance of discerning between good and evil, sacred and secular, and the Hasidic doctrine threatened to blur these crucial boundaries. The GRA maintained that Divine Providence inherently involves value discrimination, reinforcing the distinctions between right and wrong, pure and impure.

The dispute between the Hasidic and Mitnagdim perspectives reflects a broader tension within Jewish thought regarding the nature of God's relationship to the world. It highlights the contrast between a philosophy that sees divinity in every aspect of creation and one that maintains a separation between the Creator and His creations. Thus, the debate over divine immanence and transcendence within Judaism reveals the complexity of understanding God's nature and presence in the world. It underscores Jewish theology's dynamic and multifaceted nature, which continues to engage and challenge scholars and practitioners alike. [SEE ENTRY ON THE *TZIMTZUM* AND SPARKS]

אָדָם קַדְמוֹן
ADAM KADMON

In Kabbalah's rich mystical imagery, the celestial figure of *Adam Kadmon*, or the "Primordial Man," embodies divine wisdom and intention, serving as the archetypal blueprint for creation. Unlike the earthly Adam from Genesis, *Adam Kadmon* is a divine figure, free from the confines of time and space, predating the universe and life itself.[114] Born from the *tzimtzum*—God's self-limitation of infinite light — *Adam Kadmon* initiates existence, connecting the divine essence with our tangible cosmos. Existing outside of Kabbalah's four spiritual worlds, *Adam Kadmon* embodies the potentiality of all that could be. It encapsulates the cyclical and paradoxical nature of existence, being both the beginning and the end. Through *Adam Kadmon*, divine emanation illuminates the cosmos, shaping all realities that follow. This celestial blueprint represents creation's potential — the spiritual DNA encoding endless possibilities.

Kabbalists seek to understand this Primordial Man, hoping to decipher the divine intention behind our physical universe and the spiritual origins of existence. *Adam Kadmon* guides their exploration of the divine, offering glimpses into the profound mystery at the heart of life and creation. Not to be confused with the earthly Adam from Genesis, *Adam Kadmon* is the primary emanation following the *Tzimtzum*, bridging the limitless divine essence and our cosmos. This celestial figure, embodying the raw potential of creation, is seen as the metaphysical prototype of humanity and a reflection of the divine. This distinction between the physical and spiritual realms underlines the Kabbalistic belief in their interconnected yet distinct natures.

Adam Kadmon & Philo's Logos

The profound insights of Kabbalistic thought while emerging long after Philo of Alexandria's time, bear striking resemblances to the teachings of this Hellenistic Jewish philosopher from the 1st century C.E. Philo, known for his pioneering efforts to merge Jewish theology with Greek philosophy, especially Platonism, laid a foundation that, in various ways, anticipates key themes later developed in Kabbalah. In the interest of brevity, let us focus on some of the key ideas they share:

- **COMMONALITIES IN THE LOGOS AND ADAM KADMON:** Philo introduced the concept of the Logos, a divine intermediary between God and the physical world. The Logos serves as God's instrument in the creation and the manifestation of His thoughts, much like Adam Kadmon, which represents the initial divine intention and the blueprint for creation.

- **EMANATIONIST THEOLOGY:** Philo's ideas about the Logos echo the Kabbalistic concept of Sefirot and the process of divine emanation. Like the *Sefirot*, the Logos is a mediator through which God interacts with the world, a concept that closely resembles how the early Jewish mystics viewed Adam Kadmon as an emanation bridging the infinite Divine with the finite cosmos.

- **METAPHYSICAL DUALISM:** Both Philo and Kabbalah emphasize a distinction between the physical and spiritual realms. Philo's philosophy posits a higher, spiritual reality that transcends the material world. Similarly, Kabbalistic thought, as seen in the idea of Adam Kadmon, distinguishes between the spiritual origins of existence and their physical manifestations.

- **THE ARCHETYPAL SCHEME OF HUMAN CONSCIOUSNESS:** Philo viewed the biblical Adam as a symbolic representation of humanity in its ideal state, living in harmony with God and nature — a concept that aligns with the Kabbalistic view of Adam Kadmon as the archetypal human and the prototype of all creation.

- **INFLUENCE ON MYSTICAL THOUGHT:** While a direct influence of Philo's work on Kabbalah is hard to ascertain, his ideas likely contributed to the pool of Jewish mystical thought that eventually culminated in Kabbalah. His blend of Jewish theology and Greek philosophy could have laid the groundwork for later mystical interpretations of Jewish scripture, which are central to Kabbalistic teachings.

In short, while Philo of Alexandria and the Kabbalistic concept of Adam Kadmon belong to different eras and intellectual traditions, their ideas share intriguing similarities. Both deal with themes of divine intermediaries, the duality of the spiritual and material realms, and the symbolic representation of the ideal or primordial human. These similarities highlight a continuity in Jewish thought, exploring the relationship between the divine, the cosmos, and humanity.

אור LIGHT

Light as a Biblical Metaphor

The concept of light is central in numerous narratives, often appearing as a symbol of creation, order, and protection. Physical light, frequently depicted as the very origin of life, elicits a sense of awe and wonder. Light serves as a fundamental counterforce to darkness, establishing a dichotomy that pervades numerous stories and allegories. In biblical writings, light is presented as God's creation, distinct from its Creator (Ps. 148:5). In this respect, light becomes an index pointing to the divine, rather than being deified itself as depicted in numerous mythical traditions. It's an essential element in the archetypal struggle between light and darkness (Gen 1:4), symbolizing rulership and order in the universe (Gen. 1:16). It's seen as a mysterious force (Job 38:19, 38:24), whose absence instills fear (Job 12:25, Isa. 5:30).

The Illuminating Metaphor: Light in Kabbalistic Thought

Light is not merely a physical phenomenon in Kabbalah; it is deeply woven into the fabric of its teachings, illuminating profound spiritual concepts. This potent metaphor transcends the material realm, becoming a multifaceted lens through which Kabbalists contemplate the divine, creation, and their own path toward enlightenment.

❑ **MANIFESTATION OF THE INEFFABLE:** Just as physical light banishes darkness, divine light in Kabbalah represents the emanation of God, unveiling the unknowable to the human mind. It's a radiant bridge between the infinite divine essence and our finite world, offering glimpses of the ineffable through its illuminating glow.

❑ **A COSMIC DANCE OF LIGHT:** The Kabbalistic narrative of creation, particularly the *Tzimtzum* (contraction), places light at the center stage. Here, God, initially filling all existence, withdraws, creating a void into which the divine light pours forth, birthing the cosmos. This celestial ballet of light symbolizes the flow of divine energy into creation, a luminous thread connecting the transcendent and the tangible.

❑ **A PATH LIT BY INNER ILLUMINATION:** For Kabbalists, light isn't just external; it's a beacon within, guiding the journey toward spiritual enlightenment. The pursuit of wisdom and connection with the divine is itself a quest for this inner light, a gradual ascent toward an ever-brighter understanding of the universe and our place within it.

❑ **THE PRISM OF THE SEFIROT:** The Kabbalistic Tree of Life, a map of the divine attributes, becomes a canvas painted with the spectrum of divine light. Each Sefira, a facet of the divine essence, shimmers with a distinct color or aspect of light, revealing the multifaceted nature of God within creation. This metaphor showcases the interplay of unity and diversity, demonstrating how the singular divine light refracts into the multitude of attributes and experiences we encounter in the world.

❑ **PARADOXES ILLUMINATED:** Light in Kabbalah embraces the paradoxical nature of the Divine. Just as white light encompasses all colors, the Divine Presence pervades all aspects of creation, both the holy and the seemingly profane. This seemingly contradictory image illuminates the profound unity underlying the apparent diversity of the universe, revealing the omnipresence of God even in the darkest corners of existence.

When contemplating the metaphor of light in Jewish mysticism, we must realize it is not merely used as a literary flourish; Light is a dynamic instrument for comprehending the complex relationships between the divine, creation, and the human soul. By delving into its depths, we gain a deeper appreciation for the intricate mosaic of Kabbalistic thought, illuminating the path toward self-understanding and a more profound connection with the divine spark within and around us.

Light emerges as a paramount symbol that mirrors the profound relationship between God and the universe. Not merely confined to physical luminescence, the concept of light in Kabbalah transcends to reflect divine wisdom, the process of creation, and the illuminating presence of God within all creation. The intricate Kabbalistic framework employs this symbol through the metaphor of "sparks of holiness" (*nitzotzot*), which signify the fragments of divinity embedded within the material world, that humanity is tasked to elevate, marking their role in Tikkun Olam - the repair of the world.

Light According to the Kabbalah

As previously noted, underneath this kaleidoscopic canopy of divine light lies the Tree of Life, a Kabbalistic model embodying ten spheres, or *Sephiroth*. Each *Sefira* symbolizes a unique emanation of God's light, simultaneously revealing and veiling the divine, and facilitating the perpetual creation of both the physical and the metaphysical realms. An indispensable aspect of Kabbalistic thought is the concept of *Tzimtzum* - the self-constriction or withdrawal of God's light. R. Isaac Luria proposes that God's light, in order to make room for the universe, withdrew, leaving behind an "empty space" (*chalal panui*). Into this void, God projected a slender line of light (*kav*), which became the canvas upon which the universe was painted. Hence, this divine light intertwines with the fabric of all creation, infusing it with Divine Presence and guidance.

Light of the Ein Sof

Simultaneously, within the complex matrix defining Kabbalistic lore, the *Ohr Ein Sof* (אוֹר אֵין סוֹף) the "Light of the Infinite," emerges as a key notion. It epitomizes the most ethereal level of divine manifestation, capturing the transcendental facets of God, which remain ultimately beyond human comprehension. Before creation, only the *Ein Sof,* the infinite or endless, existed, a state of being beyond conceptualization and distinction. To facilitate creation, differentiation, and relationality, the *Ein Sof* radiated its light—the *Ohr Ein Sof.* This divine light, infused into the void post-Tzimtzum, initiated the creative process, eventually culminating in the formation of the ten *Sephiroth.*

Yet, even amidst this effulgence, the *Or Ein Sof* retains its transcendent nature, reflecting God's boundless aspect, while the Sephirot mirrors God's immanent, definable attributes. This delicate balance paints a vivid image of how the divine reality harmonizes transcendence and immanence, bringing both to life through the metaphor of light.

אורות כלים

OROT AND KELIM

Lights and Vessels

In Kabbalistic esoteric teachings, the concept of the *Sefirot* is essential, serving as divine dimensions that interpret and manage God's infinite essence. This makes His attributes discernible to His creations. These *Sefirot* are envisioned as both filters and vessels for the divine radiance, drawing multifaceted meanings from Hebrew words. They function as *orot* (Lights), revealing God's majesty, and as *kelim* (Vessels), channeling His boundless light into the tangible realm. This dual role of the *s* provides profound insights into the nature of divine manifestation and the purpose of creation, forming a bridge between the spiritual and physical worlds. Each *Sefirah* acts as a unique filter, shaping the expression of divine energy.

The *kelim,* as containers, are crucial in holding, regulating, and transmitting these divine energies. The nature of the *kelim* significantly affects how the divine lights are manifested. Crucially, in our world, we are tasked with creating and preparing these vessels to adequately contain and express the divine light. Our actions and intentions, therefore, play a vital role in shaping these vessels, making us active participants in the divine process.

Before proceeding, let us define our terms.

In Biblical Hebrew, the term כְּלִי (*keli*) primarily refers to an article, utensil, or vessel. It originates from the root כָּלָה, meaning something finished or made. The concept of a כְּלִי "vessel" in Kabbalah offers a rich metaphorical framework to understand the dynamics of reality and its intricate connection with the divine. This notion is multi-dimensional, encompassing various layers of spiritual and existential understanding.

At the heart of the vessel metaphor is the idea of containment and reception of divine light. Much like a physical container that holds liquids, Kabbalistic vessels are envisaged as structures capable of receiving and manifesting divine emanations. They symbolize the interface between the infinite divine and the finite world. The Kabbalistic tradition posits different types of vessels, each signifying a distinct level of capability to receive and reflect the divine light. Some vessels are depicted as robust and refined, capable of containing the divine light in its purest form. Others, less resilient, are prone to breakage, symbolizing the imperfections and imbalances that arise in creation.

The relationship between *orot* and *kelim* – the divine energies and their vessels – is essential for the harmonious unfolding of creation and spiritual evolution. Weak vessels may shatter under the force of divine energies, leading to spiritual turmoil, while overly rigid vessels can obstruct the flow of divine light, limiting spiritual expression. This highlights the importance of *tikkun* (rectification), a process of enhancing and fortifying the vessels to better align with divine energies. Through *tikkun*, the vessels are improved to channel the divine light more accurately and effectively.

In essence, the *Sefirot,* with their balance of *orot* and *kelim*, offers a complex yet enlightening framework for understanding Divine Presence and interaction in the universe. Our role in crafting these vessels underscores our responsibility in the spiritual domain, emphasizing the need for continuous personal growth and refinement in our spiritual journey. This active engagement in preparing vessels for the divine light not only deepens our connection with the Divine but also aligns the spiritual and material aspects of our existence, fostering a more integrated and holistic approach to understanding and living within the universe.

עולם התהו
THE WORLD OF TOHU

In Jewish mystical teachings, *Tohu* represents a primordial state of chaos that preceded the orderly creation of the world. It is associated with shattered vessels or flawed structures that were unable to contain the divine light. These vessels shattered due to their inability to withstand the intense divine energy and fell into a state of fragmentation. The process of repairing and rectifying this chaos is known as *Tikkun* (rectification)... These stages represent different states or levels of spiritual and cosmic development. Each stage represents a progression in the process of creation, moving from chaos and fragmentation toward unity, structure, and harmony.

> THE ANALOGY: Imagine a newly started jigsaw puzzle with pieces scattered all around. Each piece represents a fragment of potential, but they are not yet connected, resulting in a chaotic and disorganized state. This is akin to *Olam HaTohu*, where the divine light is like the potential each puzzle piece holds, yet they are scattered and uncontained, leading to

disorder and fragmentation. This realm represents the primordial state of chaos that preceded the orderly creation of the world. It is a realm where the divine light is not properly contained within vessels, leading to a state of fragmentation and disorder. The world of Tohu signifies shattered or flawed vessels that were unable to contain the flow of this intense divine energy. From *Tohu,* the divine light undergoes further refinement in the nascent spiritual evolution of the world and consciousness. These states are:

❑ AKUDIM (עֲקוּדִים = "World of Binding"): Following *Tohu*, *Akudim* represents a stage where the shattered vessels begin to be reconfigured and bound together, signifying the initial steps toward reintegration and unity, though the rectification is not complete.

> THE ANALOGY: Imagine a group of people, initially strangers, who are stranded and must work together to survive. They start to form basic connections, sharing resources and communicating to address immediate needs. These initial bonds are fragile and not deeply integrated, but they represent the first steps toward unity and collaboration. This scenario is similar to *Akudim*, where the shattered vessels of *Tohu* begin to connect and bind, forming a rudimentary but crucial framework of cohesion and unity. *Akudim* is thus the stage that follows *Olam Hatohu.* It represents a level of unity and binding, where the shattered vessels of Tohu are reconfigured and bound together. In *Akudim,* the vessels are not fully repaired or rectified, but they are brought into a state of connection and cohesion. This stage signifies the initial attempt to reintegrate the shattered elements of Tohu.

❑ NIKUDIM (נְקוּדִים = "World of Points"): After *Akudim*, comes *Nikudim.* This stage is marked by further rectification and refinement. The vessels take on the form of points or dots, indicating a more organized and structured approach to containing the divine light.

THE ANALOGY: Picture a sophisticated orchestra where each musician represents a point or vessel. Initially, the musicians play independently, each producing their own unique sound. As they start to follow the conductor's guidance, their individual notes begin to align, creating a harmonious and balanced melody. In *Nikudim*, the vessels are like these musicians, each distinct yet contributing to a collective harmony under the guidance of the divine light, akin to the conductor. This stage symbolizes a transition from individuality to a more structured and synchronized unity, reflecting the orderly and balanced nature of *Nikudim*. Here, the divine light begins to manifest within these refined vessels in a more organized and structured manner. The stage of *nikudim* is characterized by a more stable and balanced state compared to the previous stages.

❑ BERUDIM (בְּרוּדִים = "World of Connection"); *Berudim* is the final stage in this sequence. It represents a higher level of rectification, where the vessels are interconnected in a network or system, allowing for a more complete and harmonious integration of the divine light.

THE ANALOGY: This can be best compared to an intricately designed skyscraper. This skyscraper is not just a collection of floors, rooms, hallways, and staircases; each element is a vessel, thoughtfully crafted and interconnected to form a cohesive and harmonious whole. The design ensures that every component of the building is accessible, integrated, and functions seamlessly with the others, mirroring the smooth and purposeful movement of people within its confines. This architectural analogy aptly symbolizes the essence of *Berudim*. In this stage, the concept of connection and integration is paramount. The vessels, representing various aspects of the divine creation, are no longer isolated entities. They evolve, develop, and intertwine, forming sophisticated networks or systems akin to the complex pathways and junctions within a skyscraper.

As the final stage before the transition to the realms *of Atzilut, Beriah, Yetzirah,* and *Asiyah, Berudim* signifies a critical point in the creation process. The divine light within this stage undergoes a profound integration within these vessels. This integration is not just a mere aggregation of light; it represents a harmonious blending that elevates the entire structure, much like the way a skyscraper's design isn't only about individual floors but about how these floors come together to form a magnificent edifice.

> *Berudim* thus represents a significant leap in the order and structure of the divine creation process. It is a stage where the earlier fragmented and chaotic elements are connected and organized into a system greater than the sum of its parts. In its flow through these vessels, the divine light brings about a level of harmony and functionality that sets the stage for the subsequent, more advanced realms. *Berudim* is about laying down a foundation of intricate connections and relationships that prepare the path for a more complex, cohesive, and elevated form of creation.

In retrospect, the realm of *Tohu, Akudim, Nikudim, and Berudim* describes the process of creation and the spiritual evolution of the cosmos. It illustrates the journey from a state of chaos and fragmentation toward increasing levels of rectification, harmony, and divine revelation. It's important to note that these stages are complex and symbolic, and their meanings and interpretations can vary among different Kabbalistic traditions and teachings.

Olam HaTohu: The Dynamic Landscape of Chaos and Potential

Olam HaTohu, or the "World of Chaos" from Kabbalistic teachings, transcends its scriptural origins, emerging as a dynamic metaphor for personal, societal, and cosmic evolution. This concept encapsulates the unrefined, tumultuous energy at the core of creation, resonating within our inner selves, our communities, and the cosmos.

Olam HaTohu can be envisioned as the untamed wilderness of our unconscious. Here, thoughts, emotions, and impulses intermingle chaotically, reminiscent of the intense feelings of early childhood or the upheaval following trauma. In the realm of childhood development, *Olam HaTohu* is ever-present. Children's worlds are torrents of raw emotions and undefined experiences. Yet, this apparent disorder harbors transformative power. Therapy and self-reflection guide us in navigating this inner *Olam HaTohu*, helping us construct narratives that transform chaos into clarity and peace. As they grow, our children's cognitive and emotional structures form, steering them toward *Olam HaTikun*'s stability. This parallels the cosmic narrative, where chaos precedes order and structure in creation.

Society, too, experiences *Olam HaTohu* in periods of significant change, be it through revolutions, technological shifts, or natural catastrophes. These epochs fracture established norms, paving the way for new societal architectures. Amidst this chaos lies the seed for constructive change, echoing the Kabbalistic concept of *Tikkun Olam* - the healing and repair of the world. These metaphors are interconnected strands in a vast mosaic. Individual growth influences societal evolution, which in turn reflects in the cosmic scheme. Our journey through personal *Olam HaTohu* shapes the collective progression toward a more harmonious and equitable world.

Olam HaTohu's roots in Judaic mystical traditions add a mystical dimension, positioning it as a precursor to the orderly *Olam HaTikun*. This spiritual aspect enriches the metaphor, framing our encounters with chaos as integral parts of a larger divine narrative. *Olam HaTohu's* relevance extends beyond ancient texts, offering insights into today's global challenges, including environmental crises and societal upheavals. This metaphor provides a lens to comprehend and navigate these tumultuous times, highlighting the potential for profound change and rejuvenation within chaos.

By delving into *Olam HaTohu's* multifaceted nature, we uncover its profound significance. It evolves from a mere Kabbalistic concept into a versatile tool for understanding our individual experiences, societal dynamics, and our role in the universe's grand mélange. In moments of disorder and uncertainty, remember *Olam HaTohu* as a symbol that chaos is not just a state to endure but a crucible for growth, transformation, and the birth of new possibilities.

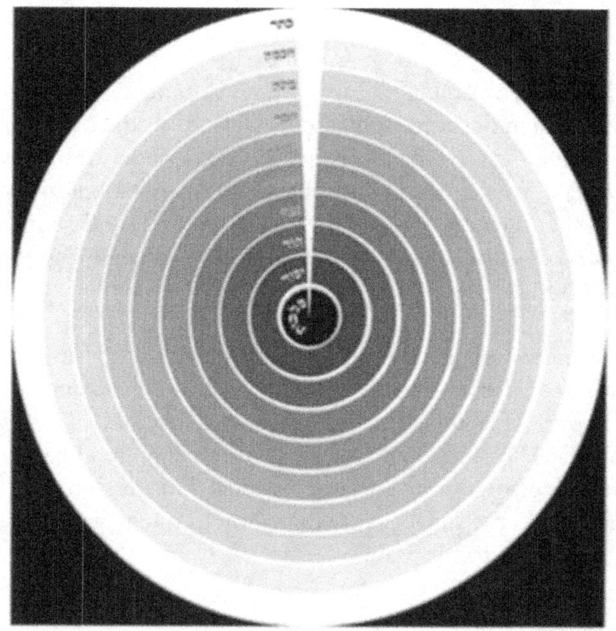

This image depicts Tzimtzum, the Kabbalistic concept of divine contraction, where God creates space for the universe by withdrawing His infinite light. The concentric circles represent the diminishing intensity of Divine Presence, layering reality from the spiritual to the material, with the central void symbolizing God's hidden Presence. The line from the center to the periphery suggests an enduring, subtle connection to the Divine, maintaining the existence of all. The Hebrew labels denote various spiritual realms, mapping the descent from pure divinity to physical existence.

סֵדֶר הִשְׁתַּלְשְׁלוּת

The Chain of Spiritual Worlds

In Lurianic Kabbalistic philosophy, "*Seder Hishtalshelut*" (Hebrew: סֵדֶר הִשְׁתַּלְשְׁלוּת) is a fundamental concept describing the descending chain of spiritual worlds (*Olam/Olamot*) that bridge the gap between God and Creation. It represents the stages through which the divine essence manifests and creates the material universe, marking a gradational process from God's infinite presence to the physical realm.

The term, meaning "order of development" or "order of evolution," signifies a sequential unfolding from the most sublime levels of divinity to the tangible world we experience. It begins with the *Ohr Ein Sof*, or "God's Infinite Light," a paradoxical state of divine self-revelation, transcending all limitations and forms. This stage precedes the creative process and is beyond any worldly constraints.

Lurianic Kabbalah, as developed by Isaac Luria in the 16th century, provides a detailed framework for understanding *Seder Hishtalshelut*. This includes various stages like the *Tzimtzum* (a metaphorical "contraction" of God's infinite light to create a space for the universe), the *reshimu* (the residual "impression" left post-*Tzimtzum*), and the subsequent emanation of divine light through a "line" or "ray" into this void.

The Four Worlds

As we noted earlier, in the mystical heart of Judaism, a profound spectrum gradually unfolds, laying out a cosmic hierarchy of existence. This encompasses the four spiritual realms, known as the Four Worlds. Each world is a layer of existence, interwoven, yet distinct, each a stepping stone from the divine to the mortal, from the ethereal to the tangible.

ATZILUTH, ALSO KNOWN AS THE "WORLD OF EMANATION," resides at the zenith of the celestial order, a realm beyond description, bathed in the luminosity of pure spiritual essence. Untouched by the constraints of physical matter, it is wreathed in a divine radiance that emanates unity in its most undiluted form. In this exalted realm, the ineffable essence of God emanates unimpeded, a testament to *Ein Sof*, the boundless and unconstrained divine entity, the wellspring from whence all creation emerges. *Atziluth* sings a silent symphony of oneness, a canticle of unblemished existence, whose echoes reverberate across the cosmic expanse, guiding all creation with its resounding melody.

Here, the celestial form of *Adam Kadmon*, the Primordial Man, is subtly discernible amidst the grand configuration of the ten sefirot, acting as a divine blueprint for all that exists. This spectral silhouette symbolizes the genesis of all emanations, forming a cosmic conduit between the divine and the manifest. Moreover, in this sacred expanse, *Atziluth* is seen as the celestial embodiment of "Emanation." It glimmers with divine luminosity, tenderly cradling the spiritual forces of divinity, each bound to a distinct name of God as engraved in the sacred verses of the Torah. Revered as the fountainhead of divine inspiration, *Atziluth* resonates with the primal force signified by the first letter of the Tetragrammaton, the *yod*. It encapsulates the potential energy that kindles the spark of all existence, thereby connecting to the profound depths of our spiritual essence, typically concealed beneath the surface of our conscious awareness.

BERIAH IS ALSO KNOWN AS THE "WORLD OF CREATION" Descending into the sphere of *Beriah*, we touch the sanctum of consciousness and ideation, a realm intricately carved from divine wisdom. This is where sacred knowledge crystallizes into palpable form, sculpting the primary conceptual blueprints for all that is yet to bloom in existence. It serves as an ethereal drafting table where nebulous ideas assume definitive contours and the groundbreaking emergence of spiritual consciousness burgeons into personalized existence. Within the majestic folds of *Beriah*, we ascend to where the radiant Throne of Glory sits in resplendent sovereignty over the seven celestial mansions. This mystical realm, wrapped in the sacred verses of *Hekhalot* literature, serves as the divine womb where creation's inception springs forth.

YETZIRAH IS ALSO KNOWN AS THE "WORLD OF FORMATION." *Yetzirah* is not just a realm of existence, it is a celestial symphony. It resounds with the harmonious music of angelic choirs, their voices echoing the ethereal letters of our mental dialogue. Yet, their communication surpasses mere speech, embodying a telepathic intertwining that reverberates in a joyous rhapsody. It is an operatic existence, a divine sonnet that embodies the spiritual resonance of creation. Each note, each rhythm, and each melody harmonize into a universal melody, underscoring the emotive reality and creating a symphony of divine consciousness.

ASIYA IS ALSO KNOWN AS THE "WORLD OF ACTION." As our celestial journey concludes, we find ourselves at *Assiyah,* the "World of Action," the realm of physical reality. Here, the divine essence, having cascaded through the higher planes, becomes wholly encased in matter. *Assiyah* is a world that thrives on action and tangibility, where the spiritual forces from the preceding realms manifest into perceivable reality. *Assiyah* is our world - a complex universe of galaxies, radiant stars, diverse planets, and a multitude of life forms. It's a stage set for the human drama of joy and sorrow, triumph and tribulation, hope and fear. In every element of this world, from the pebble on a path to the leaf rustling in the wind, divine sparks lay hidden, awaiting discovery and elevation back to their divine origin. This divine spark-finding forms our spiritual task, as we assist these sparks in their return journey. *Assiyah* also serves as the dwelling place of the ophanim, the lower order of angels. These celestial beings fulfill their divine duty of battling evil, standing as the divine receivers of humanity's prayers. *Assiyah*, with its spiritual framework, shapes the material cosmos and incorporates both the heavens and our earthly realm.

As the final link in the divine chain of existence, it is within the boundaries of *Assiyah* that the *Sitra Ahra*, the "Other Side," is most evident. This contrasting force offers a challenge and test to the forces of goodness, ensuring that every good act is a choice and not a predestined event. Thus, *Assiyah* represents the delicate balance of light and darkness, encapsulating the complex dance that drives existence forward. The four realms of the Kabbalah are thus interlinked, each a reflection of the other, each a step on a divine journey from the infinite light of Godhead to the finite world of human existence, making the ineffable accessible to the human spirit.

The Four Worlds & The Tetragrammaton

Each of the four worlds is intimately tied to a specific letter of the divine name of God, the Tetragrammaton, YHWH. The worlds emerge like stanzas of a celestial poem, each verse giving voice to a unique facet of the divine essence. At the beginning of all worlds stands *Adam Kadmon*, embodying the archetype of the Primal Man, the purest of all emanations. This realm emerges as the initial stirrings of existence following the mystical event known as *Tzimtzum*, wherein the Infinite Source, *Ein Sof*, contracted to make room for creation. *Adam Kadmon*, with its sublime divine nature, retains a perfect unity with the *Ein Sof*. Although it doesn't correspond to a specific letter of the Divine Name, it is symbolized by the subtle "thorn" of the *Yud*, a potent indicator of its transcendent status, beyond all the worlds that follow.

Descending from this lofty peak, we arrive at the realm of *Atziluth*. This is where the divine emanation, initially born within *Adam Kadmon*, continues to unfold, though with diminished intensity. The realm of *Atziluth* corresponds to the *Yud* (י) of YHWH. While the divine energy here is less intense, *Atziluth* remains close to the *Ein Sof*, ensuring its inherent divinity. It represents a realm on the brink of existence, akin to the faint mark left by a seal - a whisper of reality within the infinite possibility.

This world draws its life-force from *Atziluth*, marking a more significant shift from the divine essence. *Beriah* aligns with the first *Hei* (ה) in the Tetragrammaton. It signifies a transition from the intangible and ethereal to the rudiments of substantial existence, echoing the formative power of divine thought. *Beriah* can be likened to an engraving, with greater tangibility and visibility than the preceding realm, yet still shrouded in subtle mystery.

Yetzirah is also the realm of intense emotion, of feeling, and song. This world is characterized by the letter *vav (ו)*, which symbolizes emotional depth and connectivity. It is the spiritual home of the angels, beings that sing the praises of the divine. Imagine an eternal choir, their voices blending into a harmonious song that celebrates the glory and majesty of the divine. It is said that their melodies echo the rhythms of creation, an endless hymn that reverberates through the universe, filling it with divine energy. Here, in *Yetzirah*, the feeling is the language of existence.

This world is steeped in the emotional hues of divine energy, the spectrum of feelings that range from awe to love, from humility to boundless joy. Each feeling is a note in the celestial symphony, a unique expression of the divine attributes that ripple through *Yetzirah,* painting the realm with the colors of divine emotion. *Yetzirah* thus serves as an emotional conduit between the intellectual divine constructs of *Beriah* and the physical reality of *Asiyah.* It is a testament to the profound power of emotion in the grand scheme of creation, a realm where the heart's song finds harmony with the divine symphony. It is here that we come to understand that to feel, to feel truly, is to touch the divine.

Finally, we reach the world of *Asiyah*, the furthest realm from the *Ein Sof*, synonymous with the final *Hei* (ה) in the divine name. *Asiyah* is sustained by the life-force drawn from *Yetzira,* representing the endpoint of the divine descent into creation. *Asiyah* is the realm of action, the realm where our deeds impact all levels of reality, from the micro to the macro; *Asiya* is a world of dense substance where the divine light is fully clothed in physical form.

This is our world, a place where spirituality intertwines with physicality, where divine sparks hide in plain sight, waiting to be discovered. As we descend through these realms, the divine light becomes increasingly veiled, manifesting in forms more accessible and familiar to human perception. Each realm resonates with specific *Sefirot*, painting a cosmic tableau of the gradual transition from the infinite to the finite. The divine light becomes more comprehensible, more deeply woven into the texture of reality, embedding the unknowable within the reach of human spirituality.

בְּרִיאַת יֵשׁ מֵאַיִן

"Creation from Nothing"

The Grammar of "Creating"

Following in the sequence of divine realms is Beriah. To understand this, it's important to delve into the meaning of the Hebrew verb בָּרָא (*bärä'*)In the *Tanakh*, this term is exclusively used to describe God's unparalleled and effortless act of creation, which is distinct from human creativity that is limited by material constraints. God's creative capacity is limitless, as demonstrated by the concept of *creatio ex nihilo*, or creation from "nothing."[115] This notion illustrates God's unique power to bring into being a world endowed with consciousness.

Modern Hebraists have linked בָּרָא to the South Arabic "*br*," meaning "to build," "bring forth," or "give birth to," and the Aramaic בַּר (*bar*), meaning "child" or "son," as used in "*Bar Mitzvah*" ("son of the precept"). This interpretation aligns with the scriptural theme of "giving birth" to new realities. However, the precise meaning and origin of בָּרָא remain debated. Importantly, the principle of *creatio ex nihilo* does not solely rely on this verb. The creation of light in Genesis, through God's command "Let there be light," exemplifies *creatio per verbum*—"creation from the word"—and offers a mythopoetic insight into reality as a divine creative expression.

Ancient Views of "Creatio Ex Nihilo"

The doctrine of *creatio ex nihilo*, or "creation out of nothing," is a theological concept that has its roots in ancient religious texts and thought, although it's often regarded as a post-biblical idea introduced during the Hellenistic era. Early References: One of the earliest explicit mentions of this doctrine is in 2 Maccabees 7:28, a text written in Greek in the 2nd century B.C.E. The passage illustrates a mother urging her son, who is about to be executed for his faith, to acknowledge that God created the universe and the human race out of nothing. This implies the belief that God, who creates from nothingness, also has the power to resurrect the dead. The Letter of Aristeas, written between 150-100 B.C.E, further supports this doctrine by arguing against the deification of inventors who merely repurpose existing creations, instead of creating the substance of the thing.

Influences from Judaic and Greek Thought: The Wisdom of Solomon, a work from between the 3rd century B.C.E. and early 1st-century C.E, recounts the biblical creation story in terms similar to those in Plato's *Timaeus*, highlighting the creation of the world from "formless matter." This could be seen as a reflection of the concept of *creatio ex nihilo,* but it could also be interpreted differently, and the exact reference (Gen. 1:1 or Gen. 1:2) is uncertain. According to the first-century Judaic thinker Philo of Alexandria, Time itself also came into existence with the appearance of space and matter. However, once creation began, God took the role of an Artist, employing existing raw materials. Josephus explicitly replaced the term "made" with "created" in his writings, emphasizing the belief that God continuously creates the world *ex nihilo*, without the need for pre-existing matter.

Medieval Interpretations of Creatio ex Nihilo

Maimonides (1135-1204) presented his views on creation in his monumental work, *Guide for the Perplexed.* In it, he favored the idea of creation *ex nihilo.* He reasoned that God created the universe out of nothingness, a radical departure from the prevailing Aristotelian view of the eternal existence of matter.

Like Philo of Alexandria, Maimonides argued that the concept of time itself was created when the universe was created, and thus the question of "what was before creation?" is meaningless because time did not exist before creation. Saadia Gaon (882-942), another critical figure in Jewish philosophy, also supports the concept of creation *ex nihilo* in his famous theological work, *The Book of Beliefs and Opinions.* Saadia Gaon similarly argued against the idea of the universe's eternal existence. He provided philosophical and theological arguments to support יֵשׁ מֵאַיִן *(creatio ex nihilo).* He posited that only God is eternal, and everything else, including the universe, had a definite beginning. One of his arguments relies on the finite nature of the universe; if the universe is finite, it must have had a start. Thus, Saadia Gaon, like Maimonides, asserted that God created the world out of absolute nothingness.

"Creatio Ex Nihilo" in the Kabbalah

The Hebrew phrase יֵשׁ מֵאַיִן *(Yesh me'ayin)* translates to "creation from nothing." In Kabbalistic thought, this concept has profound implications for understanding the nature of creation and the relationship between the Divine and the universe. In theological terms, *creatio ex nihilo* expressed the idea that God brought the universe into existence from absolute nothingness. This stands in contrast to the idea of יֵשׁ מִיֵּשׁ *(yesh mi'yesh)*, or "something from something." Kabbalists interpreted the divine process of creation as an emanation (*tzimtzum*) in which God contracted Himself to create a metaphysical space where the universe could exist.

The light of the Divine, symbolizing the Divine creative energy, then filled this space, giving birth to the universe. Among the Kabbalists, R. Shneur Zalman (RSZ) of Liadi rejected the notion of the deists, who believed God abandoned the world and cosmos upon completing it. RSZ countered that creation is not a one-time occurrence, but a continuous process from utter non-being. Such a view reflects a dynamic understanding of reality, wherein the Divine is constantly present and active.[116]

God as "Ayin"

In the Jewish mystical tradition, particularly within Hasidic thought, certain thinkers conceptualize God as *Ayin* (אַיִן), a Hebrew term meaning "nothing." This paradoxical designation does not imply God's non-existence but rather conveys a profound understanding of the Divine as transcending the tangible, everyday reality we perceive. *Ayin* signifies that God is "not-a-thing"—an entity beyond the categories of ordinary existence, distinct from the material objects and beings we encounter in our daily lives. This concept underscores God's ineffable nature, existing beyond the limits of human comprehension and the confines of physical form.

This idea becomes clearer when exploring the mystical Jewish understanding of creation, centered on the concept of the *Ein Sof*—the infinite God—and the process of *tzimtzum* (divine contraction). The *Ein Sof*, being boundless and infinite, undergoes a metaphysical act of self-limitation through *tzimtzum*. In this act of divine humility, God "contracts" His infinite essence, creating a conceptual space where a finite universe can exist. Though this space appears separate from God, it remains wholly sustained by His presence. Following this contraction, God's divine light flows into the seemingly empty space, infusing it with life and forming the spiritual foundation of all existence. This light permeates every aspect of creation, becoming the unseen essence that animates every being and every particle of the universe.

From this perspective, all of creation, including humanity, serves as vessels for this divine light. Our sense of independence is an illusion, as we are, in truth, immersed in the omnipresent radiance of God. Thus, God is *Ayin*, the transcendent "not-a-thing," because everything, at its deepest level, is a manifestation of the Divine. Yet, from a human perspective, this profound unity often goes unrecognized. Spiritual shortsightedness leads many to overlook the divine presence, rendering God "nothing" not in the mystical sense of transcendence, but in the tragic sense of being ignored or absent from their awareness. This creates a poignant paradox: the Divine, though intricately woven into the fabric of existence, often fades into the background of human consciousness due to inattentiveness.

Importantly, this mystical framework does not diminish the value of the physical world or human existence. In Jewish mystical thought, the material world is the very stage where humanity fulfills its purpose: to create a "dwelling place" for God in the lower realm. This is achieved by engaging with the physical world in alignment with Divine will, thereby revealing the inherent godliness within creation. Far from negating the material, this perspective elevates it as a medium for divine service and revelation.

In summary, the concept of God as *Ayin* in Chabad Hasidic thought encapsulates three key ideas: the transcendence of God beyond ordinary categories of existence, the intrinsic unity of all creation with the Divine, and the spiritual path of self-nullification, through which one recognizes and aligns with this unity.[117] By understanding God as "nothing," Jewish mysticism invites a deeper awareness of the Divine presence that permeates all things, urging us to look beyond the illusion of separation and to live in harmony with the sacred essence that underlies reality.

תכלית הבריאה
THE PURPOSE OF CREATION

When we look at the concept of creation in Kabbalah using the lens of Carl Jung's theory of individuation, we can suggest that the divine version of individuation originates from a confrontation between God's internal opposites, essentially, between His subconscious and conscious states. Before God wakes, He embodies everything and nothing, both potentials and impossibilities. This clash between His polarities initiates a process toward individuation, a dual response—first a reaction to the strong presence of these internal contrasts and then a counter-reaction or a yearning to reconcile these opposites, a term Jung refers to as 'enantiodromia'.

To advance in the process of individuation, God creates man, thereby making man a partner in God's divine process of individuation. As Jung put it, "God is a contradiction in terms, [and] therefore He needs a man to be made One ... God is an ailment which man has to cure." Jung admired the theurgical principle in Lurianic Kabbalah, which asserts that after the initial stages of creation and subsequent shattering, mankind is destined to partner with God to repair the broken worlds. Here, Jung acknowledges for the first time that man bears a cosmic responsibility in aiding God to repair the damages from creation, marking the correlation between worldly history and the collective spirit's development.

In essence, the Kabbalists, through their individuation, contribute to God's individuation— through the creation of the world on God's part, and the repair of the broken world on humanity's part. This transformation of God allows human consciousness to mature, thus providing the same opportunity for humans. Aniela Jaffe, a close associate of Jung, wrote that Jung was keen on finding parallels in the Lurianic Kabbalah, especially the idea that humans are essential in the divine life process and redeeming the world, which ultimately lies in harmonizing the opposites within the Godhead.

Early signs of individuation occur within God's mind, and His desire to create is born. But how does He 'wake up'? According to Jung, the process of individuation involves a continuous dialogue between the unconscious and the developing consciousness, which incites an awakening in the mind. Unifying the opposites is indeed central to the process of God's individuation, both in the Kabbalistic myth and in Jungian psychology. The process of individuation can be metaphorically explained by a dream, an unconscious phenomenon that manifests chaotically and unsystematically. God initially lacks any desire or consciousness, resembling a dream state. However, something within this unconscious state triggers His desire to 'wake up,' pointing toward His inherent desire to actualize and manifest His existence. Despite His unconsciousness, there's a potential for consciousness, the only autonomous element within His unconscious mind. Applying this to various Kabbalistic teachings, we see this as the stage where God begins moving from His unconscious state to uncover His conscious mind.

פרק השירה

PEREK HASHIRAH—THE SONG OF CREATION

"*Perek HaShirah*," or the "Chapter of Song," is a fundamental element of the broader Jewish textual tradition, although not part of the Hebrew Bible. This ancient Jewish text, now part of some Jewish liturgical practices, encapsulates a list of creatures or natural phenomena, each paired with a biblical verse that its "sings" to God. This important prayer pairs various creatures and elements of the natural world with biblical verses, along with certain rabbinical teachings that serve as their respective songs of praise to God. Here are some examples:

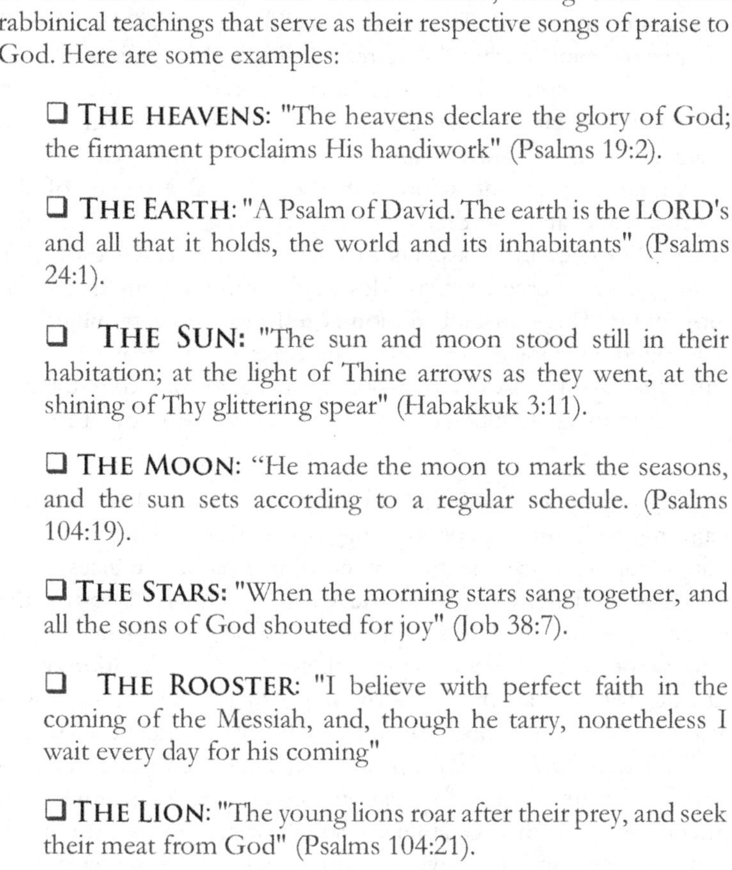

❑ **THE HEAVENS:** "The heavens declare the glory of God; the firmament proclaims His handiwork" (Psalms 19:2).

❑ **THE EARTH:** "A Psalm of David. The earth is the LORD's and all that it holds, the world and its inhabitants" (Psalms 24:1).

❑ **THE SUN:** "The sun and moon stood still in their habitation; at the light of Thine arrows as they went, at the shining of Thy glittering spear" (Habakkuk 3:11).

❑ **THE MOON:** "He made the moon to mark the seasons, and the sun sets according to a regular schedule. (Psalms 104:19).

❑ **THE STARS:** "When the morning stars sang together, and all the sons of God shouted for joy" (Job 38:7).

❑ **THE ROOSTER:** "I believe with perfect faith in the coming of the Messiah, and, though he tarry, nonetheless I wait every day for his coming"

❑ **THE LION:** "The young lions roar after their prey, and seek their meat from God" (Psalms 104:21).

❑ **THE TREES:** "Then shall all the trees of the wood sing for joy" (Psalms 96:12).

The divine orchestration envelops all facets of creation, including the earth, diverse weather conditions, and a multitude of creatures. Each organism, regardless of form, contributes to this harmonious praise to God. The symphony is echoed in daily life — from seasonal changes to tidal flows, and even in the artistry of drawing, painting, sculpture, and poetry. Each creature in creation uniquely exalts God, forming a symphony of praise that transcends physical attributes and demonstrating the interconnectedness of all beings.

In the Jewish mystical tradition of Kabbalah, *Perek HaShirah*, physical entities symbolize spiritual realities, each with a spiritual essence or "root" within divine realms. Thus, their praises to God reveal unique spiritual essences, with associated verses offering insights into their spiritual nature and role within creation's grand design. The act of studying and reciting *Perek HaShirah* can deepen the practitioner's connection with the spiritual essences of the natural world and the divine source, fostering awareness of the Divine Presence in all aspects of creation. The essence of life's beauty, as we perceive it, resides in the omnipresent quality of movement. This constant motion is reflected in everything from seasonal transitions to tidal flows and breezes. Just as we resonate with this rhythm of existence—our essence, our mind, body, and the nature that surrounds us—it echoes in the harmony of music.

This symphony, inherent in various art forms like drawing, painting, sculpture, and poetry, suggests rhythm and harmony that mimic music. Each creature in creation uniquely praises God, showcasing the myriad ways the Creator is revered across the natural world. This spiritual ecology portrays the interconnectedness of all beings in their collective adoration of the Divine, forming a symphony of praise that transcends physical attributes and behaviors. Engaging with this spiritual ecology, as embodied in *Perek HaShirah,* promotes a deeper connection to the world and its divine foundation. Each verse, creature, and phenomenon in the "Chapter of Song" offers an opportunity to pause, listen, and perceive. In doing so, we come closer to understanding the interconnected dance of existence, where every being, every moment, is a unique note in the divine symphony of life.

In every interaction, in every moment, we have the opportunity to join this universal chorus, to contribute our unique note to the divine symphony. Whether we're conscious of it or not, we are all part of this music, this rhythm, this harmony. This ancient prayer reminds us how every entity, great and small, forms a part of this divine orchestration, a guide to finding our unique rhythm, and a pathway to attuning ourselves to the divine melody that permeates the world.

"Song of Creation"

The image intricately weaves the Hebrew letters of the alphabet, which in Kabbalistic tradition are considered the building blocks of creation, into a spiraling galaxy, symbolizing the profound belief that the universe was spoken into existence through the divine language. Each letter, believed to hold specific spiritual energy and creative power, seems to emanate from the galactic core, suggesting the concept of "Otiot Yesod," or foundational letters, that channel the divine will into the fabric of reality. This cosmic depiction highlights the esoteric view of language as a tool of creation, reflecting the deep mysticism of Kabbalah where words and letters are not mere symbols but actual vessels of divine essence shaping the cosmos.

Martin Buber: "I and Thou" Also Includes Nature

In Martin Buber's mystical contemplation of a tree, as described in "I and Thou," he transcends the ordinary perception of the tree, seeing it not merely as a physical object but as a being in a profound, existential relationship with himself. Buber doesn't disregard the tree's scientific or aesthetic aspects; instead, he integrates these into a holistic view where the tree becomes a living entity engaging in a mutual, dynamic relationship with him. Buber noted:

> Throughout all of this, the tree remains my object and has its place and its time span, its kind and condition. But it can also happen, if will and grace are joined, that as I contemplate the tree I am drawn into a relation, and the tree ceases to be an It. The power of exclusiveness has seized me. This does not require me to forego any of the modes of contemplation. There is nothing that I must not see in order to see, and there is no knowledge that I must forget. Rather, is everything, picture and movement, species and instance, law and number included and inseparably fused? Whatever belongs to the tree is included: its form and its mechanics, its colors and its chemistry, its conversation with the elements and its conversation with the stars—all this in its entirety. The tree is no impression, no play of my imagination, no aspect of a mood; it confronts me bodily and has to deal with me as I must deal with it—only differently.[118]

One should not try to dilute the meaning of the relation: relation is reciprocity. Does the tree then have consciousness, similar to our own? I have no experience with that. But thinking that you have brought this off in your own case, must you again divide the indivisible? What I encounter is neither the soul of a tree nor a dryad, but the tree itself.[119] This perspective allows the tree to transcend its status as an "It" to become a "Thou," a subject in a relationship rather than an object of observation. Buber's mystical thought suggests that by recognizing and embracing this deep connection with the tree, he enters into a relationship where the tree and he are interrelated and interdependent, sharing a bond that goes beyond the physical and enters the realm of the spiritual.

For Buber, the tree's existence is not just a matter of its physical properties or its categorization in biology. It embodies a union of its form, structure, interactions with the environment, and even its cosmic relations, all converging in a singular, interconnected whole. The tree thus becomes an integral part of a larger, living cosmos, where every aspect of its being is in a meaningful dialogue with the observer. This mystical perspective emphasizes the unity and interconnectedness of all existence, where the distinction between subject and object dissolves, and a profound, reciprocal relationship emerges.

CHAPTER 7

God's Oneness in the Kabbalah

And the LORD shall be king over all the earth; in that day there shall be one LORD with one name.

—Zechariah 14:9

The Lord is our God; the Lord is one: The Lord, who is now our God and not the God of the other nations- He will be [declared] in the future "the one God," as it is said: "For then I will convert the peoples to a pure language that all of them call in the name of the Lord" (Zeph. 3:9), and it is [also] said: "On that day will the Lord be one and His name one" (Zech. 14:9).

—Rashi on Deuteronomy 6:4

God, Blessed be His name, is the absolute essence of good. And in truth, it is the nature of good to bestow good. And this is what God intended – to create beings in order that He could bestow good to them, for if there is no recipient of the good, there is no goodness.

—Moshe Hayyim Luzzato, Da'at Tenuvot 1:8

Rabbi Moshe Hayyim Luzzato's (a.k.a. "*Ramchal*") contemplations unfurl like a soul-stirring sonnet of profound wisdom and enlightened intellect. They paint a vivid canvas of an expansive cosmic blueprint, where the ultimate objective is the manifestation of a singular awareness of God's Presence in our earthly realm. Intriguingly, this monumental endeavor is not a solo undertaking by the Divine, but rather a collaborative mission shared in partnership with humankind.

In this grand schema, *Ramchal* perceives God as an unceasing advocate for universal progress and evolution. He visualizes a God who fervently hopes for everyone to delve within, unearth one's latent shortcomings, and commit to the challenging journey of self-rectification. This transformative process is imagined as a nuanced ballet between the sacred and the secular, where each pirouette of personal growth is born from the tireless honing of our inherent imperfections. In *Ramchal's* philosophical cosmos, the Divine is not a distant, detached entity but an intimately involved co-dancer in the human story. God extends an open invitation for humans to engage in a dynamic duet — a celestial choreography designed to refine our earthly existence, turning flaws into strengths, and fostering growth and evolution. This dual participation allows for a shared effort and co-creation, elevating the human experience from mundane to divine, while illuminating God's Presence within the rhythm of everyday life. And when that occurs, God's Name shall indeed become One as His name is One (Zech. 14:9).

However, *Ramchal* carefully notes that for the bestowed goodness to find its full expression, it must be earned rather than freely given. Like a farmer tilling the soil under the baking sun, each individual must put forth effort to receive and own this divine goodness. This struggle for acquisition eliminates any potential shame associated with receiving unearned gifts, much like the discomfort of accepting charity. It transforms the recipients into active participants, owners of the goodness they receive, rather than passive beneficiaries. This philosophy is beautifully encapsulated in ancient wisdom that echoes down the ages: "Whoever partakes without his own labor, it is not considered his true fulfillment."[120] Thus, through their efforts, the recipients fully enjoy the goodness, imbuing it with a sense of personal accomplishment and making it truly their own.

אֶחָד

GOD'S ONENESS

The Hebraic Usage of One in the Kabbalah

In the Jewish mystical tradition, the Hebrew word אֶחָד (*Echud*)—commonly translated as "one" or "unity"—transcends its simple linguistic definition to embody a profound and dynamic concept of divine oneness. Far beyond a mere numerical designation, "*Echud*" in Kabbalah represents the absolute, indivisible unity of God, an all-encompassing wholeness that underlies and permeates every aspect of creation. This unity is both a theological cornerstone and a lived reality, inviting contemplation and participation through practices such as *Yihud Ilah* (higher unification) and *Yichud Tata* (lower unification). To explore "*Echud*" is to peer through a radiant prism, where the infinite light of God refracts into the diverse hues of existence while remaining eternally one.

At its core, "*Echud*" signifies the foundational Jewish belief in monotheism, as proclaimed in the *Shema*: "Hear, O Israel: The Lord our God, the Lord is One" (Deuteronomy 6:4). In the Kabbalistic thought, the Hebrew word אֶחָד (*echad*)—meaning "one" or "unity"—emerges as a radiant prism, refracting the pure, unblemished light of God's absolute oneness into a breathtaking spectrum of colors. This metaphor, a luminous mosaic woven with threads of unity and diversity, unveils the profound essence of creation itself. Just as white light, when guided through a prism, blossoms into a cascade of hues—each distinct yet eternally bound to the same luminous source—so too does the world, in all its manifold forms, reflect the singular essence of YHWH, the divine artist whose boundless creativity paints existence with the brushstrokes of His infinite being.

This unity, embodied in *echad*, transcends the simplicity of a numerical count. It is a transcendent, all-encompassing wholeness, a sacred reality that enfolds every aspect of existence within its embrace. Beneath the vibrant multiplicity of forms, beliefs, and experiences that color the human journey, there lies a fundamental interconnectedness—a divine fabric where every thread, no matter how unique, is spun from the same eternal light. To contemplate *echad* is to peer into the heart of creation and recognize that all is one, held together by the invisible hand of the Divine.

At the heart of this mystery lies *Tzimtzum*, the act of divine contraction. In this sacred process, the infinite God—whose essence, known as *Ein Sof* (the Endless), defies all comprehension—withdraws His overwhelming light to carve out a metaphorical "space" for the finite world to emerge. This is not a physical retreat but a gracious act of self-limitation, akin to an artist stepping back from the canvas to allow their masterpiece to take shape. Through *Tzimtzum*, the boundless light of *Ein Sof* is dimmed just enough for creation to breathe, setting the stage for the prism of *echad* to refract the divine radiance into the myriad hues of existence.

As this light passes through the prism of *echad*, it is filtered through the Sefirot, the ten divine attributes or emanations that serve as the conduits of God's energy into the world. These *Sefirot—Keter* (crown), *Hokmah* (wisdom), *Binah* (understanding), *Chesed* (loving-kindness), *Gevurah* (severity), *Tiferet* (beauty), *Netzach* (eternity), *Hod* (glory), *Yesod* (foundation), and *Malchut* (kingship)—are like the colors of the spectrum, each a distinct hue yet inseparable from the original light. Together, they form the Tree of Life, a mystical blueprint that maps the dynamic interplay of these attributes, balancing mercy with strength, wisdom with beauty, to weave a harmonious universe.

Each *Sefirah* reflects a unique facet of the divine character: *Chesed* pours forth boundless love, while *Gevurah* tempers it with discipline; Tiferet blends them into compassionate beauty, and *Malchut* grounds this celestial flow in the tangible world. Though they appear as separate qualities, the *Sefirot* remain united in their source, teaching us that the diversity of creation is but a reflection of the singular essence of God. Like colors blending on a canvas, they dance in tension and harmony, crafting the intricate patterns of reality.

Woven Creation is the *Shekhinah*, the Divine Presence that dwells within creation, infusing every fragment of existence with holiness. The Shekhinah is the immanent aspect of God, the gentle light that shimmers in every soul, every leaf, every breath. To perceive the *Shekhinah* is to see the divine spark that animates all things, to understand that even in the seeming chaos of diversity, the presence of *echad* unites all in a sacred embrace. This recognition deepens our reverence, whispering that no corner of creation stands apart from the infinite source.

Our journey through the spectrum of human experience—its joys, sorrows, beliefs, and practices—becomes an invitation to engage with this divine prism. The concept of *echad* calls us to seek harmony amidst diversity, to honor the sacred in every hue of existence, and to participate in *tikkun,* the holy work of rectification. *Tikkun* is the process by which we, as partners with the Divine, restore creation to its original state of unity. Through acts of kindness, the study of sacred texts, heartfelt prayer, and adherence to the divine commandments, we draw down the light of *echad*, mending the fractures born of separation and revealing the underlying oneness that binds all things.

Imagine a world where every gesture of compassion, every whispered blessing, gathers the scattered shards of divine light and weaves them back into the whole. This is *tikkun*—a labor of love that aligns the human soul with the divine will, transforming the mundane into the sacred and the broken into the complete.

Ultimately, this path of restoration leads us back to the singular source of light—YHWH, whose holy name resonates with the harmony of the *Sefirot* and the eternal wellspring of all that is. Just as the colors of the spectrum, when reunited, dissolve into the purity of white light, so too does our journey through the prism of *echad* guide us back to the divine unity from which we emerged. In this return, we discover that the diversity of existence is not a departure from oneness but a celebration of it—a kaleidoscope of divine expression rooted in the infinite heart of God.

Thus, *echad* stands not merely as a theological concept but as a living call to awaken to the divine in every moment. It reminds us that no matter how far we wander through the hues of life, we remain cradled within the embrace of God's infinite oneness, forever tethered to the light that illuminates our path.

Unfolding God's Oneness in History

Rashi's commentary indeed takes a unique stance on the concept of God's Oneness in comparison to other Jewish thinkers of his time. His interpretation is steeped in a vision of a future where all nations will finally acknowledge the primacy of the One God, thereby rendering God universally recognized as "One."[121] Rashi's position is rooted in the understanding that the declaration of God's unity in Deuteronomy 6:4, שְׁמַע יִשְׂרָאֵל יְהוָה אֱלֹהֵינוּ יְהוָה אֶחָד "Hear, O Israel: The Lord our God, the Lord is one," has implications that reach beyond a theological claim about the nature of God. For Rashi, the assertion of God's Oneness is not merely about God's indivisible unity or uniqueness but is equally about His universal recognition as the singular and ultimate Being.

He draws from the prophecies in Zephaniah 3:9 and Zechariah 14:9, which envision a future time when all nations will turn toward God, acknowledging His unique and singular divinity. Until this time, Rashi suggests, God's Oneness is somehow incomplete. It's not a statement about God's essential nature changing, but rather the collective recognition and understanding of God's Oneness by humanity.

Therefore, the paradoxical claim that "so long as the nations of the world have not recognized the importance of ethical monotheism, God paradoxically is not One," could be understood not as a theological assertion that God's nature is in flux, but rather as a sociological observation that God's Oneness is not yet fully recognized and affirmed globally. This stance is consistent with Rashi's method of interpretation, which often seeks to understand the wider implications of the biblical text, considering both its theological and societal dimensions. Thus, for Rashi, the concept of God's Oneness is not only a fundamental Jewish theological principle but also a global aspiration and a future promise.

A Kabbalistic Glimpse into "Echad"

In the profound heart of Kabbalah's cosmic song, one truth resonates with an unfaltering clarity: the Oneness of God. A melody that transcends the mere arithmetic of singularity, it whispers of a divine unity that envelops every atom of existence, permeating each silent space between breaths and thoughts. God's Oneness, in Kabbalistic thought, is not a solitary figure atop a celestial throne, but a fluid, omnipresent essence that weaves itself into the intricate fabric of the universe.

Like the unseen wind that animates the autumn leaves or the silent force that pulls the tides, the Oneness of God moves through creation, silent yet irrefutably present. God's Oneness is the quiet architect of stars' orbits and the author of every heartbeat, the painter of sunsets and the sculptor of mountain ranges, yet also the quiet comfort in moments of solitude and the shared joy in times of celebration. The Jewish mystical tradition teaches that God's oneness is not a static truth, but a dynamic, ever-unfolding reality. It is a divine dance between *Ein Sof*, the endless, unfathomable aspect of God, and the *Shekhinah*, the Divine Presence that permeates our tangible world. In their eternal exchange, an intricate web of existence is spun, each thread humming with the sacred melody of unity.

The notion of *tzimtzum* illuminates this dance further. *Tzimtzum* speaks of God's act of self-contraction, of making space within the divine essence to allow for creation and for otherness. Yet, even in this gracious withdrawal, God's Oneness is not fragmented. It merely folds unto itself, contracting and expanding in the cosmic dance, allowing the universe to bloom within its infinite expanse. Hence, in the sacred labyrinth of Kabbalah, God's Oneness is an exquisite paradox, a symphony of unity played on the instruments of diversity.

It is a divine mystery that invites us not to solve it but to marvel at it, to live it, and ultimately, to find our place within its grand, divine harmony. God's wisdom unfolds as a rich blend of unity and duality, of action and stillness, of consciousness and will. These two facets emerge not as opposites but as two expressions of the Divine, intrinsically linked in their source. It is as if the Great Architect, in the boundless expanse of His Being, had spun these threads of duality from the loom of unity, the singular becoming the manifold.

This divine expression, akin to the shimmering brilliance of a jewel, reveals differing facets under the scrutiny of perception. In the dance of creation, it bursts forth as divine will, carving existence from the void. And yet, in the silence of divine repose, it becomes consciousness—a tranquil pool of awareness reflecting the universe in its depths. As the ebb and flow of tides under the moon, this dynamic yet harmonious interplay of will and consciousness forms the heartbeat of the Divine.

Drawing a parallel with the natural world, one could observe this unity in the elemental dance of sound and light. Both, though distinct in their perception, spring from the womb of vibration. The subtle shift in conditions causes these vibrations to traverse the spectrum between the audible and the visible. Just as the resonance of a note and the glimmer of a star share the same origin, so too do consciousness and will. Both are woven into the very fabric of the Divine, illuminating the innate unity within all expressions of God's Being.

More on God's Individuation

Rashi's intriguing perspective on God's evolving unity within human development and history echoes profoundly when studied alongside the Kabbalistic concept of creation, particularly through the lens of Carl Jung's theory of individuation. This theory leads us to the captivating idea that God's divine individuation arises from an internal confrontation between His conscious and unconscious states. In this unconscious domain, God personifies all and none, embracing both potential and impossibility. This inner clash initiates a journey toward individuation, characterized by a dual response: initially a reaction to the strong presence of these polarities, followed by a yearning for reconciliation of these contrasts, a phenomenon Jung terms 'enantiodromia'.

To propel this individuation process, God creates man, thereby engaging man as a participant in His divine journey. As Jung articulates, "God is a contradiction in terms, [and] therefore He needs man to be made One ... God has an ailment which man has to cure." Jung, notably admiring the theurgical concept in Lurianic Kabbalah, posits that humans are called upon to assist God in mending the shattered worlds following the initial creation. This thought marks his unique recognition of man's cosmic duty to aid in healing the creation's fallouts, bridging the gap between the physical world's history and the collective spirit's evolution.

The process of individuation is central to Kabbalists who, through their personal development, participate in God's individuation. The divine transformation is manifested in God's creation of the world and His responsiveness to humanity, resulting in the maturation of His consciousness and concurrently affording humans the same growth opportunities. Aniela Jaffe, a close associate of Jung, noted Jung's interest in finding parallels in Isaac Luria's Kabbalah, particularly in the concept of humans' vital role in the divine life process and the redemption of the world, which hinges on the harmonization of opposites within the Godhead.

Indeed, this reconciliation of opposites is fundamental to God's individuation process in both Kabbalistic mythology and Jungian psychology. Jung's view is highly speculative—a view that Maimonides would have certainly rejected. Jung argues that this process can be metaphorically likened to a dream in the psyche of God. Although God starts in an unconscious state with no desires or consciousness, akin to a dream state, an element within this unconscious state sparks His desire to 'wake up,' reflecting His inherent wish to actualize and express His existence. This potential for consciousness stands as the only autonomous element within His unconscious mind. God's desire to create arises from the early signs of individuation within His mind. But what triggers His 'awakening'?

Jung suggests that individuation unfolds through a continuous dialogue between the unconscious and the developing consciousness, prompting mental awakening. In line with various Judaic mystical teachings, this phase represents God's transition from His unconscious state toward His conscious mind.

The Human Response: As a Reverse Tzimtzum

God withdrew—a cosmic exhale, *tzimtzum*—His infinite light curling inward to carve a void where stars could blaze and souls could breathe. But what if we, too, must withdraw, hollowing our cluttered hearts to summon God back? This reverse *tzimtzum* inverts the Lurianic Kabbalistic script: as *Ein Sof* shrank to create existence, we shrink our egos to give birth to the divine within—a reciprocal dance of retreat and return, a mirror held up to the Infinite.

It's no rogue heresy, but a tremor pulsing through Kabbalah's veins. The Zohar hums of it: "The Holy One contracted His light, and the darkness shone" (I:15a), a shattering (*shevirat ha-kelim*) scattering sparks across a fractured cosmos. Luria's *tikkun olam* bids us gather those embers, mending the divine weave. Yet the Baal Shem Tov, Hasidism's wild-hearted founder, took it further—*bitul ha-yesh*, the self's dissolution, a storm-soaked dance to calm a widow's grief, his joy prying open a portal for God's grace. We're not mere pawns in this celestial drama but co-creators, echoing *Ein Sof*'s primal act with our own retreat. The *Tanya* calls it clear: "The soul is a spark of God above" (I:2), hewn from the Infinite, yearning to return—not to vanish, but to blaze.

Picture it: God's contraction cracks the silence, birthing a universe of dust and dream. Now, we crack ourselves—pride crumbling, greed fading—until *nefesh*, the soul's earthy root, softens to compassion, ruach lifts with prayer, and *neshamah* flares with insight. *Chayah* and *yechidah*, those rare upper tiers, tremble awake, kissing *Ein Sof*'s edge. Kabbalah casts us as microcosms, our inner *Sefirot*—*Chesed*'s love, Gevurah's resolve—mirroring the cosmic Tree. The Zohar's vessels broke; our egos do too, spilling light back to its source. This isn't subtraction but addition—a hollowing that fills.

Psychologically, it's Carl Jung's individuation—a soul forged whole, the shadow melding with the self. "God dwells within and beyond," Jung wrote, and we carve space for that spark, wrestling chaos into unity. The Besht's muddy twirl finds kin here: ego fades, divinity floods. Societally, it's tikkun writ large—justice (*Tzedakah*), mercy (*Chesed*), peace (*Shalom*) woven into villages and cities, repairing a world gashed by apathy. A shtetl feeds its poor; a nation shelters its lost—each act a reverse *tzimtzum*, inviting God to dwell. Metaphysically, it's symbiosis: God's retreat birthed us; our opening sustains Him. The *Sitra Achra*, that other side of shadow—anger, greed—lurks as foe, a cosmic and inner fracture we mend with every mitzvah, every breath turned holy.

No Lurianic scroll dubs it "reverse *tzimtzum*," yet the melody hums in mystic echoes. Rabbi Akiva's martyrdom (BT Berakhot 61b) radiates it—his flesh torn, his soul chanting "One," a space carved for God amid Rome's blades. Abulafia's chants to the Name (YHWH) unlock *neshamah*'s gates, a theosophical key turned anthropological tool. The Zohar's "hidden spark in every husk" (II:80b) begs us to lift it—not just God's task, but ours. We're not passive clay but smiths, hammering ego into altars. Philosophically, it's interdependence: *Ein Sof's* contraction seeded being; our contraction seeds meaning—a cycle where the finite cradles the infinite.

This summons resounds on every plane. Personally, it's shedding vanity for wonder—*nefesh* nursing a stranger, ruach singing in the dark. Communally, it's a marketplace turned sanctuary, coins swapped for kindness. Cosmically, it's humanity as God's echo, our choices—*mitzvot* or malice—rippling to the *Sefirot*, tilting *Malchut* toward *Keter*. The *Sitra Achra* snarls, tempting us to hoard the void, but reverse *tzimtzum* defies it—hollowing not to despair, but to shine. The Besht whirled in rain; Akiva bled in faith; we, too, spin holiness from dust. God's retreat carved the world; ours carves a bridge—finite eyes locking with the Infinite, the void aflame with light.

אֶהְיֶה
-- EHEYEH: I AM

The Grammar of Being and Becoming

One cannot begin to grasp the Kabbalistic significance of this mystical Name of God without first grasping the Hebrew grammar, which will clarify what precisely this divine Name implies. In Hebrew, verbs are often understood in terms of aspects rather than tenses, which can significantly shape the interpretation of the language and its meaning.

The two main aspects in Biblical Hebrew are the Perfect and the Imperfect.

- ❑ PERFECT: This aspect describes actions that are seen as complete, whether they happened in the past, are happening in the present, or will happen in the future. It's about the completeness of the action rather than when it takes place. It can also express facts or general truths.

- ❑ IMPERFECT: This aspect describes actions that are incomplete, ongoing, or continuous, or actions that will happen in the future. The focus is on the process or progression of the action rather than its completion.

With regards to אֶהְיֶה אֲשֶׁר אֶהְיֶה [*ehyeh asher ehyeh* = "I AM THAT I AM"] (Exod. 3:14), the verb *eheyeh* (אהיה) is what grammarians describe as the first-person imperfect form of the verb "to be" (היה). Given what we know about the imperfect aspect, this can suggest an ongoing, continuous existence. The phrase could be rendered as "I am becoming what I am becoming" or "I will be what I will be", indicating a continuous unfolding, a perpetual becoming. This aligns with some of the Kabbalistic interpretations that view God as an ever-evolving, dynamic presence.

אֶהְיֶה אֲשֶׁר אֶהְיֶה

This expression could stress God's self-existence and eternity. Yet, it could also depict God's unfathomable nature, a divine refusal to be defined or limited by human language. This reflects the richness and complexity of Hebrew grammar, as well as the depth of its theological concepts.

Numenius' Thoughts on Eheyeh

Greek philosophers of ancient times often deeply admired the theological teachings presented in the Jewish scriptures. These profound ideas emanating from the Jewish tradition piqued the curiosity and captured the attention of these philosophers. Among them, Numenius of Apamea, a prominent Neo-Pythagorean and Neoplatonic philosopher who flourished in the second century C.E., found himself particularly intrigued by the Jewish understanding of God as expressed in the books of Genesis and Exodus.

Numenius went as far as acknowledging Moses, as the earliest thinker of antiquity to recognize and associate God with a concept that later resonated with Greek philosophers, termed οὐσία (*ousia*) or "Being." This notion revolves around the unique essence and existence of God. Numenius drew a parallel between Mosaic insights and the philosophical thoughts that Greek scholars would explore in depth. He boldly proclaimed that Moses was the forerunner, the precursor who laid the foundation for the subsequent philosophical exploration of the nature of God. Numenius pointed to a significant event in Moses's life, namely his encounter with the burning bush. It was during this awe-inspiring moment that God revealed Himself to Moses as "I AM THE ONE WHO IS" (ἐγώ εἰμι ὁ ὤν = *egō eimi ho ōn*) (Exod. 3:14). This divine self-disclosure, the declaration of God's eternal and self-existent nature, left an indelible mark on Numenius. To him, Moses' proclamation encapsulated the essence of God's being, the core of His existence.

In his admiration for Moses and the profound impact of this encounter, Numenius boldly compared the renowned Greek philosopher Plato to a "Hellenic Moses." By drawing this parallel, Numenius sought to highlight the profound resonance between Plato's philosophical inquiries and the deep theological insights found in the Jewish tradition. He recognized the immense intellectual contributions of both Moses and Plato, attributing them with a similar level of wisdom and profundity. Through Numenius' admiration and acknowledgment of the Jewish theological message, we witness a fascinating intersection between ancient Greek philosophy and the religious teachings of the Hebrew Bible. It serves as a testament to the universal appeal and enduring impact of these ideas, as they transcended cultural and religious boundaries, captivating the minds of philosophers and leaving an indelible mark on the intellectual landscape of the time.

Philo of Alexandria: Thoughts on Eheyeh

One of the first Judaic mystics of Late Antiquity was Philo of Alexandria (20 B.C.E. to 50 C.E.). He utilized the principles of Pythagorean, Platonic, and Stoic philosophy to harmonize Jewish religious thought with the larger Greek intellectual tradition. While he predated the development of Kabbalah and its language of the Sefirot, Philo's interpretations of Jewish theology and scripture, including the concept of God as revealed in Exodus 3:14, had an indirect influence, shaping many of the neo-Platonic ideas that gave rise to medieval Judaic mystical and philosophical traditions.

In his interpretation of the phrase אֶהְיֶה אֲשֶׁר אֶהְיֶה ("I AM THAT I AM"), as found in the Book of Exodus, Philo emphasizes the timeless, unchanging nature of God. For Philo, the name *Eheyeh* signifies God's eternal, self-sustaining existence. It refers to the nature of God as the ultimate Being, the cause of all existence, and the one who is not contingent on anything else for existence. He sees God's declaration of "I AM THAT I AM" as an assertion of God's aseity — the quality of existing in and of oneself, independent of all other things. Philo's God is an eternal, self-sufficient Being, a concept that aligns with the philosophical traditions of his time, particularly Platonic and Stoic thought. He understood *Eheyeh* as indicating a God who exists beyond time and change, a God who simply IS.

It's important to note that Philo's interpretation of *Eheyeh* differs from some later Kabbalistic interpretations, which may emphasize God's dynamic and ever-becoming nature. Yet, these differing interpretations aren't necessarily contradictory but rather different facets of the multifaceted diamond of divine understanding. As such, they reflect the richness and diversity of Jewish thought on God's nature.

Eheyeh in the Kabbalah

Within the echo of אֶהְיֶה אֲשֶׁר אֶהְיֶה, also known as "I AM THAT I AM," we find a profound resonance of divine beauty, a profound hymn of perpetual creation, which harmonizes with the central tenets of Kabbalah, embracing both the dynamism of existence and the ever-unfolding mystery of the Divine. This heavenly epithet, *Eheyeh,* gives voice to a divine essence in perpetual motion as if dancing to the rhythm of the *Sefirot,* encapsulating the idea of a ceaselessly evolving Deity.

This Divine Presence, akin to the Kabbalistic concept of *Ein Sof,* portrays a divine duality, a paradoxical dance of stasis and evolution. It emerges as an eternal chorus of creation, a symphony reverberating through the cosmos. Its melody, akin to the Kabbalistic *'Or Ein Sof'* or the Light of the Infinite, weaves through time, enveloping the cosmos in a cloak of divinity. *Eheyeh,* bearing witness to the constancy of divinity, echoes the Kabbalistic concept of *Keter*, the Crown, the highest of the *Sefirot*. This recalls the image of *Ein Sof*, the Infinite One, unchanging amidst the flux of existence. It remains a constant beacon, illuminating the limits of our transient mortal understanding, similar to how the deeper truths of Jewish mysticism elude the uninitiated.

Yet, even as our reality intertwines with the divine, the true nature of this Presence remains tantalizingly beyond our grasp. It nudges the edge of our comprehension, much like the elusive insights that lie at the heart of Kabbalah, a divine enigma echoing in the cosmos, a melody of an ethereal dream. Hence, *Eheyeh* stands as a symbol of the ineffable Divine Presence, analogous to the ineffability of *Ein Sof*, encapsulating a divine paradox of perpetual transformation and eternal constancy.

This intricate interplay of contradictions reflects the complexity of the Kabbalistic Tree of Life, the divine structure of the *Sefirot.* It humbles us, evoking a sense of silent wonderment and an unceasing longing for the divine, mirroring the spiritual journey undertaken in the study and contemplation of Kabbalah. *Eheyeh* can also be seen as the divine statement of self-definition, a declaration of absolute freedom from all constraints and limitations. It implies a divine reality that is continuously unfolding, constantly becoming. It points to a God that is beyond all categories and definitions, yet is intimately involved in the process of existence and becoming.

Eheyeh is a powerful reminder of the divine mystery that lies at the heart of all existence. It hints at a God who is always present yet forever becoming, a God who is intimately connected with the world yet forever beyond our comprehension. It is the whisper of the infinite within the finite, the voice of the eternal within the transient. In essence, *Eheyeh,* when observed through the Kabbalistic lens, unfolds as a divine riddle: the infinite within the finite, the ever-changing within the unchanging, the intimately known within the perpetually elusive. It serves as a testament to the paradoxical nature of divine understanding, stirring within us a sense of awe and an insatiable thirst for divine wisdom.

יְהוָה
THE MEANING OF YHWH

The Italian Kabbalist R. Moshe Hayyim Luzzato (1707-1746) wrote on some of the most lucid material on this theme and the various permutations of the divine Name's variant spellings as discussed in the Lurianic Kabbalah:

The concept of the four permutations of the divine name *Havayah,* corresponding to numerical values 72, 63, 45, 52, is a deep and multifaceted aspect of Jewish mystical thought. These four permutations can be derived based on the full spelling of each Hebrew letter— employing full *yuds* (יוד הי ויו הי), *mushlav* (יוד הי ואו הי), full *alefs* (יוד הא ואו הא), or full *hehs* (יוד הה וו הה). They represent the accents, vowels, crowns, and letters, each intertwined with the other.

The numerical value of 72 is thought to reside within the cranium, its pathways concealed, subtly revealed through the hair strands. The 63 is associated with the region from the ears downwards, embodying three types of cantillation marks— high, medium, and low. The high ones originate from the ears, the medium from the nose, and the low ones from the mouth.

Each ear embodies ten high cantillation marks, residing internally, each captured within one of the letters "*hey*", with its form being "*dalet*" and "*vav*" (summing up to ten). They extend to the tip of the beard. The medium cantillation marks emerge from the nose, with ten on the right and ten on the left, these too residing internally. Here, the "*vav*" within the "*hey*" unveils itself, signifying six thousand, stretching down to the chest. The lower cantillation marks emanate from the mouth, including ten internal and comprehensive *Sefirot*. The "*dalet*" within the "*hey*" manifests as four thousand, made up of two "*vavs*" and two "*yuds*" corresponding to the two ears and two nostrils. Two breaths originate from the right of the mouth, and two from the left, rooted in the upper and lower cheeks, descending to the belly button.

The process begins with *Malchut*, followed by *Ze'ir Anpin*, all ultimately being consumed by the vessel's strength. The initial energy returns and enters, starting with *Keter* and followed by the rest. What remains solidifies into a vessel, imbued by sparks from the clash between the returning light of the Upper and the mark of the Lower. Initially, they were solely present within the life force of souls.

Their emergence and return involved separation, with each following a unique path suitable to its nature, until the second circling. Keter remained within the mouth of Adam Kadmon while the other nine *Sefirot* emerged, leaving *Malchut* as a vessel devoid of light. All the vessels constitute a single entity, yet contain ten lights within. This is the essence of "Bound Ones."[122]

See also EHEYEH

A Meditation: Breathing in the Name of God

The following exercise draws from the teachings of Abraham Abulafia, a 13th-century Kabbalist renowned for his ecstatic approach to Jewish mysticism. For Abulafia, reciting the Ineffable Name—the Tetragrammaton, YHWH—entwines multiple elements: mental focus, vocal articulation, and, crucially, a distinctive breathing technique. Each demands careful unpacking, but the breath stands out as foundational, anchoring the pronunciation of sacred letters in a rhythm that mirrors the pulse of life itself.

Abulafia's writings offer tantalizing hints about this method, though he shrouds it in sparse, suggestive detail. By piecing together fragments from his texts, we can glimpse its contours. Moshe Idel, a leading scholar of Kabbalah, highlights a pivotal passage from *Mafteah ha-Shemot* (*The Key of Names*) that illuminates both the physical practice and its philosophical depth. Abulafia instructs the practitioner to treat each letter of the Tetragrammaton as a subtle ripple within a single, prolonged breath—an unbroken stream of air that carries the Name's sanctity. This isn't a staccato exercise of gasps and pauses; rather, one sustains a deep inhalation through the utterance of each letter, pushing the limits of endurance. Only after this exertion does a brief rest follow, measured by the span of a single breath. In *Or ha-Sechel* (*The Light of Intellect*), Abulafia elaborates:

> When he begins to pronounce one letter with a given vocalization, one should remember that it alludes to the secret of the unity, so do not extend it more than the length of one breath, and do not interrupt it during that breath at all until you complete its expression. And extend that breath in accordance with the strength of the length of one breath, as much as you are able to extend it.[123]

Here, the breath becomes a vessel for divine unity, its continuity reflecting the oneness of God. The practitioner stretches this exhalation—whether long or short—until the letter's sound fades naturally, aligning physical effort with spiritual intent. Yet Abulafia distinguishes this sustained emission from the pauses between letters.

In *Mafteah ha-Shemot*, he equates the rest to one breath's duration, while *Or ha-Sechel* introduces nuance:

> Do not separate between one breath and the breath of the letter, but cling to it, whether one long breath or a short one... But between the letter of the Name and the Aleph, in the direct ones, or between the Aleph and the letter of the Name, in the inverted ones, you may take two breaths—no more—without pronouncing anything. At the end of each column, you may take five breaths, and no more, though you may also breathe less than five.[124]

This rhythm—two breaths per letter (one to vocalize, one to pause), with a cap of five at a sequence's end—suggests a structured dance of inhalation and silence, tailored to the practitioner's capacity. The inclusion of Aleph, a silent letter symbolizing the breath's origin, hints at a deeper interplay: the Name's consonants (*Yud, Heh, Vav, Heh*) ripple outward from this primal stillness.

Practically, this invites us to see God as the breath animating all creation—a truth we can intuit by observing the steady cadence of our own breathing. Mystically, the Tetragrammaton becomes a whisper on the wind, its letters hovering between consonants and vowels, much like breath itself. Forbidden from casual speech, this Name finds expression not in words but in the act of breathing it into being. Each prolonged exhalation weaves the practitioner into the fabric of the divine, merging the physical and the metaphysical. Abulafia's technique transcends mere mechanics; it's a meditative ascent. The extended breath mirrors the soul's yearning to touch the infinite, while the disciplined pauses ground it in human limits. As Idel notes, this practice fuses body and spirit, transforming the simple act of respiration into a ladder to the divine. The

Tetragrammaton, too vast to be spoken, lives in the silence between breaths—a sacred space where the mystic encounters the Ineffable.

A Spiritual Exercise: Inbreathing the Name of YHWH

In Abraham Abulafia's Kabbalistic practice, meditation transforms breathing into a sacred act by aligning it with the Tetragrammaton—YHWH, the four-letter Name of God (*Yod, Hei, Vav, Hei*). The practitioner subtly shapes each inhalation and exhalation to the sounds of these letters, turning every breath into a silent invocation of the Divine. Far from a mere physical reflex, breathing becomes a spiritual journey, embedding the presence of God into the rhythm of daily life.

> **HOW IT WORKS:** Breathe in deeply, whispering "*Yod*" (like "yode") in your mind as air fills your lungs—about three seconds.
>
> Exhale slowly, forming "*Hei*" (like "hay") for another three seconds.
>
> Inhale again with "*Vav*" (like "vahv"), then exhale "*Hei.*" Try this now: four breaths, one cycle, feeling the Name ripple through you.

When ready, let this focus soften. Allow your breath to flow naturally, keeping a quiet awareness of its rhythm. Here, each breath echoes YHWH, as if to breathe is to speak God's Name. This mirrors the Psalmist's insight: "Every breath praises You, God, Hallelujah" (Psalm 150:6). Each cycle becomes a silent prayer, a steady pulse of devotion woven into life's cadence. Conducted in the stillness of one's being, it reveals the power of silence—unspoken words carrying profound eloquence. Through this, breathing transcends survival, evolving into a continuous dialogue with the Divine, a testament to faith in every rise and fall of the chest.

Abulafia's practice reflects a core Kabbalistic idea: the union of physical and spiritual realms. In Hebrew, words emerge from consonants—rigid like the body—and vowels, marked by *nikud* (dots and dashes), which flow like the soul. The Tetragrammaton blends both: *Yod, Hei*, and *Vav* serve as consonants yet hint at vowels (e.g., *Yod* suggesting "i," *Vav* "o" or "u"), embodying God's multifaceted nature. Breathing, often likened to the life force (ruach in Hebrew, prana elsewhere), mirrors this duality—tangible air infused with divine essence.

By meticulously modulating their breath to echo the Ineffable Name, the practitioner engages with the divine on both physical and metaphysical levels. Abulafia's teachings illuminate a key principle of mystical traditions: the Divine is not a remote, external force but is intricately woven into the fabric of the world and our very being. Breath becomes the conduit, the inner spark allowing communion with the universe and the divine. This intimate relationship between the human and divine, the inner and outer worlds, the tangible and the transcendent, is beautifully encapsulated in the practice of breathing the Divine Name. [125]

Abulafia teaches that the Divine isn't distant but woven into existence—into our very bodies. Breath becomes the bridge, an inner spark linking the human to the cosmos. Imagine it: as you inhale "Yod," you draw in the world; as you exhale "Hei," you return it, blessed. This interplay—inner and outer, body and soul, mundane and transcendent—unfolds in each cycle.[126]

This meditation invites spirituality into the everyday. It's intimate, requiring no grand ritual—just you, your breath, and the Name. Yet it's vast, affirming God's presence within and beyond. As you sit with this now, notice your breath's gentle tide. Can you sense the sacred in its rhythm? For Abulafia, this is the mystic's art: to breathe consciously is to commune with the Divine, making every moment an act of worship.

ELOHIM—SIGNIFYING GOD'S PRESENCE IN CREATION

—

Traditionally, the word "*Elohim*" is translated as "God" or "gods," and its root "*El*" is one of the oldest designations for divinity in the Semitic languages. However, in Kabbalah, names are not just labels; they also represent different aspects of the divine reality. One might wonder why this name of God is written in the plural. Christian interpreters have often seen whispers of the Trinity here. Yet, both rabbinic scholars and many Christian exegetes have cast this view aside, declaring it absent of a true linguistic footing in the Scriptures. Let's uncover why.

- ❑ Biblical Hebrew reflects a truth that is evident in other Semitic languages, namely, an inferior addresses a superior using the plural form. This honorific dialectic convention is often dubbed the "plural of majesty" (*a pluralis excellentis*). Even in contemporary societies, such as Britain, the echo of this practice resonates in the usage of the "royal we".

- ❑ Furthermore, with its manifold meanings, this plural form reveals a myriad of majestical and powerful attributes in Hebrew parlance. It conveys an abundance of power, an intensity of majesty, and is often translated as the "God of gods," the "highest God," or the "embodiment of all divine powers."

- ❑ The roots of אֱלֹהִים (*'ělōhîm*) most likely draw nourishment from אֵל (*'ēl*), signifying "strength" or "power"—echoing in phrases like "it is within my power" (Gen. 31:29). Derived meanings include the hardy "oak tree" (*'ēlôn*) and the robust "pasticcio tree" (*'ēlâ*), testaments to the strength inherent in their very wood. In the poetic dance of language, the Hebrew term for God, אֱלֹהִים, doubles as the word for "Judge." The judges of early societies, their power incarnate, commanded warriors to implement their will. As the Author of natural law, God also crafts moral law, weaving a moral order as the foundation for ethical values and self-discipline. God—He before whom all beings of the world stand accountable.

In Kabbalistic thought, "*Elohim*" is a term that refers to one of the manifestations or aspects of God. This term is often used in the Torah and has a complex, layered significance in Kabbalistic philosophy. The Kabbalists perceived God as having both transcendent and immanent qualities. "*Elohim*" is associated with God's immanence, His presence and action within the world. In the context of the Kabbalistic Tree of Life, "*Elohim*" is often associated with the *Sefira* of *Gevurah* or *Din*, representing judgment, strength, and the law. This is in contrast with the name YHWH, which represents the aspect of God's mercy, and is associated with the Sefira of *Chesed*—God's lovingkindness.

Furthermore, it's interesting to note that in *gematria* (a Kabbalistic numerological system),"*Elohim*" equals 86, which is the same numerical value as "*HaTeva*" (הטבע), the Hebrew word for "nature." Some Kabbalists point to this as evidence of the Divine Presence in the natural world. Overall, "*Elohim*" in Kabbalah signifies an aspect of God that interacts with creation, imposes divine law, and can be discerned through the manifestations of nature.

הגשמה

ANTHROPOMORPHISM— GOD AS DESCRIBED BY HUMANKIND

In the rich network of religious literature, especially the Bible, metaphors provide a vital thread of understanding. They invite us to picture one thing in the light of another, illuminating shared qualities. For instance, a woman called a "lioness" resonates with the wild strength and courage associated with these majestic creatures. The ancient philosopher Aristotle first identified. The importance of metaphors, who viewed them as linguistic bridges, transferring meanings across disparate realms. In his view, metaphors have the unique ability to offer fresh perspectives, enabling us to glimpse resemblances within differences and to see the familiar in an unfamiliar guise.

Yet, metaphors defy literal interpretation. According to philosopher Paul Ricoeur, they create a "cunning distortion," a paradox that stretches our imagination, presenting seemingly incompatible ideas side by side. They serve as conduits, linking the known with the unknowable and offering glimpses into realities beyond the grasp of ordinary language. In their evocative power, metaphors breathe life into ideas and images that might otherwise remain linguistically untouchable.

This tantalizing quality of metaphors prompts us to engage with the images they conjure. This rings particularly true in the mythopoetic language of the *Tanakh*, where metaphors foster thoughts that deepen our understanding of the divine. Ricoeur suggests that metaphor is fundamentally a thought process, its chief function being to unveil new meanings. When it comes to anthropomorphism in Jewish mysticism, we find a careful application of this metaphorical discourse. Judaism, with its fierce monotheism, presents God as beyond human comprehension—ineffable and transcendent. Any human traits attributed to God are understood as metaphoric devices, aiding our limited minds in grappling with the Divine.

In Kabbalistic texts, anthropomorphic language is often employed as symbolic expressions of divine attributes and processes. For instance, within the framework of the *Sefirot*—the ten divine emanations through which God interacts with the world—each *Sefirah* corresponds to a metaphorical human "part." Thus, "*Hokmah*" (Wisdom) and "*Binah*" (Understanding) are represented as "Father" and "Mother," respectively, with corresponding associations with the "right brain" and "left brain." These metaphorical expressions are not literal. They do not suggest God's possession of a physical form or human emotions but rather serve as symbolic vessels carrying complex metaphysical ideas. They offer a language to articulate the inexpressible and conceive the inconceivable, delineating a framework for understanding divine influence in our world.

The gravity of this symbolic language lies in its safeguard against literal anthropomorphism, which in Judaism, would be akin to idolatry. As Maimonides emphasizes in his *Thirteen Principles of Faith*, God is devoid of physical form. Anthropomorphic depictions of God are thus metaphorical, facilitating our connection with the Divine. Reinforcing this point, the Zohar, , states that "No thought can grasp Him at all" (Zohar, 2:42b), reminding us of the ultimate unknowability of the Divine Hence, while Kabbalah uses anthropomorphic imagery, it constantly reminds us of the ultimate transcendence and unknowability of the Divine. Therefore, while anthropomorphism in Kabbalah serves as a metaphorical expression of divine attributes and processes, it is essential to remember its symbolic essence. These representations do not confer upon God human characteristics or a physical form, but serve as a guide, mediating our comprehension of the Divine.

שְׁכִינָה

SHEKHINAH: THE DIVINE FEMININE

The concept of שְׁכִינָה (*Shekhinah*), representing God's dwelling among mortals, is a profound aspect of Jewish theology. The term originates from the Hebrew root שָׁכַן (*shakhan*), meaning "to dwell" or "reside," as seen in biblical verses like Exodus 25:8, which states, "They shall make a sanctuary for me, that I may dwell in their midst." This verse, often translated to emphasize God's presence in a physical sanctuary, holds a deeper, more mystical meaning: "They shall make a sanctuary for me, so that I may dwell in them." This interpretation suggests that God's Presence is not confined to physical structures but resides within the human heart.

The Shekhinah, therefore, represents the "Divine Indwelling." After the Temple's destruction, Jewish tradition holds that the *Shekhinah* found a home in synagogues and places of study. It's believed that transgressions can repel the *Shekhinah*, while virtuous actions invite her presence. The Torah also refers to God "choosing a dwelling place for His Name," indicating that His Presence is not limited to any one location but is accessible to those who seek Him sincerely.

This Divine Presence is not just within the confines of religious buildings or specific holy places but is an all-pervasive force in our lives. Like the air we breathe, the *Shekhinah's* presence surrounds us, infusing each moment with deeper significance. Our actions, whether of kindness, comfort, or reverence, draw the *Shekhinah* closer and deepen Her presence within us. Conversely, our misdeeds can diminish this divine light, though the Shekhinah's patience is infinite, always waiting for our return.

"The Shekhinah"

This image captures the essence of the Shekhinah as a mystical and ethereal presence, embodying spirituality, wisdom, and nurturing qualities. The abstract and symbolic artwork suggests femininity, divinity, and a connection to the spiritual realm, evoking a sense of the sacred and the sublime.

God, as portrayed in the Psalms, is intimately involved in our daily lives, guiding and nurturing us. This understanding shifts our perspective, turning everyday experiences into encounters with the

Divine. The mundane becomes sacred, and every interaction is an opportunity to connect with God more profoundly. The Shekhinah is particularly attuned to human suffering and injustice. Her divine lament, "My head is heavy; My arm is heavy,"[127] reflects a deep empathy for both the innocent and the guilty. The *Shekhinah* is not just a witness to our struggles but actively shares in them.

Midrashic texts, like the interpretation of Song of Songs 5:1, portray the Shekhinah as the Divine Lover in a garden, symbolizing Eden, and the beloved as Israel. This allegory represents a deep, intimate relationship between God and His people, embodying the nurturing presence of the *Shekhinah*. The Lover's visit to the Garden is a metaphor for the divine spark within us, echoing our connection with God.

The Shekhinah's retreat after humanity's fall in Eden and its gradual return signify our ongoing journey to rebuild a dwelling for the Divine Presence. Our perception of God has evolved, often becoming more intellectual and distant. However, the *Shekhinah* invites us to rediscover a more personal, relational understanding of God, emphasizing His continuous presence in our lives.

In the sacred Song of Songs, a grand metaphor,
"I have come to My garden," God's tender command.
A tale of Divine love, so deep and so wide,
Between God and His people, forever to abide.

In the Sanctuary's construction, the *Shekhinah* did soar,
Returning to Her garden, to dwell evermore.
From the sin of the Knowledge Tree, the Presence did flee,
Ascending through heavens, from earthly decree.

Seven righteous souls, from Abraham to Moses' hand,
Brought back the *Shekhinah*, to the promised land.
In the Holy Temple, God's glory did rest,
Dwelling within each soul, in every chest.

"Make Me a sanctuary," the scripture implores,
And "I shall dwell within them," God's love outpours.

In each heart and soul, His presence to ignite,

Transforming the mundane, with celestial light.

The world, a canvas, for the Divine to paint,
Through deeds of the righteous, without taint.
In subduing darkness, in the holy fight,
Transforming it to a radiant, heavenly light.

From Above comes an all-encompassing glow,
Illuminates realms high and those below.
A transcendent light, from darkness unfurled,
Rising in glory, throughout all the worlds.

This divine interplay, a cosmic dance,
Inviting each soul, to join and enhance.
In God's grand design, we each play a part,
Bringing the *Shekhinah*, into every heart.

A Mystical Reading on Songs of Songs Rabah 4:10[128]

In Kabbalistic tradition, the *Shekhinah* symbolizes the Divine Feminine aspect of God, representing nurturing, compassion, and an immanent Divine Presence. This aspect emphasizes the sanctity of the physical world, which embodies feminine qualities, and underscores the interconnectedness of the spiritual and material realms. The *Shekhinah's* role extends to sharing in the suffering and exile of humanity, reflecting empathetic and nurturing characteristics. Practices in Jewish mysticism aimed at honoring the Shekhinah involve acts of kindness, observance of commandments, and Torah study, believed to draw the Divine Presence closer and facilitate spiritual healing. The *Shekhinah* also symbolizes God's love and compassion, offering a personal and intimate relationship with the Divine.

The Burning Bush as a Mystical Symbol

The Midrashic statement from Shemot Rabbah 2:5, referencing the Divine Presence manifesting in a thorn bush during the revelation of the Burning Bush to Moses (Exodus 3), carries profound spiritual meaning. In Jewish thought, this teaches that holiness permeates all levels of existence, even the seemingly mundane or lowly. When viewed through the lens of Kabbalah, this idea deepens into a metaphysical exploration of the Divine structure of reality, the *Sefirot*, and the interplay of concealment and revelation.

In Kabbalistic terms, the thorn bush (*sneh*) symbolizes the lowest levels of creation, often associated with the physical world or the *Sefirah* of *Malchut* (Kingdom), the final emanation of the ten Sefirot. *Malchut* represents the material realm, where the Divine light is most concealed, and it serves as the vessel that receives the flow of divine energy from the higher *Sefirot*. The thorn bush, prickly and unassuming, reflects *Malchut's* apparent lowliness—yet it is precisely here that God chooses to reveal Himself, demonstrating that even in the "lowest" place, the Divine Presence (*Shechinah*) resides.

The burning bush that "is not consumed" (Exodus 3:2) further aligns with Kabbalistic principles. The fire represents the influx of Divine light (*Ohr Ein Sof*), the infinite energy of God, descending into *Malchut*. In Kabbalah, the *Ein Sof* (the Infinite) emanates through the *Sefirot*, contracting (*tzimtzum*) and stepping down to sustain creation without overwhelming it. The unconsumed bush illustrates the harmony between the infinite (*Ohr*) and the finite (see the entry on *Ohr* and *Keli*), showing that the Divine can dwell within the material without destroying it. This mirrors the latter mystical concept of *Ratzo v'Shov* (running and returning), the dynamic interplay of Divine transcendence and immanence. (See the Glossary for a more comprehensive description of this concept).

Moreover, the thorns themselves can be understood as a symbol of *Din* (Judgment), a quality associated with the *Sefirah of Gevurah* (Severity), which imposes boundaries and limitations. The presence of the Divine within the thorny bush suggests the unification of *Chesed* (Kindness) and *Din*—a central Kabbalistic theme. The revelation in the bush teaches that even in places of harshness or concealment (Din), the Divine compassion (*Chesed*) and presence (*Shechinah*) are never absent.

From a Kabbalistic perspective, this event also hints at the purpose of creation: to reveal the Divine in the lowest realms, elevating them through human action and perception. The thorn bush, as a microcosm of *Malchut*, reflects the fallen sparks of holiness (*Nitzotzot*) scattered throughout the world, as described in Lurianic Kabbalah. The burning bush signifies the potential for *Tikkun* (rectification), where the Divine light is uncovered even in the most unlikely places, reminding us that no corner of existence is devoid of God's essence.

Thus, in mystical terms, the thorn bush teaches that the Divine Presence permeates all levels of reality—from the infinite heights of *Keter* (Crown) to the depths of *Malchut*—and that even in the lowliest, most concealed aspects of creation, the Shechinah dwells, awaiting recognition and upliftment. This revelation to Moses underscores the Kabbalistic mission: to find and reveal the Divine unity (*Yichud*) woven into the fabric of all existence.

CHAPTER 8

KABBALISTIC ANTHROPOLOGY

1. The divine philosophy [the Kabbalah] teaches us the attributes of God, the divine sefirot, that we may know it is for us to link our lives with the attributes of the Holy Blessed One.

2. We must study God's names, His attributes, and the sefirot so that we know it is incumbent on us to cleave to God's attributes, that we can cleave to them, and that we cannot cleave to God in His awesome transcendence. If this is not clear to us, then we have no understanding of the divine attributes, of the basic meaning of the sefirot, and of the fundamental significance of the mysteries of the "chariot."

3. Our ideals will always be advanced and they will bring to light each day and each moment new wellsprings of light and of a life of purity if we are convinced that there can be no morals and divine ideals in the world and in life, in the soul and in the spirit, unless there is a God, unless all existence is rooted in a source that transcends all existence.

4. We must attach ourselves to the divine ideals and we must always strive to realize them in life, in thought, in action, and in the imagination, in the life of the individual and of society, in our deepest and most zealous aspirations.

*5. One cannot avoid some semblance of idolatry unless one master the concept that the cleaving to God called for in verse "And you who cleave to the Lord your God" (Deut. 4:4), refers to the attributes of the Holy One, praised be He. One cannot cleave to the shekinah** itself. We can cleave to His ways. As He is merciful and gracious, you be merciful and gracious; as He bestows kindness, so you bestow kindness.*

—Abraham Isaac Kook, Moral Principles

We are sinful not only because we have eaten of the Tree of Knowledge, but also because we have not yet eaten of the Tree of Life. The state in which we are is sinful, irrespective of guilt.

—Franz Kafka

Defining Kabbalistic Anthropology

In Kabbalistic thought, the *Sefirot*—ten divine attributes, such as *Chochmah* (wisdom), *Binah* (understanding), and *Chesed* (compassion)—serve as conduits for God's infinite essence to flow into the finite world, much like hands channel human creativity into action. These attributes echo within humanity, forging a sacred bond between the human microcosm and the divine macrocosm. The purpose of human life is rooted in spiritual growth and the sacred mission of *Tikkun Olam*, repairing and elevating the world through acts of justice and compassion. As co-creators with the Divine, humans transmute the material realm, unveiling its hidden divine sparks to restore cosmic harmony.

The soul embarks on a transformative journey, shaped by the delicate interplay of free will and Divine Providence. Each choice and action reverberates with spiritual significance, shaping the individual soul and the broader cosmic order. Ethical growth lies at the heart of this process, cultivated through the practice of mitzvot (divine commandments), acts of compassion, and relentless self-refinement. By aligning its actions with divine will, the soul ascends through its spiritual stages—*Nefesh, Ruach,* and

Neshamah—contributing to *Tikkun Olam*, the repair of the world, and fulfilling its purpose of returning to divine unity.

This perspective highlights the interconnectedness of all beings, not only with each other but with all creation, underscoring the idea that individual spiritual actions have cosmic significance. Kabbalistic anthropology thus offers a holistic and profound view of humanity, emphasizing spiritual origins, divine purpose, ethical responsibilities, and the ultimate goal of achieving unity with the Divine.

Kabbalistic Anthropology vs. Kabbalistic Theosophy

Rooted in Kabbalah's fathomless well, theosophy maps the divine cosmos, while anthropology probes the human soul—two gazes from one sacred spring, one piercing the heavens, the other plumbing the heart's abyss. Both pulse with the same mystic fire, ignited by texts like the Zohar and the visions of medieval seers like Isaac the Blind, yet their quests diverge: theosophy unveils God's infinite dance, anthropology traces humanity's steps within it.

Kabbalistic theosophy begins with *Ein Sof*, the boundless, a light too vast for form, contracting in *tzimtzum*—a divine inhale—to birth the void where creation hums. From this, the *Sefirot* cascade: ten radiant vessels, *Keter* blazing as will, *Chesed* spilling mercy, *Gevurah* tempering might, down to *Malchut*, the earthen throne. The Zohar sings of this genesis: "Light concealed in darkness" (I:15a), a shattering (*shevirat ha-kelim*) scattering sparks across a fractured cosmos. Theosophy paints this as God's blueprint—eternal, hierarchical—where humans play bit parts, gathering embers for *tikkun olam*, mending the divine weave. It's a celestial saga, asking, "What is God?" and "How does the infinite unfurl?"—a grand tapestry of light and law.

Turn inward, and Kabbalistic anthropology unfolds—a soul not singular but a prism, refracting five hues: *nefesh, ruach, neshamah, chayah, yechidah*. Nefesh breathes life into flesh, a tether to *Malchut's* dust. Ruach stirs emotion and will, echoing *Tiferet*'s harmony. *Neshamah*, a divine ember, mirrors Binah's wisdom, as the *Tanya* whispers: "A spark of God above" (Part I, Ch. 2). *Chayah* and *yechidah*, rare and radiant, bind us to *Ein Sof's* pulse, awakened by mystic toil. Here, humanity is a microcosm, each soul a fractal of the *Sefirot—Chesed* as love, *Gevurah* as resolve—reflecting the divine in miniature. Anthropology asks, "Who are we?" and "How do we climb?"—a soul's odyssey through time's arc.

Their kinship glimmers in the *Sefirot*, threading God's essence to ours. Theosophy's cosmic Tree of Life blooms outward; anthropology's roots inward, a mirror held to eternity. Yet their songs differ. Theosophy revels in the why—*Ein Sof's* timeless now, where past and future fuse. Anthropology wrestles with the how—souls cycling through gilgul, refining *nefesh* with deeds, lifting ruach with prayer, rousing *neshamah* in silence. Theosophy's God dreams in stillness; anthropology's humans mend in motion, co-weavers of *tikkun*. Evil, too, splits: theosophy's *Sitra Achra*, a cosmic shadow; anthropology's inner tilt—anger flaring from unchecked *Gevurah*—both calling for repair.

In their sacred dance, Kabbalistic theosophy and anthropology unite in a loving embrace. Theosophy unveils God's divine structure, while anthropology illuminates humanity's spiritual calling. Abulafia's theosophy reveres the Name (YHWH) as creation's source, and his anthropology employs meditative breathing to awaken the *neshamah*, the soul's divine spark. Luria's theosophy envisions tikkun, repairing the Sefirot's cosmic brokenness through their harmonious balance, while his anthropology calls us to gather divine sparks through mitzvot, sacred acts like charity and justice.

Theosophy maps God's infinite plan; anthropology guides the soul's ascent—vision and action in perfect harmony. Without theosophy, anthropology wanders aimlessly; without anthropology, theosophy dissolves into abstraction. Masters like the Baal Shem Tov wove them as one, finding God through self-awareness and healing the self to restore divine unity. In this mystic duet, theosophy and anthropology sing Kabbalah's truth: a fractured unity, where the infinite kisses the finite, and the soul, a shard of light, becomes the bridge.

אַרְכֵטַיְפּן -- ARCHETYPE

In the vast and intricate theatre of the human psyche, Jung situates archetypes as primordial echoes passed down with the inheritance of brain structure. These are no mere vestiges of ideas but dynamic forces of instinctive preservation and adaptation, universal tendrils burrowing into the bedrock of the psyche, their roots merging with the sinews of nature.

Each archetype is an unseeable master sculptor, their invisible hands shaping the motifs and images of our psychic tableau. They are known not by their unseen form but by the distinct sculptures they create, resonating with an uncanny familiarity that transcends individual experiences and permeates all cultures. Archetypes assume the form of "instinctual images," spectral shadows cast by the infra-red dynamism of instinct, their ultraviolet auras illuminating our psychic landscapes. Their influence is not a mere absorption but a profound integration, imprinting an image that bears little resemblance to its biological progenitor yet whispers of a shared origin.

Archetypes are the compass by which human instinct navigates. They are the oceanic depths that all psychic rivers yearn to meet, the coveted prize secured in the hero's triumphant contest with the dragon. Manifesting in the personal realm through complexes and resonating in the collective consciousness as cultural traits, they persist as inescapable players on the world stage. They are primal forces we cannot negate nor neutralize. As we climb the staircase of civilization, each rise necessitates reforming our understanding of these archetypes.

We are bound to splice the lingering threads of the past within us with the emergent patterns of the present, reweaving the fabric of our interpretations at each turn. Only thus can we perpetuate the grand narrative of our shared human journey. An archetype is a core structure in our collective psyche, a universal blueprint informing our ideas, images, and behaviors. Physiology expresses archetypes as instincts. Individual experience, in its ceaseless dance with the present, endows these skeletal instincts with flesh and skin, transforming the archetypal bones into tangible forms, and the abstract into the personal.

Archetypes and the Kabbalah

Simultaneously, in a different corner of human consciousness that seeks to comprehend the divine through intricate symbolism and metaphysical contemplation. It features the Tree of Life, a diagrammatic representation of divine emanation, with ten sephiroth, or spheres, interconnected by twenty-two pathways. Each *Sefira h* embodies an aspect of God's character, resonating with the multi-faceted nature of the divine.

Here is where Jungian thought and Kabbalah converge, in the shared recognition of the rich complexity of existence, the manifold facets of the divine and the human. The archetypes and the sephiroth both serve as guides, as signposts on the journey of human understanding, each with its resonances and reflections. Consider the archetype of the mother and the Sefira h of Binah on the Tree of Life.

Binah, meaning "understanding,' represents the divine feminine, the womb of creation, just as the mother archetype embodies nurturing, creation, and unconditional love. In the Tanakh and in the Pseudepigrapha, wisdom is frequently portrayed by the feminine archetype of the Mother, and does not personify the masculine aspect of the Divine. The Hero, on the other hand, might align with *Tiferet,* the *Sefira h* of Beauty, which sits at the center of the *Tree of Life.* An image that later occurs in the Tabernacle. *Tiferet* represents balance, integration, and sacrifice—akin to the Hero's journey of self-discovery, overcoming obstacles, and eventual transformation.

Despite their similarities, there are some significant differences. Jungian archetypes mainly illuminate aspects of human psychology, while the Kabbalistic Tree of Life seeks to illustrate the structure of divine, cosmic, and earthly realms. Yet their intersection in literature, myth, and art reveals a rich network of human experience, a spiritual and psychological symphony that speaks to our shared quest for meaning and understanding. It's the echo of these shared symbols that whispers to us in the turning of pages, in the mysteries of ancient texts, and in the shared dreams and tales that stitch together the fabric of human culture. They illuminate our common journey, from the external world to the inward depths of the human soul, bridging the chasm between the earthly and the Divine.

סְפִירוֹת

SEFIROT

In our relentless pursuit to fathom the intricate nature of the Divine, we have identified ten unique aspects that facilitate our understanding of God. These dimensions not only deepen our knowledge of the Supreme Being but also invigorate our profound and personal connection to the Divine. These ten aspects, known as the *Sefirot*, function as channels for the Divine's influence in the world and, concurrently, serve as a spiritual pathway that guides us back toward God.

The *Sefirot* concerning God could indeed be compared to a violin in the hands of a concert violinist. The violin, on its own, is just an instrument— a beautiful and intricate creation, but silent and lifeless without the touch of the violinist. It does not create music by itself. But when a skilled violinist plays it, the violin comes to life, producing harmonious and captivating music that stirs the hearts of the audience. The music is not in the violin itself but in the heart, the skill, and the intentions of the violinist. The violin is merely the medium through which the violinist's inner music finds outward expression.

Similarly, the *Sefirot* are not God themselves, just like the violin is not the music. The *Sefirot* are conduits or instruments through which the Divine manifests in the world. The true essence of the Divine, akin to the music in the heart of the violinist, is beyond comprehension and transcends the *Sefirot*, but we perceive God's influence through these ten emanations.

This comparison highlights the notion that, just as a violinist conveys their inner music through a violin, God expresses the divine will and wisdom through the *Sefirot*. While we cannot fully grasp the entirety of the violinist's talent or the depth of their music from the violin alone, it gives us a means to appreciate and connect with it. Similarly, while we cannot fully understand the Infinite (*Ein Sof*) in its totality, the Sefirot provides a framework to experience and relate to the Divine.

The Ten Sefirot

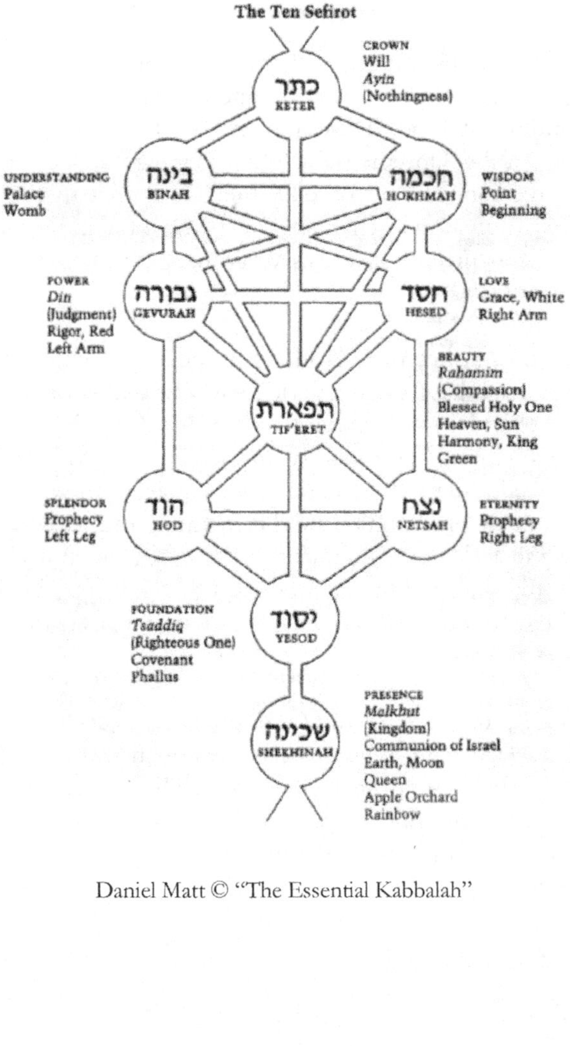

The Ten Sefirot

כתר KETER — CROWN, Will, *Ayin* (Nothingness)

בינה BINAH — UNDERSTANDING, Palace, Womb

חכמה HOKHMAH — WISDOM, Point, Beginning

גבורה GEVURAH — POWER, *Din* (Judgment), Rigor, Red, Left Arm

חסד HESED — LOVE, Grace, White, Right Arm

תפארת TIF'ERET — BEAUTY, *Rahamim* (Compassion), Blessed Holy One, Heaven, Sun, Harmony, King, Green

הוד HOD — SPLENDOR, Prophecy, Left Leg

נצח NETSAH — ETERNITY, Prophecy, Right Leg

יסוד YESOD — FOUNDATION, *Tsaddiq* (Righteous One), Covenant, Phallus

שכינה SHEKHINAH — PRESENCE, *Malkhut* (Kingdom), Communion of Israel, Earth, Moon, Queen, Apple Orchard, Rainbow

Daniel Matt © "The Essential Kabbalah"

As another metaphor, one could compare the *Sefirot* to the colors on an artist's palette. Each color represents a different attribute or quality, but they all stem from the same source - the artist's vision. Just as an artist will mix and apply colors to convey their vision on a canvas, God uses the *Sefirot* to manifest the divine will in the world. Each *Sefirah* is an individual color, but together, they form a complete picture of divine interaction with the universe. And yet, the source of the artwork, the artist's vision and inspiration, remains a mystery that transcends the colors on the canvas.

The Sefirot, each one a *Sefirah*, stand as cornerstone concepts in the Kabbalah, the enigmatic and mystical facet of Jewish philosophy. They epitomize the ten attributes or emanations by which *Ein Sof*— the Infinite Oneunveils itself and ceaselessly brings forth both the tangible, physical realm and the intangible, metaphysical one. According to Kabbalistic philosophy, these *Sefirot* act as a conduit for God to manifest and establish a relationship with the finite cosmos. Hence, they form a spiritual bridge between the earthly and the divine, a vital medium through which we can comprehend and experience the otherwise unfathomable nature of God. These ten attributes are divided into three categories: intellectual (understanding), emotional, and practical/behavioral. They are typically arranged in the shape of a tree (hence the "Tree of Life" reference) or in the human form, with three columns or pillars to represent a harmonious system.

A List of the Sefirot

Here is a thumbnail list of the ten *Sefirot*, going from top to bottom in the tree:

❑ KETER (Crown): Divine will, the source of all the other Sefirot.

❑ HOKMAH (Wisdom): The power of intuitive insight, flashing lightning-like across consciousness.

❑ BINAH (Understanding): The analytical ability to delve into the depths of wisdom.

❑ CHESED (Kindness): Love, giving, or mercy.

❑ GEVURAH (Severity): Judgment, strength, or discipline.

❑ TIFERET (Beauty): Symmetry, compassion.

❑ NETZACH (Victory): Endurance, the fortitude to carry on.

❑ HOD (Glory): Humility, the yielding power that allows others to grow.

❑ YESOD (Foundation): Connection, the power to contact and communicate.

❑ MALKUTH (Kingship): Fruition, the receptacle where all comes to completion.

In Kabbalistic thought, these *Sefirot* are not seen as separate deities, as in some forms of pagan polytheism, but as different aspects of the one God. They are like different facets of a diamond, each reflecting the light of the divine in its unique way, but all part of one unified whole. Why does God require them for creation? This is a theological question that can be interpreted in many ways.

However, one common explanation in Kabbalah is that the *Sefirot* bridges the infinite, unknowable, transcendent God (*Ein Sof*) and the finite, knowable universe. The *Sefirot* are channels for the divine energy to flow into the world; through these channels, God interacts with the world. The *Sefirot* also enables humans to have a relationship with the divine by providing a framework for understanding and relating to God's attributes.

These monikers, these celestial constellations of divine attributes, weave themselves through the fusion of both classical and modern works in and about Kabbalah. The final seven also correlate to the "lower" attributes, each corresponding to the seven days of creation –

- ❑ *Chesed* illuminates the first day, embodying the moment God decreed, "Let there be light."

- ❑ *Gevurah* aligns with the second day, signifying when God set the upper apart from the lower.

- ❑ *Tiferet* echoes the third day when God proclaimed, "It is good" twice.

- ❑ *Netzach* is reflected on the fourth day when God birthed the sun, moon, and stars.

- ❑ *Hod* reverberates on the fifth day with the creation of birds and fish.

- ❑ Yesod corresponds to the sixth day when humankind was created.

- ❑ *Malchut* is in sync with the *Shabbat* when God existed as the Sovereign.

The Kabbalists bequeathed these names and qualities to the pivotal elements of their reality map. Each one is interconnected; following this cosmic blueprint is akin to attaining the highest level of awareness accessible to a human being, but only if this enlightenment is perceived as a unified experience within oneself. You shall know if you manage to harmonize with all ten levels.

כֶּתֶר

KETER: THE CROWN SEFIROTH

Keter is sometimes omitted from the traditional structure of the *Sefirot and* occupies an otherworldly realm. So high, so inscrutable, it exists as a category unto itself. *Keter* is the fulcrum, the "intermediary", the celestial bridge that spans the divine chasm between the infinite En Sof and the lower *Sefirot*. It's the first step where the *En Sof's* Light descends, and from this point, it fuels the ensuing divine emanations. It's the root, the soul of the *Sefirot.* Symbolizing the primary lever of divine manifestations, *Keter* is the Supreme or Abysmal Will of the divine. This is not a particular will focus on a specific purpose, but rather the primordial divine willingness that underpins the creative will— the essence-will, the will to will, which precedes all divine powers or attributes, i.e., the *Sefirot.*

חָכְמָה.

WISDOM

The Hebraic Meaning of "Wisdom"

In the Tanakh, חָכְמָה (*Hokmah*), wisdom is perceived as a profound entity that transcends the confines of mere knowledge. It demands the acquisition and the deft application of knowledge in a moral compass governed by righteousness, compassion, and unwavering loyalty. It encourages us to practice ethical conduct; wisdom inspires us to observe life and be attentive to nature's lessons; it is impossible to raise children without wisdom! The absence of wisdom paves the way for folly, ultimately spiraling into self-destructive behavior and endless negative patterns of relating to others.

Unlike the view found in most Kabbalah texts, which associates חָכְמָה as a distinctively masculine energy, it is significant that this word and concept have a distinctive feminine quality. Particularly in the Book of Proverbs, wisdom evolves into a tangible entity, personified as a woman—"Lady Wisdom". She stands as a beacon, her teachings echoing in the streets, open to all who would lend an ear. An embodiment of God's first creation, she is depicted as an active participant in forming the world. Lady Wisdom calls upon the masses to abandon their folly in the bustling squares, city gates, and atop the high walls (Prov. 1:20-33). Her value surpasses that of precious jewels, her teachings outweigh worldly desires (Prov. 3:13-18). Those who embrace Lady Wisdom find life and garner divine favor. She starkly contrasts the adulterous "Woman Folly", the embodiment of destruction.

Interpretations of Lady Wisdom vary, with some viewing her as an allegory for practical wisdom grounded in sound judgment and a fear of the Lord. Others draw parallels with goddesses of the ancient Near East, though, within Proverbs' monotheistic framework, she remains a creature, not a deity.

"Lady Wisdom"

The "Lady Wisdom" image, often associated with the biblical figure of Sophia, embodies the fusion of divine knowledge and feminine insight within the mystical traditions, including the Kabbalah. The portrayal of Lady Wisdom with a book suggests the embodiment of divine knowledge and the act of revelation, aligning with the Kabbalistic theme of knowledge as a living, transformative experience. Her regal and serene presence, encompassed by celestial light, underscores the sacredness of wisdom and the higher intelligence that permeates the cosmos according to Kabbalistic belief.

Similar personifications appear elsewhere in the Tanakh and non-canonical Jewish texts. For instance, in Job, wisdom is a hidden treasure exclusive to God's grasp. In the *Apocryphal Wisdom of Solomon*, wisdom shines as God's glory, reflecting eternal light. The Gnostic literature introduces Sophia, a divine wisdom figure, more mythological and complicated, yet adding to the richness of the wisdom tradition. Sophia, as portrayed in some Gnostic systems, is a heavenly entity that creates the material world but falls from grace, only to be redeemed eventually.

Hokmah According to the Kabbalah

In the mystical labyrinth of the *sefirot. Hokmah,* or wisdom, gleams like a luminary in the cosmological structure known as the *Sefirot*, the divine emanations of God's essence. *Hokmah*, the second of the ten *Sefirot*, sits resplendent at the crown of the right column, where it plays a profound role in the celestial dialectic of creation. *Hokmah* represents the primal spark of divine consciousness, the ethereal flash of intuition, and the first revelation of the divine intellect. It is the inception of potentiality, the undiluted, pure, and unadulterated thought before it is processed and understood. It is the silence before the melody, the raw idea untrammeled by the constraints of reason.

In Kabbalistic cosmology, the initial spark of insight in *Hokmah* finds its structure and development in *Binah,* the *Sefirah* of Understanding. Located on the left side of the Tree of Life, Binah is associated with elaboration and comprehension. *Hokmah* and Binah symbolize the essential dynamics of creation: *Hokmah* is the source of creative potential, and *Binah* is the nurturing space where this potential is shaped and refined.

In this mystical framework, *Hokmah* is envisioned as the father, embodying the raw power of the creative impulse. At the same time, Binah, as its counterpart, is likened to the mother, the realm where the initial idea from *Hokmah* is cultivated and brought to maturity. The interaction between *Hokmah's* flash of inspiration and Binah's detailed understanding gives rise to the diverse realities of the multiverse. This interplay between *Hokmah* and *Binah* is a fundamental aspect of the Kabbalistic process of creation, where the union of these two *Sefirot* leads to the unfolding of existence.

Hokmah, in its unfathomable depth, represents the non-verbal experience of the divine, the silent knowing, and the ceaseless wonder. It is the initial insight into the divine mind, a point of pure potentiality from which all things originate. To use an astronomical analogy, *Hokmah* is like the silent explosion of a supernova, a moment of absolute wisdom from which cascades a universe of understanding, birthing stars and planets, galaxies and nebulae, in a brilliant display of cosmic consciousness.

Thus, in the end, *Hokmah* moves as the silent partner, the breath before the word, the idea before it takes form. It is the celestial melody that is sung in silence, the wisdom of God expressed in the unspoken language of existence. The wisdom of *Hokmah* is the wisdom of the cosmos, a wisdom not spoken, but deeply felt and understood. It is a wisdom that reaches beyond words and thoughts to touch the very essence of divine reality.

בִּינָה

UNDERSTANDING

The Hebrew Nuances of Binah

The Hebrew feminine noun בִּינָה (*bînāh*) embodies the concepts of understanding, insight, and discernment. It refers to the wisdom required to respond appropriately to the Lord and His Torah, as noted in Deuteronomy 4:6. This term also relates to the capacity to skillfully navigate life's circumstances, as seen in 1 Chronicles 12:33.

The term בִּין (*bin*), typically used as a verb, conveys the action of comprehending, distinguishing, or understanding. It implies an active process of discernment, such as in the phrases הֲבִינוֹתִי (Have I understood?) or לְהָבִין ("to understand"). In contrast, בֵּין (*bein*) is often employed as a preposition or conjunction, signifying "between" or "among." It describes the relationship of one entity to another in space, time, or metaphorically, as in בֵּין הַשָּׁמַיִם וְהָאָרֶץ ("Between heaven and earth") or בֵּין כָּךְ וּבֵין כָּךְ (Either way).

Both בִּין and בֵּין stem from the same root and share a basic meaning related to separation or being amid things. However, בִּין suggests a more active engagement with the concept of separation, involving intellectual or conceptual distinction, whereas בֵּין often denotes a more passive or physical state of being between entities. In essence, בִּינָה represents the application of understanding to live wisely in accordance with divine principles, while בִּין and בֵּין differentiate the modes of comprehension and the spatial or conceptual relationships within the Hebrew language.

A Woman's Understanding

The Talmud records a remark by the third-century Babylonian scholar, Rav *Hisda* (ca. 320 C.E.), who remarked: God endowed woman with greater intuition than men (BT Niddah 45b). This remark can be interpreted and examined through various psychological perspectives.

- ❑ **COGNITIVE ABILITIES:** The term *Binah* or intuition, in this context, might refer to several different cognitive abilities. In psychology, intuition is often related to abilities such as emotional intelligence, social cognition, or interpersonal sensitivity. These involve understanding and navigating social and emotional signals and situations, areas where some research has suggested women, on average, might outperform men.

- ❑ **EMPATHY AND PERSPECTIVE TAKING:** Women are often found to be more empathetic than men, meaning they may be more capable of understanding and sharing the feelings of others. This ability to 'put oneself in another's shoes' is a vital aspect of intuition.

❑ **COMMUNICATION SKILLS:** It takes a special talent to be an effective communicator. This multifaceted skill includes not only the ability to convey one's thoughts and feelings effectively but also the ability to perceive and interpret the verbal and nonverbal cues of others. Women are sometimes thought to have an advantage in this area, contributing to their intuitive understanding of situations.

Let us note that *Rav Hisda* only made a generalization, which may not be factually accurate when describing gender differences between women and men. There can be considerable overlap between the sexes, and individual differences often exceed gender differences. Not all women are more intuitive than all men, and vice versa. Personality traits are widely distributed and influenced by many factors, including genetics, environment, upbringing, and personal experiences. Yet, many of the points thus mentioned can be applied to how the Kabbalists viewed this particular *sefira*, which we shall now examine.

The Sefira of Binah

In the labyrinthine cosmic order of creation in the Kabbalah, *Binah*, the third emanation upon the Tree of Life, holds the mantle of comprehension and wisdom. Depicted as a maternal presence, it cradles the unrefined core of *Hokhmah*, the kernel of intuition, within its embracing warmth. One must dive into the understanding of the *Sefirot* to grasp *Binah* fully. These divine manifestations serve as conduits through which *Ein Sof*, the Infinite, presents itself. They interlace the physical and spiritual domains, and they weave the rich matrix of existence.

Among the letters of the Tetragrammaton, *Binah* is symbolized by the *Hei*. Unlike the non-dimensional point of *Yud*, the *Hei* a letter that has depth and three-dimensionality. The Zohar refers to the Sefirot of *Hokmah* and *Binah* as "The dot (*Hokmah*) in the palace (*Binah*)."[129] symbolizing the essence of these categories and their interrelation. Within Kabbalistic imagery, *Binah* is closely associated with the Divine Feminine principle. *Binah*, which translates to "understanding" or "insight," is often portrayed as a nurturing and formative force, providing structure and cultivation.

Its energies echo the maternal aspect of divinity, representing the Heavenly Mother in the Kabbalistic Tree of Life.

Like a mother, *Binah* makes significant contributions to creating and developing ideas and insights. She personifies a womb-like receptivity, a deep intuitive wisdom that patiently comprehends and nurtures. The energy of *Binah* involves a sense of discernment and patience, reflecting the attributes typically associated with motherhood, such as nurturing, caring, and forming bonds. *Binah* works in harmony with *Hokhmah*, the second *sefirah* on the Tree of Life, which represents the Divine Masculine, often described as the Heavenly Father. *Hokhmah* symbolizes the inception of thought and ideas— the initial, formless spark of inspiration. In contrast, *Binah* provides structure to these raw concepts, just as a mother would provide form and shape to a child during pregnancy.

"Binah"

In this image, Binah, the Kabbalistic *Sefirah* of understanding and intuition, is personified as a feminine figure intertwined with flowing, wave-like patterns, symbolizing the receptive and contemplative nature of Binah. Her form merges with a tree, alluding to the Tree of Life, where *Binah* occupies a pivotal position as the nurturing mother of creation, giving structure and form to the emanations of the divine. The surrounding symbols, including Hebrew letters and esoteric diagrams like the Tree of Life and geometric shapes, imply the complex interplay of cosmic forces that Binah orchestrates. The overall composition embodies Binah's role as the womb of the cosmos, where the raw insights from Hokmah are processed, shaped, and ultimately brought into existence, exemplifying the transformative power of divine understanding.

In their harmonious interaction, *Hokhmah* and *Binah* give birth to the rest of the *Sefirot,* which are the divine emanations or attributes on the Kabbalistic Tree of Life. They are considered the parents of the other sefirot, embodying the foundational energies of the cosmos. The interplay between *Binah* and *Hokhmah*, the Divine Feminine and Masculine, illustrates a profound principle: unity's dynamic, creative, and generative power. Binah gives form and structure to the abstract inspirations from *Hokhmah.*

The resultant birth of the other *Sefirot* illustrates the creative process's completeness, marking the emergence of a balanced and harmonized universe. As a realm of insight and understanding, it is a cosmic vault of enigmatic wisdom, offering an intuitive comprehension that probes the marrow of existence. As the "mother of comprehension", *Binah* nourishes the nascent flash of *Hokhmah's* wisdom, bestowing upon it form and structure, thus giving birth to existence.

In essence, *Binah* is a celestial chalice of depth and receptivity. She symbolizes divine understanding, discernment, and rationality. Acting as the universal womb, she accepts the spiritual spark of *Hokhmah's* intuition, imparts form and comprehension to it, and guides it through the remaining *Sefirot.* She is instrumental in creating and nourishing existence, reflecting the divine energy into a spectrum of intricacies, mirroring the profound depths of her understanding.

In this way, *Binah* is not just the "mother of comprehension" but also the sculptor of wisdom. She shapes the raw intuition of

Hokmah into structured thought, adding flesh to the bones of the idea and birthing it into existence. This act of creation is not solely a mental phenomenon, but also a cosmic one, mirroring the divine process that breathes life into the universe. *Binah* weaves a thread of comprehension, enlightening the spiritual seeker with her wisdom, and guiding them through the labyrinthine paths of existence.

דַּעַת

EXPERIENTIAL KNOWLEDGE

The Hebrew Nuances of Da'at

As we noted earlier, to understand Kabbalah, a basic understanding of Biblical Hebrew terms is crucial. A case in point is the understanding of the concept of 'knowledge'. In Hebrew and Aramaic, the expression of 'knowledge' is predominantly represented by the root יָדַע (*yāda'*). This Hebrew root is abundantly employed in its verb form *yāda'* ("to know"), with a staggering frequency of over 800 instances in various contexts across the Scriptures. Emerging from this root is the noun דַּעַת (*da'at,* "knowledge"), which is observed 88 times throughout the scriptural narrative. The Septuagint, the renowned ancient Greek translation of the Tanakh, primarily employs two Greek words to translate the Hebrew term *yāda'*: οἶδα (*oida,* "to have seen") and γινώσκω (*ginōskō,* "know"), thus illustrating the depth and multiplicity of meanings the original term encapsulates.

The verb יָדַע (*yāda'*), denoting understanding or recognition, is used in a variety of contexts:

❑ The noun דַּעַת (*da'at*) signifies the capacity, content, or breadth of one's knowledge or understanding. An excellent instance of its usage can be seen in Proverbs 1:7: "The fear of the LORD is the beginning of knowledge (*da'at*), but fools despise wisdom and instruction." Once again, his verse poignantly emphasizes the value of experiential knowledge and wisdom that stems from a sense of reverence, also known as the "fear of the LORD."

- ❑ The term דֵּעָה (*dēʿāh*) signifies divine knowledge or knowledge specifically imparted by God. This term is used in Isaiah 11:2, which says, "The Spirit of the LORD will rest on him—the Spirit of wisdom and of understanding, the Spirit of counsel and of might, the Spirit of the knowledge (*dēʿāh*) and fear of the LORD ." This verse beautifully conveys the profound significance of divine knowledge.

- ❑ The term דֵּעַ (*dēaʿ*) refers to personal knowledge or opinion. It makes an appearance in Job 26:3, "How you have counseled the unwise and provided abundant revelation (*dēaʿ*)!"

Each of these unique Hebrew terms illuminates the multifaceted ways in which knowledge is depicted and understood within the *Tanakh*. They range from personal and experiential knowledge to divine knowledge and wisdom, all of which are integral to the Bible's broader narrative.

The Power of 'Da'at: And Adam Knew Eve

In this context, Ramban posits that the term "to know" (ידע) is not simply an act of intellectual comprehension but denotes an intimate, experiential knowing. Before their expulsion from Eden, Adam did not experience Eve in a deeply personal way, neither as a life partner nor as a friend. Post-Eden, however, Adam begins to truly "know" Eve, discovering her as a companion and a beloved partner in life. This interpretation finds support in Midrashic writings, where the phrase "knew Eve" suggests a deepening of Adam's affection for his wife, kindled by an increased understanding of her.

A superficial reading of the Adam and Eve story might suggest a shattered bond after their exile from Eden. Yet, this view misses the profound growth woven through shared struggles and deep mutual understanding. Though their early days beyond Eden brimmed with tension and missteps, these trials crafted an enduring bond, enriching their love and unity. This ancient tale holds timeless wisdom for modern relationships, revealing that true intimacy transcends physicality, calling for a fearless commitment another, so that one may know and be known by another fully.

In today's distracted world, where sexuality is often reduced to a hollow act, stripped of emotional or spiritual depth, an aching isolation lingers. Many long for a deeper connection with their partners—a yearning often stifled in a culture that prizes hasty encounters and superficial ties. The story of Adam and Eve offers a radiant counterpoint: a vision of intimacy rooted in shared vulnerability, lived experiences, and a tender exploration of each other's innermost selves. In a society that too often cheapens and commodifies human connection, this narrative challenges the notion that intimacy hinges on physical pleasure alone. Instead, it celebrates the vital role of emotional depth and spiritual harmony.

By embracing the transformative power of truly knowing and being known, we can heal the wounds of alienation and forge connections that restore wholeness to our fragmented world. In a space where genuine caring and empathy reside, physical intimacy can facilitate a near-mystical merging of souls, a unification of consciousness that allows us to truly "know" the inner realm of the other and be "known" in return. This process offers a balm for our collective soul in an increasingly fragmented world.

The story of Adam and Eve speaks to a deep-seated yearning within us—a longing for a love that transcends the superficial and reaches the core of our being. This biblical narrative highlights that physical intimacy coupled with genuine caring and empathy can lead to a profound merging of souls. This reciprocal process of knowing and being known provides solace and healing, reminding us of our interconnectedness and the potential for deep, meaningful relationships.

Pinpointing Da'at on the Tree of Life

In the Kabbalistic Tree of Life, *Da'at* is often portrayed as floating or being in flux rather than fixed like other *Sefirot*. It functions as a vital bridge or link, providing a transition from the intellectual *Sefirot* (*Hokmah* and *Binah*) to the realm of emotion and action. According to Kabbalistic philosophy, this beautifully encapsulates the dynamic interplay between cognition and emotion in the spiritual journey.

Positioning on the Tree of Life: Unlike other *Sefirot*, which have fixed locations, *Da'at* is often depicted as floating or being in flux. It acts as a bridge or a link between the intellectual and emotional *Sefirot*, transitioning from the realm of the mind (*Hokmah* and *Binah*) to the realm of emotion and action.

It embodies conscious awareness born of deeply internalizing wisdom and understanding, transcending mere abstract intellectual grasp.

INVISIBILITY: *Da'at* is sometimes referred to as an "invisible" *Sefirah*. Since it's considered a process or a conduit rather than a standalone attribute of the Divine, some Kabbalistic traditions don't always include it in the count of the ten *Sefirot*.

INTEGRATION: *Da'at* is about integration and synthesis. It's the aspect that allows for integrating the upper Sefirot (representing the intellectual or conceptual aspects of divinity) with the lower ones (representing the emotional and behavioral aspects). In this way, *Da'at* brings harmony and unity to the Tree of Life.

CONSCIOUSNESS: *Da'at is* often equated with consciousness itself. It represents the human ability to be aware of one's own existence, sensations, and thoughts. This aspect of self-awareness sets it apart from the other *Sefirot*.

With these thoughts in mind, *Da'at* is different because of its unique positioning, its role as a channel between intellectual and emotional divine aspects, its focus on experiential knowledge and consciousness, and its inherent invisibility in certain Kabbalistic traditions.[130]

חֶסֶד

KINDNESS

Hebraic Aspects of Hesed

The Hebrew term חֶסֶד (*chesed*) occurs 246 times in the Tanakh and primarily conveys the ideas of faithfulness, steadfast love, and kindness. This term frequently describes human interactions marked by kindness and mercy (e.g., Gen. 21:23; 2 Sam. 10:2), and it also characterizes the benevolent actions and disposition of God toward His faithful, Israel, and humanity (e.g., Ps. 5:8; 36:6; 48:10). Notably, חֶסֶד is often paired with אֱמֶת (*emet*), signifying truth or faithfulness, to underscore the concept of enduring mercy or steadfast love (e.g., Gen. 24:12, 14; Exod. 20:6; Deut. 5:10).

Hesed in the Kabbalah

Chesed, often regarded as the fourth *Sefira* on the Kabbalistic Tree of Life, embodies unbounded benevolence and generosity. It arises from the harmonious union of Wisdom (*Hokmah*) and Understanding (*Binah*) and is pivotal in guiding human observance of the Torah's 248 positive commandments. *Chesed* is about selfless giving, extending beyond mere material charity to encompass the entirety of one's actions. It holds a revered place in Jewish wisdom for its capacity to benefit both the rich and poor and to assist both the living and the dead. This form of generosity requires an open-hearted giving that transcends the simple relinquishment of possessions. Within the intricate framework of the *Sefirot*, the Kabbalistic blueprint that maps out the complexities of existence, *Chesed* stands as more than just a point on the Tree of Life. It embodies an essential life force, pulsating like a cosmic heartbeat throughout the entirety of creation. *Chesed* symbolizes unlimited kindness and compassion, infusing the universe with a spirit of boundless generosity and mercy.

However, in the delicate equilibrium of the spiritual universe, unchecked *Chesed* poses the risk of creating an overly indulgent world, where spiritual growth is hindered by excessive leniency and comfort. This unbridled kindness, without proper spiritual counterweights, can lead to a state where the essential challenges and struggles necessary for growth and development are absent. Therefore, *Chesed's* expansive nature requires careful moderation. In the dynamic balance of the *Sefirot, Chesed* is tempered by other forces, ensuring that its benevolence is delivered in a way that fosters growth and resilience, rather than spiritual complacency.

This equilibrium is vital, as it prevents the overwhelming nature of boundless generosity from overshadowing the need for discipline and resilience in the spiritual journey. *Chesed,* in its essence, invites individuals to partake in acts of kindness and generosity, becoming integral contributors to the cosmic symphony of creation. It goes beyond the act of giving to embody a deeper, spiritual generosity— a divine invitation to extend oneself in lovingkindness, shaping not just individual experiences but the very fabric of reality.

גְּבוּרָה

MIGHT & DISCIPLINE

Hebraic Aspects of Gevurah

The Hebrew word גְּבוּרָה (*gevurah*) is commonly associated with strength, power, or might in the Bible. It is used to describe a commanding force or power, often evoking a sense of awe and respect due to its superiority (Job 39:19). The term also encompasses victory, indicating the successful defeat and conquest of an enemy (Exodus 32:18). Additionally, גְּבוּרָה signifies achievement, representing the completion and success of actions or deeds. In essence, גְּבוּרָה captures the themes of powerful strength, triumphant victory, and successful accomplishment (1Kgs. 15:23).

On the great tableau of the *Sefirot's* energies, *Gevurah* emerges as a symbol of divine might, encapsulating the intricate balance of strength expressed through restraint. This fifth *Sefira* on the Tree of Life represents a fusion of judgment with unwavering fortitude, standing up against injustice and enduring challenges. Known as "severity" or "strength" in Hebrew, *Gevurah* is necessary to counter *Chesed*'s infinite generosity. This equilibrium is crucial in maintaining cosmic harmony, as it prevents the potential disorder that could arise from unrestrained kindness, ensuring divine justice and order.

Gevurah in the Kabbalah

Gevurah's role involves the directed application of God's power to confine, shape, and focus energy. This disciplined approach is vital in transforming what could be chaotic into a structured and orderly system. It's through *Gevurah* that the universe experiences the necessary limits and boundaries, facilitating a balanced existence.

The dynamics of rain serve as a fitting metaphor for the function of *Gevurah*. Rain, when it falls as gentle droplets, nurtures life and growth, but an uncontrolled deluge can lead to destruction. Similarly, *Gevurah* tempers the flow of divine energy, much like the way rain must be metered to sustain rather than overwhelm life. It's this measured and purposeful restraint that characterizes *Gevurah*, illustrating how controlled power can be a source of life and order, rather than a force of overwhelming destruction. In this way, *Gevurah's* presence in the Kabbalistic Tree of Life underscores the importance of balance, strength, and discipline in the unfolding of the divine plan. *Gevurah* channels God's power to contract, limit, and concentrate energy, effectively crafting divine order from potential chaos.

Far from a negative force, *Gevurah* contributes positively to the grand cosmic scheme. The divine love, particularly expressed through *tzimtzum* or contraction, facilitates the existence and sustenance of God's creatures. Yet, like *Chesed*, an excess of *Gevurah* could disrupt the creation. In the divine framework, *Chesed* and *Gevurah* exist in harmony, neither opposing nor countering each other. *Tiferet* masterfully mediates *their successful interaction*, blending Chesed's abundance with *Gevurah's* severity to ensure the continued existence of creation. This harmonious blending of *Chesed* and *Gevurah* births *Tiferet*'s beauty, adding depth to the triadic relationship often encapsulated by the acronym חגת (*ChaGaT*). Each representing a fundamental *Midot* or attribute, their derivatives further illuminate the richness of Kabbalistic thought.

תִּפְאֶרֶת

BEAUTY & COALESCENCE

Hebrew Nuances of Tiferet

The Hebrew term תִּפְאֶרֶת (*tiferet*) primarily signifies beauty or glory, often relating to external appearances, like the adornment of jewelry or precious stones (2 Chr 3:6; Ezek. 16:17). It also denotes the honor or dignity of an object or person. For example, in Exodus 28:2, the term is used alongside כָּבוֹד (*kābôd*, "glory") to describe the splendor of the priestly garments for Aaron and his sons. Additionally, תִּפְאֶרֶת is used in the Tanakh to signify the glory or high status associated with honor (Deut. 26:19; Judg 4:9).

Tiferet in the Kabbalah

One of the primary reasons the quality of beauty is considered necessary in *Tiferet* is its role as a mediator. Situated between the *sefirot* above and below it on the Tree of Life, *Tiferet* serves as the focal point where divine attributes converge and harmonize. It acts as a unifying force, balancing and integrating the *sefirot* of *Chesed* (kindness) and *Gevurah* (severity), embodying opposing qualities such as mercy and judgment. By blending these contrasting forces, Tiferet brings forth a state of harmony and equilibrium, facilitating the flow of divine energy throughout creation. In the teachings of Kabbalah, the concept of *Tiferet* holds profound significance as it represents a *sefira* associated with beauty, harmony, and balance. Positioned at the center of the Tree of Life, a symbolic diagram representing the ten *sefirot* and their interconnectedness, *Tiferet* occupies a pivotal role in the spiritual framework. Furthermore, *Tiferet*'s beauty reflects the divine order's inherent goodness and unity. It is not limited to external appearances but also encompasses inner beauty—the harmony and alignment of one's thoughts, emotions, and actions. This holistic understanding of beauty recognizes that true beauty arises from aligning one's inner and outer worlds; *Tiferet* acts as a unifying force, blending and integrating these opposing qualities to establish harmonious equilibrium.

Tiferet plays a crucial role in sustaining harmony within the Tree of Life by balancing *Chesed* and *Gevurah*. It prevents an imbalance of excessive kindness or severity, ensuring the balanced and harmonious flow of divine energies throughout creation. Moreover, *Tiferet* serves as a convergence point where divine attributes harmonize. Beauty acts as a meeting place for the various sefirot, allowing their energies to blend and interact. This convergence creates a symphony of spiritual energies that contribute to the overall balance and order of the Tree of Life. As a mediator and harmonizer, *Tiferet* serves as a foundational principle within the Tree of Life. It bridges the gap between higher and lower *sefirot*, balancing and integrating their energies to ensure the smooth flow of divine energy across the spiritual and physical realms.

In psychological terms, the trait of *Tiferet* reminds us about how the experience of beauty is transformative, as it allows individuals to awaken and surrender simultaneously. It brings a sense of completion and sureness, a momentary transcendence of the ordinary. Without the need for calculation or analysis, one can effortlessly slip into the embrace of the Beautiful, much like surrendering to the seamless embrace of water. It is an ancient instinct within us that trusts in the holding power of beauty, providing solace, inspiration, and a profound sense of connection to something greater than ourselves.

Ultimately, *Tiferet's* role in the Tree of Life of Kabbalah is crucial for maintaining balance, harmony, and unity within the divine framework. It acts as a mediator, unifying opposing forces, blending energies, and ensuring the harmonious flow of divine attributes throughout creation. Its association with beauty reflects the Divine Presence and provides a pathway to connect with the divine. The transformative power of beauty in *Tiferet* allows individuals to transcend the ordinary and experience the profound essence of existence.

The Kabbalistic Theology of Beauty

In Kabbalistic thought, the notion of beauty, embodied in the *Sefirah* of *Tiferet* (beauty/harmony), extends far beyond mere physical appeal, resonating with the mystical symbolism of the rainbow observed by Noah after the flood. The Zohar (I:71b) interprets the rainbow as a reflection of the *Sefirot*, particularly *Tiferet*, symbolizing divine harmony and the covenant between God and creation. This perspective reveals a profound truth: within the human soul lies a deep-seated longing for *Tiferet*—a spiritual aspiration to connect with divine beauty. This yearning manifests in our appreciation of the natural world, our resonance with music and art, and even our creative expressions, such as fashion. However, these material expressions are but shadows of the soul's true desire: to experience and manifest the harmonious beauty of Tiferet, which integrates the expansive love of *Chesed* (kindness) and the restrictive strength of *Gevurah* (judgment).

Encountering beauty is akin to entering a sacred space, where the divine light of the *Ein Sof*— the infinite God —becomes perceptible. The most cherished moments of our lives often unfold in settings of profound beauty—a sunset, a melody, a work of art—instilling an immediate sense of connection and elevated existence. These experiences fulfill a spiritual need, offering solace amidst life's challenges and illuminating the transient nature of our world with a glimpse of the eternal. In Kabbalistic terms, beauty reveals both the transcendence of God, who is beyond all form, and the immanence of the divine presence, which permeates creation through the *Sefirot*. As Rabbi Isaac Luria (the Ari) teaches, the divine light that flows through *Tiferet* harmonizes the *Sefirot*, allowing us to perceive the godliness inherent in the world.

The experience of beauty involves a delicate interplay of the *Sefirot* *Tiferet*, *Netzach* (eternity/victory), and *Hod* (splendor/submission). *Tiferet* awakens us to the world's splendor, harmonizing our emotions and intellect in a moment of divine connection. *Netzach* inspires us to actively pursue and create beauty, driving us to manifest *Tiferet* through acts of creativity and perseverance, such as composing music or performing acts of compassion. *Hod*, in turn, fosters a humble receptivity, allowing us to surrender to beauty's transformative power without the need to control it. This balance of awakening and surrender is a hallmark of *Tiferet*'s harmonizing role, where we become acutely aware of the divine while releasing our ego, as described in the Hasidic concept of *bittul* (self-nullification).

Beauty, in this Kabbalistic framework, is both healing and transformative, connecting us to a shared human experience that transcends our individual existence. Yet, Kabbalah also emphasizes our active role in revealing beauty. Through the process of *tikkun* (rectification), we harmonize the *Sefirot* by using the physical world to fulfill the Divine will, transforming mundane actions into expressions of *Tiferet.* For example, an act of kindness not only reflects *Chesed* but, when balanced with *Gevurah,* becomes a manifestation of *Tiferet*'s beauty in the world. Thus, beauty is not a passive experience but a dynamic interaction: we are both receivers of divine beauty and co-creators of it, tasked with making the world a dwelling place for God.

In this light, beauty in Kabbalistic theology is far more than a sensory pleasure—it is a profound encounter with the divine. It elevates the human spirit, much like the awe-inspiring moment when Noah beheld the rainbow, a symbol of unity and revelation. Through Tiferet, supported by *Netzach* and *Hod*, we glimpse the divine harmony that underlies creation, fulfilling our soul's deepest longing to connect with the sacred essence of existence.

נֵצַח וְהוֹד

VICTORY & ENDURANCE

Hebraic Aspects of Netzach

The Hebrew term נֵצַח (*nēṣaḥ*) is derived from the verb נָצַח, which means to be perpetual or enduring. It has cognates in

Aramaic, Phoenician, Ugaritic, and Arabic, within the semantic field of success or victory. In other languages, such as Ethiopic and Arabic, it is associated with purity and reliability, likely derived from the idea of shining or brilliance. In the Tanakh, נֵצַח is used in various forms and contexts. It generally connotes eminence, enduring, everlastingness, or perpetuity (Lam 3:18). As an adverb, it translates to meanings such as "strength," "victory," "forever," "never," and "to the end," reflecting a sense of ongoing or unceasing quality. Some scholars interpret נֵצַח with slight variations, ranging from "glory" to "unceasing." This term encapsulates both the concept of temporal endurance, as in something that lasts forever, and the idea of preeminence or excellence, such as in victory or glory.

Hebraic Aspects of Hod

The Hebrew term הוֹד (*hôd*) is associated with the concepts of majesty, splendor, and vigor and is primarily used in a poetic context. It signifies grandeur, imposing form, and appearance, encompassing beauty, excellence, glory, and honor. In the context of royalty or kingship, הוֹד is used to describe the splendor and majesty of a king, as seen in verses like Psalm 45:4 and 21:6. It denotes the grandeur conferred upon a king, as in 1 Chronicles 29:25, where God bestows majesty upon Solomon.

Netzach and Hod in the Kabbalah

"*Hod*," which translates as "Glory" or "Splendor," represents the eighth *Sefirah* in the Tree of Life. As a divine attribute, *Hod* embodies the principles of humility, surrender, and receptivity. The *Sefirot* are often depicted in pairs, representing opposing or complementary forces, and *Hod* forms a pair with *Netzach.* Within the *Sefiroth*, *Netzach* stands for endurance, assertiveness, and the desire to overcome obstacles. It represents the active, outgoing energy in the world, like a force that pushes outwards.

In contrast, *Hod* embodies the more passive, inward energy. It is about yielding, acquiescing, and receiving. It represents the concept of restraint and the power of stepping back to allow other forces to act. If we were to imagine it in terms of a conversation, *Netzach* would be the force of expressing your point of view, of asserting your ideas, while *Hod* would be the art of listening, of truly hearing and receiving what the other person is saying. On a more spiritual level, *Hod* also symbolizes acknowledgment and gratitude. It is about recognizing the splendor of God's creation, the majesty of divine laws, and the blessing of divine gifts. It's about surrendering to the divine will, acknowledging that higher powers are at work in our lives, and expressing gratitude for the divine blessings we receive.

In the Kabbalistic system, each *Sefirah* also corresponds to a part of the body. *Hod*, interestingly, corresponds to the left leg. Legs, in a spiritual sense, are about movement and progress. The right leg, corresponding to *Netzach*, is the force that propels us forward, while the left leg, *Hod*, provides balance and support. In essence, Hod represents the principles of receptivity, surrender, gratitude, and acknowledgment. It's the quiet glory of the divine, the splendor of humility, the power of yielding and receiving. While *Netzach* is associated with the ability to envision and perceive divine inspiration, *Hod* is associated with the capacity to communicate that inspiration. It can be viewed as the aspect of prophecy that involves interpretation, articulation, and sharing divine wisdom. Also, it's important to note that although *Hod* is often described as a more passive quality, it should not be mistaken for a weakness.

The passive energy of *Hod* is a form of power, just as much as the active energy of *Netzach*. It represents the power to listen, yield, and receive, which is a critical part of any form of communication or interaction. On a broader level, each *sefirah* in the Kabbalistic Tree of Life contributes to the divine process of creation, manifestation, and renewal. Each one plays a critical role in maintaining the balance and harmony of the universe. In this grand scheme, Hod represents the capacity to appreciate, acknowledge, and be receptive to the glory and splendor of divine creation.

יְסוֹד

BONDING & RELATIONSHIP

Hebraic Aspects of Yesod

The Hebrew term יְסוֹד (*yesôḏ*) is multifaceted, primarily denoting foundations and bases in both literal and metaphorical senses. It refers to the base of buildings and constructions (Psalm 137:7; Micah 1:6), specifically the foundation of altars in religious contexts (Exod. 29:12). In a physical sense, it describes body parts like the foot (Hab. 3:3). Metaphorically, it symbolizes endurance and stability, akin to a building's foundation (Prov. 10:25).

The term also derives from the root יָסוֹד, which means "to found" or "establish," often used to describe God's founding of the earth or heaven, as well as in contexts of constructing buildings or setting ordinances. In addition, יְסוֹד takes on a proper name context and metaphorically extends to the concept of beginnings, as well as the foundations of structures and metaphorically to leaders or princes (Ezek. 30:4). Overall, יְסוֹד encapsulates the ideas of physical and structural foundations, bodily parts, and metaphorical concepts of foundational principles and endurance in various settings.

Yesod in the Kabbalah

Yesod, the ninth sefirah on the Kabbalistic Tree of Life, embodies the essence of "foundation" in both a literal and metaphorical sense, playing a pivotal role in the dynamics of bonding and connectivity across various relationships, including those between parent and child, teacher and student, and romantic partners. It acts as a crucial bridge in the Tree of Life, particularly in its interaction with *Netzach* ("Victory"), *Hod* ("Glory"), and *Malkuth* ("Kingdom"), thereby underscoring its integral role in relational balance and harmony.

Situated directly below *Netzach* and *Hod, Yesod* harmonizes their contrasting qualities—*Netzach's* enduring, forceful nature, and Hod's majestic, awe-inspiring presence—into a stable and foundational force. This harmonization is essential in all forms of relationships, ensuring a balance between persistence and respect, vigor and reverence. *Yesod*'s role here is akin to the foundation of a building, ensuring that the structure is both stable and able to withstand various forces.

Further, *Yesod* serves as the conduit to *Malkuth*, the *sefirah* representing the material world. It channels and translates the spiritual and emotional energies from the upper sephirot through *Netzach* and *Hod* into *Malkuth*. This reflects how foundational values and emotional bonds in human relationships manifest into tangible actions and experiences in our physical existence. For instance, a parent's love shapes a child's growth, or a teacher's guidance molds a student's path.

In the metaphorical landscape of relationships, *Yesod* is where trust, understanding, and connectivity are nurtured and maintained. It represents the undercurrents of communication and emotional exchange that form the bedrock of strong, healthy relationships. Its balancing role is critical in preventing overwhelming energies from *Netzach* or Hod from destabilizing relationships, thus maintaining a nurturing environment that is conducive to growth and mutual enrichment.

Thus, *Yesod*'s interactions with *Netzach, Hod, and Malkuth* highlight its crucial role in fostering relationship stability and balance. It embodies the foundational elements of connectivity and communication, essential for developing and sustaining healthy, meaningful bonds across various aspects of human interaction. *Yesod*, therefore, stands as a testament to the importance of a strong foundation in every relational dynamic, be it familial, educational, or romantic.

מַלְכוּת

MALCHUT & ACTUALIZATION

Hebraic Aspects of Malchut

The Hebrew term מֶלֶךְ (*melekh*), meaning "king," goes beyond mere political leadership in the Hebrew Bible (Tanakh); it carries spiritual significance. It represents not just earthly authority but often a divinely sanctioned role. For instance, King David's anointment by Samuel symbolizes divine approval and mission. The term thus embodies a concept of leadership that intertwines with spiritual duty and divine guidance.

In broader Jewish thought, מֶלֶךְ also reflects spiritual leadership and moral responsibility. A king is not merely a ruler but a steward of God's will, responsible for guiding the people in accordance with divine laws and principles. This view elevates the role of מֶלֶךְ from a secular position to one of spiritual significance, where the king's actions have both earthly and heavenly implications.

"There Cannot be a King Without a Nation."

In Kabbalistic thought, the concept of אֵין מֶלֶךְ בְּלֹא עָם "There cannot be a King without a nation" essentially means that the Divine, often referred to as the "King" or "Creator," cannot be recognized or actualized without a receptive entity, which in this case is the "nation" or creation itself. It's an expression of the reciprocal relationship between God and humanity. It illustrates the idea that God's kingship, His ruling aspect, only exists when there are subjects who acknowledge it, i.e., humanity. God is all-powerful, and yet, even Divine power has its limitations and cannot act in a totalitarian manner toward human beings.

Furthermore, this principle highlights the significance of free will within the Kabbalistic worldview. God, despite being all-powerful, does not act in a totalitarian manner toward human beings. Divine power respects human agency and freedom and does not arbitrarily impose its will. The "nation" must choose to recognize and accept the "King," which makes the interaction a consensual relationship rather than a coerced one.

This Kabbalistic concept beautifully encapsulates the reciprocity, mutual respect, and interconnectedness between the Divine and His creation. It emphasizes the significance of human free will in recognizing and accepting the Divine, and how this recognition actualizes the concept of Divine Kingship. In this paradigm, God's existence is not in question, but the recognition and manifestation of God as "King" depends on the consciousness and acceptance of his subject's consent. This consensual notion implies that people, by their spiritual choices and actions, can elevate the divine sparks in the world, thus actualizing God's sovereignty. Accepting God's reality and Will enables people to realize the Heavenly kingdom on this material plane.

"There Is No King without a People"

The image captures the Kabbalistic idea that a king's essence is defined by his people, with a silhouette of a crowned figure embodying numerous individual forms. This represents the concept that a ruler's legitimacy (Malchut) is conferred by and dependent on the collective he serves, emphasizing the symbiotic relationship between a leader and his subjects within the cosmic order.

Among Western thinkers, the French philosopher Jean-Jacques Rousseau's concept of the social contract comes relatively close to this Judaic mystical idea. The social contract theory proposes that the legitimacy of authority, in this case, the state or the sovereign, over individuals, arises from a kind of agreement, a "contract," between them. In Rousseau's version of this theory, individuals collectively agree to surrender some of their freedoms to the collective authority in exchange for protection and the establishment of an organized society.

Thus, in Rousseau's social contract, the authority's existence is contingent upon the people's consent, similar to how the Kabbalistic idea posits that the actualization of the King's authority depends on the will of the nation (as we see on election day). But they differ in nature. The mystical "contract" is spiritual and transcendent, dealing with divine-human relations and the spiritual state of the world. In contrast, Rousseau's work is socio-political, addressing the relationships among human beings and their mutual obligations within a civil society.

The Kabbalistic idea and Rousseau's social contract focus on mutual recognition and dependence —between God and humanity, and between the authority and the citizens, respectively. However, the goals and implications of these concepts in their respective contexts are very different. The former is aimed at spiritual elevation and the fulfillment of a divine plan, while the latter aims to ensure political order, justice, and the well-being of individuals within a society. *Malchut* bears the genesis of the revealed light of the *En Sof*, shedding light upon the world and its beings. Each entity derives its unique light and vitality from this source, infusing life and sustenance into it.

Malchut highlights the intimate connection between spiritual and physical realms, fostering the manifestation of divine energy in everyday life. It underscores our interconnectedness, guiding us to appreciate divinity in everyday events and interactions, revealing their role in the divine plan. This *Sefirah* is often seen as the culmination of the spiritual journey, symbolizing the merger of the individual with the universal consciousness, implying a profound sense of unity with the Divine.

Therefore, *Malchut* aligns with Shechinah, the Divine Indwelling Presence. This *Sefirah* nurtures personal transformation, aligning individual consciousness with divine intent. It signifies our physical body and our external world, transforming us into microcosms of the Tree of Life. By cultivating mindfulness, we infuse the divine's qualities into *Malchut*, recognizing the sanctity within creation and aligning our actions with divine will. Thus, we contribute to *tikkun olam* or "repair of the world."

Malchut, therefore, serves as a reminder of our potential to be divine vessels, channeling and manifesting spiritual energy into the physical world. It urges us toward spiritual growth and moral responsibility and inspires conscious contributions to the world's betterment. In essence, *Malchut* illustrates unity and interconnection, prompting us to acknowledge our divine potential and strive for a mindful, compassionate, and harmonious existence. In the enigmatic matrix of Kabbalah, a mesmerizing strand named *Ze'ir An'pin* entwines itself. Embarking on a journey to unfurl its intricate knots, let us tread lightly yet resolutely, retaining its profound literary allure.

Kabbalah's heart reverberates with the rhythm of the *Sefirot*, ten divine emanations breathing the Infinite into the finite. Far from a pantheon of deities, these *Sefirot* are radiant facets of a solitary divine essence, dancing a cosmic ballet that threads the delicate fabric of existence. Nestled within this divine constellation is *Ze'ir An'pin,* the "Small Face" or "Short Countenance." This entity, enigmatic and alive, encapsulates six *sefirot*—*Chesed* (Kindness), *Gevurah* (Strength), *Tiferet* (Beauty), *Netzach* (Eternity), *Hod* (Glory), and *Yesod* (Foundation)—each shimmering with the emotional colors of God.

Just as a mirror reflects the beholder, *Ze'ir An'pin* mirrors the divine in its microcosmic stature, encapsulating the dynamism and dualism of life's primal forces. For instance, *Chesed* and *Gevurah* echo the divine balance between grace and justice, compassion and severity. At the heart, *Tiferet* plays the peacemaker, harmonizing these contrasting forces. *Ze'ir An'pin*, perceived as the symbolic visage of God, personifies the divine facet intimately entwined with our world, forging a bridge between God's unfathomable transcendence and immanent presence.

Within the web of Kabbalistic symbology, *Ze'ir An'pin* often dons the guise of a divine groom, while the tenth *sefirah*, *Malkuth,* assumes the form of a divine bride. This mystical union recurs in Kabbalistic lore, symbolizing the fusion of divine compassion and justice, the harmonious convergence of transcendence and immanence. Yet, bear in mind that these elucidations are akin to maps of unseen territories—symbolic rather than literal. Kabbalah conveys truths that whisper beyond words, hiding in their silent interstices. Its poetic imaginings guide us beyond language's borders, deeper into the divine mysteries.

As we embark, we confront the Kabbalistic paradox: the pursuit to articulate the inarticulable, to depict God's transcendent reality in words and concepts. Thus, the *Sefirot*, including *Ze'ir An'pin*, ought to be considered celestial blueprints of divine qualities, not literal descriptions. *Ze'ir An'pin*, associated with the *midot* or God's emotional attributes, offers a counterpoint to the first three *Sefirot*, entwined with God's intellectual aspects. These "emotions" must not be mistaken for human sentiments; instead, they metaphorically delineate the dynamic facets of divine interaction with the world.

זעיר אנפין
ZE'IR AN'PIN

Each of the six *Sefirot* within *Ze'ir An'pin* has its own complex symbology:

- ❑ *Chesed* (Kindness) represents love, benevolence, and abundant generosity. It is the outpouring, giving aspect of the Divine.

- ❑ *Gevurah* (Strength) signifies restraint, discipline, and justice. It is the withholding, boundary-setting aspect of the Divine, balancing Chesed.

- *Tiferet* (Beauty) - This embodies harmony and compassion. It is the center of the Sefirot, balancing and integrating different forces.

- *Netzach* (Eternity) - This represents the drive to overcome obstacles and the endurance to carry on.

- *Hod* (Glory) stands for humility and the power of surrender, forming a balance for Netzach.

- *Yesod* (Foundation) signifies the ability to connect and relate, acting as a conduit between the other Sefirot and Malkuth.

- *Malchut* represents the sefirah associated with sovereignty, kingship, and the feminine aspect of the divine. It is often referred to as the "Kingdom" or the "Shekhinah," representing the immanent presence of the divine in the world.

In Lurianic Kabbalah, *Zeir Anpin* and *Malchut* are intimately connected. *Zeir Anpin* is considered the "husband" or the masculine aspect, while *Malchut* is regarded as the "wife" or the feminine aspect. They form a cosmic union, symbolizing the divine union of masculine and feminine principles.

Zeir Anpin is seen as the emanator and provider of energy and influence, while *Malchut* receives and channels that energy, manifesting it in the physical world. *Malchut* is the vessel through which the divine light is revealed and actualized in the material realm. Thus, while *Zeir Anpin* and *Malchut* are distinct aspects within the sefirot system, they are deeply interrelated and interdependent. *Zeir Anpin* provides the energy, and *Malchut* receives and expresses it, allowing for the manifestation of Divine Presence and influence in the world.

The interplay of these Sefirot in *Ze'ir An'pin* offers a model of divine dynamics. They suggest that God's interaction with the world involves a blend of love and justice, endurance and surrender, and balance and connection. Through the lens of *Ze'ir An'pin*, it serves as a poignant reminder of the complexity and richness of this ancient tradition, as well as the way it continually invites its students to deepen their understanding of the divine and the cosmos.

אֲרֵךְ אַנְפִּין
ARECH ANPIN

Arech Anpin: The Infinite Visage of the Divine

In Kabbalah's shadowed tapestry, *Arech Anpin*—the "Long Face" or "Extended Countenance"—rises as a divine enigma, a whisper of awe cloaked in fathomless mystery. It's no mere concept, but a portal to the Divine's deepest pulse, soaring beyond the grasp of mortal thought, a beacon of the infinite shimmering just out of reach. Within Jewish mysticism, *Arech Anpin* reigns at the heart of the *Sefirot*—ten radiant emanations tracing the Tree of Life, God's living architecture. Anchored to *Keter*, the crown of crowns, it stands as the pinnacle of divine potential, a vast will unfurling from *Ein Sof*'s boundless abyss. Here, *Keter* gleams as pure intent, and *Arech Anpin* embodies its expanse—an eternal gaze too vast for our eyes, too deep for our words.

Its nature unfolds in layers, each a revelation:

INFINITE DIVINE WILL: *Arech Anpin* is God's unbridled volition, a torrent of intent so mighty it drowns comprehension. The Zohar hints at this: "A spark from the hidden of all hidden" (I:20a), a will that births worlds yet eludes naming.

THE DIVINE DUALITY: Paired with *Zeir Anpin*—the "Short Face," tethered to six emotional Sefirot like *Tiferet*'s harmony—*Arech Anpin* looms as the arcane twin. Where *Zeir*

Anpin offers a God we can feel, *Arech Anpin* veils the unknowable, a duality weaving the tangible with the transcendent.

BRIDGE TO THE TRANSCENDENT: Bound to Keter, it's a conduit to God's most ethereal edge, a window cracked open to the divine riddle—less a face than a horizon.

DIVINE ENERGY DYNAMICS: In Kabbalah's cosmic dance, *Arech Anpin* channels divine energy, a river of light cascading from Ein Sof's silence to creation's hum, igniting the Sefirot below.

And then, the thirteen mercies—etched in Micah 7:18–20 and *Ki Tissa* (Exodus 34:6–7)—unfurl like petals from its core: "Compassionate, gracious, slow to anger…" These attributes, split between *Keter*'s crown and *Hokhmah*'s wisdom, pulse as divine breath, threading mercy through the infinite will. *Arech Anpin* isn't static—it's a living interplay, a face gazing both inward to *Ein Sof* and outward to us, its light refracted through a prism of grace.

This isn't God diminished but magnified—mysterious yet mighty, a paradox of presence and absence. The *Besht* saw it in a storm's hush, a glimpse of eternity in a widow's tear. *Arech Anpin* doesn't explain—it beckons, a divine expanse where awe meets the unknown, and the soul trembles at the edge of the infinite.

Analogies for Arech Anpin's Relation to Keter

Understanding *Arech Anpin* is indeed pivotal to grasping the nature of *Keter*, the highest *Sefirot* in Kabbalistic teachings. *Arech Anpin* is closely associated with *Keter* and helps in understanding how *Keter*, representing the divine will and crown, functions within the Sefirotic structure. Here are three analogies that can aid in comprehending the essence of *Arech Anpin*:

THE CROWN AND THE KINGDOM: Imagine *Keter* as a crown and *Arech Anpin* as the king who wears it. The crown (*Keter*) symbolizes authority, sovereignty, and the highest power level, while the king (*Arech Anpin*) embodies that power's actual exercise and manifestation. Just as a crown symbolizes royalty but requires a king to actualize its authority, *Keter* represents the potential of divine will, which is actualized through *Arech Anpin*.

THE BRAIN AND THE NERVOUS SYSTEM: Think of *Keter* as the brain and *Arech Anpin* as the nervous system of a body. The brain (Keter) is the control center, the source of thoughts and decisions, while the nervous system (*Arech Anpin*) is the pathway through which these decisions are communicated and executed throughout the body. This analogy illustrates how *Keter's* influence and directives are channeled and manifested through *Arech Anpin*.

THE SEED AND THE TREE: Consider *Keter* as a seed and *Arech Anpin* as a tree that grows from this seed. The seed (*Keter*) contains the genetic blueprint and the potential for the tree's existence. *Arech Anpin,* like the tree, is the actualization of this potential – the growth, development, and expression of the seed's inherent possibilities. This analogy demonstrates how the 'seed' of *Keter* finds its expression and fulfillment through the 'tree' of *Arech Anpin*.

These analogies help conceptualize *Arech Anpin's* role about *Keter,* portraying it as the medium through which the divine will and essence embodied in *Keter* are expressed and actualized.

עַתִּיק יוֹמִין
ATIK YOMIN
עַתִּיק יוֹמִין

Atik Yomin, translated as "Ancient of Days,"[131] is based on a mystical passage in Daniel 7:9, חָזֵה הֲוֵית עַד דִּי כָרְסָוָן רְמִיו וְעַתִּיק יוֹמִין יְתִב לְבוּשֵׁהּ כִּתְלַג חִוָּר וּשְׂעַר רֵאשֵׁהּ כַּעֲמַר נְקֵא כָּרְסְיֵהּ שְׁבִיבִין דִּי־נוּר גַּלְגִּלּוֹהִי נוּר דָּלִק "As I watched, thrones were set in place, and an Ancient One took his throne, his clothing was white as snow, and the hair of his head like pure wool; his throne was fiery flames, and its wheels were burning fire" (Dan. 7:9).

Atik Yomin, meaning "Ancient of Days" in Aramaic, is a profound and esoteric concept in Kabbalah, representing one of the deepest aspects of the divine. Within the framework of the Sefirot—the ten emanations or attributes through which the *Ein Sof* (the Infinite Divine) reveals itself and becomes accessible to human understanding—*Atik Yomin* is closely associated with *Keter*, the highest *Sefirah*. *Keter*, often translated as "Crown," symbolizes the transcendent will and primordial source of divine emanation, existing beyond comprehension and serving as the bridge between the infinite and the finite. *Atik Yomin* specifically refers to the most elevated and concealed aspect of *Keter*, embodying the eternal, unchanging essence of the Divine that precedes all creation and time. This concept underscores the mystical unity and timelessness of the Divine, evoking awe at the unfathomable depth of existence's origin.

Keter stands at the top of the Tree of Life and is often translated as "Crown." It represents the initial point of contact between the Ein Sof and the manifest universe. While *Keter* itself is a complex *Sefirah*, *Atik Yomin* is considered an inner dimension of *Keter*. It's the most concealed part, representing not just the beginning of the visible or manifest aspects of God, but the depth of the divine mind that precedes and underlies all creation. The title "Ancient of Days" conveys the idea of timelessness and eternal existence. In Kabbalistic thought, *Atik Yomin* is beyond all temporal and finite categories. It signifies a state of divine reality that exists before and beyond creation as we know it. As such, it represents the ultimate source of wisdom and understanding, containing the blueprint of all that is to unfold in the universe.

When Kabbalistic texts speak of "words of wisdom reaching *Atik Yomin*," they refer to the process by which human spiritual insights or interpretations of Torah ascend through the Sefirotic structure to reunite with their divine source. This ascent symbolizes elevating human consciousness and understanding back to its ultimate origin in the divine intellect. The concept of *Atik Yomin* further suggests that the deepest truths of existence and the highest forms of spiritual wisdom are not just ancient in a temporal sense, but are part of the eternal, unchanging fabric of reality. They are truths that transcend time and space, existing in a realm of divine consciousness that is largely inaccessible to human reason but can be approached through mystical experience.

The return of insights to *Atik Yomin* is not merely a reunion with their source, but a transformation. As human understanding merges with divine wisdom, it contributes to the continuous unfolding and evolution of the universe, revealing new aspects of divine light and truth. Thus, *Atik Yomin* represents the deepest, most hidden aspect of divine wisdom, associated with the *Sefirah* of *Keter*. It embodies the eternal, unchanging source of all existence and understanding. The journey of wisdom to *Atik Yomin* is symbolic of the mystical aspiration to return to and unite with this profound source, leading to spiritual transformation and enlightenment.

הִתְכַּלְלוּת

Inter-inclusionary Reality

In Kabbalistic thought, the universe is composed of various spiritual levels or dimensions that are deeply interconnected and interwoven. The concept of *Hitkallalut* describes this dynamic relationship, where each *Sefirah* contains aspects of the others within itself. This interconnection ensures that the divine flow, or the spiritual energy emanating from the *Ein Sof* (the Infinite), is seamlessly transmitted and shared across all levels of reality.

Hitkallalut underscores the idea that all aspects of the divine structure are united and integrated. It suggests a holistic view of the cosmos, where every part reflects and contains the whole. This principle is crucial for comprehending the intricate, interconnected nature of the divine realm and the unity that underlies the diversity of creation in the Kabbalistic cosmology. To use an analogy from "David Bohm's concept of the Implicate Order, his insights reveal intriguing parallels with the Kabbalistic concept of *Hitkallalut.* Both ideas reflect a reality where separation is only apparent, and underlying connections form the essence of existence. While there are no direct connections between Bohm's ideas and Kabbalah, one might find some interesting parallels, which, however, should be taken with caution as speculative comparisons rather than solid links:

- ❑ IMPLICATE AND EXPLICATE ORDER: One of Bohm's key ideas was that of the implicate (hidden, "enfolded") and explicate (visible, "unfolded") order. The former represents a deeper, more fundamental level of reality, while the latter is the reality we perceive directly. Similarly, Kabbalah suggests that there are hidden, mystical aspects to reality that are not immediately accessible to human perception.[132]

- ❑ HOLISM: Bohm's theory proposes that the universe is holistically interconnected, rendering the traditional concept of space and the idea of separation within reality as nonsensical. This perspective aligns with certain Kabbalistic interpretations, which suggest that every aspect of creation, no matter how minute, mirrors a part of the Divine. Both Bohm and Jewish mysticism invite us to envision existence not as a collection of isolated objects but as a dynamic, interconnected whole.

❑ PROCESS AND MOVEMENT: Bohm's concept of the "holomovement" suggests a dynamic, constantly changing universe where matter and energy are in constant flow. Some elements of Kabbalah also emphasize the dynamism and constant unfolding of divine energies in the creation and sustenance of the world.

❑ CONSCIOUSNESS AND REALITY: Bohm also ventured into the territory of consciousness and its relation to reality, arguing that they are not separate, but deeply interconnected. This echoes some views in Kabbalah, which regards human consciousness as capable of directly participating in the divine or spiritual reality, which teaches that through the power of the *mitzvah* and proper intentionality, one can impact the world and the cosmic order. It is here that the Kabbalah offers a perspective that is missing in Bohm's view of reality.

❑ HOLISM'S IMPLICATIONS FOR PRAYER: In this holistic view of the universe, where all is fundamentally interconnected and God underpins all existence, prayer is redefined. The implications of holism for prayer are profound. Introspection and spiritual awakening become paramount, guiding us toward recognizing the Divine not as a remote entity, but as an integral part of ourselves and the world around us. Prayer is not a spatial journey toward God, but rather an inward journey of the soul, which already exists within God. Every action, every thought, ripples outwards, contributing to the intricate dance of the universe. This understanding fosters a deep sense of responsibility and interconnectedness, reminding us that our choices and actions hold cosmic significance. This perspective implies that our perception of individual objects as distinct and separate in space and time could be an illusion crafted by the Divine. Such an illusion is crucial, as it upholds the sense of individuality, freedom, and distinction that characterizes our physical reality. This understanding of prayer and existence suggests a deeper, more intrinsic connection between the self, the universe, and the divine.[133]

In the larger picture, the Hassidic concept of *hitkallalut* and Bohm's Implicate Order offer frameworks for understanding an intrinsically unified reality. Yet, Jewish mystical tradition offers a perspective that is missing in Bohm's view of reality. These concepts invite us to embrace a more holistic view of existence, recognizing the profound interconnectedness of all things and the deep, often hidden, dimensions that underlie the manifest world. In Kabbalah, every action is meaningful, and the divine and physical intermingle.

Bohm's concept also has practical implications in Kabbalistic spirituality and ethics. It implies that every action and thought, no matter how seemingly small or isolated, has repercussions throughout the entire spiritual structure of the universe. Thus, *hitkallalut* serves as a reminder of the interconnectedness of all things and the importance of each individual's actions within the greater cosmic scheme. While Kabbalistic mysticism and Bohm's theoretical physics emerge from distinct traditions and are grounded in different methodologies, they converge on the idea that reality is far more integrated and whole than our ordinary perceptions suggest. They both challenge us to see beyond apparent separations to the deeper connections that unite all aspects of existence.

In drawing these analogies, we navigate a passage that links tangible reality with the esoteric, connecting the quantum mechanics of the cosmos with humanity's pursuit of spiritual elevation. By marrying contemporary physics jargon with time-honored mystical wisdom, we forge potent metaphors that encapsulate the profound enigma and unity underlying our existence. This synthesis creates a reverberation, reminiscent of the celestial harmonies in the grand orchestra of creation. In reflecting on this confluence of science and spirituality, one is reminded of a poignant observation by the astronomer Robert Jastrow in his significant work, "God and the Astronomers":

At this moment, it seems as though science will never be able to raise the curtain on the mystery of creation. For the scientist who has lived by his faith in the power of reason, the story ends like a bad dream. He has scaled the mountains of ignorance; he is about to conquer the highest peak. As he pulls himself over the final rock, he is greeted by a band of theologians who have been sitting there for centuries.[134]

CHAPTER 9
THE LANGUAGE OF SOUL

Similar to how the pupil is an integral part of the eye, God is an integral part of the soul. The way the eye gains illumination and vision through the pupil, the soul, when enlightened with divine radiance, perceives everything, encompassing not only what exists in the present but also those things not yet manifested but destined to appear in the flow of time. –

—*Philo, On Dreams, 1:15*

Antoninos: *At what times does the soul enter a person? Do we say it is from conception, or is it from the moment the embryo is formed, which is forty days after conception?*

R. Judah HaNasi: *It is from the moment of the formation of the embryo.*

Antoninos: *Your remark does not make sense. Could a piece of meat remain edible for even three days without salt as a preservative, and would it not rot? Your remark is illogical. An embryo could never exist for forty days were it not for the soul. Rather, the soul is placed in man from the moment of conception.*

R. Judah HaNasi: *I must admit that Antoninos convinced me of his point of view regarding this matter. There is a verse that supports him, as it is stated, as it is stated,* וּפְקֻדָּתְךָ שָׁמְרָה רוּחִי *"And Your Providence [ûpĕquddātkā] has preserved my spirit" (Job 10:12), indicating that it is* *from the moment of conception [פְּקִידָה = pekida] that the soul is preserved within a person.*

—*BT*
Sanhedrin 91b

Love is composed of a single soul inhabiting two bodies.
—*Aristotle*

For it was not into my ear you whispered but into my heart. It was not my lips you kissed, but my soul.
—*Judy Garland*

וּמִבְּשָׂרִי אֶחֱזֶה אֱלוֹהַּ

AND FROM MY FLESH I WILL SEE GOD

JOB 19:26

The concept of *Adam Kadmon* in Kabbalistic cosmology provides a fascinating lens through which we can explore the interconnectedness of the macrocosmic (universal) and microcosmic (individual) orders. *Adam Kadmon*, often translated as "Primordial Man," is not a physical being but a spiritual archetype that represents the first emanation of the Divine light following the act of *tzimtzum*— the contraction of the Infinite to create a space for the universe. This archetypal figure embodies the entire cosmos, with every aspect of creation reflected within it.

In this sense, *Adam Kadmon* serves as a macrocosmic mirror of the microcosmic human being, aligning with the verse from Job, "From my flesh, I see God." This principle suggests that the vast, complex structure of the universe and the Divine can be understood through the study and contemplation of our own existence, both physical and spiritual. It implies that the human form, in its complexity and intricacy, is a reflection of the cosmic order.

The concept of perceiving the Divine in our flesh is deeply rooted in the Kabbalistic interpretation of the human body and soul. Just as *Adam Kadmon* is a blueprint for the cosmos, the human body is seen as a microcosm of this larger divine structure. Each part of the body corresponds to different *Sefirot* (divine attributes or emanations), and the soul mirrors the divine light that animates the universe. In this way, understanding our own physical and spiritual makeup becomes a path to understanding the Divine. This correlation elevates the human experience, positioning our physical existence not as something separate or base, but as a vital, integral part of the spiritual world. The body and soul, in their harmonious union, reflect the unity and complexity of the divine structure, offering a tangible means to comprehend and connect with the Divine.

Furthermore, this concept underscores the transformative potential within each individual. In Kabbalistic thought, the soul's journey through the physical realm is not merely a passive experience but an active process of spiritual evolution and *tikkun* (rectification). By engaging with the physical world mindfully and ethically, we mirror the process of divine emanation and contraction. This active participation in the world becomes a form of divine service, where our actions, thoughts, and intentions have cosmic significance. The verse וּמִבְּשָׂרִי אֶחֱזֶה אֱלוֹהַּ "and from my flesh I will see God" (Job 19:26)

"From my flesh, I see God" thus becomes a call to self-awareness and spiritual responsibility. It invites us to explore the depths of our own being, to find within ourselves the reflections of the Divine, and to embrace our role in the ongoing narrative of creation and revelation. In doing so, we align our microcosmic existence with the macrocosmic divine order, participating in the sacred dance of unity and diversity that characterizes the Kabbalistic vision of the cosmos.

The Human Body as a Vessel for the Divine

The relationship between the human body and the spiritual hierarchy of the cosmos can be seen in several ways:

❑ MICROCOSM: Kabbalistic thought often viewed the human body as a microcosm of the universe. Just as the universe is seen as a manifestation of God's attributes, the human body, with its complex structure and functions, reflects these divine qualities. This analogy extends to the belief that understanding our own physical and spiritual makeup can lead to a deeper understanding of the Divine.

❑ SEFIROT AND BODY PARTS: The *Sefirot*, which are the ten emanations or attributes through which the Divine interacts with the world, are often correlated with parts of the human body. For instance, *Chesed* (kindness) and *Gevurah* (severity) are associated with the right and left arms, respectively, symbolizing the balance of mercy and judgment in human actions and divine governance.

❑ THE SOUL'S CONNECTION TO THE DIVINE: The soul is considered to be a "spark" of the Divine, a piece of the eternal that resides within the temporal human body. This perspective suggests that one can connect more deeply with God by understanding and nurturing the spiritual aspect of the soul. Kabbalistic practices, including meditation and prayer, elevate the soul toward its divine source. By engaging in these practices, individuals seek to purify their souls and, in turn, gain a clearer perception of the Divine.

❑ THE ROLE OF PHYSICAL EXISTENCE: Far from seeing the physical world as merely an illusion or a hindrance to spiritual growth, Kabbalistic thought often views physical existence as a vehicle for spiritual elevation. The body and its actions become means through which one can enact divine will and engage in a process of tikkun (repair or rectification), both personally and universally. When performed with intention and awareness, everyday actions can become acts of sanctification. This is the essence of the Kabbalistic approach to life – seeing and revealing the divine spark in all aspects of existence, from the mundane to the holy.

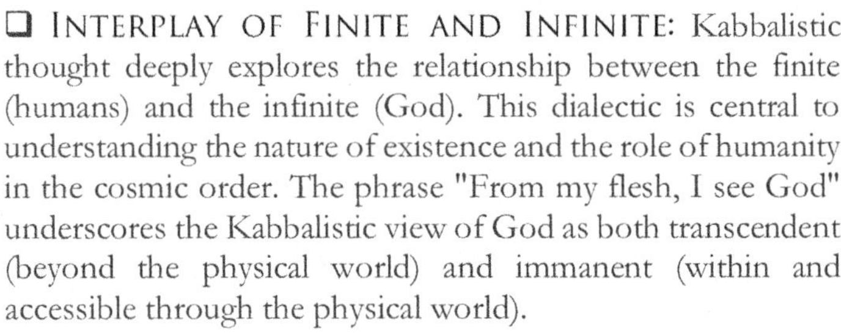

❑ **Interplay of Finite and Infinite:** Kabbalistic thought deeply explores the relationship between the finite (humans) and the infinite (God). This dialectic is central to understanding the nature of existence and the role of humanity in the cosmic order. The phrase "From my flesh, I see God" underscores the Kabbalistic view of God as both transcendent (beyond the physical world) and immanent (within and accessible through the physical world).

❑ **Self-Reflection as a Path to God:** Kabbalistic teachings often emphasize self-reflection and introspection as paths to understanding the Divine. By exploring the depths of one's own soul and existence, one can gain insights into God's nature. The soul's journey through the physical world, with its challenges and experiences, is an essential part of its development and eventual reunification with the Divine.

❑ **Ethical Conduct:** Recognizing the Divine as mirrored within one's own being fosters a profound sense of ethical responsibility. In Kabbalah, actions transcend mere personal choices; they reflect our sacred relationship with God and the interconnected world. Humanity is not a passive bystander but an active co-creator in the unfolding of existence. Through intentional thoughts, deeds, and aspirations, individuals contribute to *tikkun olam*—the repair and elevation of the world—aligning it with the divine blueprint. Every ethical act becomes a step toward harmonizing the material and spiritual realms.

The Kabbalists interprets the biblical verse, "From my flesh, I will see God" (Job 19:26), as a profound testament to the intricate bond between humanity and the Divine. It reveals that through our physical and spiritual essence, we can perceive and connect with divine truths. This understanding is not merely abstract but deeply practical, shaping how we navigate and interact with the world. It inspires a life of intentionality, sanctity, and purpose, where every thought and deed carries spiritual weight, advancing the sacred task of harmonizing the material realm with its divine origin

נֶפֶשׁ.

SOUL "ANIMA"

Terminology in the Kabbalah often goes underappreciated when a student fails to grasp the rich linguistic nuances that are embedded within familiar terms used in Jewish mystical literature. Any initiate of Jewish mysticism needs to have a rich appreciation of these linguistic nuances of the Hebrew language, the "Holy Tongue." The word נֶפֶשׁ (*nepeš*), a term of feminine attribution in Hebrew, unfolds into a mélange of meanings within the biblical narrative. It may denote the throat or neck, as echoed in passages like Job 24:12 or Isaiah 32:6, or it may signify breath, the vital gust coursing through the throat as referred to in Job 41:21 and Jeremiah 15:9. The "breath," indeed, is the lifeline linking us to existence itself, a sentiment beautifully portrayed in Job 31:39. This connection becomes more profound in Genesis 2:7, as the first man is breathed into life, evolving into a 'living being' or nepeš.

Life, or *nepeš,* is a delicate thread that slips away upon death, a concept reverberated in several biblical narratives (Gen. 1:30, 19:19, 35:18, 1 Sam. 19:11). The Tanakh, on multiple occasions, postulates that this life essence, this *nepeš,* is contained within the blood, providing the cornerstone for the prohibitive stance against blood consumption (Gen. 9:4-5; Lev. 17:14). The idea of nepeš as something reanimated and revitalized by YHWH and His Torah reverberates in the Psalms (Pss 19:7, 23:3, 34:22, 35:17, 54:6).

Further layered into the phrase נֶפֶשׁ הַחַיָּה (*nepeš haḥayyâ*), translated as "living soul", is a shared passion for life uniting human beings and animals. This term highlights common experiences of breath, awareness, and individuality—the building blocks of conscious existence. It brings into focus the shared string of life that resonates with anyone who has ever connected with a pet's gaze or admired the complex choreography of animal behavior.

Here, the "soul" transcends its metaphysical origins, morphing into a tangible essence representing any being capable of feeling, perceiving, and responding to the world around them. These traits form the foundation of conscious existence, threading a bond of shared life between us and the animal realm.

The renowned German biblical scholar Claus Westermann provides compelling insights into the nuanced interpretation of the Hebrew phrase *nefesh hachayah* (נֶפֶשׁ הַחַיָּה). This evocative term can be envisioned as an artist's palette, vividly capturing the diverse spectrum of animal life; a poetic tribute to the interconnected existence of humans and animals; or the profound concept embodying the "breath of life"—the animating essence that infuses vitality into both human and animal beings, uniting them in a shared life force.

Interpreting the term נֶפֶשׁ demands a view through the ethical lens. It molds the contours of human interactions, extending beyond human boundaries into the animal kingdom. This ethical thread is woven into the biblical proverb: יוֹדֵעַ צַדִּיק נֶפֶשׁ בְּהֶמְתּוֹ וְרַחֲמֵי רְשָׁעִים אַכְזָרִי "The just person takes care of their livestock, but even the most compassionate acts of the wicked are cruel" (Prov. 12:10). The echo of this ethical symbiosis resonates in the English term 'animal', rooted in 'anima', mirroring the essence of "soul." As entrusted caretakers of God's creation, humans are imbued with a solemn responsibility to demonstrate compassion and respect toward all sentient beings. An indifferent or dismissive attitude toward these creatures devalues our stewardship and fractures our divine commitments.

From Aristotle to the Kabbalah

The concept of נֶפֶשׁ *(nepeš), as articulated in Judaic mystical writings,* bears striking parallels with Aristotle's conception of the tripartite soul. Delving into this comparative realm, one can discern a shared thread weaving through these two seemingly disparate philosophical and mystical traditions. In his treatise *De Anima,* posits a three-part structure of the soul, or 'anima' in Latin. These are the vegetative (or nutritive) soul, the sensitive (or appetitive) soul, and the rational soul, each corresponding to different functions and aspects of being.

The vegetative soul, akin to the Kabbalistic nuance of נֶפֶשׁ, is the elemental level of the soul, responsible for growth, reproduction, and nourishment. This fundamental layer of existence is the source of life's most basic functions. It is the animating force within all living organisms, drawing a striking parallel with the נֶפֶשׁ as the life force, the primal consciousness that vitalizes the physical body. Moving up the ladder, the sensitive soul corresponds to perception, movement, and emotion. It signifies a more evolved level of existence, analogous in some respects to the Kabbalistic conception of the רוּחַ (*rûaḥ*). It is here that we interact with our environment, perceive and respond to it, just as the רוּחַ represents a heightened consciousness.

The pinnacle of Aristotle's hierarchy is the rational soul, unique to humans, and endowed with intellect and moral judgment. It echoes the Kabbalistic notion of *neshamah*, the divine breath, symbolizing a deep intellectual and moral consciousness. Thus, Aristotle's conception of the *anima* and the Kabbalistic concept of the נֶפֶשׁ can be seen as two different paths leading to a similar summit. They both portray the soul as a layered entity, each representing different functions and aspects of life.

At their base, both the נֶפֶשׁ and the vegetative part of Aristotle's soul signify the vital life force, the primal rhythm of existence. They capture the undulating dance of life, pulsating with the rhythm of breath, the ebb, and flow of the physical self in synchrony with the cosmos. In their grandest essence, these concepts invite us to ponder the profound continuity between the physical and spiritual realms, suggesting a universal truth—a singular breath animates all of life, a divine spark that infuses every living being, whether it's called *anima'* or *nepeš*.

רוּחַ

SPIRIT

The term רוּחַ (*rûaḥ*) is a force of profound strength, yet one that eludes the eye, forever unseen. A "mighty wind" offers an apt metaphor, encapsulating the unseen potency of this enigmatic force, stirring the imagination with its dynamic, elusive nature. As we delve deeper into the mysteries of this term, we find רוּחַ symbolizing a life-giving breath. This vital principle navigates the chaos of creation and births a cosmos from the formless expanse of primordial potentiality.

In the theological realms, רוּחַ assumes an even more profound resonance. It signifies an ethereal transformation, liberation, and refinement dimension that shapes human existence. The very fabric of Genesis 1:2 reveals this: "The earth was without form and void, and darkness was on the face of the deep. And the Spirit of God was hovering over the face of the waters." Here, we see the wind, the Spirit of God, as the harmonizing life force, weaving together earth, spirit, and divine creative energy.

This "spirit" denotes a living, intangible essence teeming with rational, emotional, and volitional attributes. The Tanakh frequently employs the concept of spirit to express the non-material living essence of human beings - the soul, the spirit, the inner life - and the Holy Spirit, or the Spirit of God. The Hebrew and Greek languages have no exclusive term for 'spirit'. Instead, they convey the concept primarily through words also denoting "wind" or "breath", such as רוּחַ (*rûaḥ*) or the Greek equivalent πνεῦμα (*pneuma*). These terms can refer to wind, the breath of a living creature, or the spirit as the living essence of a being. Context generally reveals the intended meaning, but at times, the concepts intriguingly overlap, blurring the boundaries between wind, breath, and life-essence.

In the creation narrative of Genesis 1, we witness the Spirit of God, the רוּחַ אֱלֹהִים (*rûaḥ ʾĕlōhîm*), hovering over the barren earth. This creative Spirit likened to the breath that the Almighty, breathes life into humankind (Job 33:4). Throughout the Tanakh, the Spirit of God is portrayed as empowering individuals to fulfill God's purposes, whether through artistic skill (Exod. 31:3), governance (1 Sam. 16:13), or prophecy (Neh. 9:30). In this divine dance of creation and life, the Spirit breathes new life into the redeemed people of God (Ezek. 37:1–10).

נשמה

SOUL-BREATH

Hebrew Nuances of Neshamah

In the lyrical and theosophical complexity of the Tanakh, the term נְשָׁמָה (*neshama*), primarily representing "soul-breath," surfaces as an emblem of both the divine and human spirit. It does not embody the wind as its kindred term רוּחַ (*rûaḥ*) occasionally does, but rather embodies an intimate, internal breeze - the breath of life itself. This breath, intertwining with *rûaḥ*, narrates tales of God's Spirit (Job 33:4) or the spirit He imparts to mankind (Isa 42:5). In the initial shadows of Genesis, *neshama* comes forth as the breath of God, breathing life into Adam, and transmuting him into a living soul, a נֶפֶשׁ (*nepeš*) vibrant with life (Gen 2:7).

The *neshama*, the highest form of individual consciousness within a person, is the spark of divinity within humans that allows us to interact with God and the realm of light. This interaction isn't just one-sided; the *neshama* also has the power to influence the divine world through various channels or צִנּוֹרוֹת (*tzinnoroth*), bringing about blessings and positive effects on the earthly realm. This multi-faceted nature of the human soul reflects the complexities and nuances of creation itself. It signifies the interconnectedness of all elements in the universe — the physical and the spiritual, the earthly and the divine, the darkness and the light. This interplay of opposing forces and the balance they bring to the universe is a central theme in Kabbalistic teachings.

The divine breath, or *neshama*, transcends the simple act of giving life. As expressed in Job 32:8 (NJB), "There is, you see, a spirit residing in humanity, the breath of God conferring intelligence," it radiates as a wellspring of wisdom, kindling insight within the human soul. This sacred essence, a divine endowment, illuminates the intricate paths of understanding, guiding us through life's profound complexities. Within humanity, *neshama* also captures our ephemeral existence—a fragile breath, briefly held in our nostrils—highlighting our delicate place within the boundless, eternal cosmos. It serves as a poignant reminder of our deep connection to the Divine and the fleeting, yet beautiful, nature of our mortal journey.

Simultaneously, the "soul breath" stands tall as a testament to the divine spark within us, aligning our spirit with the Creator's. This divine breath, as expressed through *neshama,* adopts both creative and destructive guises, igniting a flame with a hot wind (Isa 30:33), causing chaos with a devastating gust (2 Sam 22:16), or manifesting ice with a frigid breath (Job 37:10). It is a force that simultaneously creates, maintains, and alters, a perpetual reverberation of divinity in the natural world. A linguistic profile through the Tanakh via *neshama* and *nasham* unravels a multifaceted representation of the breath of life. As both a divine force and a symbol of human existence, it whispers tales of our intellectual prowess, our temporal fragility, and our divine affinity. This breath, graciously given and nurtured by God, bears witness to the life-affirming and transformative core of the divine as reflected in nature and humankind alike.

The Kabbalah of Soul

As previously noted, the soul, also referred to as the "*neshama*" or "breath of God," imbues us with spiritual awareness and moral autonomy. This divine breath serves as the life force that empowers our words, creating a profound spiritual connection with the universe through the seemingly mundane act of speech.

The power of a word is multifaceted, stemming from its intrinsic meaning, the vibrations it engenders, and how it's utilized. Different words resonate within us in various ways - some reverberate within the heart, stirring emotions, while others stimulate the mind or have a physical impact. This tangible resonance is a manifestation of life's mysteries, with each word functioning as a vessel for the divine. As such, the words we choose and how we use them can significantly influence our life paths, experiences, and interactions with others.

However, the Kabbalah also emphasizes the importance of humility in spiritual pursuits. True spiritual attainment should not be showcased for external validation or self-glorification. Rather, it is a quiet, introspective journey that deepens humility and self-understanding. The ultimate lesson of mysticism is to accumulate wisdom, attain spiritual enlightenment, and then maintain a silent reverence for the divine mystery that permeates existence. In this context, the more knowledge one accumulates, the humbler one should be, refraining from using spiritual gains as a ladder for egotistic self-elevation.

The relationship between words and breath extends beyond our common material comprehension. The rhythm of our breath, a mysterious force that sustains life, operates as a silent lute, waiting for its divine purpose to be fulfilled. The vibrations created by our words, powered by this divine breath, extend far beyond our immediate physical realm, influencing our mental and physical health and spiritual wellbeing. The key to unraveling the power of words, and thereby the mystery of life, lies within our self-understanding. Every external stimulus, be it a melody or a spoken word, is interpreted and truly understood within us. Thus, the knowledge of the self is crucial for decoding the latent power of words. This internal realization helps bridge the gap between the external and internal world, facilitating a harmonious balance between the physical and the spiritual, and paving the way for a deeper understanding of our place within the grand cosmic order.

Five Facets of the Soul

As we traverse the non-linear perception of time, we embark on a journey unshackled by chronology but woven into a unified narrative. The cornerstone of our tale is the Zohar, a mystical text that expands on teachings from the Midrash in Genesis Rabbah 14:9. This scripture introduces us to five ethereal facets of the soul. The wisdom revealed here intertwines with the Midrash, elucidating the multifaceted essence of the spirit.

Within our physical form resides *Nefesh*, akin to the life-giving blood, signifying our fundamental instinct that mirrors Aristotle's notion of "anima" or the animal spirit. Following this is ruach, which encapsulates our physical breath and the metaphysical wind of our moral direction, oscillating between earthly and divine realms. Progressing further, we encounter *neshamah*, the celestial breath bestowing us with intellect, differentiating us from all other species.

The Kabbalah, through sacred texts like the Zohar and Midrash,[135] unveils the soul's profound, multifaceted nature, encompassing *nefesh, ruach, neshama, chaya, and yechidah*. Each facet plays a distinct role in forging our connection to the Divine, yet together they form a singular essence. *Chaya*, the all-encompassing life-force, integrates every aspect of existence, linking the individual soul to the cosmic whole. *Yechidah*, the soul's eternal spark, serves as an intimate bridge to the Divine, embodying our unbreakable unity with the infinite source. These dimensions, as explored in the Zohar and Midrash, reveal the soul's intricate design, guiding humanity toward its sacred purpose.

The Zohar presents the soul's layers as a dynamic hierarchy: Nefesh, the foundation, animates the physical body, grounding us in the material realm with vital energy. *Ruach,* the wellspring of emotional and moral life, fosters bonds with God and others through love, awe, and compassion. *Neshama*, the higher consciousness, illuminates the intellect with divine wisdom, opening pathways to transcendent insight. Together, these facets—joined by *chaya and yechidah*—form a unified soul, not a collection of separate entities, but a singular essence manifesting through vitality, emotion, and intellect, as reflected in Genesis 2:7's "breath of life," which Kabbalistic teachings interpret as the soul's holistic origin.

Imagine the soul's facets as sources of light illuminating a sacred space: *Nefesh* glows like a steady candle, sustaining the flame of physical life; ruach shimmers like moonlight, casting an emotive, relational glow; *neshama* radiates like sunlight, flooding the soul with spiritual clarity. *Chaya* is the ambient energy, harmonizing and sustaining all light, while *yechidah* is the divine source from which all illumination flows. This metaphor captures the soul's unity amidst its diverse expressions, as the journey from nefesh to yechidah traces a cohesive path toward divine alignment.

Kabbalistic texts, such as the Zohar, emphasize the soul's intricate identity through the interplay of its dimensions. The linkage of *neshama's* intellectual clarity with *nefesh's* vitality and *ruach's* emotional depth, as seen in teachings on Genesis 2:7, illustrates this unity, showing the soul's evolution while remaining whole. Through contemplation and time, the soul's rich tapestry of wisdom unfolds, guiding us to understand our place in the cosmic order and our eternal bond with the Divine.[136]

Five Aspects of Soul within the Kabbalistic Hierarchy

According to the mystical psychology of R. Shneur Zalman in his kabbalistic psychological work, the *Tanya*, the *Benoni* the "inbetweener," possesses the potential for both virtue and vice, continually striving to "turn from evil and do good" (Ps. 34:15). "Turning from evil" implies extending our consciousness from *neshamah*, the ego-driven intelligence perceiving the *Beriah* world of autonomous and competitive selves, to *chayyah*, which bears the intuitive and soulful insight that sees reality as *Atziluth*, a world of interdependent and cooperative selves. "Doing good" is the act of serving both self and others, rooted in the understanding of their unity.

These, *neshamah* and *chayyah*, are two of the five intelligences accessible to us. Each intelligence perceives reality differently. Apart from *neshamah* and *chayyah*, there are *nefesh*, the instinctual intelligence of the world of *Assiyah* or preconscious matter; *Ruach*, the intelligence of the world of *Yetzirah*—a musical reality that is bound up with intense feelings and emotions; and *yechidah,* the intelligence of the world of *Adam Kadmon*, where all things are seen as the One Thing, God. All five intelligences are perpetually operational. The world you perceive is determined by the intelligence you employ to observe it.

Our journey leads us to an academic dialogue that deliberates on the nature of the soul. The dialogue draws analogies between the soul's facets and the diverse light sources illuminating a home. Here, the vegetative soul is compared to a candle, the animal soul to moonlight, and the intellectual soul to sunlight. Ramban highlights a unique element of this soul, comparing humans to lifeless stones that, through the breath of life, transform into living souls.

Is there such a thing as a "Jewish Soul"?

When we speak about a "Jewish soul," "Greek soul," "American soul," "Russian soul," or "Latin soul," we're not parsing theology but chasing the heartbeat of a people—their values, spirit, and collective fire etched across time. These metaphors distill a culture's essence, unveiling worldviews that ripple through history, each a thread in humanity's vibrant weave.

The "Jewish soul" blazes with ethics, learning, and a divine thirst unquenched by centuries of storm. Forged in Torah's flame, it weds justice to hope, enduring exile's whip with a gaze fixed on redemption. *Tikkun olam*—repairing the world—beats at its core, a vow to mend what's torn. Maimonides melded faith with reason in his Guide; Heschel marched with King, prayer on his lips—torchbearers of a resilient mission. Not a cloistered creed, it beckons all to join the dance of righteousness, a covenant carved in survival's stone.

The "Greek soul" dances with philosophy's grace and beauty's call, a legacy of daring etched in marble and mind. Socrates pierced truth's shroud, Plato dreamed of forms, Aristotle charted the cosmos—their echoes sculpting reason's dawn. The Parthenon's symmetry, Sophocles' Oedipus wrenching hearts, and Olympia's sweat-drenched glory crown this relentless quest. From democracy's cradle in Athens to Euclid's lines, Greece's spirit of inquiry—an ode to harmony—still stirs thinkers and poets across the ages.

The "American soul" strides with freedom's thunder—individualism, innovation, liberty's wild pulse. The Declaration's "life, liberty, pursuit of happiness" ignites it, birthing pioneers: Franklin's kite sparking light, Tubman's trek defying chains, Edison's bulb banishing dusk, Silicon Valley's digital frontier. Yet shadows loom—slavery's stain, suffrage's delay—its ideals wrestling with bloodied truths, a restless spirit straining to bridge dream and deed.

The "Russian soul" broods and soars, a vast lament laced with defiant joy. Dostoevsky's Karamazov abyss, Tolstoy's *War and Peace* sprawl, Tchaikovsky's mournful strings—born of endless steppes and history's iron fist—probe existence's depths. Endurance binds this collective spirit, threading mirth through tears, a shared fate forged in suffering's crucible.

The "Latin soul" blazes with passion's heat—tango's sway, samba's throb, laughter outwitting despair. Fiesta fuses kin and celebration, a vibrant weave of indigenous chants, African drums, and European strings. Resilience reigns—joy blooming in hardship's dust—a testament to life's zest from Mexico's highlands to Argentina's plains.

Each "soul"—Jewish duty, Greek wonder, American drive, Russian depth, Latin fire—carves a distinct mark. Yet beneath their hues thrums a shared human chord: to seek, to endure, to cast light where shadows fall.

Jewish "Choseness" as Noblesse Oblige

The concept of "noblesse oblige," which dictates that elevated status comes with profound responsibility, finds its deepest resonance in the idea of the "Jewish Soul" within the framework of "Jewish Chosenness."

Here's how they interrelate:

The "Jewish Soul," as understood by mystics like Judah Halevi, is not a claim of biological superiority, but rather a unique spiritual aptitude or sensitivity. It's considered a specific internal "wiring" that grants an inherent, often intuitive, capacity for a deeper connection with the Divine, a heightened receptivity to spiritual truths, and a natural inclination towards the commandments of the Torah.[137] This unique spiritual endowment is the very foundation of the "noblesse" in "noblesse oblige" as applied to the Jewish people. Their "nobility" isn't one of earthly power or privilege, but a spiritual nobility, a distinct attunement to the sacred.

A classic example illustrating a more personal application of "noblesse oblige" is the anecdote of Sir Walter Raleigh placing his costly cloak over a muddy puddle for Queen Elizabeth I. This act, while appearing to be spontaneous gallantry, was deeply rooted in the expectations of chivalry and the courtier's duty to honor and serve royalty. Raleigh's sacrifice of a valuable possession for the Queen's dignity and comfort demonstrated his commitment to the ideals of nobility and service, showcasing how those with elevated status were expected to act with grace, self-sacrifice, and honor, particularly towards those of higher standing or those they were bound to protect.[138]

When "noblesse oblige" is applied to "Jewish Chosenness," it fundamentally transforms it from a potentially problematic notion of exclusive favor into a profound spiritual burden and mission. The "special soul" or "chosen" status is not a ticket to worldly privilege, but rather an onerous responsibility to fulfill a unique covenantal role with God. It mandates serving as a moral and spiritual light for humanity. The Jewish people, through their history, their laws, and their very existence, are seen as bearing the weight of a divine mission: to embody ethical monotheism, strive for justice, and exemplify a life consecrated to God, not solely for their own sake, but for the betterment of the entire world. This framework suggests that the "privilege" of chosenness comes with the profound "obligation" to live up to the highest ideals of righteousness and compassion, holding them accountable for a greater standard of conduct that ultimately serves all of humanity.

This spiritual nobility then dictates a profound "oblige" – a unique and weighty set of obligations:

The "Jewish Soul," being specially attuned to the Divine, is inherently obligated to strive for a higher degree of holiness. This means a deeper commitment to the meticulous observance of mitzvot (commandments), a profound engagement with Torah study, and an unceasing pursuit of spiritual growth. This isn't merely external compliance but a deep internal resonance; the "special soul" makes this demanding spiritual path not only achievable but deeply meaningful. It is the spiritual capacity that enables the Jewish people to undertake their unique covenantal service to God.

Because of this unique spiritual capacity, the "Jewish Soul" and the people it animates are then "obligated" to serve as a "light unto the nations" (Isaiah 42:6). This is the external manifestation of their noblesse oblige. It means actively working to exemplify ethical monotheism, championing justice, demonstrating profound compassion, and contributing uniquely to the moral and spiritual elevation of all humanity. The "special soul" is seen as the driving force that equips the Jewish people to bear witness to God's presence in the world and to offer a model of how a people can live in covenant with the Divine, ultimately for the benefit of the entire world.

Jewish Mystics Need Maimonidean Sanity

In contrast to the provocative theological opinions cited above, Maimonides interprets the uniqueness of Jewish People as stemming not from their creation but from their ethical beliefs and philosophical tradition. Hence, a convert who learns the Torah is as much a descendant of the Patriarchs as a born Jew who is familiar with the Torah. He acknowledges a difference in the refined character traits of Jews compared to Gentiles, attributing this to the educational effects of the Torah rather than any essential difference in their souls. In his view, any human has the potential for moral perfection and spiritual achievement. Thus, Maimonides' perspective diverges fundamentally from the essentialist views of the *Kuzari* and *Tanya*. Maimonides rejected such a theological notion as myopic.

Contemporary Maimonides scholar Menahem Kellner explains that Abraham, as per Maimonides, chose God more than God selected Abraham. Considering that the Torah was granted solely to Abraham's descendants because of their lineage rather than any innate attributes, it follows that the Torah could have possessed a different form. Kellner offers an interesting speculation: Had Abraham been a Navajo instead of a Hebrew, the Torah might have been recorded in the Navajo language, embodying specific histories and laws appropriate to that culture.[139]

Rabbi Abraham Isaac Kook, A Modern-Day Hillel

R. Kook eloquently encapsulates a grand ode to the universal love for all humankind, rivaling some of the finest expressions ever conceived. He proclaims:

> Our loftiest homage to the virtue of love should be ascribed to the affection for our fellow humans, an affection that transcends the bounds of differing faiths, ideologies, and cultures, unimpeded by disparities of race or geographical origin. It is of utmost importance to understand the perspectives of various nations and communities, and to explore their distinct features and characteristics as thoroughly as possible. This knowledge serves as the groundwork upon which the love for humanity can be cemented, a love poised on the cusp of transformation into action. It is only upon a soul brimming with this universal love, this profound fondness for all living beings and mankind, that the love for one's nation can find its rightful place, elevated to its greatest spiritual and natural grandeur.

Kook further warns:

> The myopia that distorts our perception of all that lies beyond the confines of our particular nation, even beyond the borders of Israel, reducing it to the grotesque and the impure, is a malignant obscurity. This darkness wreaks havoc, obliterating all attempts at cultivating spiritual goodness and dimming the light that every discerning soul seeks.[140]

In his stirring words, R. Kook implores us to recognize the importance of a broad, inclusive love for all people, insisting that it forms the bedrock for cultivating a truly meaningful love for our nation and ourselves. His plea serves as a beacon, guiding us toward a greater understanding and love for all humankind.

Preserving the Embers of History—Not Its Ashes

The practice of uncritically embracing the teachings of Kabbalah can inadvertently perpetuate antiquated beliefs that may no longer be applicable or beneficial in a modern context. Indeed, certain aspects of this tradition have their roots in the medieval era, a time characterized by distinct societal norms, understandings, and paradigms. These concepts, if not scrutinized in the light of contemporary knowledge and socio-cultural evolution, can inadvertently promote outdated and potentially harmful viewpoints. Like any other philosophical or spiritual tradition, Kabbalah offers valuable wisdom. Its intricate exploration of the divine, the soul, and the cosmos can spark profound reflections and provide a sense of connection to something greater. To continue the metaphor, these teachings are the "embers" of Kabbalah—alive, glowing, and capable of igniting thought-provoking insights.

However, the embers are not the entirety of the fire. There are also "ashes," residues of past flames that no longer hold heat or light. These are elements of Kabbalah that might be rooted in outdated worldviews, leading to divisive or harmful beliefs if taken out of their historical and contextual basis. As we continue to explore and learn from Kabbalah, we must critically examine and discern between the embers and the ashes. The wisdom that still holds relevance and meaning —the embers —should be kept alive and nurtured. However, the ashes—those ideas and teachings that no longer serve us or align with the shared values of inclusivity, equality, and universal human dignity—should be left behind in the dustbin of history.

Such an approach enables the tradition of Kabbalah to evolve, as it has throughout its long history, aligning itself with the shifting tides of human consciousness while preserving its core essence and unique insights. It enables us to respect and honor the tradition's depth and history, while also allowing us to question, reinterpret, and, where necessary, depart from aspects that are no longer compatible with our current understanding and context.

CHAPTER 10

WHAT IS MAN?

Some years ago, one of the popular American news magazines featured an article entitled "What is Man?" The average man was roughly 5 feet 10 inches tall, and weighed about 150 pounds. To the writer's surprise, he discovered that if we were to examine man's body chemistry, we would find that he has enough:

- *Fat to make seven bars of soap.*
- *Iron to make a medium-sized nail.*
- *Sugar to fill a shaker.*
- *Lime to whitewash a chicken coop.*
- *Phosphors to make 2,200 match tips.*
- *Magnesium for a dose of magnesia.*
- *Potassium to explode a toy cannon.*

If one were to add up how much these substances would cost, it would add up to a—well under twenty American dollars. That is the extent of our bodily worth because we were made out of ground dust.

—Dr. Mayo, Los Angelos Times, 1935

No man is free who is not master of himself.

—Epictetus

Greatness lies, not in being strong, but in the right using of strength; and strength is not used rightly when it serves only to carry a man above his fellows for his own solitary glory. He is the greatest whose strength carries up the most hearts by the attraction of his own. Henry Ward Beecher

Man is condemned to be free; because once thrown into the world, he is responsible for everything he does. It is up to you to give life meaning.
—Jean-Paul Sartre, *Existentialism*

אָדָם

ADAM

The Grammar of "Adam"

In this chapter, we will explore the Kabbalistic interpretation of the Book of Genesis, delving into its rich, symbolic narratives. We'll examine the characters of Adam and Eve, not just as the first humans, but as profound symbols in Kabbalistic thought. The narrative of their creation and existence in the Garden of Eden offers insights into the nature of humanity and the spiritual dynamics of the universe.

Additionally, we will explore the intriguing concept of androgyny as it is presented in Kabbalistic literature. This concept, particularly in the context of Adam and Eve, provides a unique perspective on the ideas of unity and duality in creation, as well as the balance between masculine and feminine energies in the spiritual realm.

In the Book of Genesis, the name Adam (אָדָם) is closely linked to the Hebrew word אֲדָמָה, meaning ground or earth. This connection underscores the relationship between humans and the earth, highlighting a parallel between the color of human skin and the hue of the earth's soil. The word אָדָם can be aptly translated into English as "earthling" or "earth person," reflecting this deep bond with the earth.

While אָדָם is a masculine noun often used to denote "man," it is also understood to represent humanity, encompassing both men and women. This broader usage stems from the biblical account of Adam being created from the earth, symbolizing all human beings. Thus, אָדָם can refer to the entire human race. The term's versatility is evident in its various applications, from describing ordinary individuals to slaves and soldiers. This universal application of אָדָם in many contexts underscores its role in representing humankind, not limited to a specific gender. The phrase "son of man", בֶּן אָדָם, is used in a poetic sense to represent man in numerous scriptures. In Ezekiel, the prophet is addressed by God as "son of man", implying mortality.[141]

The Kabbalah of Adam

In the mystical realm of the Kabbalah, the name "Adam" is more than a mere identification of the first human being. It reflects the cosmic role of humanity and its profound interconnection with the Divine. "Adam," written in Hebrew as אָדָם is an acronym of three Hebrew words— *Aleph* (א), *Daleth* (ד), and *Mem* (מ).

The Aleph (א), as the first letter of the Hebrew alphabet, stands for "*Atzilut*," the highest of the four spiritual worlds in Kabbalah. This world symbolizes the realm closest to the Divine essence, where the radiance of God is most manifest. The Daleth (ד) symbolizes "*Beriah*" and "*Yetzirah*," the second and third spiritual worlds, representing creation and formation.

These are the realms of Divine attributes and angelic beings, where the raw energy of *Atzilut* is given shape and definition. The *Mem* (ם) represents "*Assiyah*," the physical world, the realm of action, and the world we inhabit. It is in this world that spiritual energy descends into material form, and it is here that human beings can elevate physical reality by infusing it with spiritual purpose. Thus, the name "Adam" encompasses the entirety of creation, from the highest spiritual echelons to the physical world, reflecting humanity's potential to traverse these realms and effect spiritual elevation.

Moreover, according to the Zohar (Zohar 1:34b), the name Adam is also a testament to humanity's Divine likeness. As it is written in Genesis (5:1), "When God created man, He made him in the likeness of God." The term used for man in this verse is "Adam," signifying that just as the name Adam embodies all aspects of creation, so too does humanity, created in the image of God, embody a microcosmic reflection of the Divine. In the hauntingly beautiful words of the Kabbalah, the name "Adam" stands as a profound testament to our divine origin and cosmic role, reminding us of our duty to elevate the physical world and bring it closer to its spiritual source. Thus, these three letters represent different aspects of reality, and together, they form a microcosm of the universe.

חַוָּה

EVE

The Hebraic Significance of Eve's Name

The name חַוָּה (*Chavah* = "Eve") is believed to derive from the Hebrew root חָוָה (*Chavah*), which means "to live" or "to breathe." In this context, the name is often interpreted to mean "living one" or "source of life," reflecting her role as the mother of all humanity. This etymology highlights the Hebrew tradition's belief that Eve is the progenitor of all human life.[142]

But was that her original name?

Not necessarily. Some exegetes, ancient and modern suggest that Eve's original name might have been "*Ishah*" (אִשָּׁה) based on the passage, זֹאת הַפַּעַם עֶצֶם מֵעֲצָמַי וּבָשָׂר מִבְּשָׂרִי לְזֹאת יִקָּרֵא אִשָּׁה כִּי מֵאִישׁ לֻקֳחָה־זֹּאת "This one at last is bone of my bones and flesh of my flesh! She is to be called 'Woman,' because she was taken from Man" (Gen. 2:23).

Originally, we are told, Adam named his wife "*Ishah*" and referred to himself as "*Ish*," departing from his original name "Adam" given before Eve's creation. This change reflected God's addition of His own name, Yah, to their names—adding the letter *Yod* (י) to "*Ish*" and He (ה) to "*Ishah*." This symbolic act signified that as long as they adhered to God's path and commandments, His divine protection would be with them. However, should they stray from this path, God's protective presence, symbolized by His name, would be removed. Without God's name, "*Ish*" would become "*Esh*" (אש), meaning "fire," signifying destructive forces that would emerge, symbolizing conflict and destruction consuming each individual.[143]

A Brief Biographical Sketch

In the earliest verses of the Torah, humanity emerges not through the lens of sex or gender, but as a mirror to the Divine, a dyadic entity forged in the image of God (Gen 1:27; 5:2). Brought into being on the sixth day of creation, they are anointed with a divine blessing and charged with a panoply of duties - to bear offspring, to inhabit and subdue the earth, and to preside over its creatures (Gen 1:28). This twofold entity is celebrated as the pinnacle of God's creation (Gen 1:31).

Genesis 5:2 reiterates the divine image imprinted on both males and females, thus engraving an equality inherent to their creation. God's inaugural commandment to them (Gen 1:28) delves into their earthly mission, their duty to procreate, and their stewardship, subtly hinting at their relationship with the Creator and with each other. This edict unveils God's intention to consign a portion of his dominion to man and woman, a delegation of divine authority initiated at the dawn of human existence.

The narrative shifts in Genesis 2, offering an alternative perspective on the creation of a woman. God forges man and sets him in an Edenic garden to the east (Gen 2:8). Observing man's solitude as an undesirable state, God resolves to create a companion for him (Gen 2:18), thereby acknowledging man's craving for companionship, even amidst divine company. From the early stages of humanity's inception, as recounted in the biblical narrative, notions of solitude and loneliness emerge. Man, it seems, harbored a deep yearning for a partner yet to be created. This longing for companionship reflects a deeper, more profound reality - that of the divine longing for a relationship. In the act of creating the world, God sought interaction with something distinct from Himself, an Other. In this way, the human longing for connection becomes a mirror, reflecting God's own desire for a relationship.

Yet, contrary to what might be expected in such a situation of deep longing, there is a moment of pause, an interlude of anticipation. God, in his wisdom, assigns man a unique task, the act of naming the animals around him. This was a precedent set earlier in Genesis 1, where God Himself had breathed names into the day, night, land, and sea, conferring identity and order to the elements of creation. It is within this divine mandate that Adam embarks on his mission, cataloging and naming the multitudes of animals. However, in this vast procession of creatures, not one reflects the companionship Adam seeks. None serve as an echo of his own kind, his own desire for an equal counterpart. The narrative thus sets the stage for a pivotal moment, one in which the divine plan for human companionship will finally take shape.

God then fulfills His pledge of creating a partner, an aide. The term "helper," *ʿēzer,* avoids implications of subordination or inferiority, instead describing a willing and capable assistant, a role God Himself assumes in subsequent scripture.[144] Eve's creation differs from earlier acts of creation. Unlike other creatures, which God speaks into existence or forms from dust as with man, a woman is sculpted from man's side during his slumber (Gen 2:21–22), implying neither subordination nor superiority. Acknowledging humanity's inherent sociability, a woman's creation facilitates a society of mutual companionship.

Adam's delight upon encountering his counterpart is palpable. Freed from loneliness, he recognizes his own reflection in her, exclaiming, "bone of my bone and flesh of my flesh!" (Gen 2:23). He calls her "woman", sprung from the side of "man," underlining their shared essence and mutual equality before God and with each other. The Scripture sanctifies sexual intimacy, portraying it as a natural, enduring, and exclusive bond between man and woman. Although God presents woman to man, it is a man who severs ties with his progenitors to unite with his wife, thereby striking a balance (Gen 2:24). In unity, they transmute into "one flesh," a novel entity recognized universally. They approach each other in their purest form, unashamed and equal, before God and in their mutual enjoyment of each other. This parity extends to their joint stewardship over creation.

"Eve"

Eve in the Kabbalah

The Kabbalah, Zohar, and Lurianic texts delve deeper into the metaphysical aspects of the characters of the early chapters of Genesis while providing allegorical, symbolic, and spiritual interpretations. The Zohar portrays Eve in a complex light. On one hand, she is viewed as the instigator of the Fall, responsible for the introduction of sin and death into the world. On the other hand, she is also depicted as a deeply spiritual figure who, through her actions, brought about the possibility of spiritual growth and redemption for humanity. Eve's creation is derived from the "left side" of Adam, signifying the aspect of judgment and restriction, as opposed to the "right side" which signifies grace and benevolence.[145]

In Lurianic Kabbalah, the concepts of *shevirat hakelim* (Breaking of the Vessels) and "*Tikkun Olam*" (Repair of the World) are central.[146] According to Luria, the sin of Adam and Eve (eating from the Tree of Knowledge) caused a cosmic shattering of divine light, leading to a state of spiritual exile and disarray. Eve, in this context, is seen as a key figure in this cosmic event. However, her actions also set in motion the process of *Tikkun Olam*, the spiritual work of repairing and restoring the world, which is the task of humanity.

אַנְדְרֹגִינִיּוּת

ANDROGYNY

Adam & Eve as an Androgynous Being

Before time's dawn, Adam and Eve were fused, a singular entity—both man and woman. Ancient scriptures whispered tales of this primal unity, a divine androgyne born of God's hand before the cleaving of genders. The Genesis tale, has sometimes been interpreted through the lens of the androgyne myth, posits their original state as a singular being. This notion finds expression in early rabbinical literature as well.[147]

The notion of early human androgyny, however, is contested by the biblical text itself. The creation narrative in Genesis 1:27 distinctly portrays humanity as male and female—a stark contrast to the androgynous or asexual nature often proposed. Thus, contrary to the biblical myth, the scripture celebrates human sexuality, thereby rendering an androgynous interpretation of humankind as improbable. Genesis 1:31 lauds sexuality, pronouncing it "very good," establishing it as a cornerstone of human nature. However, from a grammatical perspective, the term אָדָם *(adam),* although singular, denotes both genders.

Androgyny in the Zohar

The Zohar also entertains the idea of the androgynous nature of the first human beings. In one place we find: it is written that "When the Holy One, blessed be He, created Adam, He created him androgynous." The Zohar refers to the verse, "And God created man in His image, in the image of God He created him, male and female He created them," (Gen. 1:27) as a scriptural basis for this claim. This suggests that in the act of creation, both male and female elements were contained in the first human, Adam[148].Then, it adds, the original human form of Adam was split into two separate beings,[149] Adam and Eve. This separation resulted in two distinct entities: a male and a female, each reflecting a portion of the Divine. This is echoed in Genesis 2:21-22 where God takes a rib from Adam to create Eve.

However, Zohar's approach to interpreting biblical texts is deeply mystical and symbolic, often focusing on inner and hidden meanings rather than literal interpretations. The discussion of Adam and Eve's androgynous origin is not meant to represent biological realities, but rather, it illustrates the notion of divine unity and completeness, the balance of masculine and feminine aspects in the spiritual reality. It is important to mention that these interpretations are complex and contain many layers of meaning. The mystical tradition of Kabbalah, including the Zohar, should be studied with guidance from a knowledgeable teacher due to the dense and often cryptic nature of its teachings.

The Androgyne in Jungian Psychology & The Kabbalah

Carl Jung proposed that **individuation**—the process of personal growth and self-realization—requires integrating various unconscious aspects of the Self, particularly the **anima** and **animus**. These archetypes represent the feminine and masculine dimensions of the psyche, respectively, but they do not correspond directly to biological sex or societal gender roles. Instead, they embody psychological qualities that Jung believed are present in all individuals, regardless of gender.

- The **anima** is the unconscious feminine aspect within men, encompassing traits such as intuition, empathy, and emotional depth.

- The **animus** is the unconscious masculine aspect within women, associated with logic, assertiveness, and action.

Jung emphasized that these archetypes are not mere collections of traits but represent the totality of the unconscious feminine or masculine psyche. They act as bridges to the deeper, often repressed parts of the Self, guiding individuals toward wholeness.

In Jung's framework, **androgyny** does not mean a fusion of gender traits but rather the balanced integration of the anima and animus within the psyche. This balance allows individuals to access and express a full range of psychological qualities without being limited by rigid gender norms. For example:

- A man who has integrated his anima can be assertive when necessary, yet also empathetic and nurturing in other contexts.

- A woman who has integrated her animus can be intuitive and caring while also displaying strength and decisiveness when required.

This equilibrium fosters **psychological androgyny**, a hallmark of a mature and integrated personality. It enables individuals to avoid suppressing either the anima or animus, promoting a more complete self-understanding and a balanced approach to life's challenges. Jung also examined how the anima and animus shape interpersonal dynamics, especially in relationships with the opposite sex:

- Men may **project their anima** onto women, idealizing them as mysterious, alluring, or nurturing figures.

- Women may **project their animus** onto men, viewing them as embodiments of strength, rationality, or authority.

"Adam & Eve as an Androgynous Being"

In the Jewish mystical tradition, androgyny is often seen as a symbol of divine completeness, incorporating both masculine and feminine qualities. This image, showing two faces intertwined with nature, could be interpreted as a representation of the Sefirot—attributes through which the divine manifests in the world. The masculine and feminine depicted here might refer to the Sefirot of Chesed (Kindness) and Gevurah (Severity), whose synthesis is found in Tiferet (Beauty), embodying harmony and balance.

These projections can distort perceptions and lead to unrealistic expectations. However, by recognizing and withdrawing these projections, through self-awareness and introspection, individuals can develop more balanced and authentic relationships. This process is essential for personal growth, as it allows one to reclaim these unconscious aspects of the Self rather than externalizing them onto others.[150] Jungian psychology provides a rich, though complex, perspective on the interplay between gender, identity, and personal growth. While the concepts of anima, animus, and psychological androgyny offer valuable insights into how unconscious forces influence behavior and relationships, they are not without limitations. These ideas should be approached critically and considered alongside other psychological theories and models, recognizing that Jung's framework is just one of many lenses through which to explore the complexities of human behavior.

The Jungian concept of androgyny and the Kabbalistic view of the androgyne indeed share some commonalities, although they originate from vastly different philosophical backgrounds. In Jungian psychology, androgyny refers to the integration of the anima (unconscious feminine aspect in men) and animus (unconscious masculine aspect in women). For Jung, an individual's psychological growth, or individuation, involves acknowledging and integrating these aspects irrespective of one's biological sex. This psychological androgyny is characterized by a balance between traditionally masculine and feminine traits within an individual. Jewish mysticism often discusses the concept of the divine androgyne. This is based on the idea that the divine encompasses both male and female aspects. For instance, the Tree of Life in the Kabbalah consists of ten *sephirot*, or divine emanations, some of which have feminine qualities while others have masculine ones. The *sephirot* are usually grouped into pairs that represent masculine and feminine counterparts.

In Kabbalistic thought, divine unity is sometimes depicted as an androgynous being, symbolizing the perfect balance and union of the masculine and feminine aspects of divinity. This concept can be seen as an analogy to Jung's psychological androgyny, even though the context and interpretation differ. While both Jungian psychology and Kabbalah mention the concept of androgyny, the Jungian viewpoint is focused more on individual psychology and personal development, whereas the Kabbalistic perspective emphasizes divine attributes and spiritual understanding. It's important to note that while there may be similarities, these concepts are embedded in very different philosophical and theological frameworks, so they're not directly comparable.

The Alchemical Man-Woman
from the circa 1530 medieval texts
of Michael Cochem.

נהמא דכיסופא

THE BREAD OF SHAME

One of the premiere Jewish mystics of the 19th century was Rabbi Moshe Chaim Luzzatto, also known as *Ramchal*, who was a seminal figure in Jewish philosophy and Kabbalah. One of his central works, *Derech Hashem* ("The Way of God"), presents a systematic overview of Jewish metaphysics and theology. In this theological work, he discusses concepts that relate to the idea of giving and receiving, although not directly referencing the term נַהֲמָא דְכִיסוּפָא "Bread of Shame." *Ramchal* explains that God, in His infinite goodness, desired to bestow goodness upon others. However, God's desire wasn't merely to create beings to receive His goodness, but to allow these beings to merit this goodness, to avoid what could be seen as a spiritual "Bread of Shame." In the first part of *Derech Hashem*, *Ramchal* states:

> The purpose of all that was created was to bring into existence a creature who could derive pleasure from God's own good... For this good to be perfect, the creatures must earn this good themselves."

Receiving charity from a benefactor often comes with a psychological price. To put it simply, this concept encapsulates the feeling of discomfort and embarrassment that comes from receiving something we didn't earn. Consider a person in poverty receiving a loaf of bread without having done anything to earn it. This act of receiving often triggers feelings of shame; it's challenging to feel dignified when we haven't contributed anything. Consequently, we might even struggle to meet the gaze of the person who granted us this favor.

From a biblical perspective, the narrative of Adam and Eve in the Garden of Eden offers a profound reflection of the "Bread of Shame" principle. In the Garden, Adam and Eve lived in a state of receiving, enjoying the fruits of the Garden without labor. After their expulsion, however, they were tasked to work the land and earn their sustenance ("By the sweat of your brow you shall eat bread"— Gen. 3:19). This shift from a state of passive receiving to active earning can be interpreted as a transition from potential "read of shame" to a state of deserving, where their labor justified their sustenance.

Now, imagine if God gifted us directly with the "bread" of the World to Come. This unearned blessing could induce a cosmic version of this same discomfort or "shame," preventing us from fully appreciating and enjoying the goodness bestowed upon us. Moreover, it could hinder the achievement of true unity with God.

Therefore, in the divine wisdom of the Creator, we are placed in this world, providing us the opportunity to act, to earn, and to become givers ourselves, ultimately allowing us to truly savor the "bread" of the World to Come without the taste of unearned charity.

Autonomy refers to our capacity to act independently and make our own decisions, while self-efficacy refers to our belief in our ability to succeed in specific situations or accomplish a task. Self-esteem, on the other hand, is our overall subjective emotional evaluation of our own worth. When we receive without giving, we may feel that our autonomy has been undermined, our self-efficacy has been disregarded, and our self-esteem has been diminished, leading to feelings of shame.

Other Biblical Antecedents

The Israelites wandered in the wilderness for forty years. In this context, the נַהֲמָא דְכִיסוּפָא could be seen metaphorically: the Israelites were not ready to receive the "land of milk and honey," the divine gift, without the spiritual growth and maturity that would later come from their trials and experiences in the wilderness. They needed to "earn" their entry into the Promised Land, to avoid the shame and discomfort of receiving an unearned gift. The story of Joseph and his brothers in the Book of Genesis also offers a perspective on the concept of "Bread of Shame."

Joseph, the favorite son of his father Jacob, is sold into slavery by his envious brothers. Eventually, he rises to become the Viceroy of Egypt, second only to Pharaoh. During a severe famine, Joseph's brothers come to Egypt in search of food, unknowingly begging their brother, whom they do not recognize. Joseph could provide for his brothers instantly, but he instead chose a course of action that made his brothers confront their past actions.

In the context of the "Bread of Shame" Joseph's handling of the situation is of interest. Rather than giving his brothers grain outright, he devises a situation that requires his brothers to engage in a process of self-examination and, ultimately, repentance for their previous actions. When Joseph finally reveals his identity, his brothers have already confronted their guilt and recognized their past mistakes. This emotional and spiritual process transforms the act of receiving food from what could be a "Bread of Shame" into something the brothers have earned through their own introspection and repentance. In this narrative, the נְהֱמָא דְכִיסוּפָא is avoided through the process of *teshuvah* (repentance), which is a form of spiritual work that the brothers had to undergo before receiving Joseph's generosity. Through this process, the brothers transformed from mere receivers into individuals who have merited their sustenance, thereby avoiding the potential discomfort or "shame" associated with unearned receiving.

לְבוּשֵׁי הַנְּשָׁמָה
GARMENTS OF THE SOUL

In Jewish mystical thought, the concept of "garments of the soul" presents a nuanced understanding of the soul's expression in the physical world. Unlike the simplistic view of the soul as merely a passive entity, Kabbalah envisions it as a dynamic entity clothed in layers that actively engage with the material realm. These garments, namely thought, speech, and action, are essential channels through which the soul manifests its divine essence.

The first garment, thought, represents the innermost workings of the soul. It's a realm where ideas and dreams are conceived, reflecting the soul's silent yet profound contemplation. This is where the soul's perception of the world is shaped, forming the foundation for external expression. Speech, the second garment, serves as a conduit for these internal thoughts and feelings, transforming them into communicable forms that interact with the outer world.

This garment bridges the internal and external, allowing the soul to share its essence and influence others. Action, the third and most tangible garment, is where thoughts and words find their ultimate expression. It's through actions that the soul's intentions are brought into reality, leaving a lasting impact on the physical world. The alignment of these garments is crucial for spiritual harmony. Kabbalah teaches that misalignment leads to spiritual discord, dimming the soul's divine light. The process of aligning thought, speech, and action with divine will is known as *Tikkun*, or cosmic repair, and is central to the soul's journey toward purity and perfection.

Beyond these practical garments, Jewish mysticism introduces the *Sefirot*— ten divine attributes or emanations through which the soul experiences and interacts with the world. These *Sefirot* act as deeper, more intrinsic layers of the soul, each representing a different facet of spiritual experience, such as wisdom, understanding, or love. When viewed as garments of the soul, the *Sefirot* become tools through which the soul navigates its existence, using these divine attributes to grow, learn, and influence the cosmos.

The relationship between the soul and the *Sefirot* is dynamic, not static. As we journey through life, these divine attributes channel energy in and out, continuously shaping our experiences and our responses to the world around us. Each challenge, each moment of growth, weaves a new pattern into the mosaic of our soul, reflecting the interplay between the individual and the divine.

This intricate connection extends beyond the individual to the cosmos. As microcosms of the universe, our alignment with the *Sefirot* mirrors our alignment with the grand order of existence. Engaging with these attributes, refining our thoughts, purifying our speech, and elevating our actions, we shed the limitations of our earthly existence and move closer to realizing our true spiritual essence.

In sum, the "garments of the soul" and the *Sefirot* in Kabbalah provide a profound framework for understanding our spiritual journey. They offer a pathway for transformation, guiding us in integrating spirituality into every aspect of our lives and aligning ourselves with the divine rhythm of the universe.

CHAPTER 11

THE REALITY OF EVIL

This brings us to a further aspect of the doctrine of Tikkun, which is also the most important for the system of practical theosophy. The process in which God conceives, brings forth, and develops himself does not reach its final conclusion in God. Certain parts of the process of restitution are allotted to man. Not all the lights which are held in captivity by the powers of darkness are set free by their own efforts; it is man who adds the final touch to the divine countenance; it is he who completes the enthronement of God, the king and the mystical Creator of all things, in His own Kingdom of Heaven; it is he who perfects the Maker of all things! In certain spheres of being, divine and human existence are intertwined. The intrinsic, extramundane process of Tikkun, symbolically described as the birth of God's personality, corresponds to the process of mundane history. The historical process and its innermost soul, the religious act of the Jew, prepare the way for the final restitution of all scattered and exiled lights and sparks.[151]

— Gershom Scholem, Major Trends in Jewish Mysticism

The serpent represents the following situation: in the historical experience of man, every individual finds evil already there; nobody begins it absolutely . . . Evil is part of the interhuman relationship, like language, tools, institutions; it is transmitted,

> *it is tradition and not only something that happens. There is thus an anteriority of evil to itself, as if evil were that which always precedes itself . . . That is why, in the Garden of Eden, the serpent is already there; he is the other side that begins. Let us go further; behind the projection of our lust, beyond the tradition of evil already there, there is perhaps even more radical externality of evil, a cosmic structure of evil—not, doubtless the lawlessness of the world as such, but its relation of indifference to the ethical demands of which man is both author and servant. From the spectacle of things, from the course of history, from the cruelty of nature and men, there comes a feeling of universal absurdity, which invites man to doubt his destination . . . There is thus a side of our world that confronts us as chaos and the chthonic animal symbolizes that. For a human existent, this aspect of chaos is a structure of the universe . . .. thus, the serpent symbolizes something of man and something of the world, a side of the microcosm, a side of the macrocosm, the chaos in me, among us, and outside. But it is always chaos for me, a human existent destined for goodness and happiness.*[152]
>
> PAUL RICOEUR, *The Symbolism of Evil*

מציאות הרע

EVIL'S EXISTENCE

"Bad" vs. "Evil" – A Linguistic Distinction

As we delve into the complex linguistic maze of "evil," we find that Biblical Hebrew lacks an equivalent that captures its precise English nuance, largely because each language trails its unique etymological labyrinth. The term "evil," journeying from its Old English precursor 'feel' and venturing further into the cradle of the Proto-Germanic 'bill,' finds itself nestled amidst a constellation of Germanic dialects, casting a somber reflection in the Dutch 'level' and the German *'übel.'* In these linguistic forebears, this term assumed the most extensive connotation of disapproval and abhorrence, marking the malicious, the foul, the defective, and the injurious.

In the richly woven lexicon of language, parsing the difference and connection between "evil" and "bad," especially in the context of the Hebrew term רָעָה (*ra'ah*), requires a nuanced understanding. It resembles a sunlit prism: when a singular ray of light enters, it will give birth to a kaleidoscope of colors. When we consider "bad," we visualize inferiority or undesirability. This term may depict a dearth in quality, morality, or functionality. It's a wide-ranging term, sweeping from the sour taste of spoiled fruit to the neglect of duties. It signals displeasure, a labeling of what fails to meet expectations or standards. While it can signify harm, it lacks an inherent malicious intent; for instance, a storm could be "bad" for a picnic, but it does not bear an ill will to ruin the day. In contrast, "evil" signifies profound malevolence. It hints at an ingrained immorality, an active intent to inflict harm, whether physical or emotional. Evil implies an intense, deliberate deviation from the perceived good, righteous, or just. It evokes images of intense wickedness, usually reserved for the most heinous breaches of societal moral norms.

Therefore, when aligning "bad" and "evil" with רָעָה (*ra'ah*), the translation often veers toward the former. Although the term does indeed denote undesirability or harm, it does not necessarily mirror the profound malevolence associated with "evil" in English. Rather, it encapsulates a wider spectrum of negative attributes or conditions, akin to "bad." This comprehension underscores the nuances in translation and interpretation, particularly when transposing concepts between languages. The expanse of רָעָה (*ra'ah*) bridges the gap between "bad" and "evil," occasionally brushing against the latter's malicious undertones but generally mirroring the former's wider, negative connotations.

The Hebrew word רָעָה (*ra'ah*) illustrates the complexity of language, as it encompasses a spectrum of meanings, from "bad" to "evil." Understanding its nuances is key to capturing its true essence. Like a prism refracting light, *ra'ah* reveals a range of connotations rather than a single definition. While it may indicate deficiency or deviation, it often carries a moral weight, highlighting corruption or a departure from righteousness. However, ra'ah does not always equate to "evil," as some biblical translations suggest.

Why Did God Create Evil?

Often, we feel perplexed by questions regarding the existence of suffering in a universe birthed by God. This question rests upon an implicit belief that life should be harmonious, but from where does such an expectation originate? It is equally conceivable to conjecture that life might be fraught with difficulty, or simply indifferent. Why then, do we anticipate something different? The answer seems to lie in the human spirit's intuitive understanding of the intrinsic goodness of God, a belief that is shocked into disbelief when confronted with circumstances that seem to contradict it.

Let us assume for a moment that the rabbis and the allegorical school correctly identify the serpent as a metaphor for the Evil Inclination. But why did God create the impulse for evil? Would humankind have been better off not dealing with such an urge? The Zohar raises this important question and offers the reader a most intriguing, thought-provoking response concerning the phenomenon of moral evil.[153]

> The question arises, "How can one love God amidst the temptations of the evil inclination, which seems to hinder serving the Divine?" The answer is profound: subduing the evil inclination through love for God is a supreme act of divine service. When one overcomes and breaks the power of this inclination through love, they become a true lover of God, transforming even their basest impulses into instruments of devotion. This concept is a deep esoteric truth: everything in creation, both celestial and earthly, exists to manifest God's glory and serve His purpose.
>
> Consider this analogy: would a master allow his servant to work against him and constantly plot to undermine his will? God wishes for people to worship Him and

follow the path of truth, reaping rewards and benefits. How, then, can the evil inclination, seemingly a contrary force, fit into this divine plan? The answer lies in the notion that the evil inclination, too, fulfills God's will, albeit in a complex way.

Imagine a king with a beloved son. He warns against the seductions of immoral women, for such defilement would bar entry into the palace. The son agrees to adhere to his father's wishes. Near the palace, there's a beautiful harlot. In time, the king decides to test his son's devotion and instructs the harlot to tempt him. She tries her utmost to lure the son, but he, being virtuous, resists her seductions and remains true to his father's command.

His son's obedience overjoys the father and rewards him with treasures and honors within the palace. The source of this joy? The harlot. Is she to be praised or blamed? In this case, praised. She not only followed the king's command and executed his plan but also became the catalyst for the son's reward, deepening the bond of love between the king and his son.[154]

Zohar's passage can be better understood through Mircea Eliade's philosophical concept of *coincidentia oppositorum,* or the "union of opposites." This principle, with both philosophical and spiritual undertones, encourages the peaceful integration and reconciliation of opposing forces or dualities. Eliade believed that humans have an innate desire to transcend these inherent dualities and overcome the fragmented realities that followed the Fall. After this event, our perception often divides the world into contrasting pairs, such as light and darkness, love and hate, or life and death. However, Eliade suggests that beneath this divisive layer lies a faint memory of a unified existence, a place where these polar opposites merge into a single entity.

"Human Duality"

The image captures the dualistic interplay of good and evil, depicted through a visual metaphor reminiscent of the yin-yang symbol. Two figures, one illuminated and one in shadow, are set within a circle that spirals into a central point, suggesting the interconnectedness and balance of opposing forces. The light figure with radiant head suggests purity, wisdom, or divine spark, while the dark figure seems to embody the hidden, unknown, or potentially negative aspects of existence. The swirling designs around them evoke the constant motion and coexistence of these principles in the universe. This portrayal suggests that good and evil are not separate and isolated, but rather integral to the whole, each defining the other and maintaining the equilibrium of the cosmic order.

The concept of *coincidentia oppositorum*, deeply rooted in mystical traditions, serves as a potent tool for comprehending the complex nature of the universe and our role within it. It envisions a world where traditional foes, such as light and darkness or good and evil, aren't merely linked, but are intrinsically merged in a deeper, hidden reality. Through this principle, these apparently conflicting elements cease their battle and find a harmonious balance.

The Zohar, a central text in Jewish mysticism, offers a transformative perspective on the "evil inclination" (*yetzer hara*). Rather than viewing it as a hindrance to spiritual growth, the Zohar sees this primal impulse as a powerful tool that, when properly understood and directed, can deepen our connection to the Divine and enhance our devotion to Him. This reimagined viewpoint reveals a divine spark concealed within what is often called the "heart of darkness"—the instincts or desires typically labeled as negative. By recognizing and redirecting this spark, we can transform these seemingly unholiness impulses into a force for profound spiritual growth, fostering a closer relationship with the Divine.

This innate desire to overcome duality and reunite with the ultimate reality is encapsulated in what Eliade describes as "pre-systematic thought." In this liberated mindset, primed to perceive the enigmatic totality that encompasses all contrasts, the Satanic angel is no longer an adversary. Instead, it transforms into a stimulant, a catalyst driving us toward the good. This is a vibrant interplay, a cosmic dance where opposing forces merge, culminating in an evolution of consciousness and spiritual maturation. The principle of i, thus, provides a unique perspective to perceive, comprehend, and embrace the rich diversity of life. It guides us on our spiritual path, instructing us to transcend duality, not merely choosing one over the other, but to experience unity, harmony, and wholeness.

In the grand theatre of existence, the "evil inclination", akin to a seductive courtesan, plays a crucial role in the divine narrative. It encourages us to grapple with our lower instincts, climb spiritual peaks, and rejoice in the triumph of good over evil. One's evil inclination does not hinder life's journey; instead, it fuels our pursuit of the Holy Blessed One, achieving the magnificent goal of manifesting His glory. The "evil inclination," like the serpent representing our inner demons, becomes an unlikely conduit of divine service, embodying a captivating paradox hidden within the enigma of human existence.

"The Fall" According to the Kabbalah

> *These things are not mere fabulous inventions in which the race of poets and sophists delight, but are rather types shadowing forth some allegorical truth and mystical explanation.*
>
> —PHILO of ALEXANDRIA, *On the Creation,* 55:157

Within the ancient narrative of Genesis 3 lies a profound invitation to venture beyond literal interpretations and embrace the profound wisdom woven into its mythical mosaic. While contemporary perspectives often equate myth with fabrication, Jewish mysticism views it as a conduit for timeless values and metaphysical truths, passed down through generations.

In contrast to James Frazer's reductionist approach in "The Golden Bough," which frames myth as a primitive form of science,[155] the French anthropologist Claude Lévi-Strauss offers a more nuanced understanding. He posits that myths serve as fundamental elements within a culture's symbolic communication system. Through archetypal characters and profound symbolism, myths mirror the hopes, dreams, fears, and conflicts inherent in the human experience, striving toward a reconciliation of opposing forces within a given culture. Ultimately, as the French anthropologist Claude Lévi-Strauss observed, myths shape a community's identity, defining its core values and offering a vision of its place within the grand mosaic of reality.[156]

This perspective is more aligned with the Kabbalistic interpretation.

Within this context, Jewish mysticism offers a profound reinterpretation of the "Fall" in Genesis 3. Rather than merely transgressing divine law, the Kabbalistic lens reveals a nuanced, allegorical panorama of cosmic and psychological significance. Adam and Eve's consumption of the forbidden fruit from the Tree of Knowledge marks a pivotal transformation in human consciousness and a profound shift in humanity's relationship with the divine.

According to this mystical perspective, the "Fall" signifies the differentiation of divine unity into the multiplicity of the created world. It represents a transition from a state of unified consciousness, where humanity existed in seamless union with God, to a state of differentiated consciousness, characterized by a perceived separation from the divine and the rest of creation. Prior to the "Fall," Adam and Eve existed as spiritual beings, dwelling in a state of divine androgyny, their minds and souls intertwined in perfect oneness. Consuming the fruit from the Tree of Knowledge shattered this unity, leading to their expulsion from the Garden of Eden. This descent into the physical realm—a realm characterized by duality, diversity, and separation—signified a profound transformation in human existence.

However, the Kabbalistic tradition does not perceive the "Fall" as solely a catastrophic event. Instead, it marks the commencement of a remarkable spiritual journey known as *tikkun*, or repair. In this paradigm, humanity is responsible for mending the fractured unity of divine light, which scattered during the "Fall." This restoration process unfolds through ethical living, adherence to divine commandments, and the relentless pursuit of spiritual wisdom. Through these intentional actions, humanity elevates the "sparks" of divine light that reside within the physical world, contributing to the repair of the world (*tikkun olam*) and the ultimate reunification with the divine source. The "Fall," therefore, is not a condemnation of humanity, but rather a catalyst for spiritual growth, moral development, and active participation in the co-creation of a more perfect world.

In essence, the Kabbalistic interpretation of the "Fall" invites a profound shift in perspective, revealing a journey of spiritual evolution and cosmic restoration. It highlights humanity's integral role as co-creators, empowered to elevate the material realm and restore a state of harmony with the divine. This profound narrative offers a message of hope, resilience, and the boundless potential for transformation that resides within the human spirit. It calls upon us to embrace the challenges and imperfections of the world as opportunities for growth, recognizing that even amid perceived separation, we remain inextricably bound to the Divine. The story of Genesis 3 regarding the "Fall" can teach us that each of our moral decisions can contribute greatly to the healing of our world and our lives.

Through these actions, humans elevate the "sparks" of divine light trapped in the physical world, contributing to the repair of the world (*tikkun olam*) and the ultimate reunification with God. Thus, the "Fall" need not be viewed as an act that irrevocably condemns humanity but rather as an event that gives humans the moral responsibility and capacity to choose good, grow spiritually, and contribute to the world's repair and perfection. When viewed from a different perspective, the "Fall" could also be seen as a necessary stage in humanity's development, and he didn't view Adam and Eve's transgression as a catastrophe. Rather, he saw it as a mistake made by humans in their infancy, a step in their maturation process.

In conclusion, while the "Fall" of Genesis 3 introduces separation and duality, in the Kabbalistic view, it also opens the way for a spiritual journey of growth, moral development, and the possibility of a conscious return to unity with God. It is part of a divine plan where humans are co-creators, tasked with the work of repairing and perfecting the world.

יֵצֶר הַרַע

THE EVIL (OR "BAD") INCLINATION

> When the LORD saw how great the wickedness of human beings was on earth, and how every desire that their heart conceived was always nothing but evil,
>
> —Genesis. 6:5

> *When the LORD smelled the sweet odor, the LORD said to Himself: "Never again will I curse the ground because of human beings, since the desires of the human heart are evil from youth; nor will I ever again strike down every living being, as I have done."*

—Genesis 8:21

"You shall love the LORD your God with all your heart, with all your soul, and with all your being" (Deut. 6:5) The Sages ask: "What is the intent of: 'with all your heart'? With both of your inclinations, the good and the evil'

BT BERACHOTH 54a.

The fact that evil confronts good, gives man the possibility of victory

—R. YEHIEL MICHAEL OF ZLOTSHOV, *Hassidic Aphorism*

The Talmudic literature portrays the "*Yetzer Hara*," or the "evil inclination," as an intrinsic part of human nature, which drives physical desires such as sexual urge. However, it's not inherently malevolent but can lead to damaging actions, including licentious behavior, if unchecked.[157] According to the Talmud, this inclination is pivotal for societal stability and continuity, stimulating activities like building a house, marrying, procreation, and work. It is not exclusively destructive but can be steered toward either virtue or vice depending on personal choices (BT Berachot 61b).

This Talmudic and Kabbalistic dualistic perspective of human nature associates the *Yetzer Hara* with physicality and worldly desires (especially regarding human libido), and the *Yetzer Hatov*, or "good inclination," with spirituality and moral virtues. The objective is to balance these two forces, where the energy of the *Yetzer Hara* is harnessed and guided by the ethical insights of the *Yetzer Hatov* toward positive actions, thereby mitigating the potential harm of licentious behavior.[158] Maimonides, in his legal code, echoes this sentiment, advocating for a middle path in behaviors and inclinations as the way to balance the *Yetzer Hara* and *Yetzer Hatov*.[159] This balance enables the fruitful use of *Yetzer Hara's* energy, channeling ambition and creativity toward positive ends and preventing its unchecked expression from leading to damaging behaviors.

However, Kabbalistic interpretations often present a more nuanced and complex understanding of this concept, considering it not simply as a negative force but as a necessary part of the human spiritual journey and growth. Here's a summary of what Kabbalah might teach about the Evil Inclination:

- ❑ **BALANCE BETWEEN GOOD AND EVIL:** In Kabbalistic thought, both the good inclination (*Yetzer HaTov*) and the evil inclination are part of human nature and are necessary for free will. This balance enables people to make moral decisions and strive for spiritual growth.

- ❑ **SPIRITUAL GROWTH:** The Evil Inclination is an essential catalyst for spiritual growth. Overcoming and controlling it can lead to spiritual advancement. Some interpretations suggest that the struggle with the Evil Inclination is a part of the soul's journey and development.

- ❑ **GOD'S CREATION:** The Talmud says God created the Evil Inclination. This idea is also present in Kabbalah, suggesting that the Evil Inclination has a purpose in the divine plan, often related to free will and the possibility of moral and spiritual growth. The purpose of creation was for God to bestow goodness upon something Other than God Himself.[160]

- ❑ **TRANSFORMATION:** According to various mystical texts influenced by Kabbalah, the goal isn't to destroy the Evil Inclination but to transform it. This can be achieved by redirecting the energy and passion associated with our base desires toward serving God and doing good. This transformation is often considered the ultimate victory over the Evil Inclination.

- ❑ **LINKED TO MATERIAL WORLD:** Evil Inclination is often associated with the physical and material world, while good Inclination is linked to the spiritual realm. This reflects the Kabbalistic belief in the interconnectedness of the physical and spiritual worlds and the human role in bridging these two dimensions through their actions.

שבירת הכלים

SHATTERING OF THE VESSELS

Once upon a time, before time itself, in the vast realm of the divine, a desire to fill the infinite void sparked. This gave rise to ten vessels— the *Sefirot,* each emanating from the limitless light of *Ein Sof,* carrying unique divine principles. These vessels, each an embodiment of life, love, justice, beauty, and more, were flooded with divine light, leading to a dance of divine interaction.

However, the intensity of the divine light was too potent for these vessels. They quaked under its overpowering radiance until they could bear it no more, leading to a catastrophic shattering. The shards, each carrying a spark of divine light, scattered across the cosmos, giving rise to a world of duality, a realm where the divine is concealed, waiting to be discovered. Kabbalists refer to this cataclysmic event as "the shattering of the vessels" (שְׁבִירַת הַכֵּלִים = *šəbîrat hakkēlîm*).

This is the mystery of the "shattering of the vessels," a tale of brokenness, healing, fragmentation, and wholeness. It signifies our constant endeavor to repair this cosmic disarray through acts of kindness, truth, and love. According to Kabbalah, this ancient event is not merely of the past but continues to happen in our lives, shaping our destiny and our journey.

In Kabbalah, this spiritual journey is often represented by two stages, *Olam HaTohu*, "the World of Chaos," and *Olam HaTikun*, the "world of rectification." These stages, conceived by R. Isaac Luria, the father of modern Jewish mysticism, symbolize the archetypal spiritual states of being and consciousness, encompassing concepts of free will, evil, spiritual and physical exile and redemption, commandments, and the messianic rectification of existence. The process of *tikkun* involves the sifting and clarification of hidden Sparks of Holiness that are scattered within the physical creation, symbolizing a dynamic process of embodiment and manifestation.

The *sheviratbakelim* is related to the multifariousness and origin of evil. The concept explains the building and destruction of the primordial world, and the mystical account of the eight Edomite kings who reigned before any king over the children of Israel. The *Sefirot,* a series of divine attributes in Jewish mysticism, are envisioned as vessels of varying sizes, each progressively smaller, symbolizing a hierarchy of spiritual principles and their capacity to contain the divine light of the *Ein Sof* (the Infinite). When the overwhelming light of the *Ein Sof* flowed into the vessel of *Keter*, the first and highest *Sefirah*, the vessels were unable to withstand its intensity, leading to the "breaking of the vessels" (*shevirat ha-kelim*), a pivotal event in Kabbalistic cosmology.

"Humpty Dumpty's Fall"

Humpty Dumpty as a Kabbalistic Parable

Over fifty years ago, as I sat in the quiet solitude of an Israeli *yeshiva,* my study of the ancient Kabbalistic texts prompted a curious interpretation of a well-known nursery rhyme:

Humpty Dumpty sat on a wall,
Humpty Dumpty had a great fall.

In the figure of Humpty Dumpty, often depicted as an egg, I found parallels with the divine vessels in *Olam HaTohu*, the "World of Chaos." They, like Humpty Dumpty in his elevated position atop the wall, represented an original, serene state of unity. Humpty's "great fall" resonates with the shattering of these divine vessels, an event of cosmic magnitude caused by the overpowering intensity of the Divine light.

All the king's horses and all the king's men
Couldn't put Humpty together again.

This verse echoes the echoes of divine attempts to restore the shattered primordial unity. The futile efforts of 'the king's horses and king's men' symbolize the deep cosmic disruption that birthed the new realm of *Olam HaTikkun*, the "World of Repair." Humpty Dumpty's fragmented state after the fall mirrors this realm, where the divine sparks dispersed upon the breaking of the vessels lie concealed within our physical world, trapped within the 'shells' or 'husks' known as *kelipot.* With this perspective, the simple nursery rhyme of Humpty Dumpty expands to become a profound allegory of our role in *Tikkun Olam*, the repair of the world. It mirrors the universal "cosmic egg" archetype found across different cultures,[161] symbolizing the shift from unity to multiplicity—a theme echoed in Kabbalistic teachings.

Humpty Dumpty as a Jungian Metaphor

Turning to Jungian psychology, developed by Swiss psychiatrist Carl Jung, we find more layers to the Humpty Dumpty story that parallel our Kabbalistic interpretation. Jungian thought suggests that Humpty Dumpty can symbolize the Self, the psyche's unifying center that seeks to balance the disparate forces within an individual. Sitting atop the wall represents a precarious state of balance or equilibrium.

Humpty Dumpty's great fall can be seen as a psychic crisis, reflecting significant life changes that often disrupt the unity of the

Self, leading to transformative experiences. This resonates with the Jungian concept of the Shadow, the unconscious aspects of the personality that the conscious ego doesn't identify with. Once these shadow elements are conscious, they cannot be repressed or wished away.

Just like Humpty Dumpty, the shattered Self needs to be reintegrated. This reintegration acknowledges and incorporates all parts of the Self, leading toward wholeness. The efforts of "all the king's horses and all the king's men" highlight the fact that reintegration and the subsequent journey toward wholeness are not a task for external forces but rather a process of inner work and personal transformation.

So, the seemingly simple nursery rhyme of Humpty Dumpty, when viewed through the lens of Kabbalistic interpretation and Jungian psychology, becomes a potent metaphor for creation, disarray, restoration, transformation, and growth. It serves as an allegorical call to action and self-realization, inviting us to participate in the grand mission of repairing the world—of moving from chaos and fragmentation toward unity and wholeness, both within our own selves and in the world around us. to participate in the ongoing work of healing and wholeness.

בֵּירוּרִים

PURIFICATION OF THE SPARKS

The Hebraic Meaning of "Purification"

In Biblical Hebrew, the Hebrew verb בָּרוּר, meaning "purge," "select," or "purify," which expresses ideas of purification, selection, and cleansing. In Akkadian, the similar root *bararu* implies a sense of glistening or shining, while in Ugaritic, it denotes purity, particularly about metals, and freedom in the context of slaves. [162]

Across these Semitic languages, the roo*t b-r-r* reveals a shared cultural framework where purification transforms materials, people, or statuses, yielding clarity, beauty, or distinction. In ancient Near Eastern societies, refining metals, performing rituals, or granting freedom were practical and symbolic acts of achieving perfection. The Hebrew use of בָּרוּר, with its moral and theological depth, builds on this heritage, emphasizing spiritual purity and divine discernment. The Akkadian focus on brightness and Ugaritic's social applications highlight the root's versatility, showing how purification was valued for its visual, moral, and societal outcomes. In the Hebrew Bible, בָּרוּר underscores God's role as a refiner, testing and purifying His people, while its sense of selection resonates with the idea of a chosen nation, set apart for a sacred purpose

Lurianic Thoughts About the Divine Sparks

Isaac Luria, known as the Ari, profoundly reshaped Jewish mysticism with his Kabbalistic teachings. As we noted earlier, according to Luria, the act of Creation itself triggered this cosmic exile. He introduced the concept of *Tzimtzum*, where God contracted His Divine Light to make room for the universe. This contraction, however, led to the shattering of divine "vessels," resulting in the scattering of heavenly sparks and the introduction of evil into the world. These divine sparks, according to Luria, are embedded in all aspects of the world. Human actions play a crucial role in elevating and redeeming these sparks. This redemptive process is emphasized by Luria's disciples and followers of Kabbalah. They teach that everyone, regardless of their life stage or background, is responsible for creating meaning and spirituality in daily life. This process involves deep intentionality known as savannah, which emerges from our entire being and strives to help redeem the world.

The mission to liberate these sparks is at the heart of Lurianic Kabbalah. Figures like the Baal Shem Tov, a later mystical teacher, echoed Luria's teachings. He preached that every act when performed with the right intention, aids in cosmic redemption from darkness and confusion. According to this view, Divine Presence can be accessed through various paths in life, with each person's unique abilities being crucial for serving God.

Lurianic Kabbalah also introduces the concepts of *Assur* (forbidden) and *Birur* (refining). In this framework, "*Assur*" actions stemming from impurity contain bound sparks that cannot be directly elevated. On the contrary, "*Birur*" involves refining or elevating these sparks, a process key to spiritual rectification. This idea is further elaborated in the concept of *Partzufim*, a restructured universe designed to balance divine abundance and lack and facilitate the restoration of scattered sparks. An important aspect of this concept is that some sparks are embedded in forbidden realms or objects, encapsulated within *kelipot* (shells or husks) that represent impurity or negativity.

This implies that the material world contains hidden holiness, including its forbidden aspects. However, sparks in such elements don't justify engaging with them directly. Instead, it acknowledges the complex nature of creation, where holiness is concealed within impurity. The redemption of these sparks is a delicate process and involves navigating the world with awareness and making choices that align with divine will. It is believed that particularly righteous individuals, known as *tzadikim*, can redeem these sparks without being tainted by the negativity they are embedded in.

A Kabbalistic Debate Regarding the "Sparks"

The Vilna Gaon (GRA) critically addressed Hasidic interpretations of divine immanence, particularly in the works *Tzavaat haRivash* and *Likkutei Amarim*. He contested the Hasidic belief that holy sparks were present in all physical matter, including wood, stones, and dust, viewing this as a misinterpretation akin to idolatry, exemplified by Israel's worship of the molten calf. The GRA argued that the prophet's mention of "Blessed be the glory of the Lord from His place" did not signify God's immanence within all creation, but rather His transcendence and providence. Furthermore, the GRA opposed the Hasidic reading of "Thou preserves them all," arguing that it was blasphemous to suggest God actively enlivened or participated in sinful actions. He stressed that God's essence cannot be contained within every place, emphasizing His transcendence over immanence.

Contrasting with this view, Rabbi Jacob Joseph of Polonnoye, a disciple of the Baal Shem Tov (*Besht*), articulated a Hasidic perspective. He emphasized that no obstacle could separate man and God during Torah study or worship. Even "strange thoughts" during these practices were seen as mere veils for the divine. The *Besht* taught that such thoughts, including inappropriate ones, could be elevated to their spiritual root, such as transforming lustful thoughts through the concept of *Hesed* (loving-kindness).

The Vilna Gaon and Hasidic teachers, such as the Baal Shem Tov (Besht), offered contrasting perspectives on divine immanence within Jewish mysticism. The Vilna Gaon warned against misinterpreting God's presence, emphasizing the risks of equating the Divine with mundane or impure matter. In contrast, the Besht and other Hasidic masters viewed every facet of creation—however ordinary or seemingly impure—as infused with divine potential, offering opportunities for spiritual elevation and deeper connection with God. This core distinction highlights the diverse approaches within Jewish mysticism to understanding how God's presence manifests in the world.

אִסּוּר /"ISSUR"

"FORBIDDEN," "IMPRISONED"

In Kabbalistic thought, the concept of אִסּוּר (*issur*) extends beyond its literal meanings of restriction, prohibition, and imprisonment and conveys several profound spiritual implications. It symbolizes the soul's limitations within the physical world, mirroring how chains restrict physical movement. These material constraints are seen as hurdles in the path of spiritual growth and enlightenment, challenges that the soul must transcend to achieve a higher state of consciousness.

Simultaneously, אִסּוּר represents moral and ethical boundaries. Far from mere restrictions, these prohibitions are divine guidelines meant to align human actions with God's will. Adherence to these boundaries is crucial for *Tikkun Olam*, the Kabbalistic principle of repairing or healing the world. Shabbatai Sevi often cited the biblical verse, עֹשֶׂה מִשְׁפָּט לָעֲשׁוּקִים נֹתֵן לֶחֶם לָרְעֵבִים יְהוָה מַתִּיר אֲסוּרִים "It is He who secures justice for those who are wronged, gives food to the hungry. The LORD sets prisoners free" (Ps. 146:7) whenever he wished to justify the abrogation of Mosaic Law by envisioning himself as the Messiah, a virtual new Moses, who introduces a new Torah. This Messiah is seen as liberating followers by permitting previously forbidden actions, leading to a state where "everything is permitted," a concept Scholem describes as nihilistic.

Shabbatai Sevi utilized this concept also metaphorically depict the state of divine sparks, or *nitzotzot,* entrapped within the physical realm, particularly in impure or forbidden aspects (*kelipot*). The Kabbalistic mission of humanity involves liberating these sparks from their imprisonment, elevating them to their celestial origin. He argued that by doing so, humans release these sparks and contribute to the cosmic restoration of balance and harmony.

Yet, true Kabbalah is intertwined with normative Jewish observance and law. Moreover, Shabbatai Sevi and his followers forgot that אִסּוּר is reflective of the internal struggles and conflicts that must act as barriers to prevent an individual's spiritual journey from becoming harmed. In the grand scheme of creation, אִסּוּר aligns with the concept of the *tzimtzum*, where God contracts His infinite light to make space for the universe. This act of divine self-restriction symbolizes the essential nature of limitation within the Infinite, allowing for the existence of a finite, diverse universe. Through these interpretations, Kabbalah perceives אִסּוּר not just as a physical, legal, or moral concept but as a multi-dimensional symbol encapsulating the dynamics of spiritual growth while creating the necessary boundaries for ethical living, thus enhancing the soul's journey toward divine unification.

מַתִּיר / MATTIR

"RELEASING" AND "PERMITTED"

The Kabbalistic term מַתִּיר (*Mattir*), meaning "releasing" is semantically related to the word מוּתָּר (*mutar)* or "permitting."[163] In Jewish mystical texts, this word signifies the act of elevating divine sparks, *nitzotzot*, which are embedded in all aspects of creation. According to the teachings of Isaac Luria, the Ari, these sparks were scattered throughout the material world during the primordial event known as *Shevirat HaKeilim*, the shattering of the divine vessels, which we discussed several times earlier in this book.

Human beings must liberate these sparks by performing mitzvot and engaging in activities allowed by Jewish law, thus contributing to *tikkun olam*, the rectification of the world. When an action is *mutar,* it's not just permitted by law but is also an opportunity for spiritual elevation. The intention behind such actions, known as *kavanah*, is what transforms mundane activities into vessels for the ascent of divine sparks.

This balance between the physical and the spiritual is pivotal. While forbidden actions can trap these sparks further in the material realm, permitted actions can liberate them. Thus, the material world is not merely a space to be transcended but a platform for spiritual service. *Mattir* is a central concept in Kabbalah, emphasizing the sanctification of the physical through observance of divine laws and the pursuit of permitted acts, thereby aiding in the cosmic process of healing and divine unification.

קְלִיפָּה
KELIPAH

Beyond the divine domain of the Sefirot embodiments of light and goodness, an equivalent realm characterized by darkness and evil also exists. A *Sefira* of darkness counterbalances each of the light-emitting *Sefirot.* This duality is analogous to the dichotomy of right and left, with light—*Sefirot* representing the right side and the darkness— *Sefirot* representing the left side, often referred to as "*sitra achra*". This darker realm is metaphorically described as the kingdom of Cain, Esau, and Pharaoh, according to Zohar (Zohar, I, 55a).

In Kabbalistic thought, malevolent forces, often referred to as evil powers, perpetually disrupt the harmony of creation. These forces entice humans to stray from their connection to God, thereby strengthening the realm of evil and amplifying the influence of the *keliphot*—spiritual "shells" that obscure divine light. This disruption is symbolically depicted as a rift between the "king" and "queen," representing divine masculine and feminine aspects, which hinders their joint role in nurturing the world's well-being. However, this discord can be healed through acts of repentance, self-discipline, prayer, and meticulous observance of sacred rituals, restoring the original state of cosmic harmony. Notably, the concept of opposing spiritual kingdoms emerged later in Kabbalistic tradition, gaining prominence in the 13th century.

The term *kelipah,* translated as "husk" or "shell," signifies not a mere physical shell but a spectral veil cloaking the Divine, a metaphorical embodiment of spiritual obscurity. Much like the fruit's succulent pulp veiled by its protective casing, the Divine essence is hidden by the *kelipah's* shroud. Intriguingly, this concealment is a deliberate Divine design, creating a metaphysical space where humanity grapples with good and evil choices. *Kelipah* stands as a spiritual challenge to humanity, provoking us toward a quest to pierce through these spiritual shells and unveil the Divine within.

Kelipah underscores our moral and spiritual responsibility, transforming our life journey into a relentless battle against forces obscuring the Divine. As we observe commandments, perform acts of kindness, and engage in spiritual contemplation, we chip away at the k*elipah*, unmasking the Divine light within. *Kelipah* extends beyond spiritual symbolism, actively driving us toward spiritual awakening and the world's illumination. It transforms every action, every word, and every thought into a potential tool to weaken the k*elipah,* encouraging us to peel away layers of spiritual concealment to reveal the Divine essence. Within the framework of Kabbalistic interpretation, *kelipot* exists in dynamic interaction with human actions. Actions in accord with divine commandments, guided by kindness and contemplation, can weaken the grasp of the *kelipot*, liberating the spark of holiness encased within. Meanwhile, contrary actions can strengthen these husks, further dimming the divine light.

Particularly, the significance of *kelipat nogah* is accentuated. It's the liminal space, the gray area where what is permissible resides, neither commanded nor prohibited by Torah. It reflects our daily choices, not inherently good or evil, but dependent on our intent. When we act with a higher purpose, even in mundane tasks like eating and drinking, we elevate this neutral energy toward holiness. Conversely, actions driven by mere sensuality, without intending to serve a divine purpose, push this energy into the dominion of the impure *kelipot*. However, this fall is not irrevocable. The inherent neutrality of actions within *kelipat nogah* allows for redemption.

When we return to the path of divine service, the degraded energy ascends, realigning with the realm of holiness. Conversely, actions that violate Torah prohibitions emanate from the three impure *kelipat* and are bound tightly in their grasp. These cannot ascend to holiness until the final day when all impurity will be eradicated, or until the sinner experiences profound repentance, transforming sins into merits through a love-driven return to the Divine.

Clinical psychologist Sanford L. Drob compares the notion of the *kelipot* to the concept of karma that pervades Jainism and nearly all spiritual traditions of India. This similarity lies in that both concepts wield the imagery of a spark or a divine crystal of light. This light is seen as the individual's authentic or godlike self, enveloped by layers of darkness (*kelipot* in Kabbalah, *lesyas* (colors) in Jainism) that burden and hinder the self from attaining divine realization.[164]

In sum, the complex concept of *kelipot* guides us in our spiritual navigation, providing us with a metaphysical map for our moral and spiritual choices. It underscores the potent impact of our actions and intentions, illustrating the transformative power we hold within us to shape the spiritual cosmos. In every moment, with every choice, we're interacting with these divine husks, either strengthening or weakening their grasp. Through awareness and intentional living, we can ensure our life becomes a continuous journey toward piercing these spiritual shells and unveiling the Divine within.

סִטְרָא אַחֲרָא

SITRA ACHRA – THE "OTHER SIDE"

In the beguiling theater of Kabbalistic thought, a character intrigues and unsettles in equal measure — the *Sitra Achra.* Its name is from ancient Aramaic, translated as the "Other Side." The *Sitra Achra* is not merely an antagonist but embodies the mystery and complexity of the human condition and the universe itself.

As conceived in the Kabbalistic tradition, the world is a canvas painted with the brushstrokes of dualities. There's the radiant light of the divine, the *Sitra D'Kedushah*, the "Side of Holiness," a realm radiant with love, wisdom, and grace. Opposing it is the shadowy realm of the *Sitra Achra*, a territory born of separation, fragmentation, and imbalance. It is not a demon to be exorcised but rather a challenge to be navigated, a paradox to be understood.

The *Sitra Achra* represents those aspects of reality that are veiled from the divine light, shrouded in opacity. It is a realm that encapsulates the impurities, imperfections, and dissonance of creation. It is the resistance that comes with the pursuit of virtue, the shadow cast by the radiant light of goodness. Yet, the presence of the *Sitra Achra* does not diminish the profound wisdom of the Kabbalah. Rather, it deepens it, and generates a rich understanding that is complex and profound. For it is in wrestling with the *Sitra Achra*, in navigating its shadowy labyrinth, that we unearth our potential for growth and transformation. It is a cosmic mirror, reflecting our own vulnerabilities and fears, inviting us to transcend them.

The *Sitra Achra* is not a villain in this grand narrative. Instead, it embodies the perpetual tension between light and darkness, purity and impurity, wholeness and fragmentation. It is the friction that sparks growth, the challenge that fuels evolution. For only in acknowledging and confronting the *Sitra Achra* can we truly appreciate the radiant beauty of the *Sitra D'Kedushah*, the "Side of Holiness." Thus, in the dance of cosmic dualities, the *Sitra Achra* has its role to play. It contributes to the grandeur of the cosmic symphony, not by playing a discordant note, but by providing the contrast necessary for the divine melody to unfold in its sublime harmony. It is the canvas upon which the brilliant hues of the divine can be vividly appreciated, the depth against which the heights of spiritual ascension can be truly measured. In the eternal dance of creation, the *Sitra Achra* and the *Sitra D'Kedushah* whirl together, partners in the divine ballet of existence.

A GLOSSARY OF KABBALISTIC CONCEPTS

Adam Kadmon: Refers to the primordial human archetype God used in the creation of the universe, which everyone is believed to reflect. In Kabbalah, Adam Kadmon (אָדָם קַדְמוֹן, *ʾāḏām kaḏmōn,* "Primordial Man") also called Adam Elyon (אָדָם עֶלְיוֹן, *ʾāḏām ʿelyōn,* "Most High Man"), or Adam Ila'ah (אָדָם עִילָּאָה, *ʾāḏām ʿīllāʾā* "Supreme Man").[165]

Philo of Alexandria was the first Judaic thinker to introduce the concept of the "original man," or "heavenly man" (οὐράνιος ἄνθρωπος = *ouranios anthropos).* From his perspective, the heavenly man, being created in God's image, does not partake in any corruptible or earthly essence. This contrasts with the earthly man ("πλαστός ἄνθρωπος"= *plastos anthropos*), who is made of a loose material, often referred to as a lump of clay. The heavenly man is the perfect embodiment of the Logos and is neither male nor female but a pure, incorporeal intelligence— essentially an idea. On the other hand, the earthly man, created by God later, is tangible, perceivable by the senses, and possesses earthly qualities.[166]

Amulet: In Kabbalah, an amulet or "*kamea*" (קָמֵיעָא in Hebrew) is considered a physical object with spiritual value, often inscribed with Hebrew letters or Torah verses. These inscriptions are believed to channel divine energy, offering protection or other benefits. However, the amulet's effectiveness is attributed more to the wearer's faith and the divine force it symbolizes. It is viewed as a manifestation of faith, potentially providing protection, healing, or bringing good fortune. Historically significant in Hebrew biblical tradition, amulets have been widely used and accepted in Jewish culture, especially during the Talmudic period. They were crafted from various materials, including herbs, stones, or animal parts, and were endorsed by rabbinical authorities for their protective and healing properties against evils like the evil eye.

Atik Yomin is also known as *Atika Kadisha* (the Holy Ancient One), a term rooted in Daniel 7:9, 13, and 22, and is widely used in the Zohar.[167] Predominantly, it refers to the *En Sof* (the Infinite) as the First Cause or Most Ancient Being. It's also applied to the highest aspect of *Keter,* the foremost Sefirah, symbolizing the most "ancient" or primal emanation. It is an aspect of *Keter,* the highest *Sefirah*, representing the most hidden and profound level of divine wisdom.

Baal Shem Tov: Israel ben Eliezer (1698-1760), also known as the Baal Shem Tov or "*Besht*", was the influential founder of Hasidism. His title, meaning 'Master of the Good Name', reflects his spiritual prowess and his use of Kabbalistic practices, including the arrangement of divine names for miraculous healings. Initially known for his white magic, his role as a spiritual guide is most celebrated.

Bahir: The *Sefer HaBahir,* or "Book of Brightness" in English, is an important text in Jewish mystical literature, specifically Kabbalah. It is believed to have been written in Provence, France, around 1175. The book is a collection of mystical interpretations of biblical verses and homilies, and it is one of the earliest works to elaborate on the *sefirot*, the ten divine emanations or attributes through which God created and continues to sustain the world.

Besht: See "Baal Shem Tov."

Bittul Ha-Yesh: In Chabad theology, *Bittul Ha-Yesh* is a key concept in Hasidic thought, emphasizing nullifying the ego to achieve a profound connection with the Divine. This self-abnegation is often likened to a drop of water merging with the vast ocean, symbolizing the dissolution of individual identity into divine consciousness. This process facilitates a heightened spiritual awareness and a deeper understanding of one's place in the universe.

Breslov: The Breslov Hasidic movement is a branch of Hasidic Judaism founded by Rabbi Nachman of Breslov in the late 18th century. Breslov's teachings emphasize faith, joy, and personal connection to God through prayer and meditation. Unlike other Hasidic groups, Breslov does not have a hereditary leadership, reflecting Rabbi Nachman's wish that each follower should strive to be his own master. Unlike Chabad, Breslov focuses on refining the heart rather than shaping the mind.

Chabad: A metaphysical system developed by Rabbi Shneur Zalman of Liadi (1747-1812), forming the basis for Lubavitcher Hasidic thought. Chabad, also known as Lubavitch, is a major branch of Hasidic Judaism known for its intellectual approach to Jewish mysticism and its extensive outreach efforts. Founded in the 18th century in Russia, the movement emphasizes study, meditation, and social service. It is now globally active with institutions in many countries.

Chalal The concept of "*Chalal*" (חלל), often translated as "empty space" or "vacuum," is central to the Kabbalistic doctrine of *Tzimtzum*, introduced by the 16th-century mystic Rabbi Isaac Luria, also known as the Ari. In Lurianic Kabbalah, *Tzimtzum* describes a process where God, *Ein Sof* (the Infinite), voluntarily contracted Himself to create a conceptual space for the universe to exist. The *Chalal* represents this metaphorical space that emerged as a result of God's self-contraction. It is not "empty" in the usual sense, as it does not imply the absence of God. Rather, it is a state where God's presence is hidden or diminished, allowing for the existence of a finite, diverse world that is not overwhelmed by divine omnipresence. This concealment is necessary for creation to maintain its distinct existence and for free will to operate.

Devekut: Devekut is a term in Jewish mysticism that refers to the spiritual state of being closely attached or "cleaving" to God. It represents a deep, personal connection with the divine. *Devekut* is achieved through intense prayer, meditation, and spiritual practices, leading to a profound sense of unity with the Divine.

Dybbuk: In Jewish folklore, a *dybbuk* is a malevolent wandering spirit of a deceased person that possesses and inhabits a living person, often causing mental illness or strange behavior. Originating in 16th-century Kabbalistic traditions, the term "*dybbuk*" means "to cling," reflecting the spirit's attachment to its host. Typically believed to be souls of sinners seeking rectification or refuge, *dybbuks* are expelled through exorcism rituals, usually led by a rabbi. These rituals aim to release the spirit to the afterlife and free the afflicted person. *Dybbuk* stories, rich in moral and spiritual themes, have influenced Jewish literature and culture.

Ein Sof: In Kabbalah, *Ein Sof* refers to the infinite divine essence, the ultimate reality of God that is beyond all understanding and description, and from which all creation emanates. *Ein Sof*, literally meaning "without end" in Hebrew, is often associated with God's most concealed aspect, transcending any anthropomorphic conception of the divine. It represents the state of God prior to His self-manifestation in the creation of the spiritual and physical realms.

Emunah: Understanding faith in the context of Kabbalah requires exploring its Hebraic roots, particularly the word אָמַן (*'āman*), which signifies confirmation and support. This root leads to terms like אֱ·ונָה (*emunah* = faith) and אֱמֶת (*emeth* = truth), highlighting their deep connection. 'āman represents certainty and assurance, essential to both faith and truth. "Amen," derived from this root, is an affirmation of truth and faith. *Emunah* implies steadfast trust and loyalty, particularly in

God's benevolence, while *emeth* emphasizes truth rooted in reliability and faithfulness.

Evil Eye: Jewish tradition, the "evil eye," or עַיִן הָרַע (*ayin hara*), is viewed as more than mere superstition. Maimonides interprets it as animosity or envy toward others, which can escalate into malevolent intentions. Kabbalistic teachings regard it as a powerful negative force causing physical and spiritual harm, often linked to jealousy or greed. Protection against the evil eye in Kabbalah includes wearing a red string bracelet and incorporating specific prayers like the "*Birkhat HaBayit*" for safeguarding homes. The Talmud also advises modesty and humility to avoid attracting this harmful influence.

Frankists: In the 18th century, Jacob Frank (1726–1791), a charismatic Polish Jew, founded a heretical sect claiming to succeed Shabbatai Zevi. Styling himself as an Eastern potentate after absorbing Turkish cultural influences, Frank declared himself the reincarnated Patriarch Jacob and Zevi. His doctrine, a mix of Christian theology, Kabbalistic mysticism, and antinomian practices, elevated the Zohar above the Bible and Talmud, aiming to create a new religion. The Frankists gained followers in Poland amid Jewish spiritual unrest, but their ritualistic violations, including sexual rites and mass conversion to Christianity to "conquer it from within," provoked outrage. Rabbinic authorities issued a cherem (excommunication), and the sect's excesses tarnished Kabbalah's reputation, leading to restrictions on its study. Despite gentile protection and Frank's imprisonment for apostasy, his influence lingered through his daughter until the sect's decline by the late 19th century. The Frankist heresy intensified Jewish intellectual and spiritual crises, paving the way for Hasidism's rise.

Gematria: In Jewish numerology, *gematria* is where each Hebrew letter is assigned a numerical value. By calculating the numerical value of words and phrases, hidden connections and deeper meanings can be discovered between different words that share the same numerical value, even if their meanings are not obviously related. This technique is often used in mystical and interpretative Jewish texts to uncover hidden layers of meaning within the Torah and other sacred texts.

Gilgulim: The concept of *Gilgul*, central to Kabbalah and other mystical Jewish teachings, refers to the soul's transmigration through various lifetimes. It posits that a single soul can experience multiple existences, inheriting the consequences of its actions, both good and bad, from one life to the next. This cycle of rebirth allows the soul to evolve spiritually, rectify past wrongs, and adhere to divine commandments. It also provides an explanation for the seeming injustices in the world, where virtuous individuals may endure hardship while the wicked appear to thrive, viewed as reflections of the soul's past life deeds. Kabbalists often connect this idea to scriptural passages, such as Exodus 20:5, which speak of divine retribution extending across generations, reinforcing the notion of actions' enduring impact on the soul's journey.

Golem: In Jewish mysticism, particularly Kabbalah, the concept of a *golem* involves creating a life form from inanimate materials, such as clay or mud, through spiritual and esoteric methods. This ancient tradition is rooted in the belief that knowledgeable and spiritually adept individuals, such as sages or rabbis, could bring a *golem* to life using divine names and incantations. These practices are considered potent acts of creation. Talmudic texts, such as BT Sanhedrin 65b, describe *golems* as entities that lack speech and true human essence, often portrayed as temporary beings commanded to return to dust. The medieval fascination with golems was inspired by the *Sefer Yetzirah*, where it was believed that inserting a paper with a divine name (*shem*) into a golem could animate it.

Halacha: *Halakha* is the comprehensive legal system that governs the religious, ethical, and day-to-day life of practicing Jews. It is derived from the Torah (the Five Books of Moses), as well as subsequent interpretations and rulings by rabbinic authorities. For Kabbalists, *Halakha* is not just a set of laws, but a divine blueprint that reflects profound spiritual truths and hidden meanings. They believe that the commandments (*mitzvot*) and their detailed observance in Halakha are physical manifestations of divine wisdom, and by following them, one can connect more deeply with the divine reality. This perspective adds a mystical dimension to the practice of Jewish law.

Hasidism: Hasidism is a spiritual and social movement that emerged among Eastern European Jews in the late 18th century. Founded by Rabbi Israel Baal Shem Tov, it emphasizes personal spirituality, joy in worship, and the importance of charismatic leadership, often in contrast to more intellectual and legalistic forms of Judaism. Hasidism has profoundly influenced Jewish life and continues to thrive in various communities worldwide. Hasidism is not a monolithic movement but is divided into numerous groups, or "courts," each typically following a particular spiritual leader or Rebbe. These groups, such as Chabad-Lubavitch, Satmar, Breslov, and Belz, vary in their customs, practices, and interpretations of Hasidic teachings. Despite these differences, they all emphasize the inner dimensions of faith, the pursuit of spiritual ecstasy, and the guidance of a Rebbe.

Hekhalot: *Hekhalot* literature is a genre of Jewish mystical texts primarily concerned with descriptions of ascents into the heavenly halls (*Hekhalot*), the Throne of God, and the divine chariot (*Merkavah*) as practiced by Jewish visionaries from the first century B.C.E. through the tenth century C.E. These texts, dating from late antiquity, are some of the earliest forms of Jewish mystical literature and provide important insights into early Jewish mysticism and speculation about the divine realm. *Hekhalot* literature also includes detailed accounts of mystical experiences, angelology, and practices such as incantations and magical seals, offering a glimpse into early Jewish mystics' spiritual and mystical practices.

Hitbodedut: Abraham Ibn Maimon (1186–1237), son of Maimonides, developed a profound approach to הִתְבּוֹדְדוּת (*hitbodedut* = "seclusion"), emphasizing it as a path to spiritual intimacy with God. Influenced by Jewish tradition and Sufi mysticism, he described *hitbodedut* as comprising three elements: withdrawal from physical stimuli, focusing on the divine, and achieving *devekut* (attachment to God) through concentrated meditation. This practice aimed to quiet the mind, purify the soul, and foster a direct connection with God.

Ibn Maimon found inspiration in biblical examples of prophetic seclusion. Moses withdrew to Mount Sinai, Elijah encountered God in a "still, small voice" at Horeb (1 Kings 19:12), and Isaac meditated in the fields (Genesis 24:63), all exemplifying the transformative power of solitude and spiritual focus. He extended *hitbodedut* to all seekers of divine connection, encouraging withdrawal from distractions and inward focus to attune the soul to God's wisdom.

This vision influenced later mystical traditions. The 13th-century Kabbalists of Acre and the 16th-century Safed mystics adopted *hitbodedut* as a tool for divine inspiration and uncovering the Torah's hidden truths. Rabbi Nachman of Breslov later emphasized *hitbodedut* as personal prayer, fostering a heartfelt and direct relationship with God. Ibn Maimon's legacy frames *hitbodedut* as a timeless practice, linking biblical models of seclusion with universal spiritual devotion and enabling seekers to transcend the material and connect with the Divine. Through the lens of Abraham Ibn Maimon, *hitbodedut* is a timeless practice that integrates biblical models of prophetic seclusion with universal principles of spiritual devotion. By withdrawing from external distractions and turning inward, one can transcend the material and connect deeply with the divine, continuing the legacy of the prophets who found God in the stillness.[168]

Hitlahavut: *Hitlahavut*, in Hasidic Judaism, refers to a fervent, passionate zeal in serving God, especially during prayer. It's a sought-after state of emotional rapture and spiritual upliftment, signifying a profound, personal bond with the divine. This concept is closely tied to the Hasidic focus on joy and love in religious practice. It's seen as a crucial element of individual spiritual experience, aiming to surpass intellectual limits and establish a direct connection with the divine. This can be described as a state of "burning enthusiasm" for the divine in all life aspects.

Kabbalah: The term "Kabbalah" is derived from the Hebrew root "kbl," which means "to receive" or "to accept." Thus, Kabbalah can be interpreted as "received tradition" or "received wisdom," indicating its status as the esoteric aspect of Jewish tradition that is passed down from one generation to the next. Kabbalah is a form of Jewish mysticism that seeks to understand the nature of God and the universe. It explores the mystical aspects of the Torah and Jewish ritual. Kabbalah encompasses a range of doctrines and methods, including the sefirot (divine emanations), gematria (numerological interpretations of the Torah), and meditative practices. It has greatly influenced Jewish thought and has also had a significant impact on non-Jewish mystical and esoteric traditions.

Kavanah: *Kavanah* is a Hebrew term that translates to "intention" or "direction of the heart." In Jewish spiritual practice, it refers to the mindset of sincere focus, concentration, and emotional involvement that a person should adopt during prayer, the performance of a *mitzvah* (commandment), or any other religious act. *Kavanah* is seen as essential for these acts to be fully meaningful and effective. It's about not just going through the motions, but truly connecting with the spiritual significance of the action. In addition to its role in prayer and religious observances, *Kavanah* is also considered important in the study of the Torah and other sacred texts. It encourages an attitude of mindfulness and presence, making the act of study not just an intellectual exercise, but a form of spiritual devotion.

Keliphot: *Keliphot,* also spelled *Qliphoth* is a term in Kabbalah that refers to the "shells" or "husks" that encapsulate holiness. They are considered the realm of evil or impurity, representing the spiritual forces of chaos and disorder. According to Kabbalistic cosmology, these "shells" or forces of impurity arose during the creation of the universe as a result of the "breaking of the vessels" (*Shevirat HaKelim*), a cataclysmic event in the divine realm that occurred during the process of creation. In addition to representing impurity and evil, the *Keliphot* are also understood as spiritual obstacles that individuals must overcome in their spiritual journey. They can be seen as spiritual challenges or negative traits that one must confront and transform in order to achieve personal and spiritual growth.

Keter: The hierarchy of the Tree of Life, *Keter*, which means "crown" in Hebrew, is the highest of the ten sefirot, or divine emanations, in the Kabbalistic Tree of Life. It represents the will of God and the divine plan, and it is associated with the highest levels of divine consciousness, often beyond human comprehension. *Keter* is seen as the source from which all other sefirot flow. *Keter* is also associated with the divine aspects of compassion and loving-kindness. It is often considered the bridge between the infinite, unknowable aspect of God (*Ein Sof*) and the manifest, knowable aspects represented by the other sefirot. The "crown" or highest of the ten *Sefirot*; it is also regarded as the active, penetrating force in the cosmos.

Lekutei Halakhot: The *Likutey Halakhot*, a multi-volume work by Rabbi Nathan of Breslov, Rabbi Nachman's primary disciple, masterfully integrates the legal structure of the Shulchan Aruch with the mystical insights of Breslov Hasidism. This commentary reimagines traditional Jewish law as a pathway for spiritual transformation, showing how fulfilling mitzvot—such as prayer, Shabbat observance, and acts of charity—nurtures the soul and fosters a deeper connection with God. Unlike conventional legal commentaries that focus solely on rulings, *Likutey Halakhot* imbues each law with profound spiritual significance; for instance, charity is presented as a practice that purifies the soul and mirrors divine compassion. Written in clear, engaging language and enriched with stories and parables, it resonates with both scholars and spiritual seekers, reflecting Breslov's core values of joy, faith, and heartfelt personal prayer.

Maggid: In Kabbalah, a "*maggid*" is an angelic or celestial being that imparts divine wisdom and mystical insights to individuals, typically rabbis or mystics. These communications often occur in dreams, visions, or during meditation, and are considered to provide profound spiritual teachings. This term is distinct from its general use in Judaism as a preacher, focusing instead on the esoteric role of conveying hidden knowledge and understanding of divine mysteries. The concept became prominent in the 16th century, with notable figures like Rabbi Joseph Karo documenting their spiritual encounters with a *maggid* in works like "*Maggid Meisharim*."

Maggid of Mezritch: Dov Baer, the *Maggid of Mezritch*, was a key figure in early Hasidic Judaism, succeeding its founder, the Baal Shem Tov, as the movement's leader in the 18th century. He shifted the focus from scholarly study to a more accessible, heartfelt form of worship, emphasizing spiritual connection and the omnipresence of God. Known for interpreting Kabbalistic ideas like *Tzimtzum* (God's self-contraction) in ways central to Hasidic thought, his teachings, though largely unwritten, were disseminated by his disciples and significantly influenced the spread and development of Hasidism in Eastern Europe.

Maimonides: *Maimonides*, or Rabbi Moses ben Maimon, was a leading medieval Jewish philosopher and scholar from Spain, known for his works on Jewish law and ethics. As a rationalist, he sought to reconcile faith and reason, prioritizing intellectual understanding over emotional conviction and ethical action. Although he lived before Kabbalah fully developed, his philosophical and rational approach to understanding God and the Torah suggests he would likely have been skeptical of Kabbalah's mystical interpretations. And yet, there is a profound mystical aspect to *Maimonides'* writings that we will soon explore in the next volume of this new series on the Kabbalah.

Makom: Judaic thought since the time of the biblical writers, and Jewish thinkers such as Philo have long contemplated the theme of God's Presence and absence in the world. In Jewish mysticism, the term הַמָּקוֹם "the *Makom*," translated as "Omnipresent One," which posits the Divine as the fundamental existential space in which the universe is situated. This profound conception, while it underscores God's omnipresence, also skirts the edge of pantheistic interpretations, potentially obfuscating the essential distinctions between the sacred and the secular, as well as between good and evil.

Malkhut, which translates to "kingdom" in Hebrew, is the tenth and final *sefira*, or divine emanation, in the Kabbalistic Tree of Life. It represents the physical world and the presence of God in creation. Unlike the other *sefirot*, which are associated with active qualities of God, *Malkhut*, is considered a vessel or recipient that receives and integrates the divine energies from the other sefirot. *Malkhut* is also associated with the *Shekhinah*, the indwelling presence of God in the world, and with the divine feminine. It symbolizes the final stage of the creative process, where the divine plan becomes manifest in the physical world. In the human soul, *Malkhut* is associated with speech and action, in how our inner thoughts and feelings are expressed in the world.

Understanding Jewish mystical views on the Messiah requires exploring diverse ancient interpretations of the end times, a complex task given the prophetic nature of these events. Deuteronomy 29:28 distinguishes between "secret things" known only to God, including the mysteries of the end times, and "revealed things" given to humanity, like the wisdom of the Torah. This implies that while the exact details of the end times remain hidden in God's domain, humanity is entrusted with the wisdom to live by the Torah's teachings, even as the end times approach. The Talmud, through Rabbi Zera's words, underscores this unpredictability, likening the Messiah's arrival to encountering a scorpion or finding a lost item, emphasizing the sudden and transformative nature of these prophetic events.

Messiah: In Kabbalah, the *Messiah's* concept transcends the traditional Jewish view of a political savior, focusing instead on spiritual and metaphysical redemption. Central to this is the idea of *Tikkun Olam*, or the repair of the world. This concept stems from the belief that the world's creation involved a

'Breaking of the Vessels' (*Shevirat HaKelim*), scattering divine sparks across the physical realm. The Messiah's role, in this context, is seen as crucial in gathering these sparks and restoring them, thus healing the world and re-establishing spiritual harmony.

The arrival of the *Messiah* in Kabbalistic thought marks a universal spiritual awakening and a deeper understanding and revelation of God. This era is characterized by the unification of the spiritual and physical realms, leading to a profound shift in human consciousness and the nature of existence. The Messiah is envisioned as a guide to this transformative journey, ushering in an age of divine enlightenment where the knowledge of God permeates all. This Messianic era signifies the culmination of *Tikkun*, achieving the world's ultimate purpose in a state of divine unity and perfection.

Metatron: In Jewish angelology, Metatron is a principal angel known as the divine vice-regent and a minor embodiment of God's Name. Featured in texts like the 3 Apocalypse of Enoch, Metatron is depicted with divine-like attributes and is the only angel allowed to sit in heaven, as noted in the Babylonian Talmud. His origin is complex, intertwining elements from Enochic lore and traits of other angelic figures like Michael and Yahoel. Gershom Scholem identified two strands in Metatron's lore: one relating him to Enoch, and another aligning him with Yahoel and Michael.[169] The etymology of Metatron's name is debated, with suggestions linking it to Latin and Greek origins. Some scholars identified him with the Zoroastrian deity Mithra. In rabbinical literature, he is also known as the "Prince of the Countenance," indicating his unique proximity to the Deity, and holds roles as a celestial choirmaster, priest, and divine secretary.[170] While Metatron's development is typically traced to the rabbinic period, it may have roots in the Second Temple period, reflecting a response to traditions about exalted patriarchs and prophets. His character symbolizes an integration of theological and mystical ideas in Jewish tradition.[171]

Mitnagdim: The terms "*Mitnagdim*" (opponents) and "*Hasidim*" (pious ones) refer to two distinct movements within Eastern European Jewry that emerged in the 18th century and represent different approaches to Jewish thought and practice. The term "*Mitnagdim*" literally means "those who oppose" in Hebrew and refers to the opponents of the Hasidic movement. The *Mitnagdim* were led by figures such as Rabbi Elijah ben Solomon Zalman, known as the Vilna Gaon. They emphasized traditional rabbinic scholarship and a more intellectual approach to Judaism. The *Mitnagdim* were concerned that the Hasidic focus on mysticism and the central role of the Rebbe might lead to heretical beliefs and behaviors. They stressed the importance of intensive Talmudic study, *halakhic* (Jewish law) observance, and a more reserved form of worship.

Nefesh: *Nefesh* is a Hebrew term often translated as "soul," but it can also refer to the life force or vital spirit within a living being. In Jewish thought, particularly in Kabbalah, *nefesh* is considered the lowest level of the soul, associated with physical and instinctual desires. It is the aspect of the soul that animates the body and is involved with worldly, physical life. According to Kabbalistic teachings, the other, higher levels of the soul are the *ruach* (spirit) and *neshamah* (higher soul), each associated with progressively more spiritual and divine aspects of consciousness. In addition to its role as the life force, the *Nefesh* is also seen as the seat of personality and emotions. It's the part of the soul that grows and evolves through our actions and experiences in the physical world, and our moral and ethical choices directly influence it.

Neshamah: This dimension of the soul that is considered one's transcendent part of the Self. *Neshamah* is a Hebrew term that translates to "breath" or "soul." In the context of Jewish mysticism, particularly Kabbalah, it is considered the highest level of the soul that is accessible to humans. *Neshamah* is associated with intellectual understanding and the awareness of the divine within oneself. It represents the innermost divine spark in every individual and is the part of the soul that connects us with God. It's believed that through spiritual practice and ethical living, one can access and cultivate the *neshamah*, leading to a deeper understanding of the divine and one's place in the universe. In addition to its spiritual significance, the *Neshamah* is also seen as the source of moral conscience and spiritual insight. It's the aspect of the soul that enables individuals to distinguish right from wrong and to strive toward higher spiritual ideals. It's through the *neshamah* that individuals can experience a deep sense of unity with all of creation and with the divine.

Niggun: A *niggun* (plural: *niggunim*) is a form of Jewish religious song or tune that is often wordless and is used in Hasidic Judaism as a means of elevating the soul and connecting with the divine. *Niggunim* are typically repetitive and can be deeply emotional, ranging from joyous to melancholic. They are often sung in groups, with the repetition and melody intended to induce a spiritual and meditative state. The *niggun* is seen as a form of prayer and spiritual expression that transcends the limitations of language. In some ways, a *niggun* can be compared to a mantra in that both are used as spiritual tools to focus the mind and facilitate a deeper state of consciousness. Both involve repetition and are often used in a meditative context. However, a *niggun* is typically a melody, often without words, while a mantra is a word or phrase. The cultural and religious contexts in which they are used are also different, with *niggunim* being a part of Hasidic Jewish tradition and mantras being used in various Eastern spiritual traditions.

Nitzotzot: The concept of נִיצוֹצוֹת (*nitzotzot*), or "sparks," in Kabbalah is a profound and central idea, particularly in the teachings of Isaac Luria, also known as the Ari or Arizal, a 16th-century Kabbalist.

In Lurianic Kabbalah, the sparks of divinity—*nitzotzot*—originated from the cataclysmic event known as the "Shattering of the Vessels" (*Shevirat HaKelim*). During the process of creation, the divine light (*Ohr Ein Sof*) was channeled into vessels (*Kelim*). These vessels were meant to contain and structure the divine light, but they were overwhelmed by its intensity and broke apart. The shards of these vessels fell into the lower realms of existence, and with them, the divine sparks were scattered throughout the material world.

The self-proclaimed Messiah, Shabbatai Sevi, manipulated the Lurianic Kabbalistic concept of "elevating the sparks" of God. Lurianic Kabbalah, founded by Rabbi Isaac Luria, posits that divine sparks are trapped in all aspects of creation, and faithful actions can liberate these sparks. Sevi, however, claimed that as the Messiah, he could redeem these sparks by engaging in sinful or forbidden acts, thus challenging traditional Jewish law.

Olam: In Biblical Hebrew, עוֹלָם (*olam*), from the root ע-ל-ם (*ayin-lamed-mem*), means "world" or "universe" (e.g., Genesis 1:1, "the heavens and the earth") and "eternity" (e.g., Ecclesiastes 3:11, "eternity in their hearts"). Kabbalists, however, see it as a veil of *he'elam* (concealment), cloaking the infinite divine, the Ein Sof. This echoes הַעְלֵם (*ha'lem*) in Leviticus 20:4, where people "hide their eyes" from justice—a hint that *olam*, as the physical world, obscures a truer reality. The Sefirot, divine emanations, bridge this divide, yet the material realm remains a dim reflection, like shadows on a wall.

Beyond space, *olam* weaves into time and timelessness. Its "eternity" evokes endless years—time stretching beyond human grasp—but Kabbalists see it concealing an atemporal truth. The *Ein Sof* exists outside the past, present, or future, a boundless now. In the *Zohar*, each *olam* (e.g., *Olam Ha'Atzilut*, the realm of emanation) unfolds in temporal layers, yet their source transcends time's flow. Leviticus 20:4's "hiding" mirrors this: *olam*'s ticking moments veil the eternal, revealed only through a mystical ascent.

Linguistically, ע-ל-ם ("hiddenness") binds *olam* to *ha'lem*. From "obscurity," it grows into "world" (space), "eternity" (time), and—for Kabbalists—the absence of time altogether. *Olam* is both mask and portal: the physical and temporal conceal the timeless divine, yet hint at it. Through insight, mystics peel back this veil, glimpsing existence's infinite heart—the *Ein Sof's* radiant unity.

Or Makif: Within the spiritual hierarchy of creation is what is sometimes referred to as אוֹר מַקִּיף (*Or Makif* = the "Encompassing Light") or as אוֹר סוֹבֵב (*Or Sovev* = the "Surrounding Light"). This divine emanation represents the aspect of the divine light that is beyond the grasp of creation. And while it does not directly manifest within the physical world, it can still exert a profound influence on it. This concept emphasizes the idea that the Divine is both immanent within and transcendent beyond the universe, involved in its everyday workings while also surpassing its limitations of what people consciously imagine as possible.

Or Sovav: In Kabbalah, אוֹר סוֹבֵב (*Or Sovev*, or "Surrounding Light") refers to a divine, transcendent energy that envelops all of creation, yet is inherently beyond human grasp. This concept contrasts with אוֹר פְּנִימִי (*Or Pnimi*, or "Indwelling Light"), which permeates and is accessible within the physical world. *Or Sovev*, as "Surrounding Light," represents a higher, more hidden level of divinity, associated with God's boundless and infinite aspect, the *Ein Sof*. It signifies the transcendent nature of the Divine, an omnipresent yet intangible force that surrounds and transcends the structured universe. This concept is key to understanding Kabbalistic views of the relationship between the finite, tangible world and the infinite, unknowable Divine.

Philo of Alexandria was a Hellenistic Jewish philosopher of the first century C.E., who played a pivotal role in blending Jewish religious thought with Greek philosophy, notably Platonism. While Philo himself was not directly involved in Kabbalistic thought, his allegorical interpretation of the Hebrew Scriptures and his concept of the Logos— a mediatory divine principle —profoundly influenced later Jewish mysticism, particularly the development of Kabbalah. His ideas about the nature of God, the spiritual interpretation of religious texts, and the intermediary forces between God and the material world laid foundational concepts that resonated with, and arguably influenced, the mystical doctrines of Kabbalah. Philo's synthesis of Jewish theology and Greek philosophy provided a philosophical framework that later Kabbalists, consciously or unconsciously, echoed in their own mystical explorations of Jewish spirituality.

Practical Kabbalah is also known as קַבָּלָה מַעֲשִׂית (*kabbalah ma'asit*) applies esoteric knowledge to produce tangible effects, such as crafting amulets, casting spells, or summoning angels for healing or other supernatural outcomes. It's contentious, with some warning of its risks if misapplied, while proponents argue for its value when properly supervised. Distinguished Kabbalist *Ramban* championed this approach, contrasting with the theoretical focus of his contemporaries. He advocated for practical Kabbalah; he further believed in using divine names and symbols as a direct means to connect with the spiritual realm.

Providence: The Kabbalistic view of Divine Providence is rooted in Jewish tradition. The Tanakh depicts God as an omnipresent overseer, with verses like Psalms 33:13 ("He closely observes all inhabitants of the earth"), Genesis 28:15 ." Medieval Jewish philosophers, influenced by Greek and Islamic thought, systematized the concept of hashgahah (הַשְׁגָּחָה), or Divine Providence, into two distinct categories:

- *Hashgahah kelalit* (הַשְׁגָּחָה כְּלָלִית), or general providence, refers to God's broad governance over the natural world, ensuring the stability and continuity of species and ecosystems as a whole.

- *Hashgahah peratit* (הַשְׁגָּחָה פְּרָטִית), or particular providence, denotes God's specific attention to individual beings, particularly humans, guiding their lives with intentional care.

Kabbalah, particularly Hasidism, teaches that every detail, like a falling leaf, is divinely ordained,[172] with the righteous receiving direct guidance through Torah and mitzvot, aligning their lives with divine purpose.

Ratzon Elyon in Kabbalah, symbolizing the "Supernal Will," is an abstract concept best understood through various analogies:

- **Ocean and Waves:** Ratzon Elyon is like an immense, unfathomable ocean of potential, with every creation akin to a wave originating from it. Though the waves change, the ocean remains constant, symbolizing the unchanging source of all existence and potential.

- **Seed and Tree:** It's comparable to a dormant seed containing the potential for a tree. This seed holds the blueprint for future growth, representing the undifferentiated potential within the divine will.

- **Light and Prism:** Ratzon Elyon is like pure, white light split into a spectrum of colors by a prism. Each color symbolizes different divine aspects, but the source light remains unchanged, illustrating the unity and diversity within the Divine.

- **Silence and Music:** It's akin to the silence before music begins, containing the potential for all melodies and rhythms. The silence represents infinite possibilities, out of which the manifest world unfolds.

- **Uncarved Block and Sculpture:** Ratzon Elyon is also like an uncarved block of marble, embodying the potential for any sculpture. It highlights the divine will as the raw material for all creation.

The relationship between *Ratzon Elyon* and Keter in Kabbalah is intricate. In terms of the *Sefirot* hierarchy*, Keter* is the highest *Sefirah*, It marks the point where the Divine will become manifest and become somewhat comprehensible. It's the first tangible expression of the Supernal Will. While *Keter* is the highest emanation, it is not the ultimate source. *Ratzon Elyon*, transcending even *Keter,* remains the source beyond the *Sefirot* structure, representing the divine intention preceding all emanations. *Keter* is associated with the divine will to create and is where the unmanifest *Ratzon Elyon* transitions into the manifest universe. Thus, the relationship between *Ratzon Elyon* and Keter is one of source and expression, with *Ratzon Elyon* as the transcendent divine will and Keter as its first, finite emanation.

Rebbe: While both a traditional Rabbi and a Rebbe are religious leaders within the Jewish community, their roles and the expectations surrounding them can differ significantly. A Rabbi, which means "teacher" in Hebrew, is a religious scholar and legal authority. Rabbis are trained in and teach Jewish law and tradition, lead services, and often run religious institutions like synagogues or schools. They teach their followers the interpretation of Jewish law and serve as spiritual leaders in their communities. A Rebbe, on the other hand, is a title used primarily in Hasidic Judaism.

While a Rebbe also deeply understands Jewish law and tradition, his role extends beyond that of a teacher or scholar. A Rebbe is seen as a spiritual guide with a higher level of divine insight. Hasidic Jews often turn to their Rebbe for religious guidance and advice on personal matters. The relationship between a Hasid and their Rebbe is often deeply personal and spiritual. Furthermore, the position of Rebbe is often hereditary, passed down from one generation to the next. The term "Rebbe" is not limited to any particular Hassidic branch; any small-town rabbi who cares about the spiritual welfare of his or her community can be a "Rebbe" regardless of their Jewish religious affiliation.

During the Holocaust, the Reform Rabbi Leo Baeck exhibited remarkable courage by refusing to leave the Theresienstadt Concentration Camp until every Jewish inmate was liberated. His selfless decision to remain in such horrific conditions underscored his deep commitment to his community, offering them spiritual support and hope amidst the atrocities. Rabbi Baeck's actions during this dark period stand as a testament to the resilience of the human spirit and the profound impact of steadfast faith and compassion.

Reshimu: In Lurianic Kabbalah, as previously noted, the *Tzimtzum*, or Divine contraction, is a pivotal concept depicting God's withdrawal of infinite light to create the universe. This process, occurring in the "*chalal*" or void, is not an actual alteration of the Divine Light but its concealment, allowing for the emergence of finite creation. Central to this is the *reshimu,* a subtle "trace" of Divine Light remaining in the void after the *Tzimtzum*. This remnant, though not substantial, is vital for creation's unfolding. *Tzimtzum* is metaphorical, representing God's self-limitation rather than spatial withdrawal, and sets the stage for human free will and diverse manifestations of creation. The *reshimu* acts as a connector between the infinite and the finite.

Rotzo and Shuv: The concepts of *Ratzo* and *Shov* in Kabbalistic thought vividly describe the soul's dynamic relationship with God and its purpose in the physical world. *Ratzo,* meaning "running forward," captures the soul's passionate yearning to transcend its earthly limitations and unite with its Divine Source, the infinite light of the Ein Sof. This ecstatic pull is often felt during moments of intense prayer, awe, or spiritual elevation, as the soul seeks to ascend toward the higher *Sefirot* (divine attributes). In contrast, *Shov*, meaning "return," reflects the soul's deliberate descent back to the material world, where it fulfills its mission to refine the mundane, reveal God's presence, and align with the divine purpose of creating a dwelling place for God in the physical realm, particularly through the Sefirah of Malchut. This continuous cycle of ascent and descent weaves together transcendence and immanence, as the soul navigates its longing for the Divine with its responsibility to transform the world.

Ruach: *Ruach* is a Hebrew term that translates to "wind," "breath," or "spirit." In the context of Jewish mysticism, particularly Kabbalah, *Ruach* is considered one of the five levels of the soul. It is the second level, above *Nefesh* (associated with basic, instinctual drives) and below *Neshamah* (associated with higher spiritual consciousness). *Ruach* is associated with moral feelings and the ability to distinguish between good and evil. It represents the part of the soul that connects to the emotional aspects of the divine and is the bridge between the physical and the spiritual.

Sabbatean Movement: Born in Smyrna in 1626, Shabbati Tzvi's life was a whirlwind of mysticism, messianic fervor, and political drama. From an early age, he displayed exceptional academic and spiritual promise but also exhibited volatile moods and unorthodox practices. As a young man, he proclaimed himself the Messiah, attracting a fervent following across the Ottoman Empire and Europe. His charismatic personality and audacious claims ignited hope for Jewish redemption, leading to widespread messianic frenzy. However, his unorthodox actions, including embracing aspects of Islam under pressure, ultimately fractured his movement and brought him into conflict with both Jewish and Ottoman authorities. Imprisoned and forced to convert to Islam, Shabbati Tzvi died in 1676, leaving behind a legacy of shattered messianic dreams and a lasting impact on Jewish history and thought. His followers, known as Sabbateans, continued to carry his torch in various forms beyond his death.

Satmar: The Satmar Hasidic group, a sect within Judaism known for its strict adherence to Jewish law and conservative values, originated in the town of Satu Mare, now in Romania but part of Hungary when the group emerged. The town's name, Satu Mare, derives from the 13th-century Hungarian "*Szatmárnémeti*," linked to "*Zotmar*," a historical figure noted as a fort founder, and later evolved into the Romanian "*Satu Mare*," meaning "big village." The Yiddish "*Satmar*" reflects its Hungarian roots. Founded by Rabbi Yoel Teitelbaum, who served as the rabbi of Satu Mare before World War II, the group has preserved its distinct identity. This history resonates personally for some, including my father, who knew the Rebbe's nephew—also named Yoel Teitelbaum—and aided his family's survival during the Holocaust at Auschwitz.

Sefer Yetzirah: The *Sefer Yetzirah*, or "Book of Creation" in English, is one of the earliest extant books on Jewish mysticism. Its exact date of composition is unknown, but it is generally believed to have been written between the 3rd and 6th centuries. The book is a concise, enigmatic text that explores the mysteries of creation through the lens of the Hebrew alphabet and numerical symbolism. The *Sefer Yetzirah* describes how God created the universe through the "32 paths of wisdom," which consist of the ten sefirot (divine emanations) and the 22 letters of the Hebrew alphabet. These elements are seen as the universe's building blocks, and by understanding their workings, one can gain insight into the divine structure of existence. The *Sefer Yetzirah* has had a profound influence on the development of Jewish mysticism and Kabbalah, and it has also been studied in various non-Jewish mystical and philosophical traditions.

Sefirot: The ten energy essences that are said to be in constant interplay and underlie all the universe. *Sefirot*, also spelled *Sephirot* or *Sefirot*, are the ten divine emanations or attributes through which the Kabbalah, a form of Jewish mysticism, interprets God's actions in the world. They represent different aspects of God's character, such as wisdom, understanding, love, and justice. The *sefirot* is often depicted as a tree, known as the Tree of Life, which maps the divine structure of the universe and the soul. The Tree of Life in Kabbalah, with its ten *sefirot*, can be viewed as a map or diagram of God's personality and attributes, as well as how they interact to bring about divine action. Each *sefira* represents a different aspect of God, such as wisdom, understanding, mercy, judgment, etc. These aspects are not separate from God but are ways in which the divine reality is manifested. The Tree of Life thus provides a way to understand God's complex, multifaceted nature and divine influence on the universe.

Shefa: In Kabbalistic thought, the concept of שֶׁפַע (*shefa*), or "divine abundance," represents the continuous flow of divine energy and blessings from the Creator, particularly through the ten sefirot that shape reality. *Shefa* embodies God's attributes—mercy, wisdom, and understanding—nourishing both the material and spiritual realms, and it emphasizes the necessity of human participation in this divine flow. Kabbalists believe that through acts of righteousness, prayer, and intentionality, individuals can access and channel *shefa*, enhancing their spiritual development and the welfare of their community. This connection signifies the interdependence between the divine and humanity, making *shefa* a foundational principle that is associated with theurgy—a practice that aims to establish a closer relationship with the divine through intentional actions. Through devotion and righteous behavior, practitioners seek not only to receive blessings but to manifest the divine will in their lives, contributing to the restoration and harmony of creation.

Shekhinah: In early rabbinical literature, the *Shekhinah* is a term from Jewish theology that refers to God's indwelling or imminent presence in the world. The term is often used to express the Divine Presence in specific places, such as the Temple in Jerusalem, or in association with certain religious actions or experiences.

In Kabbalah and other forms of Jewish mysticism, *Shekhinah* is often personified as the feminine aspect of God. It is associated with the divine attribute of kingship (*Malkhut*) and is sometimes depicted as a divine mother or bride. The concept of *Shekhinah* plays a central role in many mystical interpretations of Jewish rituals and commandments, as well as in mystical understandings of Jewish history and the exile of the Jewish people. In addition to its role in Jewish mysticism, the concept of *Shekhinah* has also had a profound influence on Jewish liturgy, worship, and poetry. The welcoming of the *Shekhinah* is a central part of the Sabbath and festival rituals, symbolizing the Divine Presence entering one's home and community. The term is also used in a broader sense to refer to any experience of a Divine Presence or spiritual inspiration.

Shelemut: *Mussar* literature emphasizes that the purpose of life is to work toward שְׁלֵמוּת (*shelemut* = integrative wholeness), a state of completeness that reflects our ultimate potential. In Kabbalistic thought, שְׁלֵמוּת represents the ultimate unity and perfection inherent in the divine plan. *Mussar* and Kabbalah both center on *shelemut*—wholeness—as life's purpose. In Kabbalistic thought, the universe is intentionally incomplete, and humans are tasked as co-creators to restore balance by aligning with divine forces, such as the sefirot, balancing energies like kindness (*chesed*) and restraint (*gevurah*). *Mussar*, by contrast, emphasizes personal growth, viewing human imperfections as opportunities to cultivate virtues through disciplined effort. Together, these traditions show that striving for *shelemut* fulfills both a cosmic role—harmonizing creation—and an individual one—refining character. Rabbi Moshe Chaim Luzzatto teaches that God deliberately made us imperfect, not as a flaw but as a gift, enabling us to participate in our own creation. This journey toward wholeness, blending personal transformation with divine purpose, becomes a sacred act that aligns us with God's will and elevates the world.

Steibel: A *steibel* is a specific type of prayer house or informal gathering place for worship, often associated with Hasidic or Orthodox communities. The term can describe a small synagogue or a gathering place for study and prayer, usually less formal than a traditional synagogue. *Steibels* often serve as spaces for communal prayer, learning, and socializing, particularly within closely-knit communities.

Shtetl: A *shtetl* is a small town or village with a significant Jewish population, particularly in Eastern Europe. *Shtetls* were often characterized by their close-knit communities, where Jewish life included a range of social, cultural, and religious activities. These towns typically had synagogues, schools, and marketplaces, and they served as centers of Jewish life before World War II and the Holocaust.

Talmud: The body of oral traditions discussed in the Talmud, a pivotal text in Judaism, is an extensive compilation of Jewish laws, ethics, philosophy, and history, consisting of the Mishnah and the Gemara. Compiled around 200 C.E. by Rabbi Judah the Prince, the *Mishnah* documents Jewish oral traditions, while the Gemara, completed between 400 C.E. and 500 C.E., provides commentary and analysis of the Mishnah.

The Talmud exists in two versions: the Jerusalem Talmud, finished around 400 C.E. in the Land of Israel, and the more authoritative Babylonian Talmud, completed around 500 C.E. in Babylonia. Created in response to the changing needs of the Jewish Diaspora after the Second Temple's destruction, the Talmud remains a crucial source of Jewish legal and moral guidance.

Tanya: Shneur Zalman of Liadi's *Tanya*, written in the late 18th century, is a foundational text in Chabad Hasidism that masterfully blends Jewish mysticism with spiritual psychology. This influential work explores the nature of the soul, the internal struggle between good and evil inclinations, and maps the pathway to achieving divine consciousness. Throughout, Shneur Zalman encourages a balance of intellectual understanding and emotional devotion, making *Tanya* a timeless guide for spiritual growth and a deeper connection to the divine.

Theurgy: *Theurgy* and white magic both involve engaging with spiritual forces, but they differ in intent and tradition. Theurgy, rooted in Neoplatonic philosophy and intertwined with mystical traditions like Kabbalah, seeks spiritual unity and enlightenment, often through complex rituals and prayers. It's a sacred practice aimed at divine communion. White magic, conversely, aims at producing beneficial outcomes, such as healing or protection, believed to be ethically positive. It's more eclectic and can be practiced by individuals without needing a philosophical or religious framework, using various spells and rituals to work with benevolent forces. While both practices tap into metaphysical energies, theurgy focuses on spiritual ascent, and white magic on bringing about positive changes in the material realm.

Tikkun: *Tikkun* is a Hebrew word that means "repair" or "rectification." In Jewish thought, it is often used in the phrase "*Tikkun Olam*," which translates to "repair of the world." This concept suggests that it's the responsibility of individuals to improve the world and make it a better place through acts of kindness and social action. In Kabbalah, *Tikkun* has a more specific meaning. It refers to the spiritual rectification needed because of the "breaking of the vessels" (*Shevirat HaKelim*), a cosmic catastrophe that occurred during creation. According to this belief, sparks of divine light were trapped in the material world, and humans, through their actions and spiritual practices, can help liberate these sparks and return them to their divine source. This process of *Tikkun* is seen as a central task of humanity.

Torah: The term "Torah" has evolved over time, reflecting the development of Jewish tradition and religious literature. In its narrowest sense, "Torah" can refer to the Ten Commandments, which, according to the Bible, were given by God to Moses on Mount Sinai.[173] The term can also refer specifically to the Book of Deuteronomy, presented as a long speech by Moses recapping the laws given in earlier books. More commonly, "Torah" refers to the first five books of the Hebrew Bible, also known as the Five Books of Moses or the Pentateuch. These books contain narrative and a wide range of laws and commandments. In its broadest sense, "Torah" can refer to the entirety of Jewish religious teaching, including the rest of the Hebrew Bible, the Talmud and other rabbinic literature, and even the mystical teachings of Kabbalah. This reflects the idea that all Jewish teaching continues the divine revelation that began with the Torah.

Tree of Life: The Tree of Life is a central symbol in the Kabbalah, a form of Jewish mysticism. It is a diagram representing the ten sefirot, or divine emanations, through which God created the world. These *sefirot* are considered attributes of God and are arranged in a specific pattern on the Tree of Life, connected by paths corresponding to different stages or aspects of the creative process. The Tree of Life is often used as a tool for meditation and contemplation, and it serves as a guide to understanding the divine structure of the universe and the soul. From the top to the bottom, the sefirot on the Tree represent the process by which the infinite divine reality manifests in the finite physical world. The Tree of Life also represents the ideal state of spiritual and physical existence before the fall of Adam and Eve in the Garden of Eden. In this context, the Tree of Life symbolizes complete harmony and unity with God.

Zohar: The Zohar is a foundational work in the literature of Jewish mystical thought known as Kabbalah. The Zohar is largely a midrashic commentary on the Torah, but it includes various material covering mysticism, myth, and symbolism. It explores the nature of God, the origin and structure of the universe, the nature of souls, redemption, the relationship of Ego to Darkness and "true self" to "The Light of God," and the dynamic interrelationship of the universal energy known as Ein Sof (the "Endless One" or "Infinite") and the manifest world.

The Zohar's interpretations of the Torah are often parables and allegories. It is the source of many key ideas in Kabbalah, such as the four worlds of reality, the structure of the soul, and the Tree of Life. The Zohar has been widely studied and commented upon throughout the centuries and continues to influence various forms of Jewish, Christian, and even non-Western esoteric and mystical thought.

BIBLIOGRAPHY

Abulafia, Abraham ben Samuel. *The Path of the Names.* Translated by Aryeh Kaplan. Trigram, 1976.

Bahir. *Bahir: The Early Kabbalah.* Translated by Aryeh Kaplan. Newburyport, MA: 1980.

Bokser, Ben Zion. "The Religious Philosophy of Rabbi Kook." *Judaism* 9, no. 4 (Fall 1970): 396-405.

Book of Creation. *Sepher Yetzirah: The Book of Creation.* Translated by Irving Friedman. Newburyport, MA: Weiser, 1977.

Buber, Martin. *I and Thou.* Charles Scribner's Sons, 1958.
---. *Hasidism and Modern Man.* Horizon, 1958.
---. *Tales of the Hasidim: The Early Masters.* New York: Schocken, 1961.
---. *The Tales of Rabbi Nachman.* New York: Avon, 1970.

Cordovero, Moses. *The Palm Tree of Deborah.* New York: Sepher-Hermon Press, 1981.

Dov Baer of Lubavitch, and Louis Jacobs, trans. *Tract on Ecstasy.* New York: Valentine Mitchell, 1963.

Dweck, Yaacob. *The Scandal of Kabbalah: Leon Modena, Jewish Mysticism, Early Modern Venice.* Princeton: Princeton University Press, 2011.

Ergas, Yosef and Avinoam Fraernkel (Trans.) *Shomer Emunim: The Introduction to the Kabbalah.* Jerusalem: Urim, 2021.

Etkes, Immanuel. *The Gaon of Vilna: The Man and His Image.* Berkeley: University of California Press, 2002.

Fine, Lawrence. *Physician of the Soul, Healer of the Cosmos: Isaac Luria and His Kabbalistic Fellowship.* Palo Alto: Stanford University Press, 2003.

Heschel, Abraham Joshua, *A Passion for Truth.* New York: Farrar, Straus, and Giriux, 1973.

Idel, Moshe. *Kabbalah: New Perspectives.* New Haven: Yale University Press, 1988.

Kaplan, Aryeh. *Inner Space: Introduction to Kabbalah, Meditation and Prophecy.* New York: Moznaim Pub Corp, 1990.

Kook, Abraham Isaac. *Orot HaKodesh Vol. II.* Jerusalem: Bnei Akiva "Or Etzion" and Merkaz Shapiro, 1950.

---. *The Lights of Penitence, the Moral Principles, Lights of Holiness, Essays, Letters, and Poems.* New York: Paulist Press, 1978.

Matt, Daniel C. *The Zohar: Pritzker Edition.* Redwood City, CA: Stanford University Press, 2004.

---. *The Essential Kabbalah: The Heart of Jewish Mysticism.* New York: HarperOne, 2009.

Ruderman, David B. *The World of a Renaissance Jew: The Life and Thought of Abraham ben Mordecai Farissol.* Cincinnati: Hebrew Union College Press, 1981.

---. *Jewish Thought and Scientific Discovery in Early Modern Europe.* Detroit, MI:
Wayne State University Press, 2001.

---. *Early Modern Jewry: A New Cultural History.* Princeton, NJ: Princeton University Press, 2010.

Rosenblatt, Samuel and Abraham Ibn Maimon. *The Highways to Perfection.* New York: Columbia University, 1927.

Schachter-Shalomi, Zalman. *Spiritual Intimacy: A Study of Counseling in Hasidism.* Lanham MD: Rowman & Littlefield, 1991.

Schechter, Solomon. *Studies in Judaism, 2nd series.* Philadelphia: Jewish Publication Society, 1908.

Sheneir Zalman of Liady. *Tanya.* Brooklyn: Kehot Publication Society, 1973.

Scholem, Gershom. *Sabbatai Sevi: The Mystical Messiah.* Princeton: Princeton University Press, 1973.
---. *Jewish Gnosticism, Merkabah Mysticism, and Talmudic Tradition.* New York: Jewish Theological Seminary of America, 1965.
---. *On the Kabbalah and Its Symbolism.* Schocken, 1965.
---. *The Messianic Idea in Judaism, and Other Essays on Jewish Spirituality.* New York: Schocken Books, 1971.
---. *Kabbalah.* New York: Meridian Books, 1974.
---. *From Berlin to Jerusalem.*
---. *The Messianic Idea in Judaism, and Other Essays on Jewish Spirituality.* New York: Schocken Books, 1971.
---. *Major Trends in Jewish Mysticism.* New York: Schocken Books, 1995.

Steinsaltz, Adin. *The Essential Talmud.* New York: Basic Books, 1976.
---. *The Thirteen Petalled Rose.* Boulder, CO: Shambhala, 1975.

Susskind, Leonard. *The Cosmic Landscape: String Theory and the Illusion of Intelligent Design.* New York: Hachette Book Group, 2006.

Tishby, Isaiah. *The Wisdom of the Zohar.* New York: Littman Library, 1991

Trachtenberg, Joshua. *Jewish Magic and Superstition.* New York: Behrman's Jewish Book House, 1939.

Weiner, Herbert. *Nine and a Half Mystics: The Kabbala Today.* New York: 1969, 1992.

ENDNOTES

[1] In Hebrew, diacritical markings are not typically used in the word "Kabbalah." The Hebrew word for Kabbalah is generally written as קַבָּלָה, without any diacritical markings. Diacritical markings, also known as vowel points or niqqud, are used in Hebrew to indicate the vowel sounds in words. However, in the case of "Kabbalah," the word is spelled with the consonants קבלה (KBLH)and the specific vowel sounds are understood based on the context and the reader's familiarity with the Hebrew language.

[2] The word μύειν (*muein*) is an ancient Greek verb that means "to initiate" or "to close." According to Aristotle, the verb μύειν means to close the eyes with the inner eyelids (*De partibus animalium* 657b). The word's meaning of "to close" specifically refers to closing the eyes or mouth, which symbolically points to the secrecy and sacredness involved in these initiation rituals. This is where the English word "mystery" is derived. It is often used in the context of religious initiation rites, such as the Eleusinian Mysteries, a set of secretive ceremonies held annually in the city of Eleusis near Athens.

[3] Daniel Matt, *Zohar, the Book of Enlightenment* (Philadelphia: Paulist Press, 1983), pp. 43-44.

[4] See *QG* 2:6; 3:6; 4:152; 4:167, passim. Regarding Philo's accusation that Heraclitus did not originate his thought, reflects an attitude that existed in the Hellenistic world of the Jewish intelligentia. The first Hellenisic Jewish philosopher, Aristobulus, argued that if the Pentateuch was properly understood, people would see that the best of Greek philosophical thought was already contained in the teachings of the Pentateuch. He further asserted that Pythagoras, Socrates, Plato—even Homer and Hesiod borrowed their doctrines from the Jews and that Moses was the godfather of Greek philosophy. See Emil Schürer, *The Literature of the Jewish People in the Time of Jesus*, second division. (Edinburgh: T&T Clark, 1890) Vol. 5, pp. 239-240. Let us also add that Philo expressed a profound respect for Greek philosophy, which Wolfson noted, "However, Wolfson goes on to observe Philo often acknowledged the parallels existing between Greek and the Hebraic traditions, "...Thus referring, again, to Heraclitus' theory of the harmony of the opposites, he merely says that he was anticipated in it by Moses. 1 4 Similarly, referring

to a moral maxim of Zeno, he says rather cautiously that "he seems to have drawn his maxim as it were from the fountain of the legislation of the Jews," and again, referring to some moral maxims of the philosophers, he merely points out that Moses had said the same thing before them. Evidently Philo assumes here that philosophers discovered the same truths by their native reason." *Philo*: *Foundations of Religious Philosophy in Judaism, Christianity, and Islam* (Cambridge: Harvard University Press, 1947), Vol. 1, pp. 141-142. Ultimately, it is important to note that both Philo and Aristobulus paid a gigantic complement to Greek culture. Regarding Hesoid and Homer, several of the early Greek creation stories about Pandora, or the demigods and the flood—do reflect a cross-fertiliztion of ideas that occurred in the ancient Near Eastern and Mediterranean world.

[5] Moshe Idel, *Kabbalah in Italy 1280-1510: A Survey* (New Haven: Yale University Press, 2011), pp. 169-171.

[6] Leone Ebreo and Cosmos Damian Bacich (trans.), *Dialogues of Love* (Toronto: University of Toronto Press, 2009), p. 241.

[7] Moshe Idel, *Kabbalah in Italy 1280-1510: A Survey* (New Haven: Yale University Press, 2011), pp. 179-180..

[8] Hava Tirosh-Rotschild. *Between Worlds: The Life and Thought of Rabbi David ben Judah Messer Leon* (Albany: SUNY Press, 1991). p. 49.

[9] Gershom Scholem suggests that while there are notable parallels between Philo of Alexandria's allegorical interpretations of scripture and Kabbalistic thought, these similarities do not necessarily indicate Philo's direct historical influence on medieval Kabbalists. Scholar Y. F. Baer has argued for a deep structural resemblance between Philo's ideas and Kabbalistic conceptions, seeing both as extensions of Rabbinical thought underpinning the Halakhah. However, Scholem contends that any such parallels likely arise from a common goal rather than a direct historical connection. See Gershom Scholem, *On the Kabbalah and Its Symbolism* (New York: Schocken, 1965), p. 34.

[10] In the scriptural account from Exodus 25:18-22, the biblical narrative details a commandment from God to Moses, wherein he is directed to create figures of *cherubim*. These are not mere decorative elements; they are imbued with profound symbolism and are to be positioned precisely upon the Ark of the Covenant. The Ark itself is a central artifact in the religious rites of the Israelites, believed to house the very Presence of God. Therefore, the cherubim, often associated with

---

guardianship and divine mystery, are to serve as an integral feature of this sacred object, overseeing the space where God promises to meet and communicate with Moses.

[11] Moshe Idel, *Absorbing Perfections: Kabbalah and Interpretation* (New Haven: Yale University Press, 2002), pp. 235-238.

[12] Gershom G. Scholem, *Jewish Gnosticism, Merkabah Mysticism and Talmudic Tradition* (New York: Jewish Theological Seminary of America, 1960).

[13] Hans Jonas examines Greek Mystery religions as integral to the broader cultural and religious context in which Gnosticism emerged. In his seminal work, *The Gnostic Religion,* he opens with a discussion of the Greek Mediterranean as a dynamic cultural crossroads, highlighting its role as a melting pot of diverse traditions. This framing suggests that Jonas considers Greek Mystery religions not as isolated practices but as vital elements within the intricate religious landscape of Late Antiquity.

Jonas's approach to Gnosticism is notably multidimensional, weaving together historical, philosophical, and existential dimensions. He applies this comprehensive lens to his analysis of Greek Mystery religions as well, recognizing their significance in shaping the spiritual milieu that influenced Gnostic thought. By exploring these interconnections, Jonas illuminates how Greek Mystery religions contributed to the complex mosaic of beliefs and ideas in Late Antiquity, enriching our understanding of Gnosticism's origins. See Hans Jonas, *The Gnostic Religion: The Message of the Alien God and the Beginnings of Christianity* (Boston: Beacon Press, 1958).

[14] J.M. Robinson, *Introduction to The Nag Hammadi Library in English.* (New York: Harper & Row, 1977).

[15] See BT Chag. 14b.

[16] Moses Idel, *Absorbing Perfections: Kabbalah and Interpretation* (New Haven: Yale University Press, 2002,) pp, 433-34

[17] Daniel Matt, *Zohar, The Book of Enlightenment* (Philadelphia: Paulist Press, 1983), 43-44.

[18] Thomas Aquinas, a key 13th-century Christian theologian, outlined a method of scriptural interpretation based on four senses: the *literal* (historical

meaning), the *allegorical* (symbolic, often Christological), the *moral* (ethical guidance), and the *anagogical* (eschatological or heavenly significance) (*Summa Theologica*, I, Q.1, A.10). This approach shares striking parallels with the PaRDeS method from Jewish tradition, which also identifies four layers of meaning in the Torah: *peshat* (literal), *remez* (hinted), *derash* (interpreted), and *sod* (hidden). In both systems, interpretation begins with the literal sense and progresses to deeper spiritual insights—Aquinas's allegorical sense aligns with *remez*, his moral sense with *derash*, and his anagogical sense with *sod*'s mystical dimension. However, Aquinas's method is grounded in Christian theology, often emphasizing Christological themes, while PaRDeS reflects Jewish exegesis rooted in Torah study. Despite these differences, both approaches underscores the richness of multi-layered interpretation, revealing the diverse wisdom embedded in sacred texts.

[19] This is exemplified by Isaac the Blind, a prominent figure in Jewish mysticism, and Didymus the Blind, an esteemed Christian theologian in the Alexandrian Church. Isaac, despite his blindness, played a critical role in the development of Kabbalistic thought, while Didymus (c. 313 – 398 C.E.), blind from childhood, headed the Alexandrian catechetical school and emerged as one of the era's most erudite individuals. Despite their physical impediments, both individuals used oral tradition and exceptional memory to contribute significantly to their respective religious traditions. Their parallels, however, end at their recognition. While Isaac's teachings continue to influence the texture of Kabbalistic thought, Didymus's works were neglected following the Second Council of Constantinople's condemnation of his teacher Origen. Despite their similar circumstances, these two scholars' legacies have had differing degrees of impact and preservation within their respective faith traditions.

[20] Ramban employs this expression 98 times in his commentary on the Pentateuch.

[21] Ramban employs this expression 167 times in his commentary on the Pentateuch.

[22] Ramban is known for his methodical approach in biblical commentary, often starting with a literal explanation before exploring mystical interpretations. A prime example of this is found in his analysis of Exodus 2:23-25. Here, Ramban first offers a straightforward interpretation, then delves into the esoteric dimensions, notably referencing the Midrashic work of R. Nehunya ben HaKanah, specifically "Sefer Ha-Bahir #76". This approach is not isolated; Ramban consistently employs such methodology, as evidenced by his references to the "Sefer Ha-Bahir" in various parts of his Pentateuch commentary. These include

Genesis 1:1 (#2), 2:7 (#57), 38:29 (#196), 46:1 (#135), 49:24 (#193, #148), Exodus 2:25 (#76), 20:8 (#182), Numbers 25:39 (unknown reference), and Deuteronomy 22:6 (unknown reference).

[23] The closest parallel in Hindu tradition is niyoga, an ancient custom mentioned in texts like the Manusmriti (9.59–70) and the Mahabharata. Niyoga allowed a widow or a woman whose husband was infertile to conceive a child with a designated male—often a brother-in-law or another relative—to ensure heirs. Unlike yibbum, this was not a full marriage; it was a temporary union strictly for procreation, after which the relationship ended. The child was legally considered the offspring of the deceased or infertile husband. By the medieval period, niyoga had largely fallen out of practice, criticized as outdated or morally ambiguous by later commentators. Hinduism does not institutionalize levirate marriage as a religious practice. Niyoga shares some functional similarities but differs in intent, scope, and permanence, while localized customs reflect practical adaptations rather than doctrinal mandates.

[24] Christopher Partridge and Peter J. Forshaw, eds., "Kabbalah," in *The Occult World* (London: Routledge, 2015), p. 542.

[25] See Herman Graetz, *History of the Jews,* Chapter 1(Philadelphia: Jewish Publication Society, 1894), Chapter 1.

[26] Joseph Gikatilla, *Sha'arei Orah: Gates of Light,* trans. Avi Weinstein (San Francisco: HarperCollins, 1994), xxv–xxvii.

[27] Jonathan Garb, *A History of Kabbalah: From the Early Modern Period to the Present Day* (New York: Cambridge University Press, 2020), pp. 14-16.

[28] For a modern English translation of this work, see Leone Ebreo, and Cosmos Damian Bacich *Dialogues of Love* (Toronto: University of Toronto Press, 2009).

[29] See Moses Cordovero and Louis Jacobs (Trans.) *Tomer Devorah -- The Palm Tree of Deborah* (New York: Sepher-Hermon Press, 1960).

[30] MT *Hilkhot De'oth* 1.6.

[31] See G. Scholem, *Major Trends in Jewish Mysticism*, 1941, op. cit., pp. 244-251.

[32] Lawrence Fine, *Physician of the Soul, Healer of the Cosmos: Isaac Luria and His Kabbalistic Fellowship* (Palo Alto: Stanford University Press, 2003), p. 83.

[33] *Physician of the Soul,* 2003, p. 159.

[34] Ibid., p. 83.

[35] R. Yosef Karo's mystical encounters with an angelic being on the Pentateuch.

[36] See *Igrot Ramchal* entries 39 and 53 (*Machon HaRamchal,* Jerusalem 2001), it was considered unusual for a Kabbalah teacher not to sport a beard.

[37] Batya Gallant, "The Alleged Sabbateanism of Rabbi Moshe Hayyim Luzzatto" *Tradition*, Vol. 22, No. 3 (FALL 1986), pp. 44-53.
[38] Heinrich Graetz, *History of the Jews, Vol. 5* (Philadelphia, Jewish Publication Society, 1895), pp. 233-241.
[39] *History*, 236.
[40] Tishby, 36; Scholem, 255.

[41] David Sclar, *'The Rise of the "Ramchal": Printing and Traditional Jewish Historiography in the 'After-Life' of Moses Hayyim Luzzatto', in Ramchal*: Pensiero ebraico e Kabbalah tra Padova ed Eretz Israel, Edited by Gadi Luzzatto Voghera and Mauro Perani, Esedra editric,e s.r.l., Padua, 139–153.

[42] *Tzavat HaRivash,* Sect. 5 and 22.

[43] *Maggid Devarav LeYaakov*, Section 12. "The Creator is present in every movement and word, as nothing occurs without His power (per Micah 7:18). Human speech forms the "world of speech," and thought the "world of thought." Speaking good and aligning thought with speech unites these realms, generating good, while evil speech causes harm. The Zohar advises integrating the Shekhinah into one's actions—walking, sitting, waking—for her sake, not oneself. Like a tree planted (Psalm 1:3), the righteous draw sparks from their soul's root in worldly things, elevating them to God, using speech as a vessel for thought, and avoiding "breaking the vessels" by infusing words with intent."

[44] *Likkutei Amarim*, Part 1, Section 23.

[45] Martin Buber, *Tales of the Hasidim: The Early Masters.* Translated by Olga Marx (New York: Schocken Books, 1947), p. 82.

[46] *Maggid Devarav LeYaakov*, Section 45)

[47] *Likkutei Amarim (Maggid of Mezritch)*. Compiled by various disciples (Jerusalem: Machon Toras HaMaggid, 2003, Part 2:17).

[48] *Maggid Devarav LeYaakov*, Section 68.

[49] Immanuel Etkes, *Rabbi Shneur Zalman of Liady: The Origins of Chabad Hasidism*. Translated by Jeffrey M. Green. (Waltham: Brandeis University Press, 2015), p. 34.

[50] *Likkutei Amarim*, Part 1, Section 39

[51] *Maggid Devarav LeYaakov,* Section 91.

[52] Martin Buber, *Tales of the Hasidim: The Early Masters*. Translated by Olga Marx (New York: Schocken Books, 1947), p. 95.

[53] *Likkutei Amarim*, Part 2, Section 44.

[54] See Spinoza's *Tractatus Theologico–Politicus* t Part IV, Preface (*Deum seu Naturam, Deus seu Natura*); twice in Part IV, Proposition IV, Proof (*Dei sive Naturæ, Dei seu Naturæ*). Baruch Spinoza, in his posthumously published *Ethics* (1677), presents a radical view of God and nature as identical—coining the phrase "God or Nature" (Deus sive Natura) four times. He asserts that whether events follow natural laws or divine decree, the outcome is the same, suggesting a unified system where distinctions between the two dissolve. This reflects his pantheism: God is not a personal deity but the infinite, eternal, and necessary substance of the universe, encompassing all existence. As he writes in *Ethics* (Part I, Proposition 15), everything exists within this active, self-sustaining whole. Spinoza clarifies this in a letter to Henry Oldenburg, distancing himself from materialism. Nature, for him, isn't mere physical matter but a metaphysical reality—the singular substance with infinite attributes (e.g., thought and extension). By equating God with nature, he rejects traditional theism, framing God as the immanent cause of all things, not a transcendent creator. This monistic vision underpins Ethics, where understanding this unity through reason leads to the intellectual love of God (amor dei intellectualis), free of anthropomorphic illusions. In short, Spinoza's "God or Nature" fuses divinity and the cosmos into one rational, eternal system—a cornerstone of his philosophy that contrasts sharply with theistic traditions like RSZ's Kabbalah.

[55] *Ethics*, Part I, Proposition 14: "Except God, no substance can be or be conceived".

[56] Part I, Proposition 29: "In nature there is nothing contingent, but all things have been determined from the necessity of the divine nature."

[57] Part I, Proposition 33: "Things could have been produced by God in no other way and in no other order."

[58] Part I, Proposition 15: "Whatever is, is in God".

[59] Steven Nadler, *A Book Forged in Hell: Spinoza's Scandalous Treatise and the Birth of the Secular Age* (Princeton*: Princeton University Press, 2011)* pp. 57-58.

[60] For one of the most comprehensive works on the *Tzimtzum*, see RSZ's *Lekutei Torah Appendix to the Book of Leviticus*, entitled: להבין מ"ש באוצ"ח בתוזלתו כאשר עלה ברצונו להאציל הנאצלים מ' צמצם עצמו באמצע האור שלו כו' ונשאר החלל בנתיים כו' עד שנמצא עולם האצילות וכל העולמות נתונים בתוך החלל הזה והאור א"ס מקיפו בשוה מכל צדדיו עכ"ל

[61] *Derech Chaim,* Part 2, Chapter 14.

[62] See Immanuel Etkes, *The Gaon of Vilna: The Man and His Image* (Berkeley: University of California Press, 2002), pp. 80-86.

[63] Hasidic prayer often prioritized *kavanah* (spiritual intent) over strict adherence to clocked schedules, a point of contention with Mitnagdic critics who valued precision in halachic observance.

- **Ecstatic Worship Context**: Hasidic sources, like those from the Maggid's circle, emphasize prayer as a transformative act, sometimes extending beyond fixed durations. Rabbi Abraham, influenced by the Maggid's focus on *devekut* (cleaving to God), likely encouraged prolonged sessions to achieve ecstatic states.
- **Mitnagdic Critique**: The Vilna Gaon and Mitnagdim opposed Hasidism partly over such practices, accusing them of laxity in halachic rigor, including prayer timing. Immanuel Etkes, in *The Gaon of Vilna* (2002), mentions the Gaon's 1772 excommunication of Hasidim, citing their "deviant" prayer behaviors as disruptive to traditional norms (p. 103). While not specific to Rabbi Abraham's

group, this reflects a broader perception that ecstatic prayer might override set times.

[64] Nissan Mindel, *Rabbi Sheneur Zalman of Liadi: A Biography* (Brooklyn: Kehot Publication Society, 1969), pp. 21-22.

[65] *Likutey Moharan* 2:24.

[66] *Likutey Moharan* 1:52.

[67] *Lekutei Maharan* 2:11,44.

[68] Abraham Joshua Heschel, *A Passion for Truth* (New York: Farrar, Straus, and Giroux, 1973), pp. 308-309.

[69] See Kotzk Blog. "What Did the Kotzker Rebbe Say?" July 2024. Accessed [Date]. https://www.kotzkblog.com/2024/07/480-what-did-kotzker-rebbe-say.html.

[70] In *I and Thou*, translated by Walter Kaufmann, (New York: Scribner's, 1970), 169–82. See also Ronald Gregor Smith {Edinburgh: T. & T. Clark, 1937).

[71] Buber, 1970, p. 59.

[72] Buber, 1970, p. 69.

[73] Buber, 1970, p. 123.

[74] Buber, 1970, p. 59

[75] Martin Buber and Maurice Friedman (ed.) *Knowledge of Man: A Philosophy of the Interhuman* (New York: Harper & Row Publishers, 1965), p. 31.

[76] This essay was originally published in 1967 as part of *The Philosophy of Martin Buber*, edited by Paul Arthur Schilpp and Maurice Friedman, published by Open Court in 1967. According to Friedman, Buber wrote this tract in 1917 under the name, *Events and Meetings (*New York: Routledge , 1973.

[77] *The Philosophy of Martin Buber*, Buber, 1967, p. 12.

[78] *The Philosophy of Martin Buber,* Buber, 1967, p. 45.

[79] *I and Thou*, 1923, p. 75.

[80]Buber, 1967, p. 31-32.
[81] *Meetings*, p. 62-65.

[82] Buber, 1967, p. 91.

[83] Martin Buber, *The Way Of Man According To The Teachings Of Hasidism* (Wallingford, PA: Pendle Hill Publications, 1960), pp. 24-25

[84] Martin Buber, *The Way Of Man,* pp. 27-28.

[85] BT Berachot 57b.

[86] Rabbi Zalman M. Schachter-Shalomi, *Gate to the Heart A Manual of Contemplative Jewish Practice (*Boulder: Albion-Andalus Books, 2013).

[87] See *Teshuvot HaRivash* Responsum 157.

[88] Louis Jacobs, *Theology in Responsa* (Oxford: *The Littman Library* of *Jewish Civilization* , 1975), pp. 82-84.

[89] See Zohar 1:4b, 2:43b, 3:281b-282a, and many others.

[90] Tishby noted Rabbi Moses' wife swore that her husband never owned the book he claimed to copy from. Instead, he composed his writings independently, using his intelligence and creativity. She questioned why he didn't admit his authorship for greater recognition. He responded that if he revealed his work as his own, people wouldn't value it or pay for it. But by saying his writings were extracts from the Zohar, authored by Rabbi Simeon ben Yohai under divine inspiration, people were willing to pay handsomely. This conversation was later repeated between Rabbi Joseph's wife and Rabbi Moses' daughter, who gave the same account as her mother, offering strong evidence of the truth of the matter. See Isaiah Tishby, *The Wisdom of the Zohar: An Anthology of Texts* (Oxford, UK: The Littman Library of Jewish Civilization, 1989, repr. 2008), pp. 13-14.

[91] See Yehuda Liebes and Arnold Schwartz, Stephanie Nakache, Penina Peli (Trans.), *Studies in the Zohar* (Albany, NY: SUNY Press, 1993), pp. 141-142,

[92] *Zohar* 3:134.

[93] See Joseph Dan, *The Christian Kabbalah: Jewish Mystical Books & Their Christian Interpreters* (Cambridge: Harvard University Library, 1996) p. 24.

[94] Gershom Scholem, *Major Trends in Jewish Mysticism* (New York: Schocken Books, 1995), p.78.

[95] Isaiah Tishby, *The Wisdom of the Zohar* (Oxford: The Littman Library of Jewish Civilization, 1989), p.42.

[96] Yaacob Dweck, *The Scandal of Kabbalah: Leon Modena, Jewish Mysticism, Early Modern Venice* (Princeton: Princeton University Press, 2011), p. 92.

[97] Ibid., op. cit., p. 87.

[98] Several examples include:

The Book of Enoch: Attributed to the biblical figure Enoch, the great-grandfather of Noah, this text is rich in apocalyptic and mystical visions.

The Testaments of the Twelve Patriarchs: Purportedly the final words and instructions of the twelve sons of Jacob, this text combines moral teachings with future predictions.

The Life of Adam and Eve: Also known as the "Apocalypse of Moses," this work expands on the Genesis story, detailing Adam and Eve's life after their expulsion from Eden.

The Books of Jubilees: Known as the "Little Genesis," this text retells the events of Genesis and parts of Exodus, with additional details and interpretations.

The Assumption of Moses: A Jewish apocalyptic text that supposedly details the death of Moses and includes prophecies about Israel's history.

The Psalms of Solomon: A collection of 18 psalms, attributed to Solomon but likely written during the period of the Second Temple.

The Sibylline Oracles: A collection of prophetic writings attributed to the Sibyls, prophetic women of the Greco-Roman world.

The Apocalypse of Baruch: Also known as 2 Baruch, this text, attributed to Baruch, the scribe of Jeremiah, contains apocalyptic and theological themes.

The Testament of Abraham: A narrative focused on the death of Abraham, portraying his journey to heaven and the divine judgment.

3 Maccabees: Despite its name, it is not a continuation of the Maccabean histories but a story about an attempt by Ptolemy IV Philopator of Egypt to persecute the Jews in his realm.

These texts, while not considered canonical in most Jewish or Christian traditions, provide valuable cultural, religious, and historical insights and are often studied for their literary and theological contributions. They often became the precursor of the Midrashic literature of the rabbis.

[99] Yakov Dweck's biography, *The Scandal of Kabbalah: Leon Modena, Jewish Mysticism, Early Modern Venice,* (Princeton: Princeton UP. 2111*),* pp 116-118.

[100] Moshe Idel, "Appendix: Kabbalah in Elijah Benamozegh's Thought". In M. Luria & B. McGinn (Eds.), & M. Luria (Trans.), *Elijah Benamozegh: Israel and Humanity* (Mahwah, NJ: Paulist Press, 1995), p. 386.

[101] See Avinoam Fraernkel's fine translation of Rabbi Yosef Ergas' *Shomer Emunim: The Introduction to the Kabbalah* (Jerusalem: Urim, 2021), p. 35.

[102] In *Judaism and Its History*, published in 1871, Abraham Geiger addresses "Mysticism" in Volume 3 (pp. 64–78) with a critical eye, firmly rooted in an Enlightenment perspective. He portrays Kabbalah as a fanciful and baseless form of wisdom, exploited by zealous opportunists to captivate vulnerable, downtrodden individuals.

[103] Maimonides, *Guide for the Perplexed*; Hegel, *Phenomenology of Spirit,* 1807; Kant, Critique of Pure Reason, 1781].

[104] Daniel Klein, "Let Him Bray: The Stormy Correspondence Between Samuel David Luzzatto and Elia Benamozegh." *Hakirah*, vol. 31, 2022, pp. 269-300, esp. p. 69.

[105] Herbert Weiner, *Nine and a Half Mystics: The Kabbala Today* (New York: 1969, 1992), p. 62.

[106] The philosopher A.J. Ayer's view of "nonsense" as statements lacking empirical verifiability or logical coherence (*Language, Truth and Logic*, 1936) relates to the Lieberman-Scholem dynamic over Kabbalah. Lieberman's quip, "Nonsense is nonsense, but the history of nonsense is scholarship," aligns with Ayer's dismissal of untestable claims—like Kabbalah's esoteric doctrines—as meaningless, reflecting his Talmudic preference for rational precision. Scholem, however, mirrors the quip's second half, treating Kabbalah's "nonsense" (e.g., Sefirot, Messianic visions) as historically significant, not true, akin to Ayer's shift toward analyzing language without endorsing its content (*Language, Truth and Logic*, 1946 ed.). Lieberman sees Kabbalah as fluff; Scholem, its history as scholarship—echoing Ayer's split between nonsense and its study.

[107] Burton Dreben, a philosopher influenced by Ludwig Wittgenstein, adapted a quip originally from Saul Lieberman—"Nonsense is nonsense, but the history of nonsense is scholarship"—to frame his view of philosophy. Wittgenstein argued that much of traditional philosophy (e.g., ethics, aesthetics) was "nonsense" because it lacked the clear truth criteria of science or logic, reducing classical problems to mere linguistic confusion. Dreben echoed this, suggesting philosophy's content was often meaningless, but its history remained a worthy scholarly pursuit. Variants like "Philosophy is rubbish, but the history of rubbish is scholarship" (Leiter 2005) misalign with Wittgenstein's precise "nonsense," which isn't just garbage but discourse beyond analytic grasp. Lieberman's Talmudic rigor contrasted Scholem's esoteric focus, yet he validated studying its history—a resonance Dreben, linked to Jewish scholarship through his first wife's father, Shalom Spiegel, embraced. For Dreben, this crystallized a deconstructionist stance: philosophy's "nonsense" lacks sense, but its historical study holds academic value.

[108] Lawrence Fine, *Physician of the Soul, Healer of the Cosmos Isaac Luria and His Kabbalistic Fellowship* (Stanford, CA: Stanford University Press, 2003), pp. 128-129.

[109] See Chapter 11, יושר לבב - ריקי, רפאל עמנואל חי בן אברהם, 1687-1743 (page 23 of 113) (hebrewbooks.org).

[110] It is important to note that R. Immanuel Chai Ricchi, was a highly esteemed figure in the realm of Kabbalistic scholarship, authored *Yosher Levav.* This work was published in 5497 (1737), just a year after the release of *Shomer Emunim.* Ricchi was also responsible for the creation of the much-acclaimed *Mishnat Chassidim,* a pivotal work that effectively organized and encapsulated the teachings of Isaac Luria. Within the sphere of eighteenth-century Kabbalistic thought, R. Ricchi was revered as one of the most, if not the most, prominent and influential figures. See Avinoam Fraenkel's encyclopedic *Understanding Nefesh HaTzimtzum* (New York, Jerusalem: 2020), Vol. 2., noted The terms *Tzimtzum Kipshuto* and *Tzimtzum Lo Kipshuto*, while common in some modern circles, were primarily found in only two pre-1750 Kabbalistic works, "Shomer Emunim" and "Yosher Levav." Notably, these terms were absent in most other contemporary Kabbalistic texts of that era, as well as in the writings of the Vilna Gaon and the *Nefesh HaChaim. (Understanding Nefesh HaTzimtzum* , p. 80).

[111] Mordechai Willensky, *Chassidim U-Misnagdim* (Jerusalem: Mossad Bialik, 2nd ed. vol. 1 p. 187ff. and pp. 200-201.

[112] It is debatable whether the Vilna Gaon ever subscribed to a literal notion of the *tzimtzum* as alleged against him by R. Sheneir Zalman of Liadi. Gershom Scholem, in his analysis of the various interpretations of *tzimtzum* questioned the accuracy of this assertion, suggesting it may not fully represent the Gaon's teachings. This point of contention is highlighted in Scholem's work "Kabbalah," published by Dorset Press in 1987, where he explores the complexities of these interpretations on page 135.

[113] See Gershom Scholem, "Redemption through Sin," in *The Messianic Idea in Judaism and Other Essays on Jewish Spirituality*, trans. Hillel Halkin (New York: Schocken Books, 1971),pp. 88, 92.

[114] Philo views human reality as a manifestation of spiritual reality. The higher aspect is what he called "the heavenly man" (ὁ οὐράνιος ἄνθρωπος made in a special image made by the Divine. See *Allegories to Genesis* 1:31. R. Akiba expressed a similar thought, see From *The Letters of Rabbi Akiva*; Mid. Ps. 139:5; Sanhedrin 38a and Rashi on Genesis 1:27. Louis Ginzberg and I. Singer (Ed.) "Adam Kadmon" *The Jewish Encyclopedia: A Descriptive Record of the History, Religion, Literature, and Customs*

of the Jewish People from the Earliest Times to the Present Day, 12 Volumes (New York; London: Funk & Wagnalls,1901-1906), Vol. 1, pp. 181-183.

[115] However, Ibn Ezra challenges this interpretation, suggesting that בָּרָא might also imply fashioning from existing materials, as seen in the creation of man from earth's dust and God's breath. Ibn Ezra's view could imply that the universe was formed from pre-existing matter, which does not necessarily indicate a dualistic universe but might suggest a substance that is "pre-eternal" relative to the world but not to God. Ibn Ezra primarily interprets בָּרָא as "to cut down" or "set a boundary," a perspective supported by S.R. Driver, who also notes the Arabic roots of the word, implying "to fashion" or "shape by cutting." Despite this, Driver acknowledges that בָּרָא typically denotes God's unique, creative power.

[116] Tanya, *Sha'ar Yichud V'Emunah* Chapter 2.

[117] Zohar III:256b; *Tanya*: Part 4: *Igeret Hakodesh*, sect. 17.

[118] Martin Buber and Walter Kaufmann (Trans.) *I and Thou,* (New York: Charles Scribner's Sons, 1970), *op. cit., p.* 58.

[119] Martin Buber and Walter Kaufmann (Trans), op. cit., pp. 57–58.

[120] JT *Orlah*, Chapter 1, Halacha 3.

[121] Rabbi Shlomo Yitzhaki, better known as "Rashi" (1040-1105), was a preeminent medieval French commentator on the Bible and Talmud. Famed for merging literal and nonliteral interpretation methods, Rashi's commentary, despite some criticism, profoundly influenced Jewish biblical exegesis. Notably, his work was the first Hebrew book printed, solidifying its historical significance.

[122] R. Moshe Hayyim Luzzato, *Asarah Perakim L'Ramchal*, chp. 1.

[123] Moshe Idel, *The Mystical Experience in Abraham Abulafia* (Albany, NY: State University of New York Press, 1988), p. 26.

[124] Moshe Idel, *The Mystical Experience in Abraham Abulafia* (Albany, NY: State University of New York Press, 1988), p. 26.

[125] Arthur Waskow, an important figure in contemporary Judaic spiritual thought, perceives the name YHVH (YHWH) not just as a sequence of letters but as a representation of breath itself. He envisions the divine name as "YyyyHhhhWwwwHhhh," the auditory embodiment of inhalation and exhalation, a ceaseless rhythm mirroring the cyclical nature of life itself. Waskow, thus, portrays God as the "Interbreathing of all life," a divine breath that simultaneously encompasses and emanates from every creature. This interpretation can be explored further in his writings such as "The Breath of Life/Prayer" and "Nishmat: The Breath of All Life," available on The Shalom Center's website. The delicate interplay between the divine and all forms of life, as reflected in our shared breath, underscores his philosophy (referenced works: The Shalom Center, Philadelphia, Sep. 8, 2001).

[126] Arthur Waskow, an important figure in contemporary Judaic spiritual thought, perceives the name YHVH (YHWH) not just as a sequence of letters but as a representation of breath itself. He envisions the divine name as "YyyyHhhhWwwwHhhh," the auditory embodiment of inhalation and exhalation, a ceaseless rhythm mirroring the cyclical nature of life itself. Waskow, thus, portrays God as the "Interbreathing of all life," a divine breath that simultaneously encompasses and emanates from every creature. This interpretation can be explored further in his writings such as "The Breath of Life/Prayer" and "Nishmat: The Breath of All Life," available on The Shalom Center's website. The delicate interplay between the divine and all forms of life, as reflected in our shared breath, underscores his philosophy (referenced works: The Shalom Center, Philadelphia, Sep. 8, 2001).

[127] See BT Sanhedrin 46a. The Mishnah, as taught by Rabbi Meir in BT Sanhedrin 46a, conveys a profound message about divine empathy. It states: "In moments of human suffering, what does the Shechinah, the Divine Presence, say? 'My head is heavy, my arm is heavy,' meaning, I, too, suffer when the wicked are punished. From here it is derived: **If God suffers** such distress **over the blood of the wicked that is spilled,** even though they justly deserved their punishment, it can be inferred ***a fortiori*** that He suffers distress **over the blood of the just."** This teaching underscores the profound connection and empathy that the Shekhinah feels for all of humanity, reflecting God's feminine and compassionate nature. (based on Steinsaltz's translation).

[128] *A Mystical Reading on Songs of Songs Rabah 4:10* by Rabbi Michael Leo Samuel ©

[129] Zohar 1:6a; Tanya *Igeret Hakodesh,* sect. V, note 15.

[130] The intricate dynamics of the Sefirot within Kabbalah exhibit varying interpretations among scholars. For instance, Rabbi Moses Cordovero consistently includes Keter as part of the ten Sefirot, relegating Da'at as a distinct, non-counted Sefirah (as outlined in Pardess Rimonim and Or Ne'erau). However, Rabbi Isaac Luria's system positions Da'at as one of the ten Sefirot, omitting Keter (as referred to in the Tree of Life configuration)...

[131] Alternatively, "the Ancient One" (as per NAB, NRSV, NLT). This translation retains the traditional expression "Ancient of Days" due to its familiarity among many readers. Compare this to TEV's "One who had been living forever" and CEV's "The Eternal God."

[132] David Bohm, *Wholeness and the Implicate Order* (New York: Routledge Classics, 2002).

[133] David Bohm, *Wholeness and the Implicate Order* (New York, London: Routledge, 1980), ch. 1.

[134] Robert Jastrow, *God and the Astronomers* (New York: Warner Books, 1978), p. 105.

[135] For insights into the doctrine of the soul, one can reference several key works. See Gershom Scholem, *Major Trends in Jewish Mysticism* (New York: Schocken, 1946) provides relevant information on pages 240-41. Additional insights can be gleaned from Tishby, *Wisdom of the Zohar,* on pages 684-92. The Zohar itself, in sections 1:109a–b (*Midrash ha-Ne'elam*) and *Zohar Hadash* 6d, 9a, 14b.

[136] Jewish classical literature sometimes speaks about the three aspects of the soul from a different perspective:

- ❑ Nestled within the peak of this spiritual triad is the נֶפֶשׁ הַשֵּׂכְלִית ("intellectual soul" = *Nefesh HaSechlit*). This sphere resonates with the intellectual abilities of the individual, encapsulating cognition, wisdom, and thoughtful contemplation. It stands as the loftiest expression of the soul, a conduit to the divine intellect. See *Zohar Hadash Parshat Bereshit* 12a

- ❑ The הַנֶּפֶשׁ הַמְּדַבֶּרֶת *(Nefesh HaMidaberet* "the speaking soul" constitutes the next stratum of the soul. It houses our emotional landscape, a myriad of desires and drives. From love to fear, compassion to anger, it embodies both our angelic and devilish predispositions. The Tanya underscores the necessity of harnessing and directing these emotions toward constructive and spiritual ventures. (*Zohar Hadash Parshat Bereshit* 12a an 16a; *Derech Hayyim* on Avoth 1:17; 2:8; *Hidushei Aggadot on Sanhedrin* 107a; *Netivot Olam Netiv HaToah* Ch. 15; passim; *Hafetz Hayyim*; *Hovat Shemeirah* h. 4.

❑ At the bottom rung, we encounter the נֶפֶשׁ הַבְּהֱמִית (*nefesh habehamit* = ("animal soul" (This soul echoes our primitive instincts, our physical necessities, and earthly desires. It remains tethered to the tangible aspects of human existence. However, the Zohar encourages disciplining and subjecting this animalistic soul to the superior tiers, creating a harmonious spiritual hierarchy. (Zohar Reyeh Mehmemya Vol. 3 -- Parshat Tzav 29b; *Kad Hakemach* s.v. Ta'anit Ch. 24; Maharal *Tifereth Yisael* Ch. 6; Shelah on Yom Ch. 54, *Tanya* 1:2 passim.

[137] Some kabbalistic texts, notably the Zohar, advanced a controversial doctrine asserting a fundamental distinction between Jewish and non-Jewish souls. This view posits that Jewish souls, deriving from a divine source, are inherently holy, while non-Jewish souls stem from a different, animalistic spiritual origin. See Zohar Ha-Ḥadash (Sulam Edition, Jerusalem, 1975), Gen., no. 407 & 412; R. Chayim Vital, in *'Sha'ar ha-Kedushah'* and *'Etz Chayim'*, explains that every Jew has two souls, one from *kelipah* and *sitra achra* (infusing life through blood) and another of divine origin. In contrast, non-Jewish souls emanate from other, impure *kelipot*, entirely devoid of good, with seemingly benevolent actions often motivated by self-interest. *Tanya*, Chapter 2] Menachem Mendel Schneerson, *Letters from the Rebbe* (Brooklyn: Otsar Sifrei Lubavitch, 1997), pp. 106-107.

Despite this mystical perspective, it's crucial to note that broad Jewish law and rabbinical tradition generally reject such exclusive views, recognizing the spiritual potential and righteousness in all human beings. Figures like Maimonides emphasized valuing virtues from all cultures and affirmed a place in the world to come for the righteous of all nations. An exclusively essentialist view risks promoting harmful hierarchies and contradicts the vast contributions of non-Jews to morality and spirituality, underscoring the need for inclusive approaches in modern Kabbalistic and Judaic thought.

[138] Historically, European aristocrats were expected to use their inherited wealth and power for the public good. This often included funding public works, patronizing the arts, establishing charities, and

providing for their local populace or serfs. Such actions, even if paternalistic, were seen as a fulfillment of their inherent duty, a justification for their privileged position. For instance, a lord was expected to ensure the protection and well-being of tenants on his land, especially during hardship.

In contemporary society, this translates into the expectation that the wealthy and successful engage in significant philanthropy. Figures like industrialist Andrew Carnegie famously articulated this ideal, believing that substantial wealth should be actively deployed to improve society. This ethos continues to drive numerous charitable foundations and large-scale giving by today's billionaires.

Those in positions of leadership or influence, such as politicians, military leaders, or prominent public figures, are also subject to this expectation. They are anticipated to uphold higher ethical standards, prioritize the common good over personal gain, and demonstrate exemplary conduct. Princeton University's unofficial motto, "In the nation's service and the service of humanity," embodies this ideal, urging its graduates to utilize their education and status for broader societal benefit.

[139] Menachem Kellner, *Maimonides' Confrontation with Mysticism* (London: Oxford, 2006), pp. 31-33.

[140] Abraham Isaac Kook, *Mussar Avikha* (Jerusalem, 1985), p. 58, no. 10; *Orot ha-Kodesh* (Jerusalem, 1990), vol. 4, p. 405.

[141] Ezek. 2:1,3,6,8, passim. The term "son of man" is used 93 times in the Book of Ezekiel, emphasizing YHWH's supreme authority to instruct and guide His subjects as He wishes. Each instance where Ezekiel is addressed as "son of man" is a potent reminder of his absolute duty to comply promptly and fully with YHWH's commands.

[142] The name "Eve" (חוה) has diverse interpretations. Some link it to the Aramaic word for "serpent" (חיויא, = *ḥiwyā›*), suggesting Adam named her as such in rebuke for her role in the Genesis narrative (G. Wenham). Others connect it to the Hebrew word חיה (*ḥayyāh*), meaning "life," aligning with the Greek translation "Zoe" and the biblical text's explanation of her as "the mother of all living."

[142] The Hebrew terms for "woman" (' אִשָּׁה = ishah) and "man" (' אִישׁ = ish) present an interesting case of linguistic play. Although phonetically similar, suggesting 'ishah as the feminine form of 'ish, they are etymologically distinct. This similarity, however, adds symbolic depth

to Hebrew, symbolizing the unity and complementarity of men and women. In the biblical context, this language reflects the profound connection between man and woman. Initially, the first woman was not named "Eve"; it was only after God's curse that Adam named her "Eve," meaning "mother of all life" (Gen. 3:20), as she was made from his rib, not from earth (*'adamah*). Adam himself might have originally been named "Ish," fitting for 'Ishah. This renaming incorporated God's name 'Yah' into both 'Ish' and 'Ishah', symbolize divine protection for their adherence to God's commands.

This particular interpretation, discussed in sources like R. Akiba's teachings, Eusebius's "Praeparatio Evang.," Origen's "Ad Afric.," and Ginsberg's "Legends of the Jews," highlights the nuanced understanding of these names in biblical and historical contexts.

[143] The Hebrew words for "woman" (אִשָּׁה, 'ishah) and "man" (אִישׁ, 'ish) demonstrate a notable case of paronomasia, or wordplay. While they appear phonetically similar, suggesting *'ishah* is the feminine form of *'ish,* they are not etymologically related. This phonetic similarity, however, enriches the Hebrew language with symbolic meaning, reflecting the interconnectedness and complementary nature of men and women. In the Hebrew biblical narrative, this linguistic connection goes beyond mere style, symbolizing the deep-rooted relationship and interdependence between man and woman, and adding layers of interpretation to the understanding of gender roles in ancient Hebrew culture.

[144] Comp. Gen 49:25; Exod. 18:4; Deut. 33:26; Ps. 121:1–2; 146:5; Hos. 13:9.

[145] See Zohar 1:36b-37a, which delves into Eve's creation and her relationship with Adam. Additionally, the Zohar discusses the role of Eve in the narrative of the Tree of Knowledge (*Zohar* 1:35a-35b).

[146] The concept of *She'virat Hakelim* can be found in various works of the Lurianic system. It is discussed in books such as Etz Chayim and *Hechel Hanekudim* (Sha'ar 8, etc.), as well as in *Me'ah She'arim* II:2:1-11 and *Sha'ar Hahakdamot, Derush Be'oh Hanekudim (*pp. 81-109). In the writings of R. Shenier Zalman, this concept is explained in Torah Or, specifically in sections such as *Vayesheu* (27c, etc.), *Va'eira* (56d, etc.), and Yitro (110d). It is also discussed in Likutei Torah, particularly in sections II:37c onwards and III:82c.For additional insights, one can also refer to R. Tzvi Hirsh Horowitz's *AspakZuya Hameirah* on Zohar (111:135a, etc.).

[147] BR 8.1 and 17.6; BT Berakhot 61a; BT Erubin 18a, passim.

[148] Zohar 1:37a.

[149] Zohar 1:34b, 1:37b, 3:44a.

[150] Jung's concepts of anima, animus, and psychological androgyny have influenced various psychological disciplines, particularly in discussions of gender, identity, and personal development. His ideas introduced the notion that psychological health often involves transcending strict gender binaries and embracing a more fluid, integrated sense of self. That said, Jung's theories were shaped by the cultural and historical context of his era, and modern psychology has both built upon and critiqued them. For example:

- Contemporary gender studies often challenge the binary framework of anima and animus, arguing that gender identity and psychological traits exist on a spectrum rather than in fixed categories.

- Feminist critiques have questioned whether Jung's characterizations of the anima and animus unintentionally reinforce traditional gender stereotypes, even as they seek to transcend them.

Despite these critiques, Jung's focus on integrating unconscious aspects of the psyche remains a significant contribution to understanding human development. His work encourages individuals to explore the full scope of their psychological potential beyond societal constraints.

[151] Gershom Scholem, *Major Trends in Jewish Mysticism, op. cit.,* p. 273.

[152] Paul Ricoeur, *The Symbolism of Evil* (Boston: Beacon Press, 1967), pp. 257-258.

[153] For more information regarding the relationship concerning natural evil and God, see my notes on Genesis 1:2.

[154] Zohar 2:162b–163a.

[155] James Frazer in his *Golden Bough* describes myth as a primitive form of science or pseudo-science.

[156] The French anthropologist Claude Lévi-Strauss explains that myth functions as a basic element of a culture's underlying system of symbolic communication; through its amalgam of archetypal characters, myths reflect the hopes, dreams, fears, and conflicts of the human condition aiming toward the reconciliation of opposites within a given culture. In the final analysis, myths define a community's identity and core values, providing a vision of how a community sees itself within the greater picture of reality (*Structural Anthropology* [New York: Basic Books, 1968], p. 224.

[157] BT Berachot 61a, BT Kiddushin 30b, BT Sukkah 52a-b, BT Nedarim 32b.

[158] Avot D'Rabbi Natan 16.

[159] MT *Hilkhot De'ot* 2:2.

[160] Ramchal, *Derech HaShem* 1:2:1.

[161] The symbolism of the cosmic egg may be found in various cultures around the world, including ancient Greece (which subscribed to the Orphic tradition), and from South Africa to China. In India, this concept, known as the *brahmanda* ("egg of Brahma"), the Absolute (Brahman) becomes increasingly more personal and oriented to the world with each subsequent creation.

[162] The Hebrew term בָּרוּר, meaning "purge" or "purify," appears in various contexts in the Bible. In Ezekiel 20:38, the verb בָּרוּר, is used to describe how God will cleanse Israel of its rebellious transgressors. In the book of Daniel (11:35; 12:10), it refers to many individuals purifying themselves in the future. Zephaniah mentions a "pure language" (Zephaniah 3:9)."

[163] In terms of its grammar. מוּתָּר (*mutar*): In the Nifal conjugation, it indeed means "to be severed or loosened." This signifies something being separated, detached, or released from a previous connection or condition. נִיתַּר (*nit'ar)* and נִיתּוֹר (*nit'or*): Both forms are grammatically correct and carry similar meanings. They primarily signify "to be torn loose or released," emphasizing a more forceful or violent separation compared to the Nifal of מוּתָּר. the concept of being "untied or released from an obligation" is related to the idea of something becoming permissible.

This is a common association with these verbs, particularly relevant in religious and legal contexts where being "released" from certain restrictions implies permission or authorization.

[164] See Sanford J. Drob, *Symbols of the Kabbalah: Philosophical and Psychological Perspective* (Northvale, NJ: Jason Aronson Northvale NJ, 2000), p. 52.

[165] See Gershom Scholem, *On the Kabbalah and Its Symbolism* (New York: Schocken Books, 1969), p. 107.

[166] Philo, *Allegorical Interpretations* 1:52; *Questions on Genesis* 1:4.

[167] See Zohar Introduction 1:2b; :2:177a–b, 122b; Zohar 3:130b, 139a–140b

[168] Abraham Ibn Maimon and Samuel Rosenblatt (Trans) *The Highways to Perfection* (New York: Columbia University, 1927), Chapters 29-30.

[169] See Gershom Scholem, 1971, "Metatron," *EncJud* 11: pp. 1443–46.

[170] See I. Singer, *Jewish Encyclopedia* "Metatron," Vol. 8, pp. 518-519.

[171] See S. Libermann, "Metatron, the Meaning of His Name and His Functions," in I. Gruenwald, *Apocalyptic and Merkabah Mysticism* (Leiden: Brill, 1980) pp. 235–41.

[172] Baal Shem Tov, Keter Shem Tov 1:75.

[173] Exod. 20:17; Deut. 6:6.

Made in the USA
Monee, IL
23 July 2025